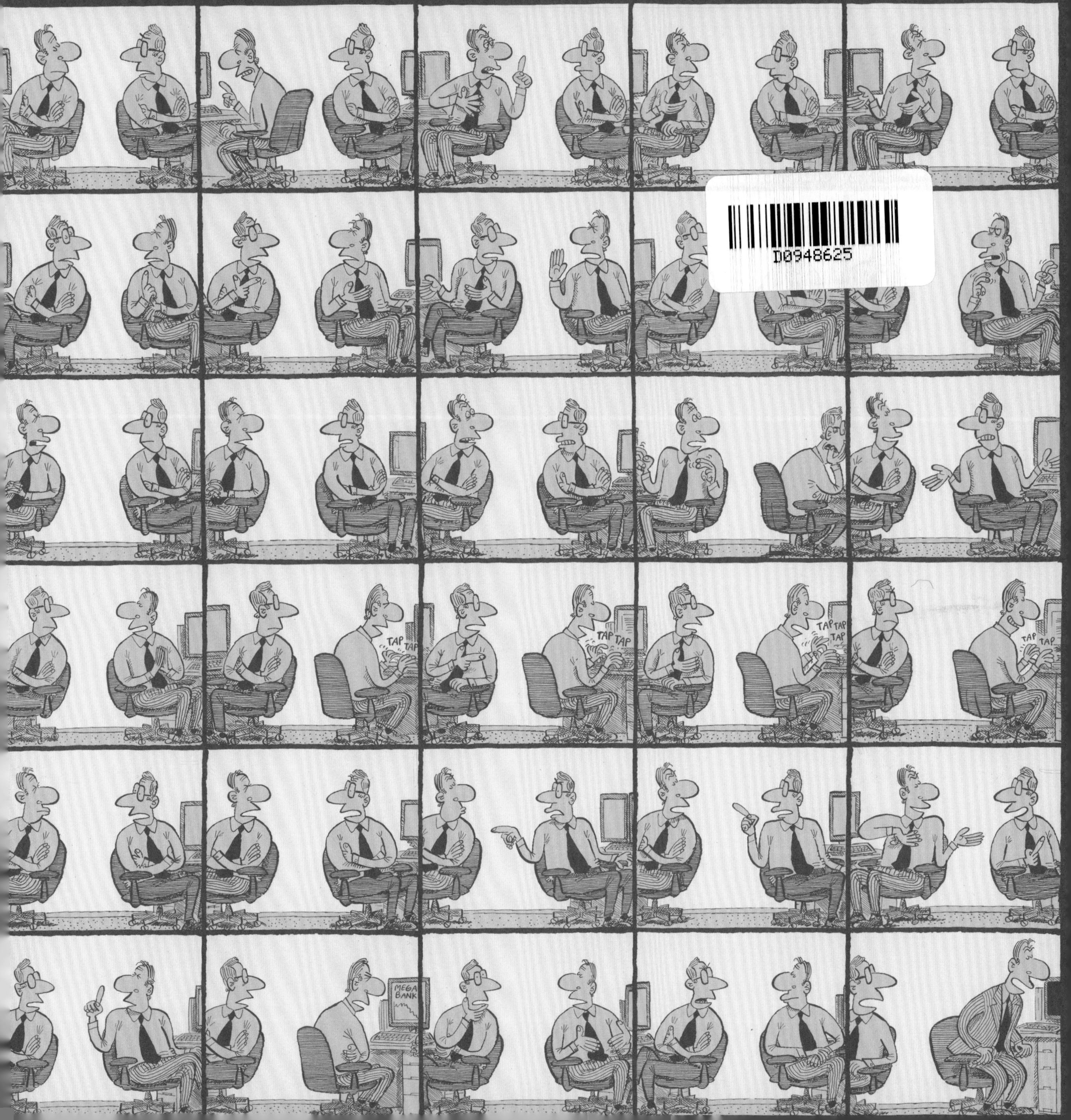
TAP TAP
TAP TAP
TAP TAP TAP
TAP TAP
MEGA BANK

The Best Of Alex 2017

Charles Peattie & Russell Taylor

Masterley Publishing

The Best Of Alex 2017

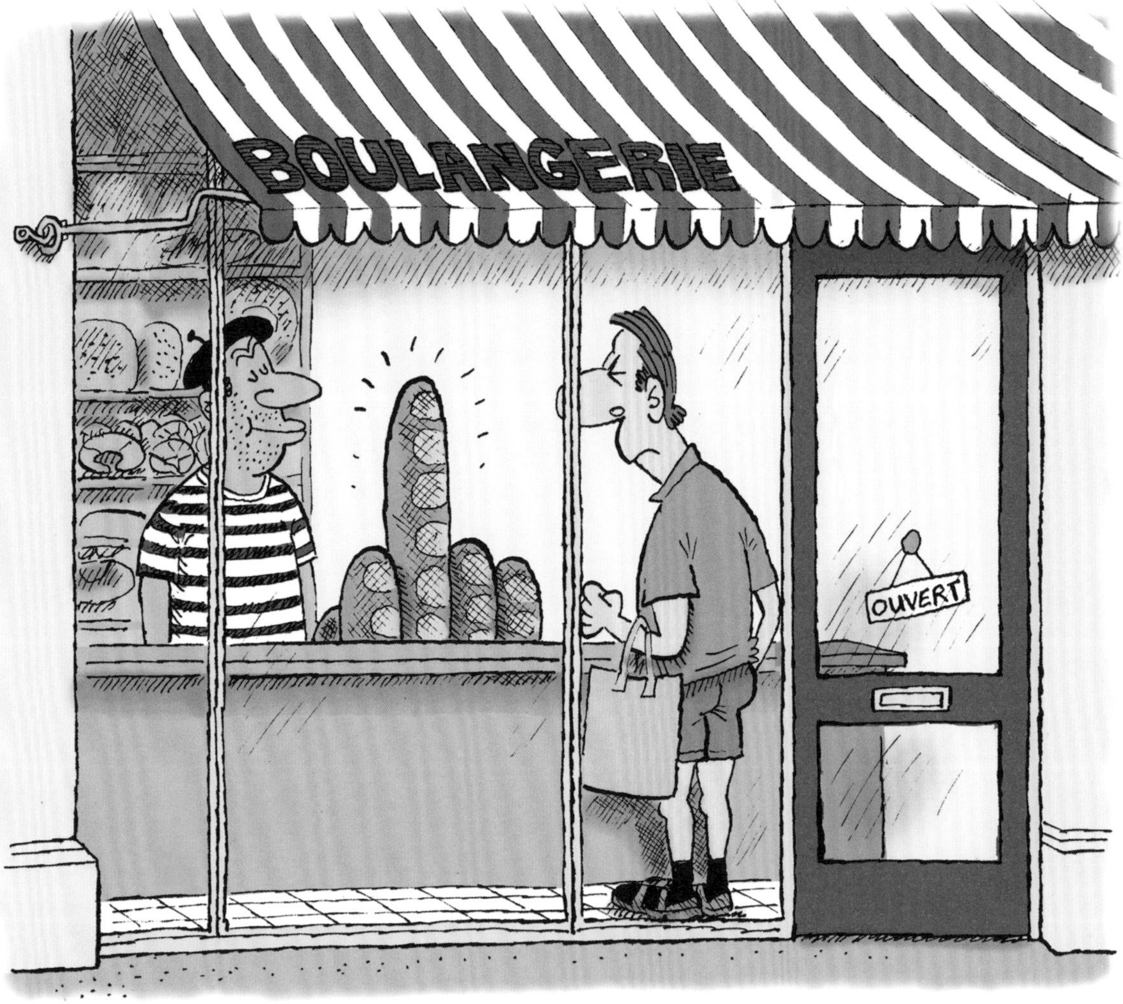
BOULANGERIE
OUVERT

First Published in 2017 by MASTERLEY PUBLISHING

Layout and Design: Suzette Field

Colouring and Artworking: Sofie Dodgson and Miki Lowe

ISBN: 978-1853759871
Printed in the UK by CPI William Clowes Beccles NR34 7TL

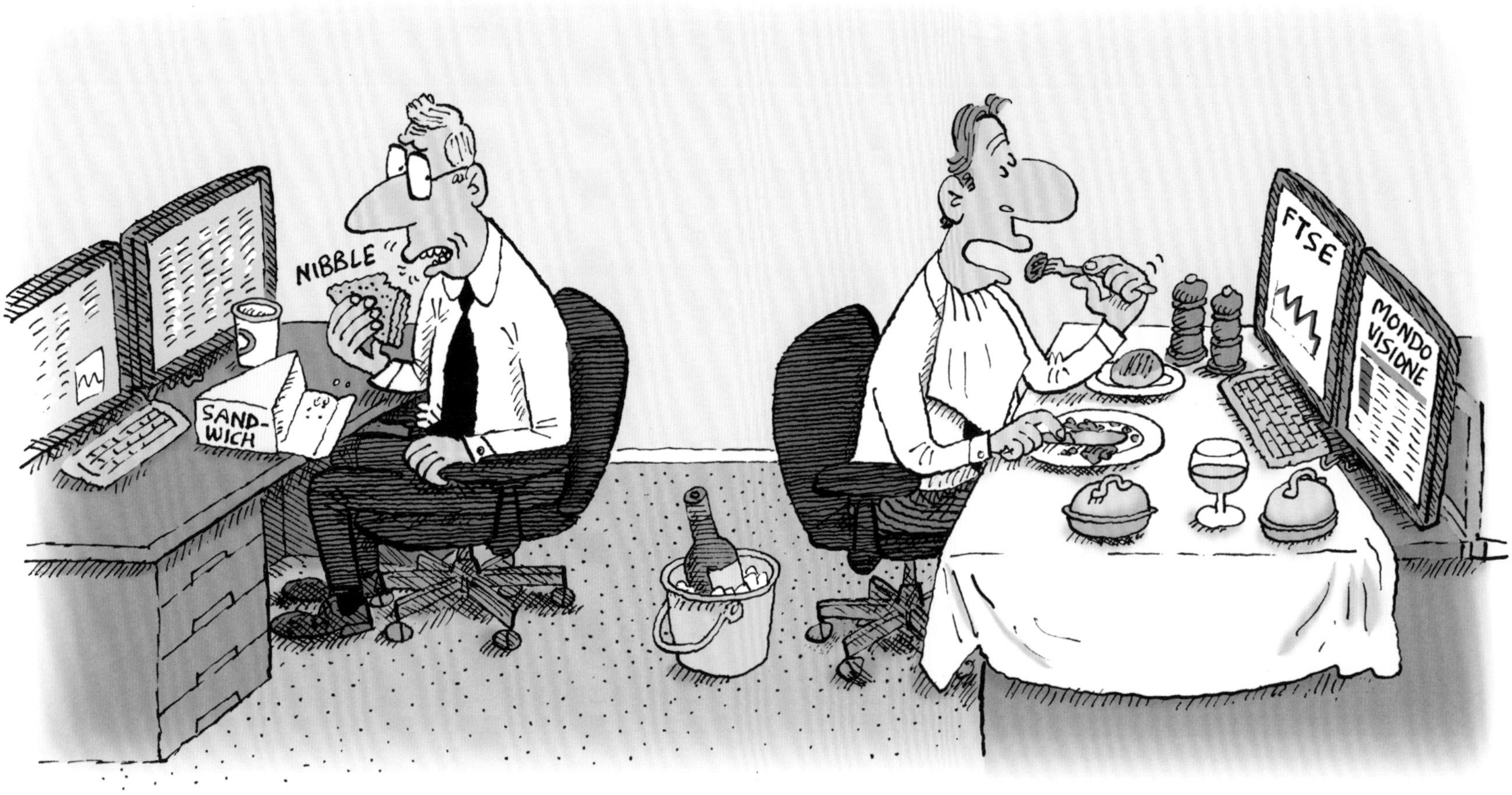
NIBBLE
SAND-
WICH
FTSE
MONDO
VISIONE

Our usual gratitude goes to our generous sponsors.

FTSE Russell is a leading global provider of benchmarks, analytics and data solutions with multi-asset capabilities.

Mondo Visione is the leading source of insight and knowledge about the world's exchanges and trading venues. As a conference and event organiser it helps to shape the development of markets.

FOREWORD

Unbelievably it is 30 years since a brash young banker named Alex Masterley first donned his pinstripes and embarked on what must now rank as an impressively long career in the City of London. Over the decades he's weathered many economic cycles, watched new generations come and go and seen many of the values and traditions he once stood for eroded.

But recently the tide has started to turn back in his favour. We are told that pinstripe suits are fashionable again among young bankers and there's a healthy eBay market for clunky old mobile phones. More to the point there has been a recent uptick in sales of physical books as Kindle and eBooks lose ground.

This change in our reading habits may have various causes. Perhaps it's that with an eBook you aren't able to impress strangers sitting opposite you on the train with your highbrow literary taste. Or maybe it's about the comfort of the reading experience. You can't stretch out and lay back on a bed, sofa or sun lounger with a digital book. You have to sit hunched over your tablet or phone, which is bad for posture (though good for chiropractors).

And with particular regard for those of us who write cartoon books, you can't leave an eBook in your downstairs loo for visitors to flick through in idle moments.

This cheering news has inspired us to bring out this year's Alex annual not only in hardback for the first time but also in full colour. So all those questions you've always asked yourself can now finally be answered. Yes, Bridget is a redhead; bank juniors do indeed wear brown shoes; and Porsches come in one colour (red).

We hope you enjoy this new augmented reality Alex.

Charles Peattie and Russell Taylor

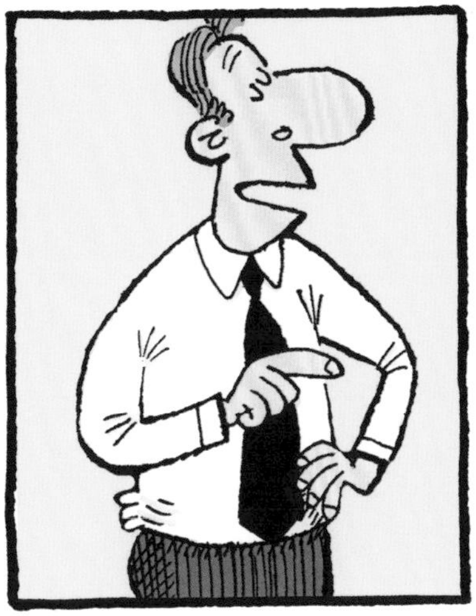
Alex - investment banker

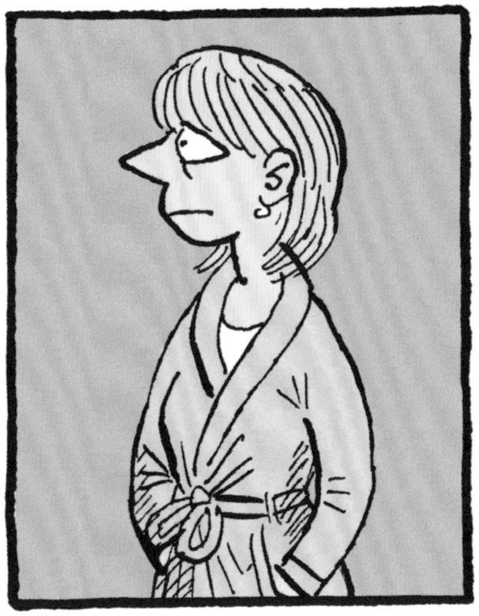
Penny - Alex's wife

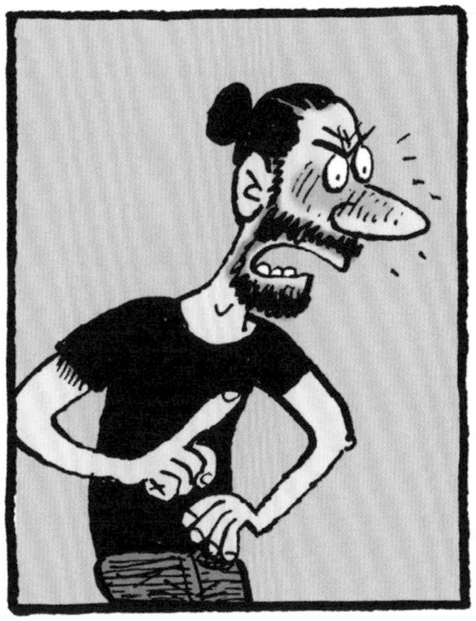
Christopher - their son

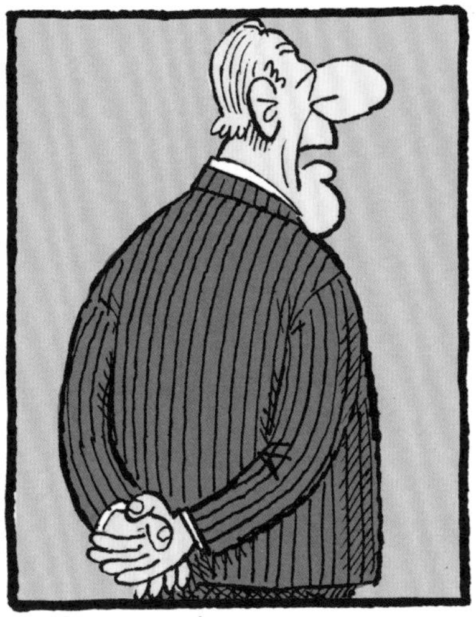
Rupert - senior banker

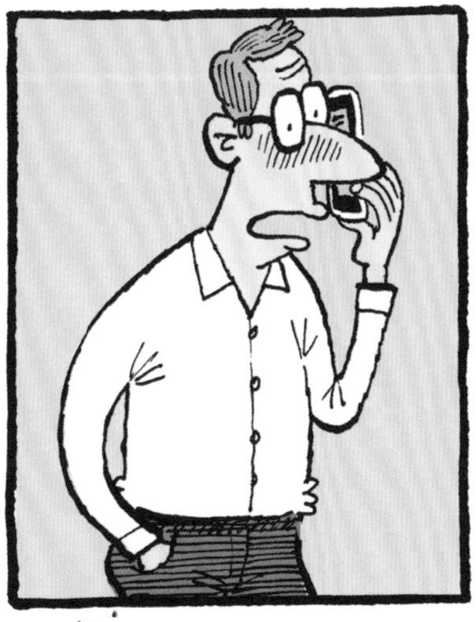
Clive - Alex's colleague

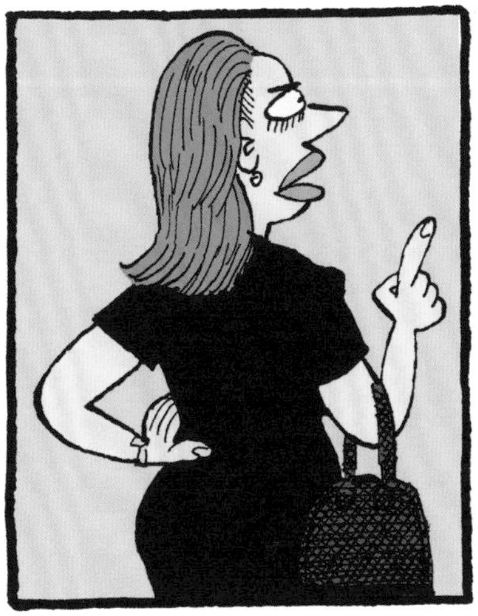
Bridget - Clive's wife

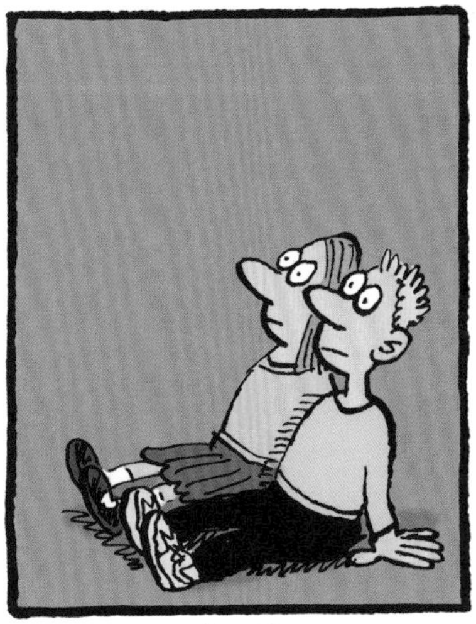
Clive's Twins

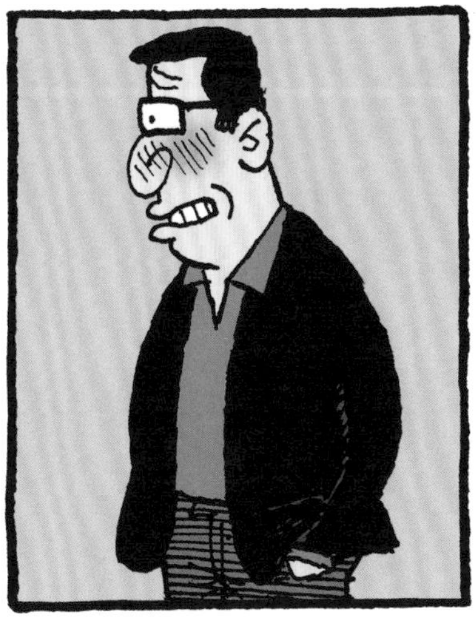
Cyrus - Alex's boss

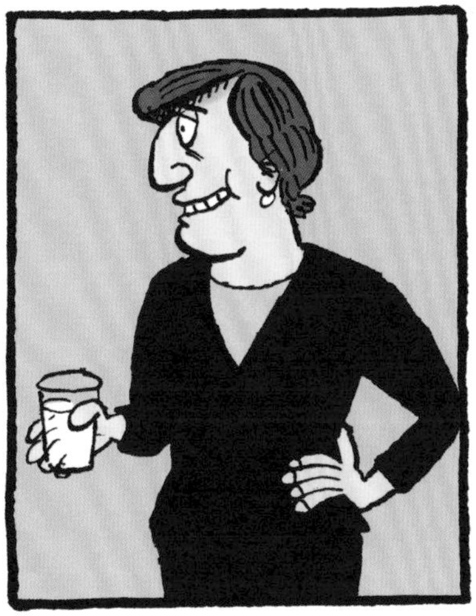
Stephanie - transgender banker

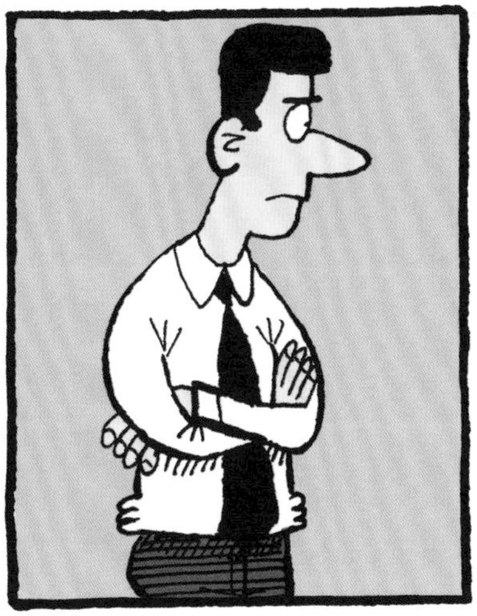
Leo - graduate trainee

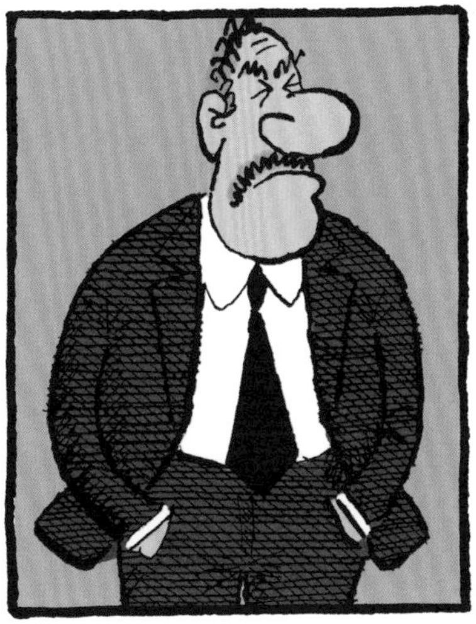
Hardcastle - Alex's client

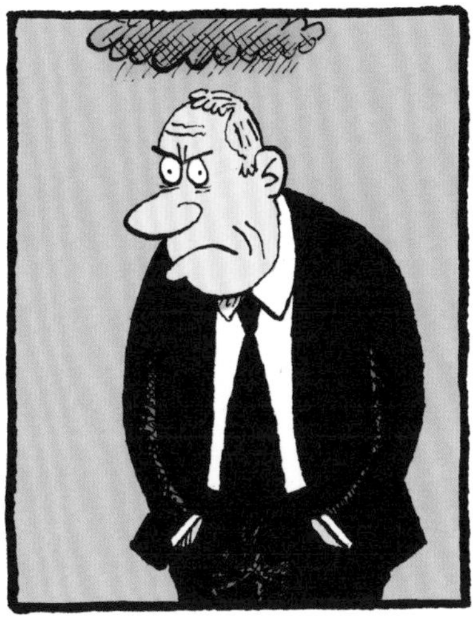
William - fund manager

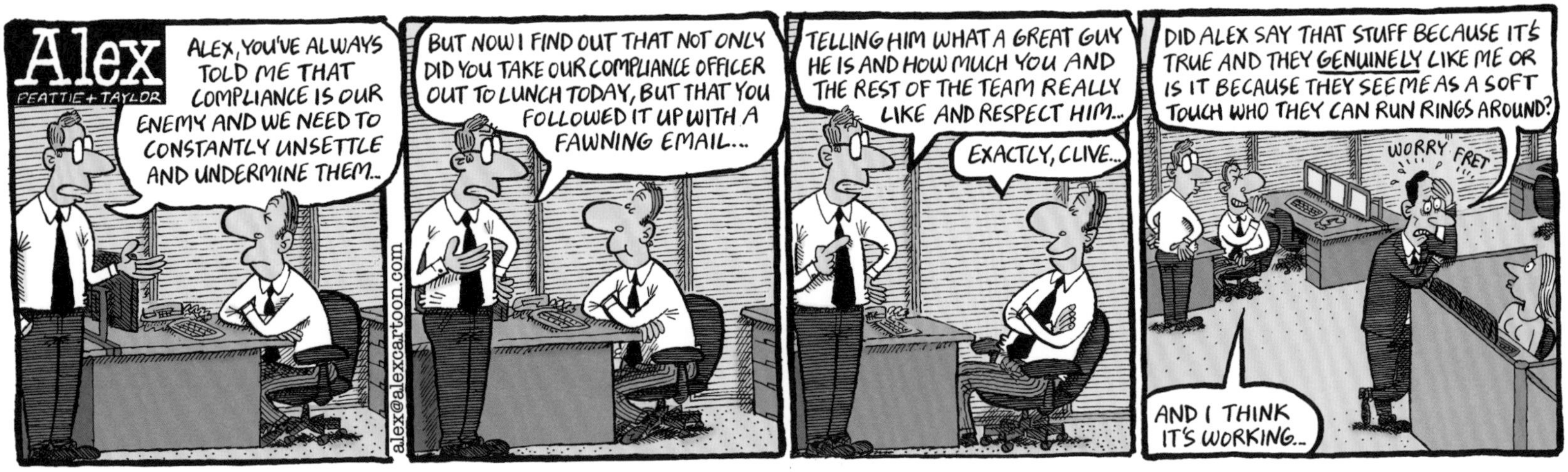
Alex
PEATTIE + TAYLOR
ALEX, YOU'VE ALWAYS TOLD ME THAT COMPLIANCE IS OUR ENEMY AND WE NEED TO CONSTANTLY UNSETTLE AND UNDERMINE THEM...
alex@alexcartoon.com
BUT NOW I FIND OUT THAT NOT ONLY DID YOU TAKE OUR COMPLIANCE OFFICER OUT TO LUNCH TODAY, BUT THAT YOU FOLLOWED IT UP WITH A FAWNING EMAIL...
TELLING HIM WHAT A GREAT GUY HE IS AND HOW MUCH YOU AND THE REST OF THE TEAM REALLY LIKE AND RESPECT HIM...
EXACTLY, CLIVE...
DID ALEX SAY THAT STUFF BECAUSE IT'S TRUE AND THEY GENUINELY LIKE ME OR IS IT BECAUSE THEY SEE ME AS A SOFT TOUCH WHO THEY CAN RUN RINGS AROUND?
WORRY
FRET
AND I THINK IT'S WORKING...

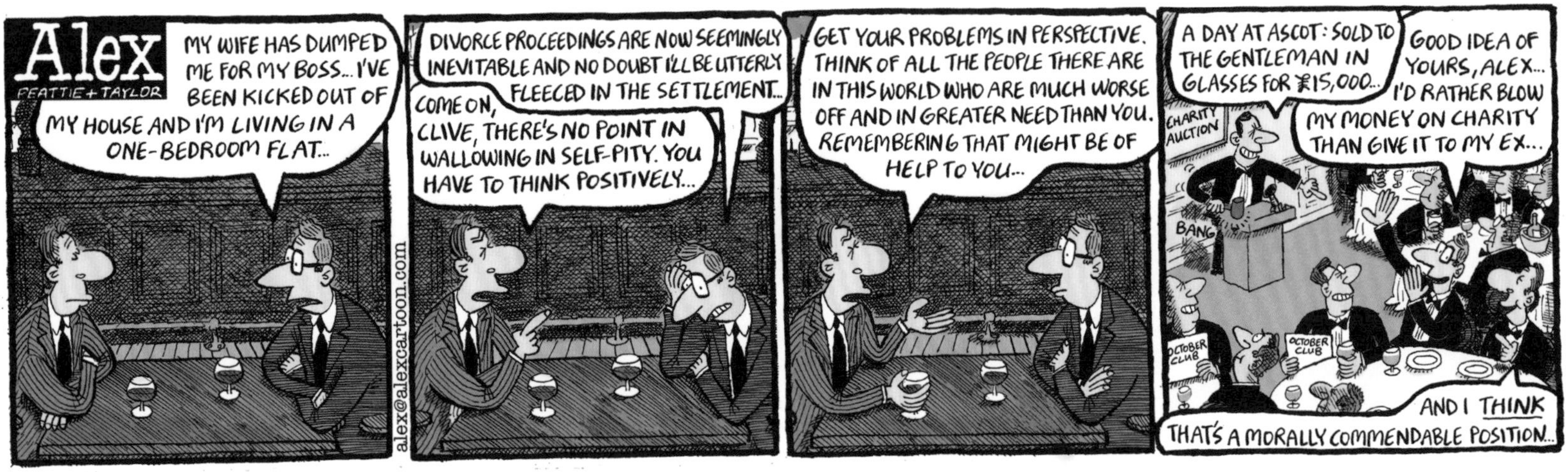
Alex
PEATTIE + TAYLOR
MY WIFE HAS DUMPED ME FOR MY BOSS... I'VE BEEN KICKED OUT OF MY HOUSE AND I'M LIVING IN A ONE-BEDROOM FLAT...
alex@alexcartoon.com
DIVORCE PROCEEDINGS ARE NOW SEEMINGLY INEVITABLE AND NO DOUBT I'LL BE UTTERLY FLEECED IN THE SETTLEMENT...
COME ON, CLIVE, THERE'S NO POINT IN WALLOWING IN SELF-PITY. YOU HAVE TO THINK POSITIVELY...
GET YOUR PROBLEMS IN PERSPECTIVE. THINK OF ALL THE PEOPLE THERE ARE IN THIS WORLD WHO ARE MUCH WORSE OFF AND IN GREATER NEED THAN YOU. REMEMBERING THAT MIGHT BE OF HELP TO YOU...
A DAY AT ASCOT: SOLD TO THE GENTLEMAN IN GLASSES FOR £15,000...
GOOD IDEA OF YOURS, ALEX... I'D RATHER BLOW MY MONEY ON CHARITY THAN GIVE IT TO MY EX...
CHARITY AUCTION
BANG
OCTOBER CLUB
OCTOBER CLUB
AND I THINK THAT'S A MORALLY COMMENDABLE POSITION...

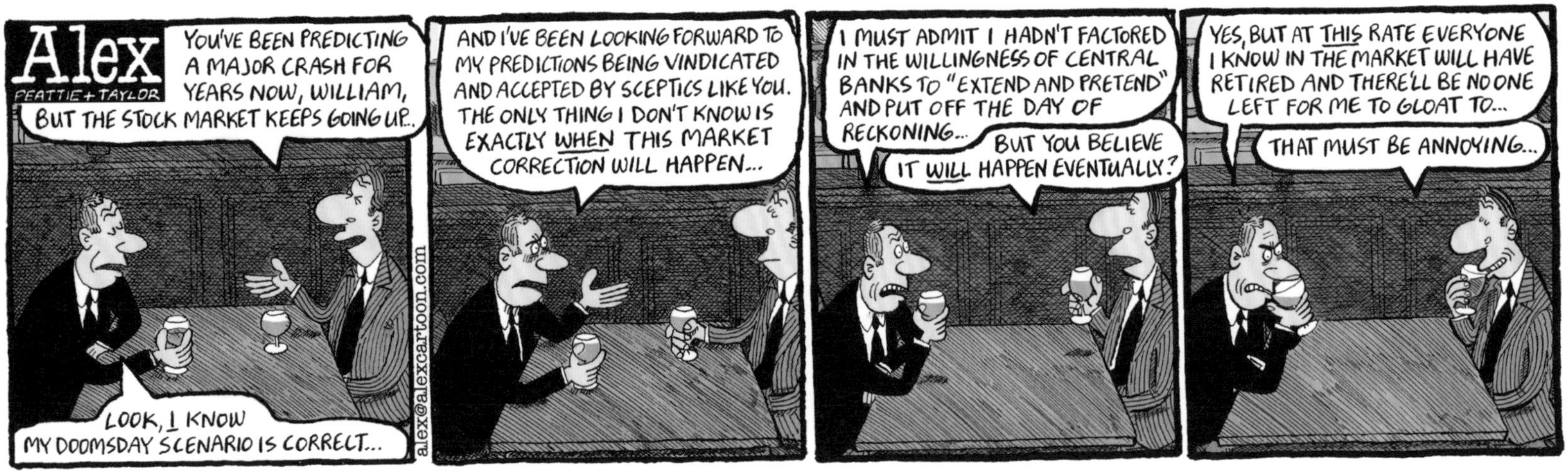
Alex
PEATTIE + TAYLOR
YOU'VE BEEN PREDICTING A MAJOR CRASH FOR YEARS NOW, WILLIAM, BUT THE STOCK MARKET KEEPS GOING UP...
LOOK, I KNOW MY DOOMSDAY SCENARIO IS CORRECT...
alex@alexcartoon.com
AND I'VE BEEN LOOKING FORWARD TO MY PREDICTIONS BEING VINDICATED AND ACCEPTED BY SCEPTICS LIKE YOU. THE ONLY THING I DON'T KNOW IS EXACTLY WHEN THIS MARKET CORRECTION WILL HAPPEN...
I MUST ADMIT I HADN'T FACTORED IN THE WILLINGNESS OF CENTRAL BANKS TO "EXTEND AND PRETEND" AND PUT OFF THE DAY OF RECKONING...
BUT YOU BELIEVE IT WILL HAPPEN EVENTUALLY?
YES, BUT AT THIS RATE EVERYONE I KNOW IN THE MARKET WILL HAVE RETIRED AND THERE'LL BE NO ONE LEFT FOR ME TO GLOAT TO...
THAT MUST BE ANNOYING...

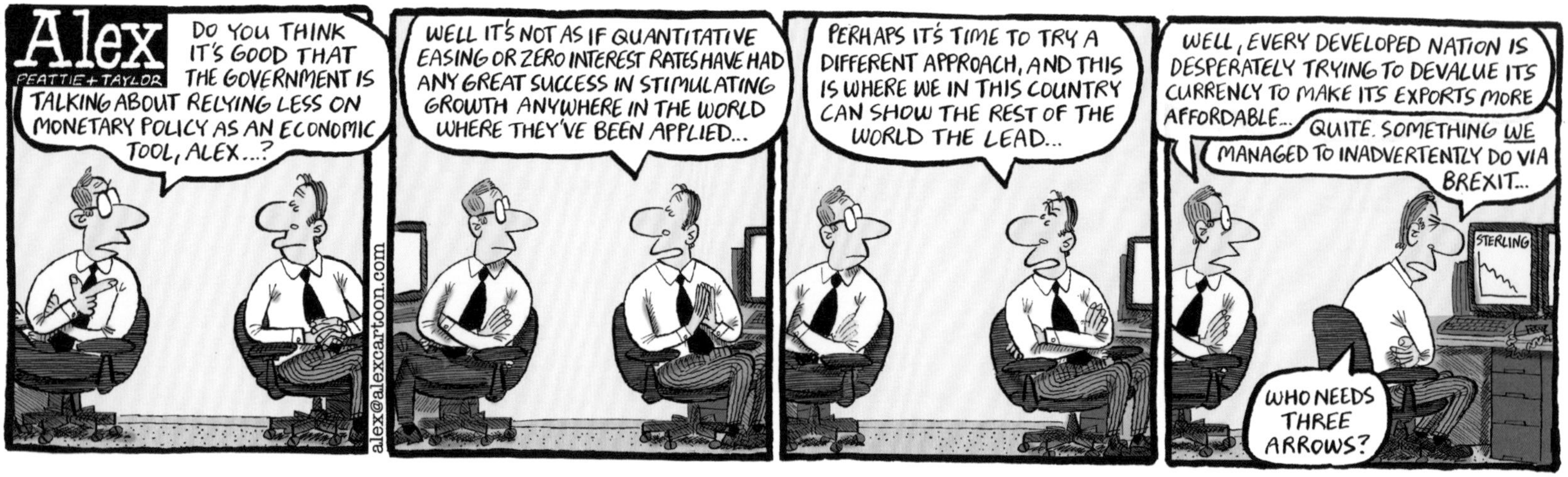
Alex
PEATTIE + TAYLOR
DO YOU THINK IT'S GOOD THAT THE GOVERNMENT IS TALKING ABOUT RELYING LESS ON MONETARY POLICY AS AN ECONOMIC TOOL, ALEX...?
WELL IT'S NOT AS IF QUANTITATIVE EASING OR ZERO INTEREST RATES HAVE HAD ANY GREAT SUCCESS IN STIMULATING GROWTH ANYWHERE IN THE WORLD WHERE THEY'VE BEEN APPLIED...
PERHAPS IT'S TIME TO TRY A DIFFERENT APPROACH, AND THIS IS WHERE WE IN THIS COUNTRY CAN SHOW THE REST OF THE WORLD THE LEAD...
WELL, EVERY DEVELOPED NATION IS DESPERATELY TRYING TO DEVALUE ITS CURRENCY TO MAKE ITS EXPORTS MORE AFFORDABLE...
QUITE. SOMETHING WE MANAGED TO INADVERTENTLY DO VIA BREXIT...
STERLING
WHO NEEDS THREE ARROWS?
alex@alexcartoon.com

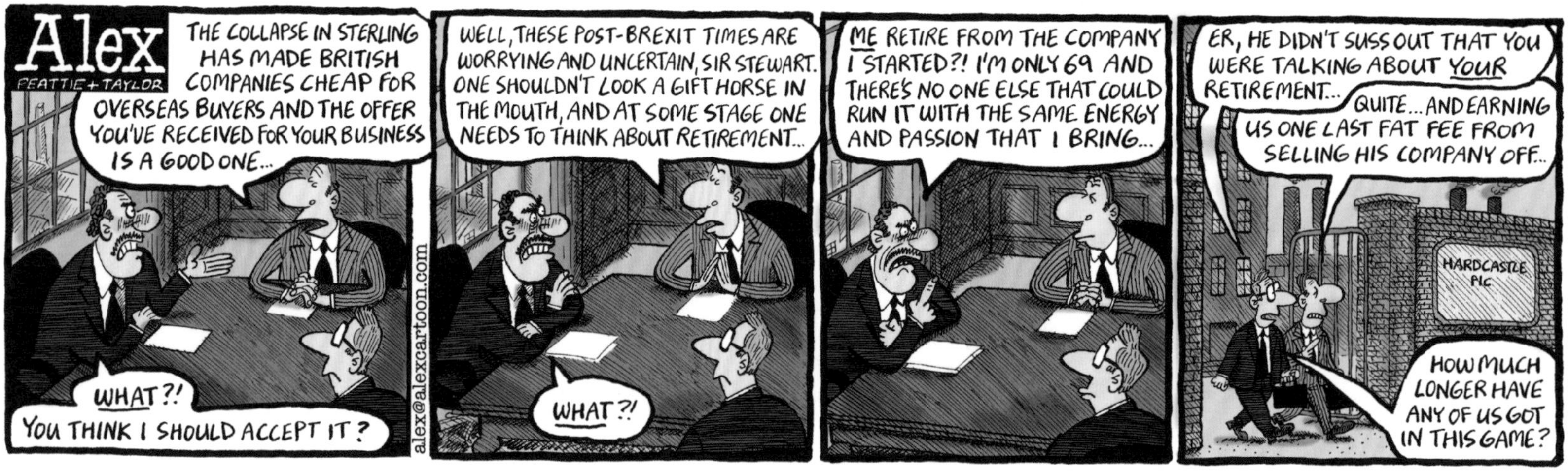
Alex
PEATTIE + TAYLOR
THE COLLAPSE IN STERLING HAS MADE BRITISH COMPANIES CHEAP FOR OVERSEAS BUYERS AND THE OFFER YOU'VE RECEIVED FOR YOUR BUSINESS IS A GOOD ONE...
WHAT?! YOU THINK I SHOULD ACCEPT IT?
WELL, THESE POST-BREXIT TIMES ARE WORRYING AND UNCERTAIN, SIR STEWART. ONE SHOULDN'T LOOK A GIFT HORSE IN THE MOUTH, AND AT SOME STAGE ONE NEEDS TO THINK ABOUT RETIREMENT...
WHAT?!
ME RETIRE FROM THE COMPANY I STARTED?! I'M ONLY 69 AND THERE'S NO ONE ELSE THAT COULD RUN IT WITH THE SAME ENERGY AND PASSION THAT I BRING...
ER, HE DIDN'T SUSS OUT THAT YOU WERE TALKING ABOUT YOUR RETIREMENT...
QUITE... AND EARNING US ONE LAST FAT FEE FROM SELLING HIS COMPANY OFF...
HARDCASTLE PLC
HOW MUCH LONGER HAVE ANY OF US GOT IN THIS GAME?
alex@alexcartoon.com

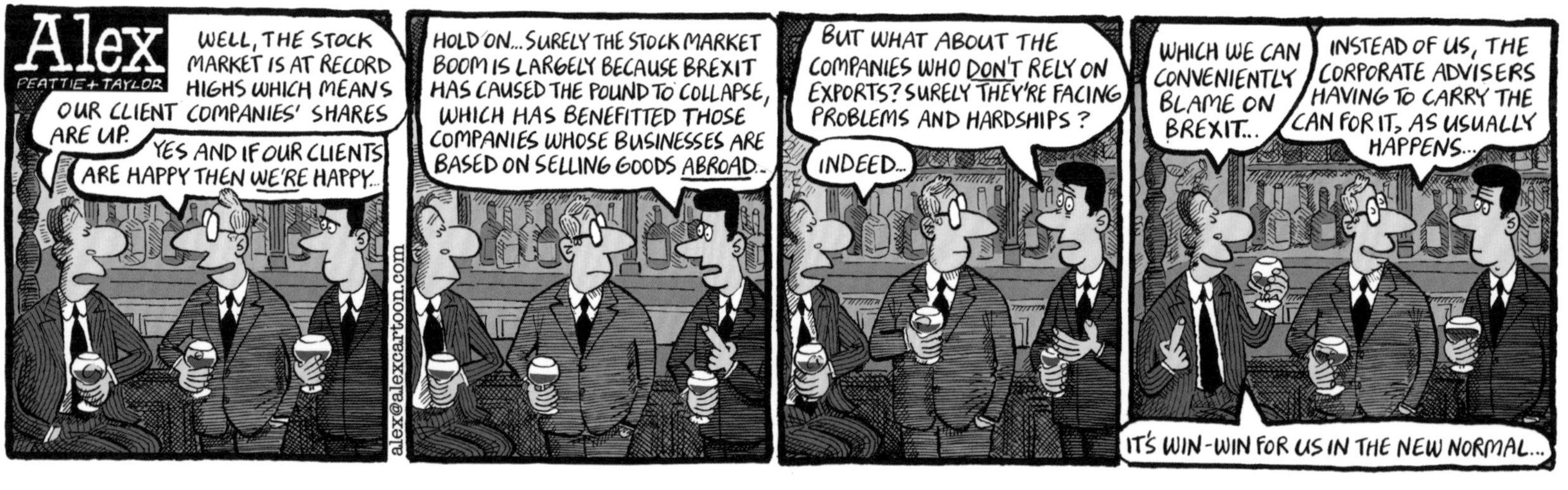
Alex
PEATTIE + TAYLOR
WELL, THE STOCK MARKET IS AT RECORD HIGHS WHICH MEANS OUR CLIENT COMPANIES' SHARES ARE UP.
YES AND IF OUR CLIENTS ARE HAPPY THEN WE'RE HAPPY...
HOLD ON... SURELY THE STOCK MARKET BOOM IS LARGELY BECAUSE BREXIT HAS CAUSED THE POUND TO COLLAPSE, WHICH HAS BENEFITTED THOSE COMPANIES WHOSE BUSINESSES ARE BASED ON SELLING GOODS ABROAD...
BUT WHAT ABOUT THE COMPANIES WHO DON'T RELY ON EXPORTS? SURELY THEY'RE FACING PROBLEMS AND HARDSHIPS?
INDEED...
WHICH WE CAN CONVENIENTLY BLAME ON BREXIT...
INSTEAD OF US, THE CORPORATE ADVISERS HAVING TO CARRY THE CAN FOR IT, AS USUALLY HAPPENS...
IT'S WIN-WIN FOR US IN THE NEW NORMAL...
alex@alexcartoon.com

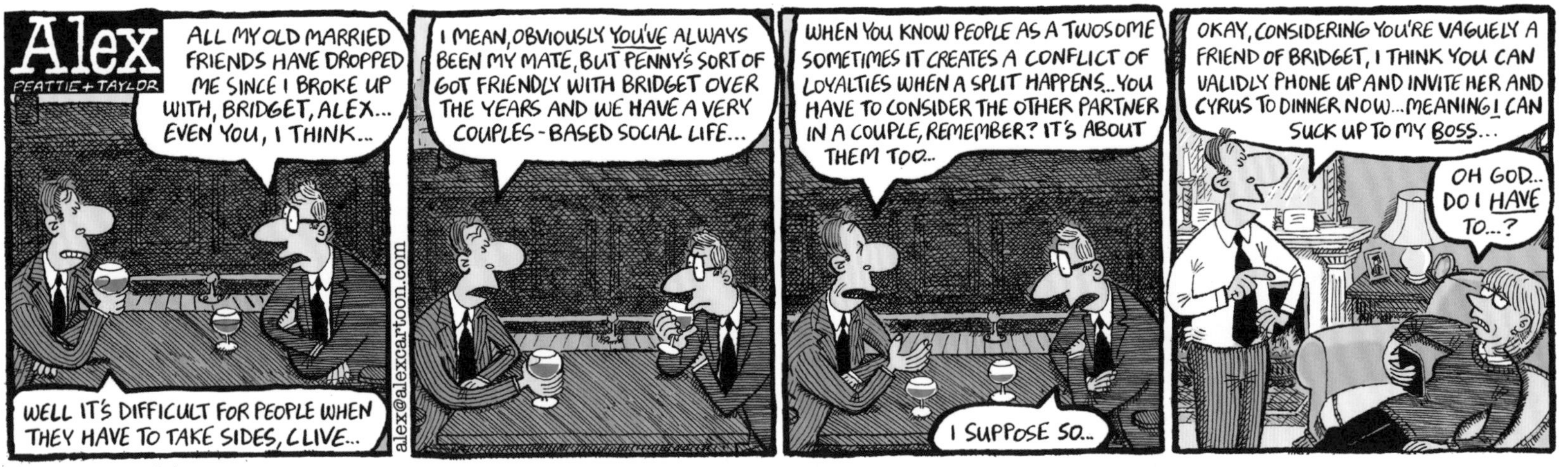
Alex
PEATTIE + TAYLOR
ALL MY OLD MARRIED FRIENDS HAVE DROPPED ME SINCE I BROKE UP WITH, BRIDGET, ALEX... EVEN YOU, I THINK...
WELL IT'S DIFFICULT FOR PEOPLE WHEN THEY HAVE TO TAKE SIDES, CLIVE...
alex@alexcartoon.com
I MEAN, OBVIOUSLY YOU'VE ALWAYS BEEN MY MATE, BUT PENNY'S SORT OF GOT FRIENDLY WITH BRIDGET OVER THE YEARS AND WE HAVE A VERY COUPLES-BASED SOCIAL LIFE...
WHEN YOU KNOW PEOPLE AS A TWOSOME SOMETIMES IT CREATES A CONFLICT OF LOYALTIES WHEN A SPLIT HAPPENS... YOU HAVE TO CONSIDER THE OTHER PARTNER IN A COUPLE, REMEMBER? IT'S ABOUT THEM TOO...
I SUPPOSE SO...
OKAY, CONSIDERING YOU'RE VAGUELY A FRIEND OF BRIDGET, I THINK YOU CAN VALIDLY PHONE UP AND INVITE HER AND CYRUS TO DINNER NOW... MEANING I CAN SUCK UP TO MY BOSS...
OH GOD... DO I HAVE TO...?

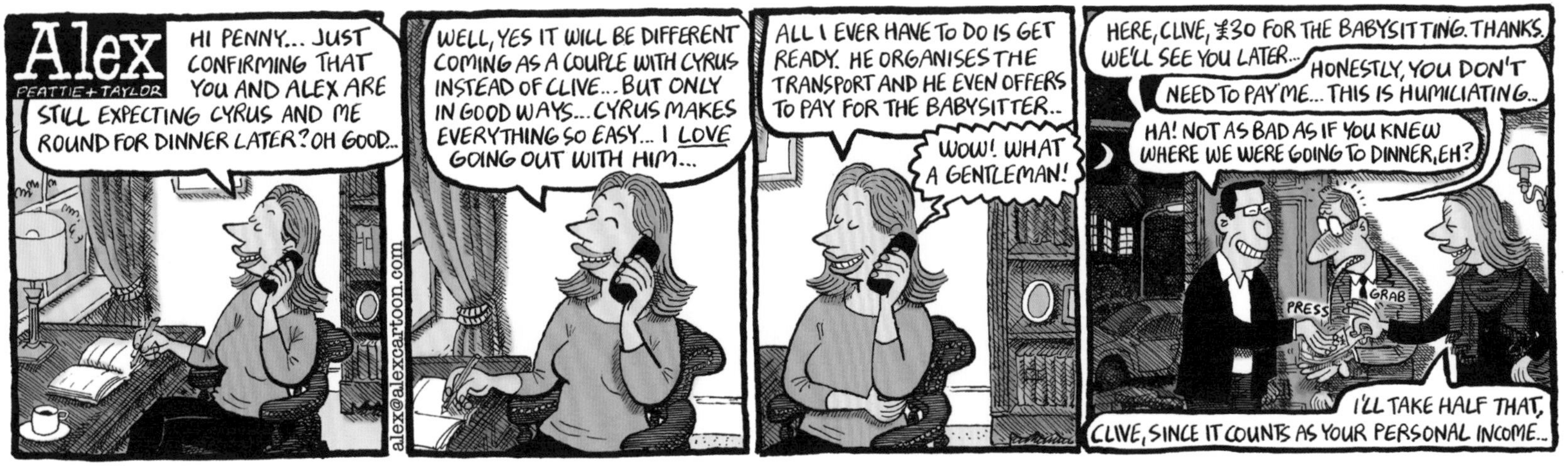
Alex
PEATTIE + TAYLOR
HI PENNY... JUST CONFIRMING THAT YOU AND ALEX ARE STILL EXPECTING CYRUS AND ME ROUND FOR DINNER LATER? OH GOOD...
alex@alexcartoon.com
WELL, YES IT WILL BE DIFFERENT COMING AS A COUPLE WITH CYRUS INSTEAD OF CLIVE... BUT ONLY IN GOOD WAYS... CYRUS MAKES EVERYTHING SO EASY... I LOVE GOING OUT WITH HIM...
ALL I EVER HAVE TO DO IS GET READY. HE ORGANISES THE TRANSPORT AND HE EVEN OFFERS TO PAY FOR THE BABYSITTER...
WOW! WHAT A GENTLEMAN!
HERE, CLIVE, £30 FOR THE BABYSITTING. THANKS. WE'LL SEE YOU LATER...
HONESTLY, YOU DON'T NEED TO PAY ME... THIS IS HUMILIATING...
HA! NOT AS BAD AS IF YOU KNEW WHERE WE WERE GOING TO DINNER, EH?
PRESS
GRAB
I'LL TAKE HALF THAT, CLIVE, SINCE IT COUNTS AS YOUR PERSONAL INCOME...

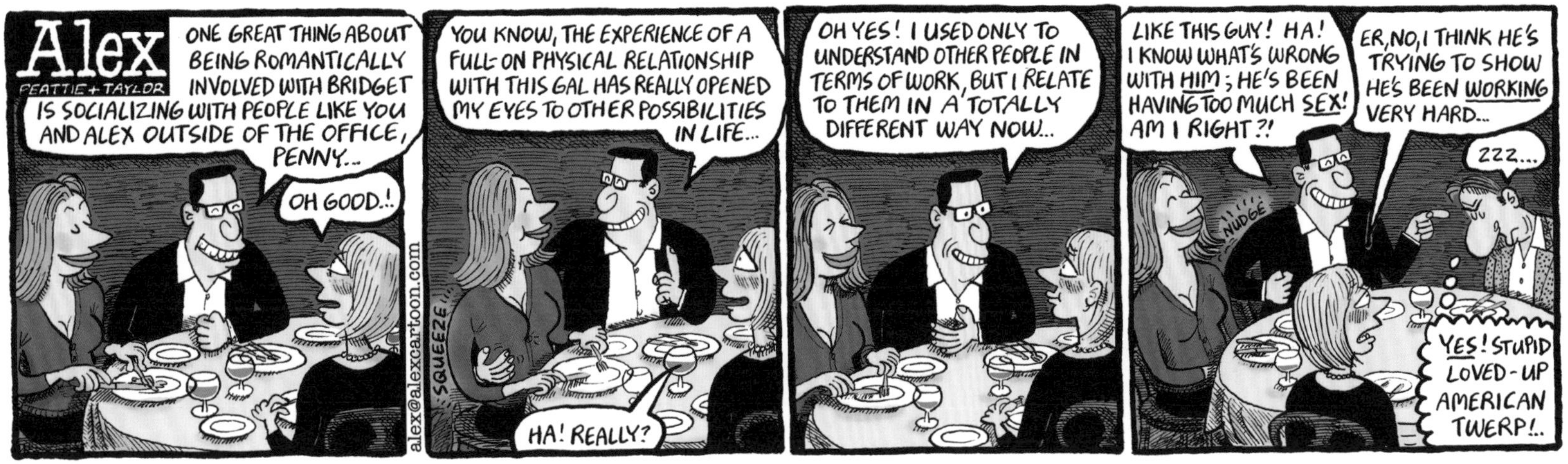
Alex
PEATTIE + TAYLOR
ONE GREAT THING ABOUT BEING ROMANTICALLY INVOLVED WITH BRIDGET IS SOCIALIZING WITH PEOPLE LIKE YOU AND ALEX OUTSIDE OF THE OFFICE, PENNY...
OH GOOD..!
alex@alexcartoon.com
YOU KNOW, THE EXPERIENCE OF A FULL-ON PHYSICAL RELATIONSHIP WITH THIS GAL HAS REALLY OPENED MY EYES TO OTHER POSSIBILITIES IN LIFE...
SQUEEZE
HA! REALLY?
OH YES! I USED ONLY TO UNDERSTAND OTHER PEOPLE IN TERMS OF WORK, BUT I RELATE TO THEM IN A TOTALLY DIFFERENT WAY NOW...
LIKE THIS GUY! HA! I KNOW WHAT'S WRONG WITH HIM; HE'S BEEN HAVING TOO MUCH SEX! AM I RIGHT?!
NUDGE
ER, NO, I THINK HE'S TRYING TO SHOW HE'S BEEN WORKING VERY HARD...
ZZZ....
YES! STUPID LOVED-UP AMERICAN TWERP!..

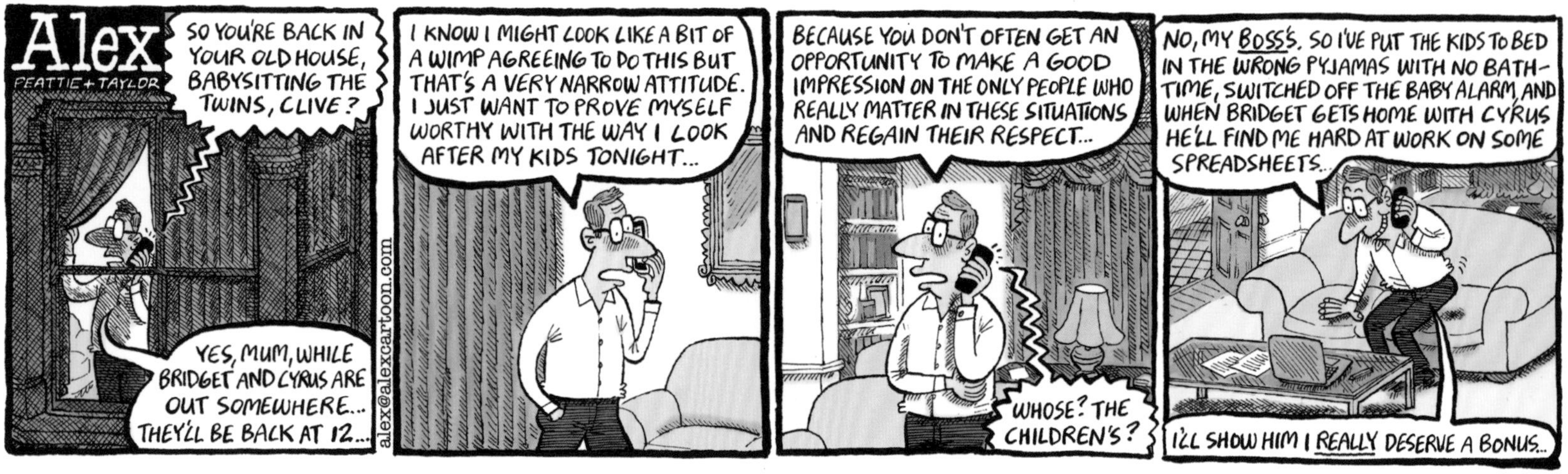
Alex
PEATTIE + TAYLOR
SO YOU'RE BACK IN YOUR OLD HOUSE, BABYSITTING THE TWINS, CLIVE?
YES, MUM, WHILE BRIDGET AND CYRUS ARE OUT SOMEWHERE... THEY'LL BE BACK AT 12...
alex@alexcartoon.com
I KNOW I MIGHT LOOK LIKE A BIT OF A WIMP AGREEING TO DO THIS BUT THAT'S A VERY NARROW ATTITUDE. I JUST WANT TO PROVE MYSELF WORTHY WITH THE WAY I LOOK AFTER MY KIDS TONIGHT...
BECAUSE YOU DON'T OFTEN GET AN OPPORTUNITY TO MAKE A GOOD IMPRESSION ON THE ONLY PEOPLE WHO REALLY MATTER IN THESE SITUATIONS AND REGAIN THEIR RESPECT...
WHOSE? THE CHILDREN'S?
NO, MY BOSS'S. SO I'VE PUT THE KIDS TO BED IN THE WRONG PYJAMAS WITH NO BATH-TIME, SWITCHED OFF THE BABY ALARM, AND WHEN BRIDGET GETS HOME WITH CYRUS HE'LL FIND ME HARD AT WORK ON SOME SPREADSHEETS...
I'LL SHOW HIM I REALLY DESERVE A BONUS...

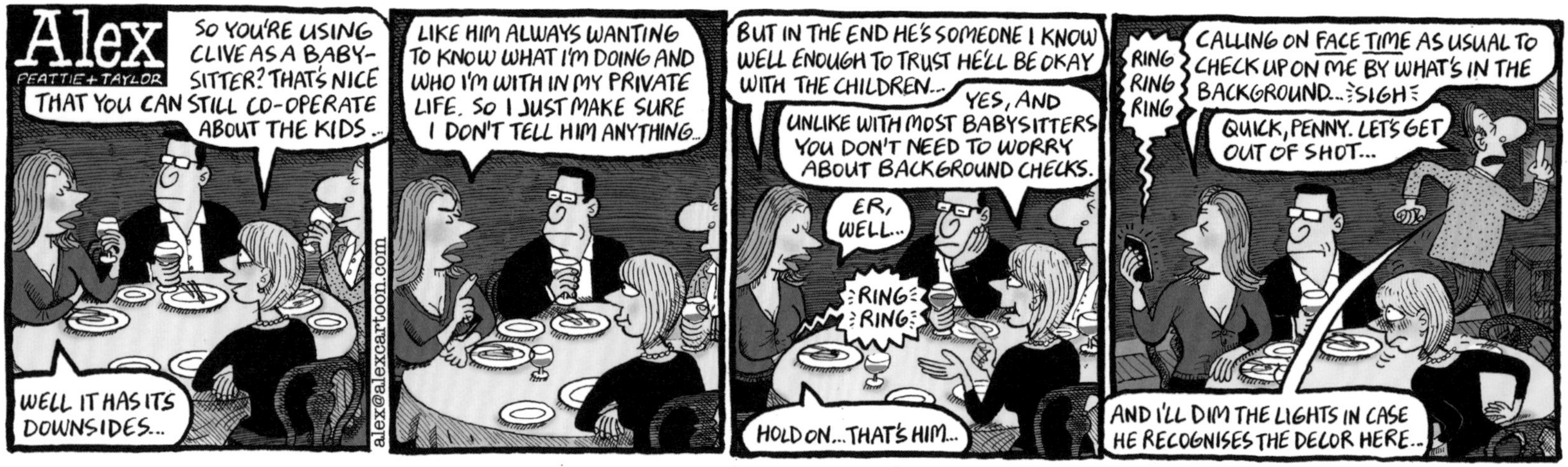
Alex
PEATTIE + TAYLOR
SO YOU'RE USING CLIVE AS A BABY-SITTER? THAT'S NICE THAT YOU CAN STILL CO-OPERATE ABOUT THE KIDS...
WELL IT HAS ITS DOWNSIDES...
alex@alexcartoon.com
LIKE HIM ALWAYS WANTING TO KNOW WHAT I'M DOING AND WHO I'M WITH IN MY PRIVATE LIFE. SO I JUST MAKE SURE I DON'T TELL HIM ANYTHING...
BUT IN THE END HE'S SOMEONE I KNOW WELL ENOUGH TO TRUST HE'LL BE OKAY WITH THE CHILDREN...
YES, AND UNLIKE WITH MOST BABYSITTERS YOU DON'T NEED TO WORRY ABOUT BACKGROUND CHECKS.
ER, WELL...
RING RING
HOLD ON... THAT'S HIM...
RING RING RING
CALLING ON FACE TIME AS USUAL TO CHECK UP ON ME BY WHAT'S IN THE BACKGROUND... SIGH
QUICK, PENNY. LET'S GET OUT OF SHOT...
AND I'LL DIM THE LIGHTS IN CASE HE RECOGNISES THE DECOR HERE...

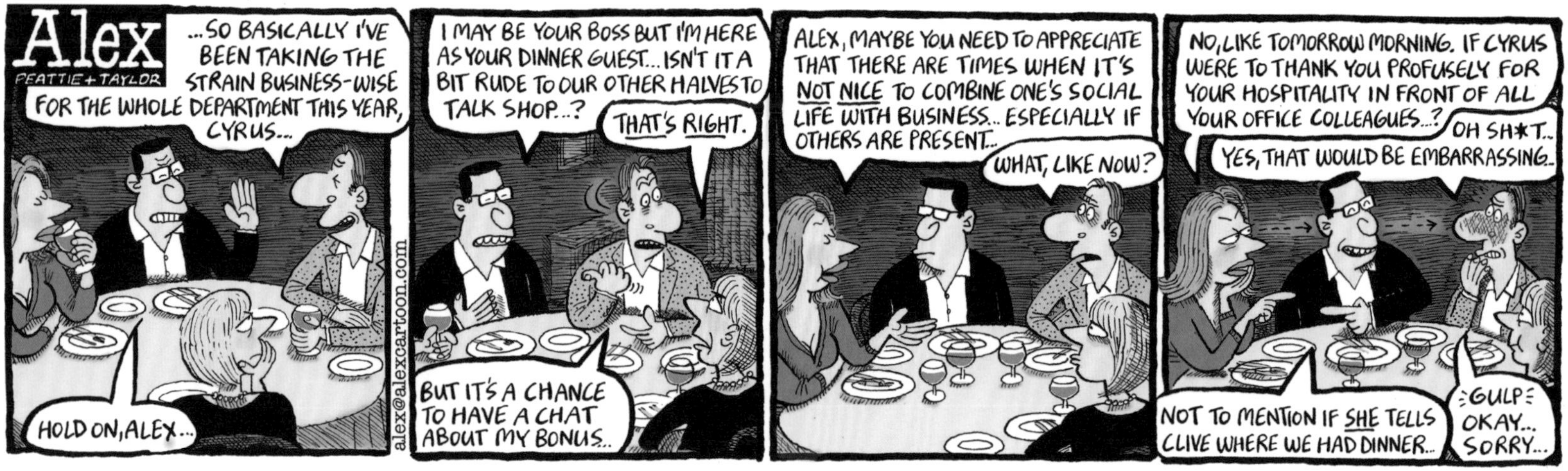
Alex
PEATTIE + TAYLOR
...SO BASICALLY I'VE BEEN TAKING THE STRAIN BUSINESS-WISE FOR THE WHOLE DEPARTMENT THIS YEAR, CYRUS...
HOLD ON, ALEX...
alex@alexcartoon.com
I MAY BE YOUR BOSS BUT I'M HERE AS YOUR DINNER GUEST... ISN'T IT A BIT RUDE TO OUR OTHER HALVES TO TALK SHOP...?
THAT'S RIGHT.
BUT IT'S A CHANCE TO HAVE A CHAT ABOUT MY BONUS...
ALEX, MAYBE YOU NEED TO APPRECIATE THAT THERE ARE TIMES WHEN IT'S NOT NICE TO COMBINE ONE'S SOCIAL LIFE WITH BUSINESS... ESPECIALLY IF OTHERS ARE PRESENT...
WHAT, LIKE NOW?
NO, LIKE TOMORROW MORNING. IF CYRUS WERE TO THANK YOU PROFUSELY FOR YOUR HOSPITALITY IN FRONT OF ALL YOUR OFFICE COLLEAGUES...?
OH SH*T..
YES, THAT WOULD BE EMBARRASSING...
NOT TO MENTION IF SHE TELLS CLIVE WHERE WE HAD DINNER...
GULP OKAY... SORRY...

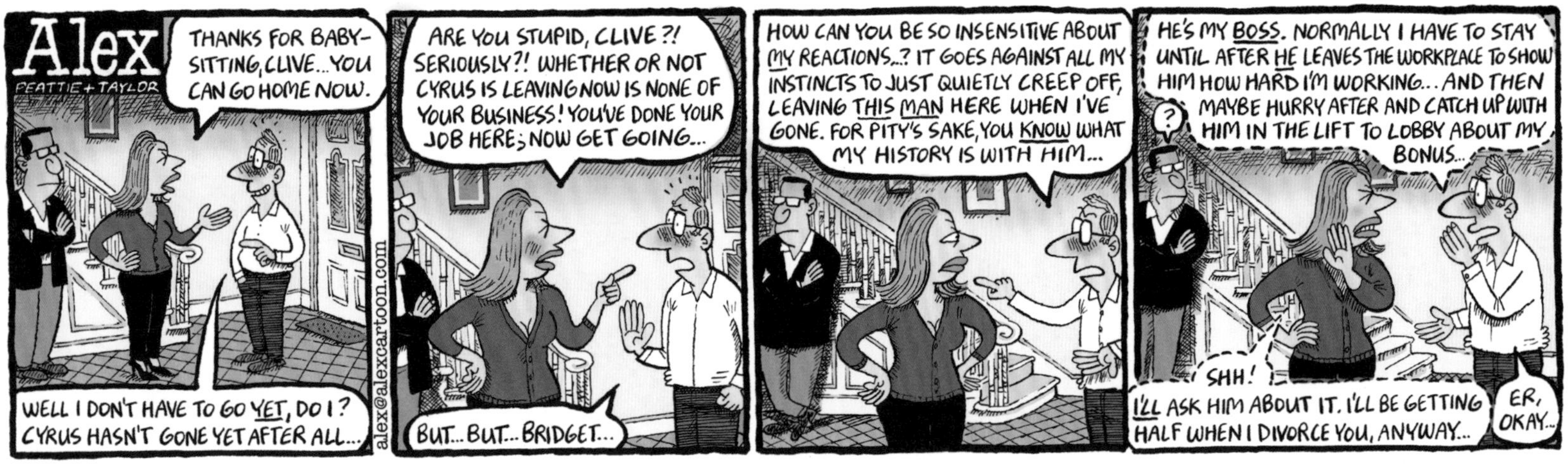
Alex
PEATTIE + TAYLOR
THANKS FOR BABY-SITTING, CLIVE... YOU CAN GO HOME NOW.
WELL I DON'T HAVE TO GO YET, DO I? CYRUS HASN'T GONE YET AFTER ALL...
alex@alexcartoon.com
ARE YOU STUPID, CLIVE?! SERIOUSLY?! WHETHER OR NOT CYRUS IS LEAVING NOW IS NONE OF YOUR BUSINESS! YOU'VE DONE YOUR JOB HERE; NOW GET GOING...
BUT... BUT... BRIDGET...
HOW CAN YOU BE SO INSENSITIVE ABOUT MY REACTIONS...? IT GOES AGAINST ALL MY INSTINCTS TO JUST QUIETLY CREEP OFF, LEAVING THIS MAN HERE WHEN I'VE GONE. FOR PITY'S SAKE, YOU KNOW WHAT MY HISTORY IS WITH HIM...
HE'S MY BOSS. NORMALLY I HAVE TO STAY UNTIL AFTER HE LEAVES THE WORKPLACE TO SHOW HIM HOW HARD I'M WORKING... AND THEN MAYBE HURRY AFTER AND CATCH UP WITH HIM IN THE LIFT TO LOBBY ABOUT MY BONUS...
?
SHH!
I'LL ASK HIM ABOUT IT. I'LL BE GETTING HALF WHEN I DIVORCE YOU, ANYWAY...
ER, OKAY...

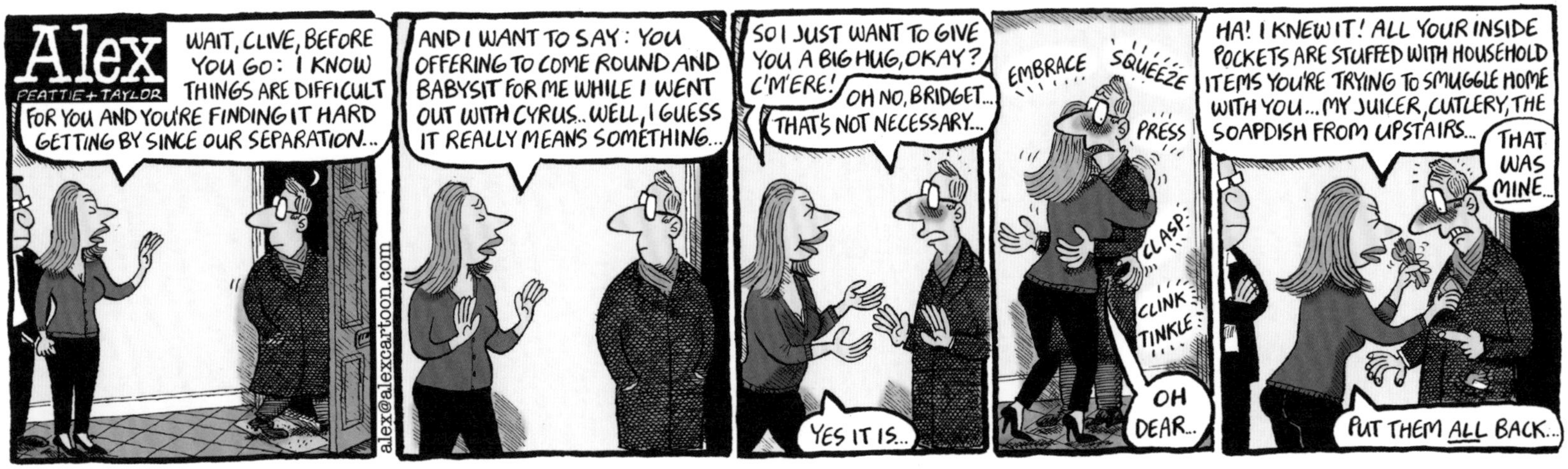
Alex
PEATTIE + TAYLOR
WAIT, CLIVE, BEFORE YOU GO: I KNOW THINGS ARE DIFFICULT FOR YOU AND YOU'RE FINDING IT HARD GETTING BY SINCE OUR SEPARATION...
alex@alexcartoon.com
AND I WANT TO SAY: YOU OFFERING TO COME ROUND AND BABYSIT FOR ME WHILE I WENT OUT WITH CYRUS.. WELL, I GUESS IT REALLY MEANS SOMETHING...
SO I JUST WANT TO GIVE YOU A BIG HUG, OKAY? C'M'ERE!
OH NO, BRIDGET... THAT'S NOT NECESSARY...
YES IT IS...
EMBRACE
SQUEEZE
PRESS
CLASP
CLINK
TINKLE
OH DEAR...
HA! I KNEW IT! ALL YOUR INSIDE POCKETS ARE STUFFED WITH HOUSEHOLD ITEMS YOU'RE TRYING TO SMUGGLE HOME WITH YOU... MY JUICER, CUTLERY, THE SOAPDISH FROM UPSTAIRS...
THAT WAS MINE...
PUT THEM ALL BACK...

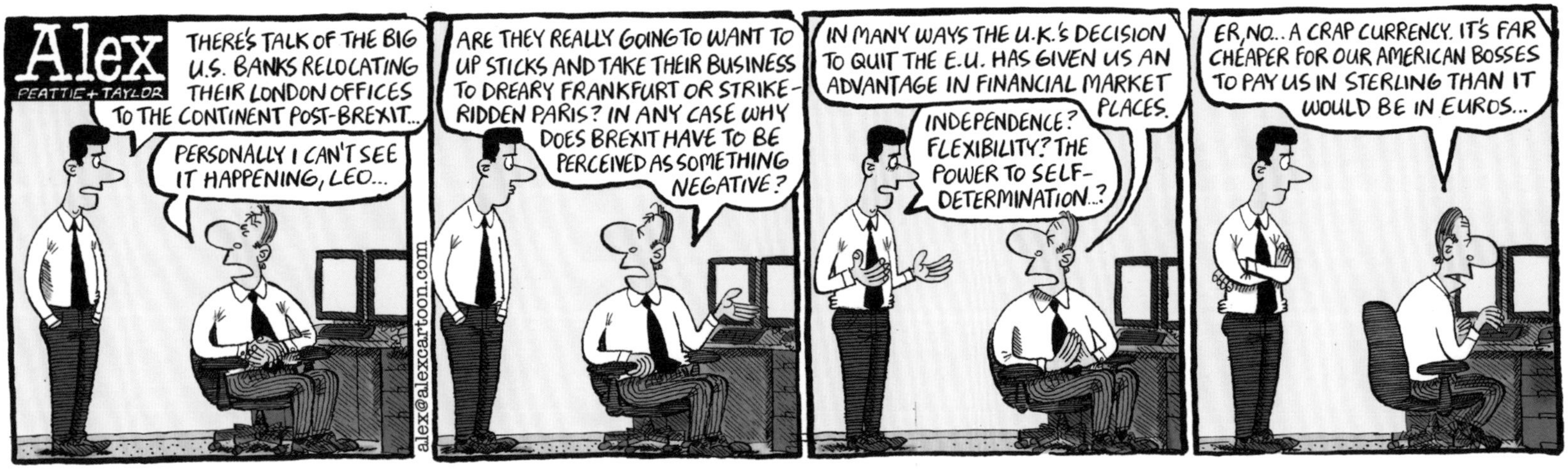
Alex
PEATTIE + TAYLOR
THERE'S TALK OF THE BIG U.S. BANKS RELOCATING THEIR LONDON OFFICES TO THE CONTINENT POST-BREXIT...
PERSONALLY I CAN'T SEE IT HAPPENING, LEO...
alex@alexcartoon.com
ARE THEY REALLY GOING TO WANT TO UP STICKS AND TAKE THEIR BUSINESS TO DREARY FRANKFURT OR STRIKE-RIDDEN PARIS? IN ANY CASE WHY DOES BREXIT HAVE TO BE PERCEIVED AS SOMETHING NEGATIVE?
IN MANY WAYS THE U.K.'S DECISION TO QUIT THE E.U. HAS GIVEN US AN ADVANTAGE IN FINANCIAL MARKET PLACES.
INDEPENDENCE? FLEXIBILITY? THE POWER TO SELF-DETERMINATION...?
ER, NO... A CRAP CURRENCY. IT'S FAR CHEAPER FOR OUR AMERICAN BOSSES TO PAY US IN STERLING THAN IT WOULD BE IN EUROS...

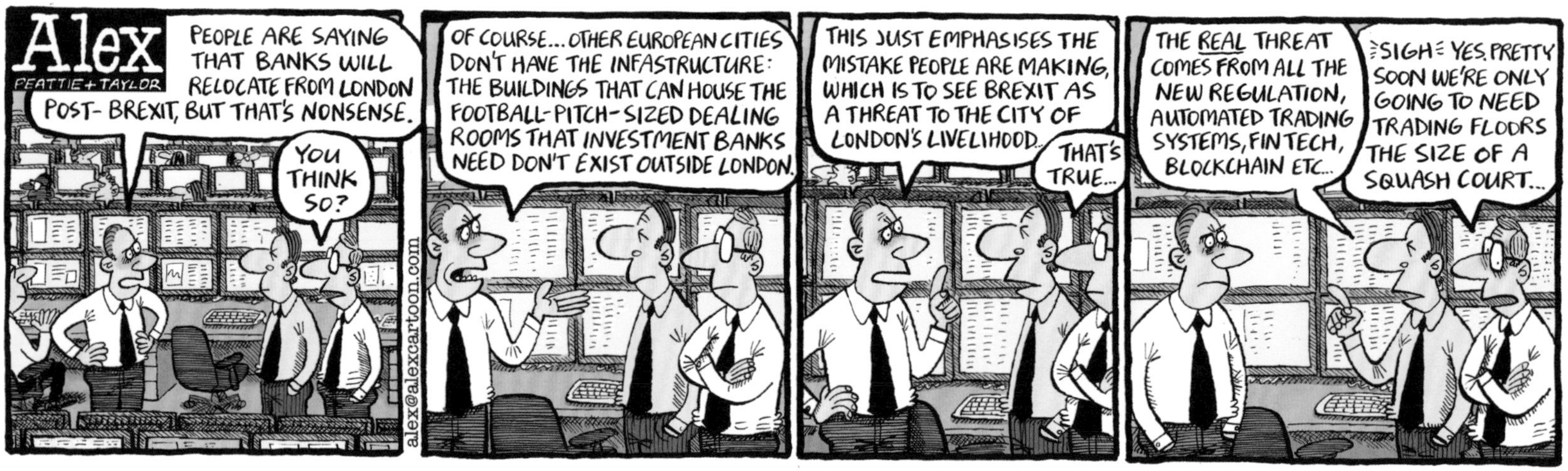
Alex
PEATTIE + TAYLOR
PEOPLE ARE SAYING THAT BANKS WILL RELOCATE FROM LONDON POST- BREXIT, BUT THAT'S NONSENSE.
YOU THINK SO?
alex@alexcartoon.com
OF COURSE... OTHER EUROPEAN CITIES DON'T HAVE THE INFASTRUCTURE: THE BUILDINGS THAT CAN HOUSE THE FOOTBALL-PITCH-SIZED DEALING ROOMS THAT INVESTMENT BANKS NEED DON'T EXIST OUTSIDE LONDON.
THIS JUST EMPHASISES THE MISTAKE PEOPLE ARE MAKING, WHICH IS TO SEE BREXIT AS A THREAT TO THE CITY OF LONDON'S LIVELIHOOD...
THAT'S TRUE...
THE REAL THREAT COMES FROM ALL THE NEW REGULATION, AUTOMATED TRADING SYSTEMS, FINTECH, BLOCKCHAIN ETC...
SIGH YES, PRETTY SOON WE'RE ONLY GOING TO NEED TRADING FLOORS THE SIZE OF A SQUASH COURT...

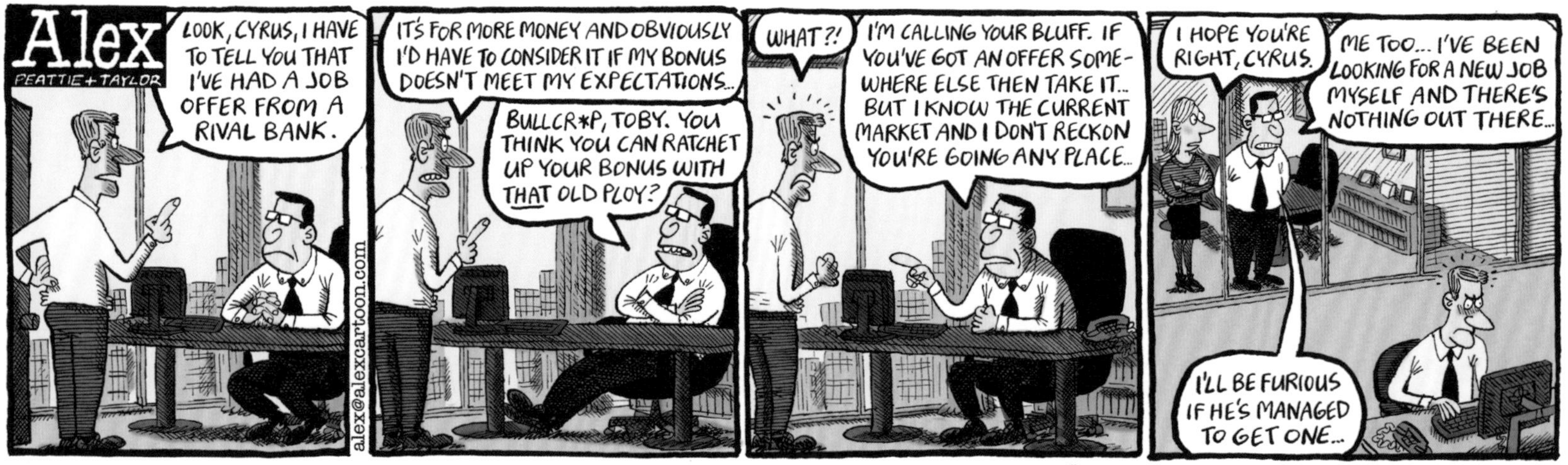
Alex
PEATTIE + TAYLOR
LOOK, CYRUS, I HAVE TO TELL YOU THAT I'VE HAD A JOB OFFER FROM A RIVAL BANK.
alex@alexcartoon.com
IT'S FOR MORE MONEY AND OBVIOUSLY I'D HAVE TO CONSIDER IT IF MY BONUS DOESN'T MEET MY EXPECTATIONS...
BULLCR*P, TOBY. YOU THINK YOU CAN RATCHET UP YOUR BONUS WITH THAT OLD PLOY?
WHAT?!
I'M CALLING YOUR BLUFF. IF YOU'VE GOT AN OFFER SOMEWHERE ELSE THEN TAKE IT... BUT I KNOW THE CURRENT MARKET AND I DON'T RECKON YOU'RE GOING ANY PLACE...
I HOPE YOU'RE RIGHT, CYRUS.
ME TOO... I'VE BEEN LOOKING FOR A NEW JOB MYSELF AND THERE'S NOTHING OUT THERE...
I'LL BE FURIOUS IF HE'S MANAGED TO GET ONE...

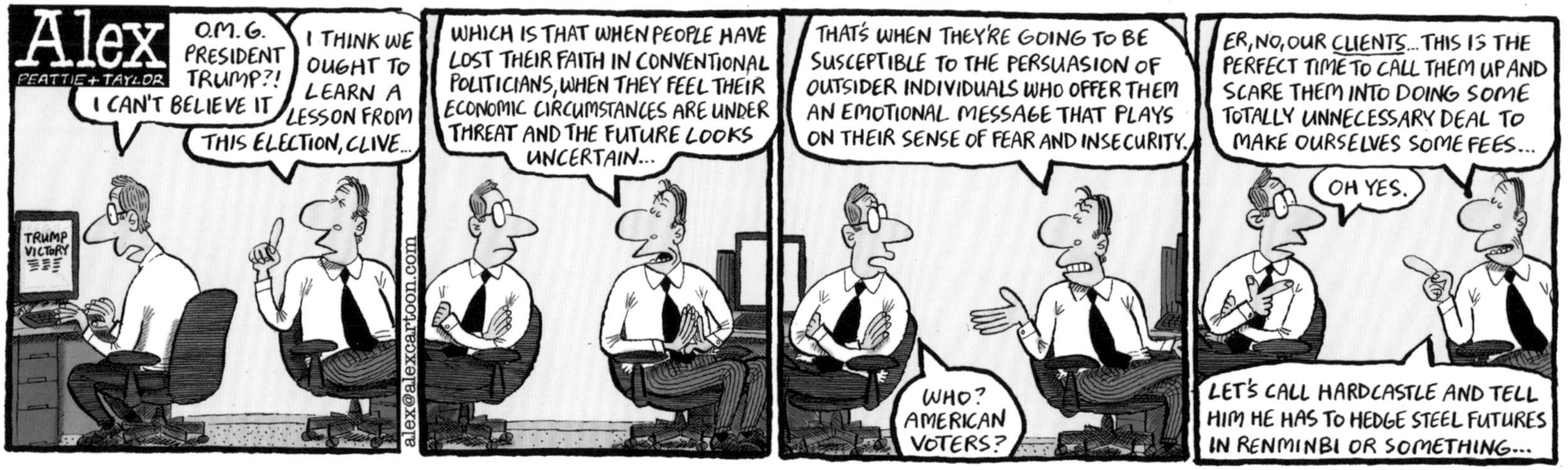
Alex
PEATTIE + TAYLOR
O.M.G. PRESIDENT TRUMP?! I CAN'T BELIEVE IT
I THINK WE OUGHT TO LEARN A LESSON FROM THIS ELECTION, CLIVE...
TRUMP VICTORY
alex@alexcartoon.com
WHICH IS THAT WHEN PEOPLE HAVE LOST THEIR FAITH IN CONVENTIONAL POLITICIANS, WHEN THEY FEEL THEIR ECONOMIC CIRCUMSTANCES ARE UNDER THREAT AND THE FUTURE LOOKS UNCERTAIN...
THAT'S WHEN THEY'RE GOING TO BE SUSCEPTIBLE TO THE PERSUASION OF OUTSIDER INDIVIDUALS WHO OFFER THEM AN EMOTIONAL MESSAGE THAT PLAYS ON THEIR SENSE OF FEAR AND INSECURITY.
WHO? AMERICAN VOTERS?
ER, NO, OUR CLIENTS... THIS IS THE PERFECT TIME TO CALL THEM UP AND SCARE THEM INTO DOING SOME TOTALLY UNNECESSARY DEAL TO MAKE OURSELVES SOME FEES...
OH YES.
LET'S CALL HARDCASTLE AND TELL HIM HE HAS TO HEDGE STEEL FUTURES IN RENMINBI OR SOMETHING...

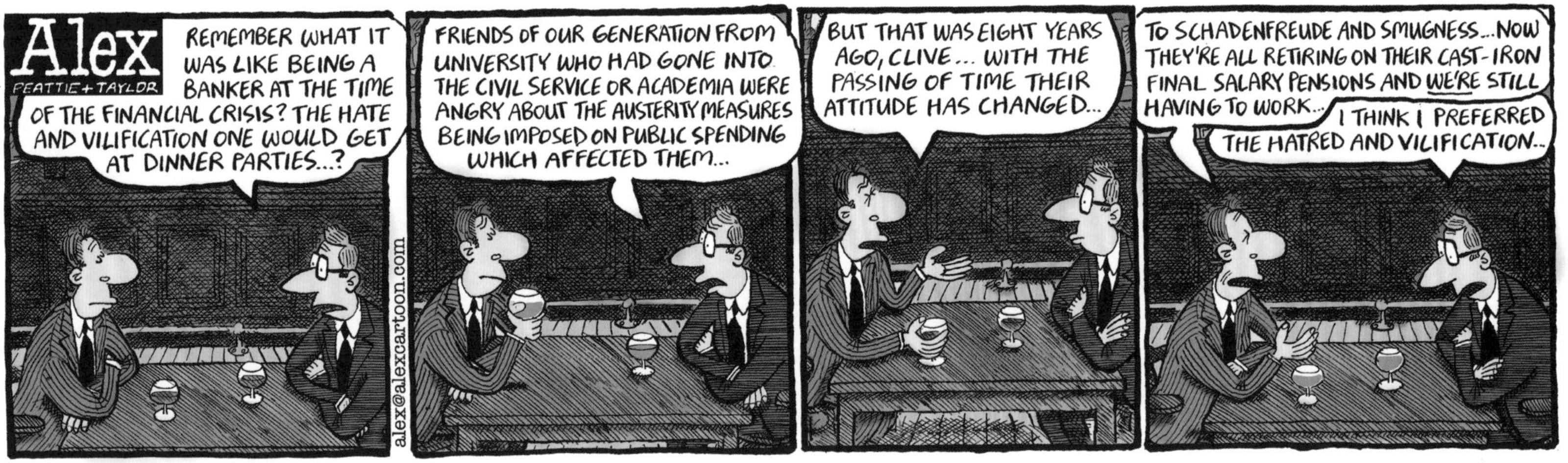
Alex
PEATTIE+TAYLOR
REMEMBER WHAT IT WAS LIKE BEING A BANKER AT THE TIME OF THE FINANCIAL CRISIS? THE HATE AND VILIFICATION ONE WOULD GET AT DINNER PARTIES...?
alex@alexcartoon.com
FRIENDS OF OUR GENERATION FROM UNIVERSITY WHO HAD GONE INTO THE CIVIL SERVICE OR ACADEMIA WERE ANGRY ABOUT THE AUSTERITY MEASURES BEING IMPOSED ON PUBLIC SPENDING WHICH AFFECTED THEM...
BUT THAT WAS EIGHT YEARS AGO, CLIVE... WITH THE PASSING OF TIME THEIR ATTITUDE HAS CHANGED...
TO SCHADENFREUDE AND SMUGNESS... NOW THEY'RE ALL RETIRING ON THEIR CAST-IRON FINAL SALARY PENSIONS AND WE'RE STILL HAVING TO WORK...
I THINK I PREFERRED THE HATRED AND VILIFICATION...

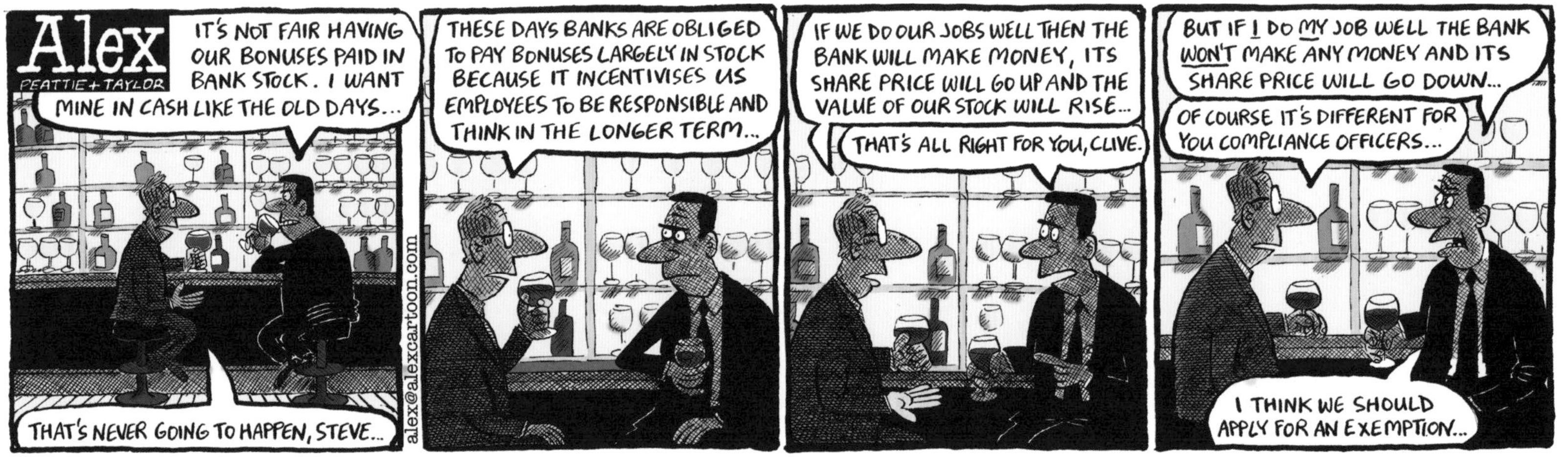
Alex
PEATTIE+TAYLOR
IT'S NOT FAIR HAVING OUR BONUSES PAID IN BANK STOCK. I WANT MINE IN CASH LIKE THE OLD DAYS...
THAT'S NEVER GOING TO HAPPEN, STEVE...
alex@alexcartoon.com
THESE DAYS BANKS ARE OBLIGED TO PAY BONUSES LARGELY IN STOCK BECAUSE IT INCENTIVISES US EMPLOYEES TO BE RESPONSIBLE AND THINK IN THE LONGER TERM...
IF WE DO OUR JOBS WELL THEN THE BANK WILL MAKE MONEY, ITS SHARE PRICE WILL GO UP AND THE VALUE OF OUR STOCK WILL RISE...
THAT'S ALL RIGHT FOR YOU, CLIVE.
BUT IF I DO MY JOB WELL THE BANK WON'T MAKE ANY MONEY AND ITS SHARE PRICE WILL GO DOWN...
OF COURSE IT'S DIFFERENT FOR YOU COMPLIANCE OFFICERS...
I THINK WE SHOULD APPLY FOR AN EXEMPTION...

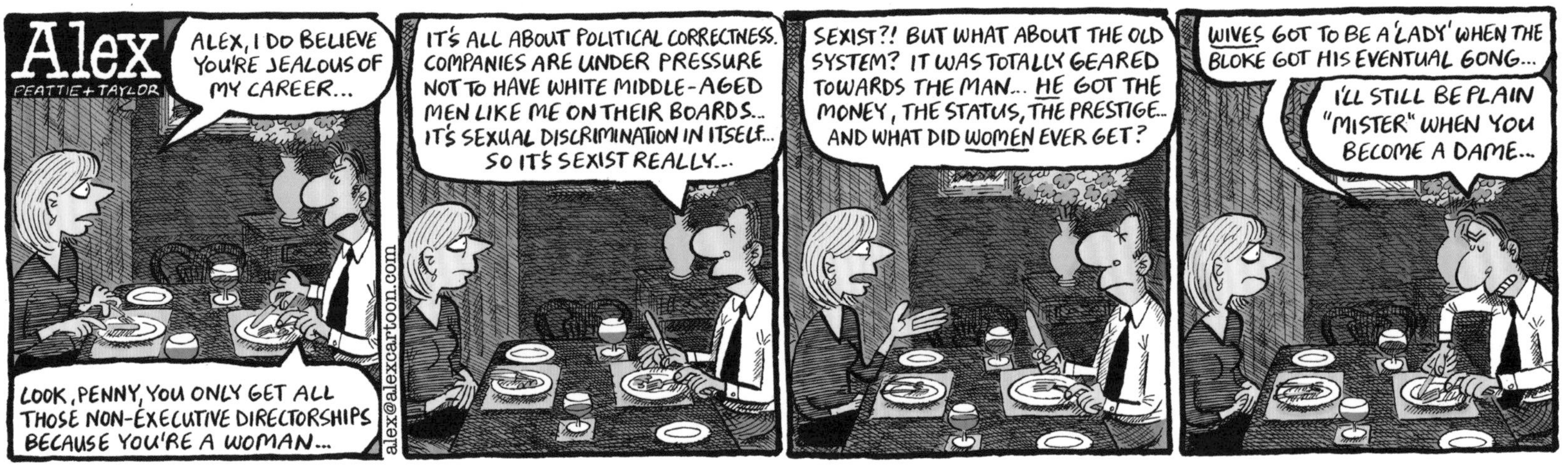
Alex
PEATTIE+TAYLOR
ALEX, I DO BELIEVE YOU'RE JEALOUS OF MY CAREER...
LOOK, PENNY, YOU ONLY GET ALL THOSE NON-EXECUTIVE DIRECTORSHIPS BECAUSE YOU'RE A WOMAN...
alex@alexcartoon.com
IT'S ALL ABOUT POLITICAL CORRECTNESS. COMPANIES ARE UNDER PRESSURE NOT TO HAVE WHITE MIDDLE-AGED MEN LIKE ME ON THEIR BOARDS... IT'S SEXUAL DISCRIMINATION IN ITSELF... SO IT'S SEXIST REALLY...
SEXIST?! BUT WHAT ABOUT THE OLD SYSTEM? IT WAS TOTALLY GEARED TOWARDS THE MAN... HE GOT THE MONEY, THE STATUS, THE PRESTIGE... AND WHAT DID WOMEN EVER GET?
WIVES GOT TO BE A 'LADY' WHEN THE BLOKE GOT HIS EVENTUAL GONG...
I'LL STILL BE PLAIN "MISTER" WHEN YOU BECOME A DAME...

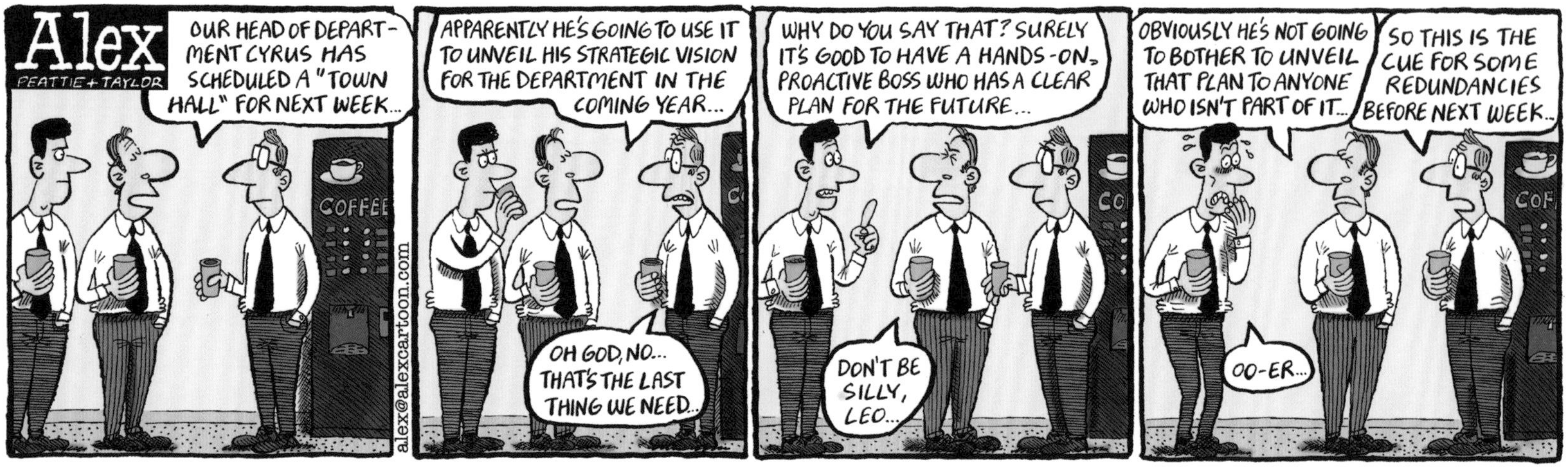
Alex
PEATTIE + TAYLOR
OUR HEAD OF DEPARTMENT CYRUS HAS SCHEDULED A "TOWN HALL" FOR NEXT WEEK...
COFFEE
alex@alexcartoon.com
APPARENTLY HE'S GOING TO USE IT TO UNVEIL HIS STRATEGIC VISION FOR THE DEPARTMENT IN THE COMING YEAR...
OH GOD, NO... THAT'S THE LAST THING WE NEED...
WHY DO YOU SAY THAT? SURELY IT'S GOOD TO HAVE A HANDS-ON, PROACTIVE BOSS WHO HAS A CLEAR PLAN FOR THE FUTURE...
DON'T BE SILLY, LEO...
OBVIOUSLY HE'S NOT GOING TO BOTHER TO UNVEIL THAT PLAN TO ANYONE WHO ISN'T PART OF IT...
SO THIS IS THE CUE FOR SOME REDUNDANCIES BEFORE NEXT WEEK...
OO-ER...

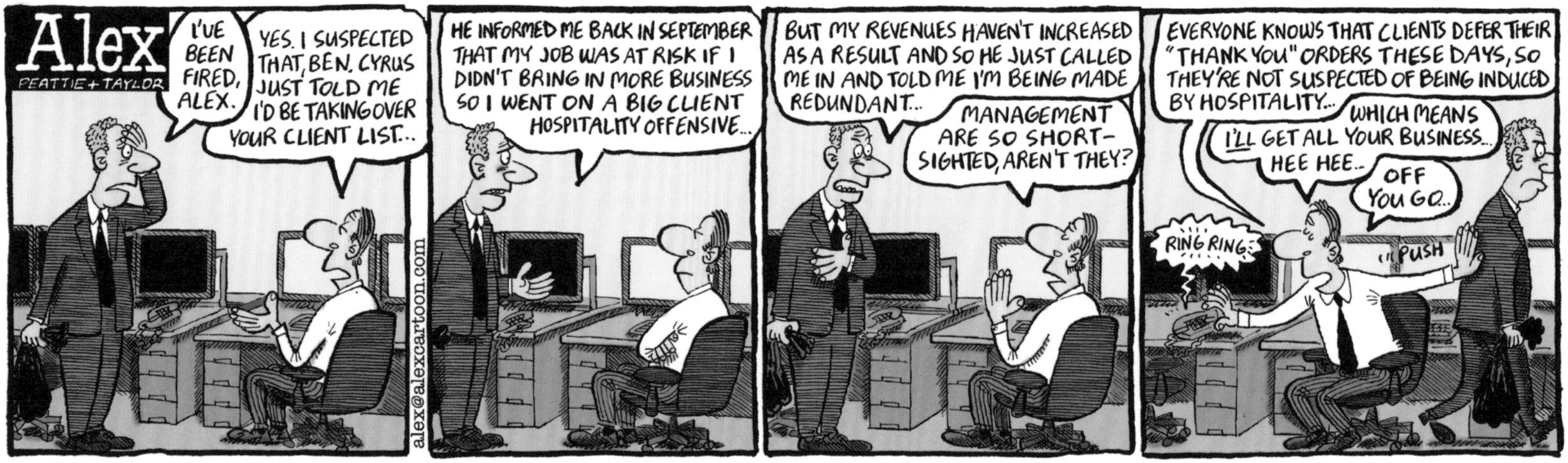
Alex
PEATTIE + TAYLOR
I'VE BEEN FIRED, ALEX.
YES. I SUSPECTED THAT, BEN. CYRUS JUST TOLD ME I'D BE TAKING OVER YOUR CLIENT LIST...
alex@alexcartoon.com
HE INFORMED ME BACK IN SEPTEMBER THAT MY JOB WAS AT RISK IF I DIDN'T BRING IN MORE BUSINESS SO I WENT ON A BIG CLIENT HOSPITALITY OFFENSIVE...
BUT MY REVENUES HAVEN'T INCREASED AS A RESULT AND SO HE JUST CALLED ME IN AND TOLD ME I'M BEING MADE REDUNDANT...
MANAGEMENT ARE SO SHORT-SIGHTED, AREN'T THEY?
EVERYONE KNOWS THAT CLIENTS DEFER THEIR "THANK YOU" ORDERS THESE DAYS, SO THEY'RE NOT SUSPECTED OF BEING INDUCED BY HOSPITALITY...
WHICH MEANS I'LL GET ALL YOUR BUSINESS... HEE HEE...
RING RING
OFF YOU GO...
PUSH

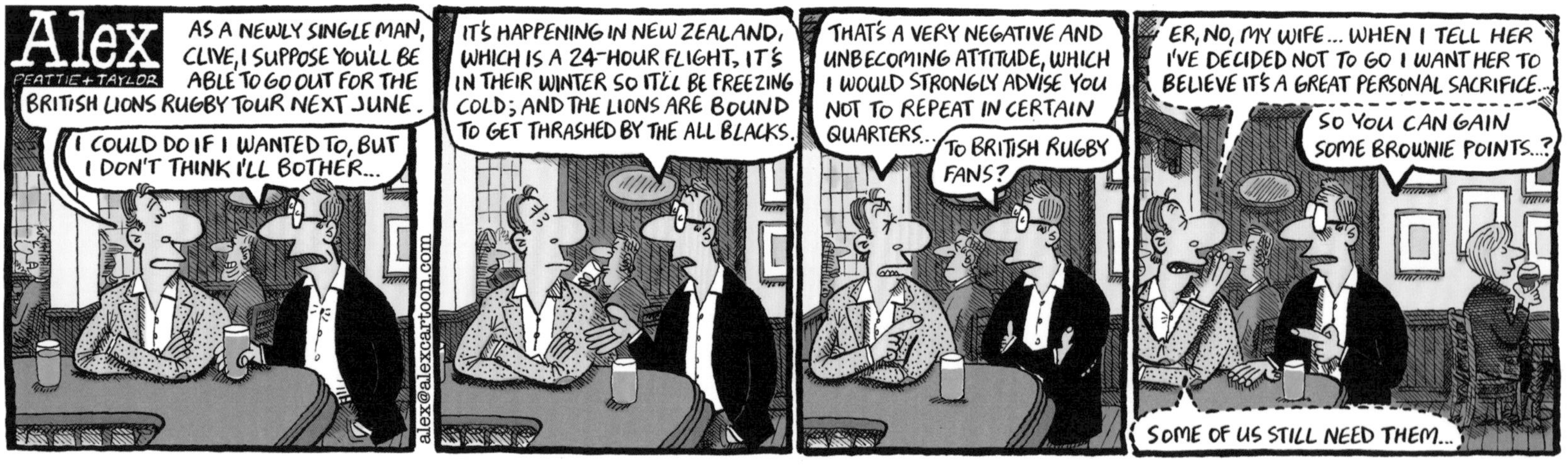
Alex
PEATTIE + TAYLOR
AS A NEWLY SINGLE MAN, CLIVE, I SUPPOSE YOU'LL BE ABLE TO GO OUT FOR THE BRITISH LIONS RUGBY TOUR NEXT JUNE.
I COULD DO IF I WANTED TO, BUT I DON'T THINK I'LL BOTHER...
alex@alexcartoon.com
IT'S HAPPENING IN NEW ZEALAND, WHICH IS A 24-HOUR FLIGHT, IT'S IN THEIR WINTER SO IT'LL BE FREEZING COLD; AND THE LIONS ARE BOUND TO GET THRASHED BY THE ALL BLACKS.
THAT'S A VERY NEGATIVE AND UNBECOMING ATTITUDE, WHICH I WOULD STRONGLY ADVISE YOU NOT TO REPEAT IN CERTAIN QUARTERS...
TO BRITISH RUGBY FANS?
ER, NO, MY WIFE... WHEN I TELL HER I'VE DECIDED NOT TO GO I WANT HER TO BELIEVE IT'S A GREAT PERSONAL SACRIFICE...
SO YOU CAN GAIN SOME BROWNIE POINTS...?
SOME OF US STILL NEED THEM...

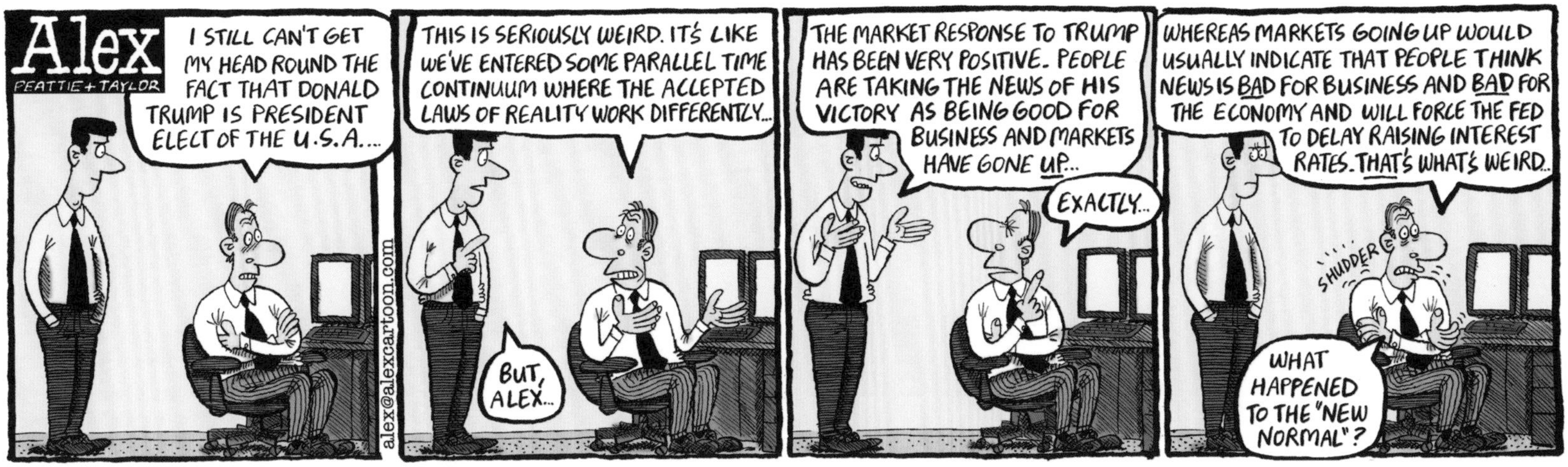
Alex
PEATTIE + TAYLOR
I STILL CAN'T GET MY HEAD ROUND THE FACT THAT DONALD TRUMP IS PRESIDENT ELECT OF THE U.S.A....
alex@alexcartoon.com
THIS IS SERIOUSLY WEIRD. IT'S LIKE WE'VE ENTERED SOME PARALLEL TIME CONTINUUM WHERE THE ACCEPTED LAWS OF REALITY WORK DIFFERENTLY...
BUT, ALEX...
THE MARKET RESPONSE TO TRUMP HAS BEEN VERY POSITIVE. PEOPLE ARE TAKING THE NEWS OF HIS VICTORY AS BEING GOOD FOR BUSINESS AND MARKETS HAVE GONE UP...
EXACTLY...
WHEREAS MARKETS GOING UP WOULD USUALLY INDICATE THAT PEOPLE THINK NEWS IS BAD FOR BUSINESS AND BAD FOR THE ECONOMY AND WILL FORCE THE FED TO DELAY RAISING INTEREST RATES. THAT'S WHAT'S WEIRD...
SHUDDER
WHAT HAPPENED TO THE "NEW NORMAL"?

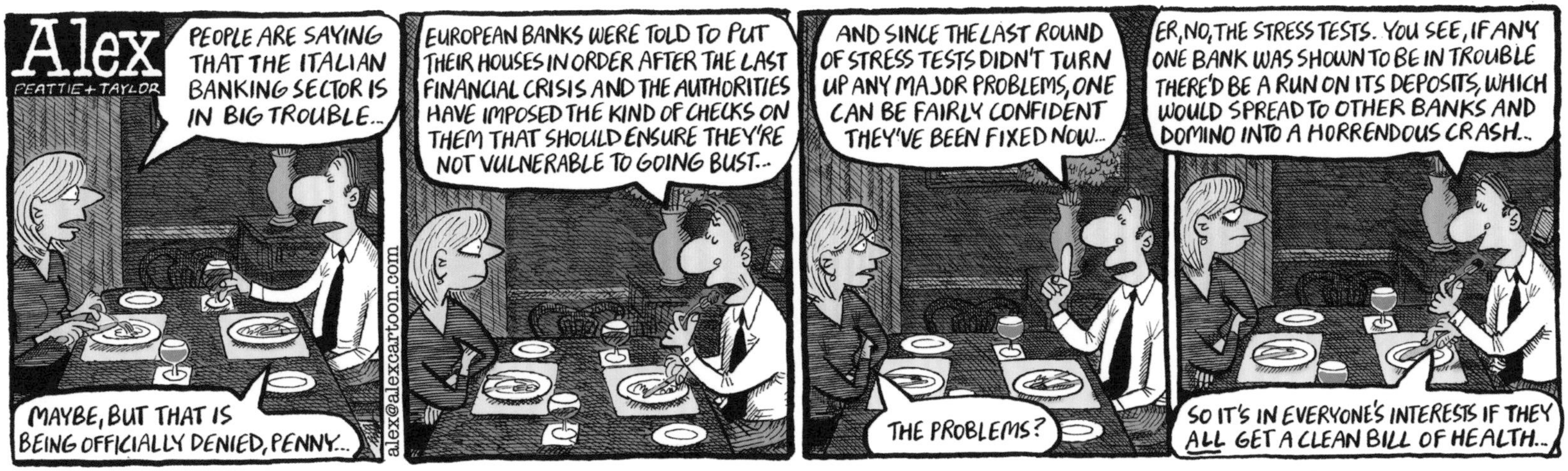
Alex
PEATTIE + TAYLOR
PEOPLE ARE SAYING THAT THE ITALIAN BANKING SECTOR IS IN BIG TROUBLE...
MAYBE, BUT THAT IS BEING OFFICIALLY DENIED, PENNY...
alex@alexcartoon.com
EUROPEAN BANKS WERE TOLD TO PUT THEIR HOUSES IN ORDER AFTER THE LAST FINANCIAL CRISIS AND THE AUTHORITIES HAVE IMPOSED THE KIND OF CHECKS ON THEM THAT SHOULD ENSURE THEY'RE NOT VULNERABLE TO GOING BUST...
AND SINCE THE LAST ROUND OF STRESS TESTS DIDN'T TURN UP ANY MAJOR PROBLEMS, ONE CAN BE FAIRLY CONFIDENT THEY'VE BEEN FIXED NOW...
THE PROBLEMS?
ER, NO, THE STRESS TESTS. YOU SEE, IF ANY ONE BANK WAS SHOWN TO BE IN TROUBLE THERE'D BE A RUN ON ITS DEPOSITS, WHICH WOULD SPREAD TO OTHER BANKS AND DOMINO INTO A HORRENDOUS CRASH...
SO IT'S IN EVERYONE'S INTERESTS IF THEY ALL GET A CLEAN BILL OF HEALTH...

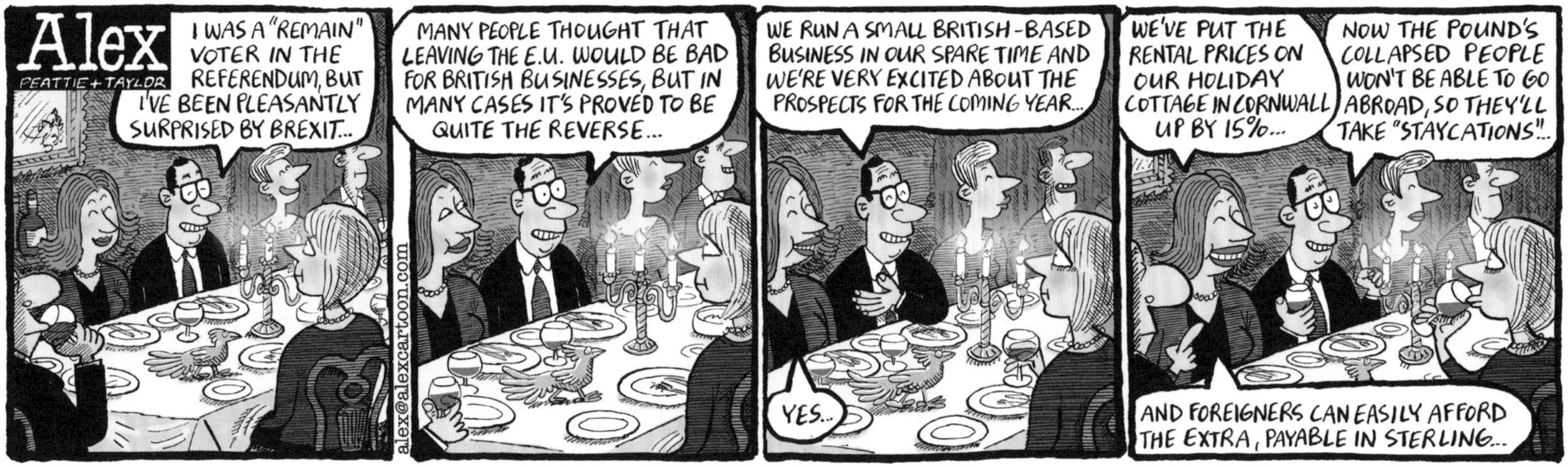
Alex
PEATTIE + TAYLOR
I WAS A "REMAIN" VOTER IN THE REFERENDUM, BUT I'VE BEEN PLEASANTLY SURPRISED BY BREXIT...
alex@alexcartoon.com
MANY PEOPLE THOUGHT THAT LEAVING THE E.U. WOULD BE BAD FOR BRITISH BUSINESSES, BUT IN MANY CASES IT'S PROVED TO BE QUITE THE REVERSE...
WE RUN A SMALL BRITISH-BASED BUSINESS IN OUR SPARE TIME AND WE'RE VERY EXCITED ABOUT THE PROSPECTS FOR THE COMING YEAR...
YES...
WE'VE PUT THE RENTAL PRICES ON OUR HOLIDAY COTTAGE IN CORNWALL UP BY 15%...
NOW THE POUND'S COLLAPSED PEOPLE WON'T BE ABLE TO GO ABROAD, SO THEY'LL TAKE "STAYCATIONS"...
AND FOREIGNERS CAN EASILY AFFORD THE EXTRA, PAYABLE IN STERLING...

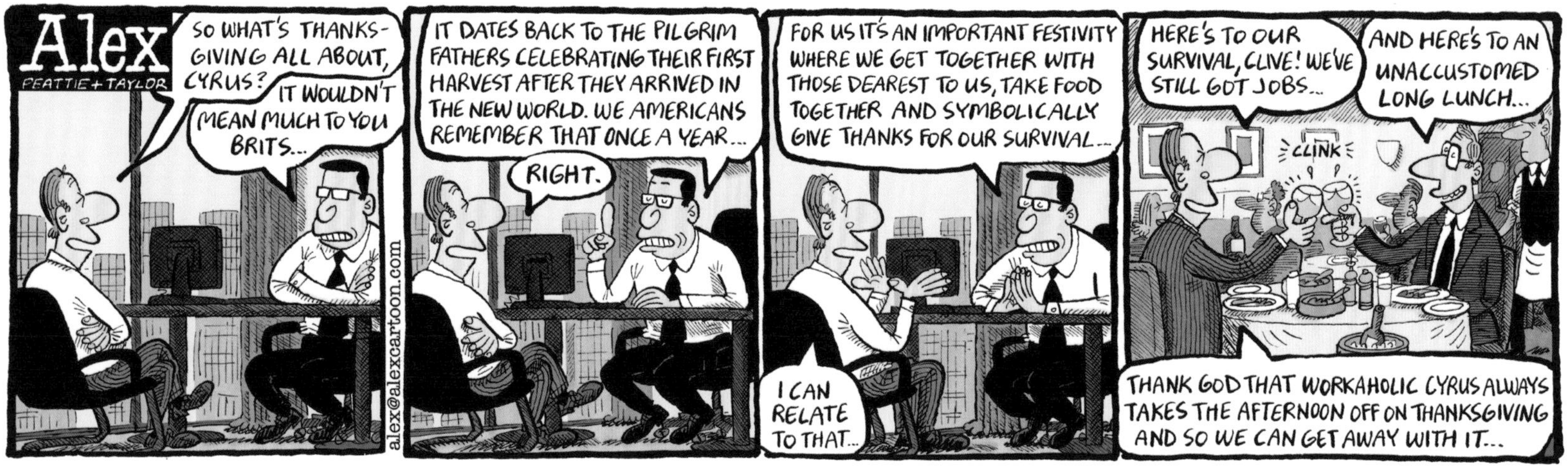
Alex
PEATTIE + TAYLOR
SO WHAT'S THANKSGIVING ALL ABOUT, CYRUS?
IT WOULDN'T MEAN MUCH TO YOU BRITS...
alex@alexcartoon.com
IT DATES BACK TO THE PILGRIM FATHERS CELEBRATING THEIR FIRST HARVEST AFTER THEY ARRIVED IN THE NEW WORLD. WE AMERICANS REMEMBER THAT ONCE A YEAR...
RIGHT.
FOR US IT'S AN IMPORTANT FESTIVITY WHERE WE GET TOGETHER WITH THOSE DEAREST TO US, TAKE FOOD TOGETHER AND SYMBOLICALLY GIVE THANKS FOR OUR SURVIVAL...
I CAN RELATE TO THAT...
HERE'S TO OUR SURVIVAL, CLIVE! WE'VE STILL GOT JOBS...
AND HERE'S TO AN UNACCUSTOMED LONG LUNCH...
CLINK
THANK GOD THAT WORKAHOLIC CYRUS ALWAYS TAKES THE AFTERNOON OFF ON THANKSGIVING AND SO WE CAN GET AWAY WITH IT...

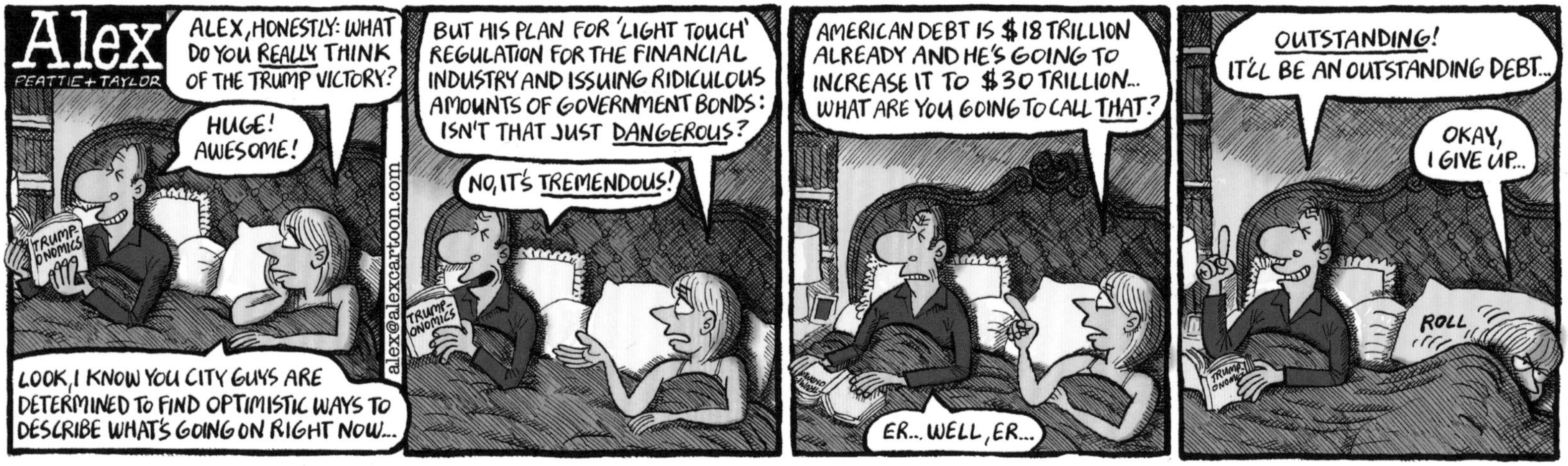
Alex
PEATTIE + TAYLOR
ALEX, HONESTLY: WHAT DO YOU REALLY THINK OF THE TRUMP VICTORY?
HUGE! AWESOME!
TRUMPONOMICS
LOOK, I KNOW YOU CITY GUYS ARE DETERMINED TO FIND OPTIMISTIC WAYS TO DESCRIBE WHAT'S GOING ON RIGHT NOW...
alex@alexcartoon.com
BUT HIS PLAN FOR 'LIGHT TOUCH' REGULATION FOR THE FINANCIAL INDUSTRY AND ISSUING RIDICULOUS AMOUNTS OF GOVERNMENT BONDS: ISN'T THAT JUST DANGEROUS?
NO, IT'S TREMENDOUS!
AMERICAN DEBT IS $18 TRILLION ALREADY AND HE'S GOING TO INCREASE IT TO $30 TRILLION... WHAT ARE YOU GOING TO CALL THAT?
ER... WELL, ER...
OUTSTANDING! IT'LL BE AN OUTSTANDING DEBT...
OKAY, I GIVE UP...
ROLL

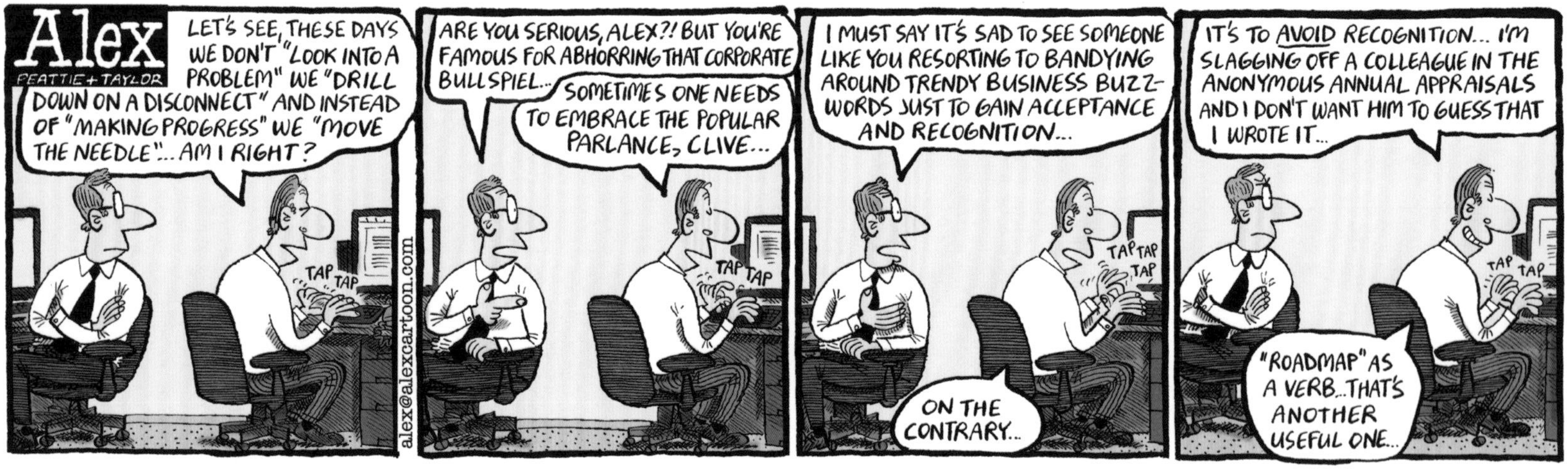
Alex
PEATTIE + TAYLOR
LET'S SEE, THESE DAYS WE DON'T "LOOK INTO A PROBLEM" WE "DRILL DOWN ON A DISCONNECT" AND INSTEAD OF "MAKING PROGRESS" WE "MOVE THE NEEDLE"... AM I RIGHT?
TAP TAP
alex@alexcartoon.com
ARE YOU SERIOUS, ALEX?! BUT YOU'RE FAMOUS FOR ABHORRING THAT CORPORATE BULLSPIEL...
SOMETIMES ONE NEEDS TO EMBRACE THE POPULAR PARLANCE, CLIVE...
TAP TAP
I MUST SAY IT'S SAD TO SEE SOMEONE LIKE YOU RESORTING TO BANDYING AROUND TRENDY BUSINESS BUZZWORDS JUST TO GAIN ACCEPTANCE AND RECOGNITION...
TAP TAP TAP
ON THE CONTRARY...
IT'S TO AVOID RECOGNITION... I'M SLAGGING OFF A COLLEAGUE IN THE ANONYMOUS ANNUAL APPRAISALS AND I DON'T WANT HIM TO GUESS THAT I WROTE IT...
TAP TAP
"ROADMAP" AS A VERB... THAT'S ANOTHER USEFUL ONE...

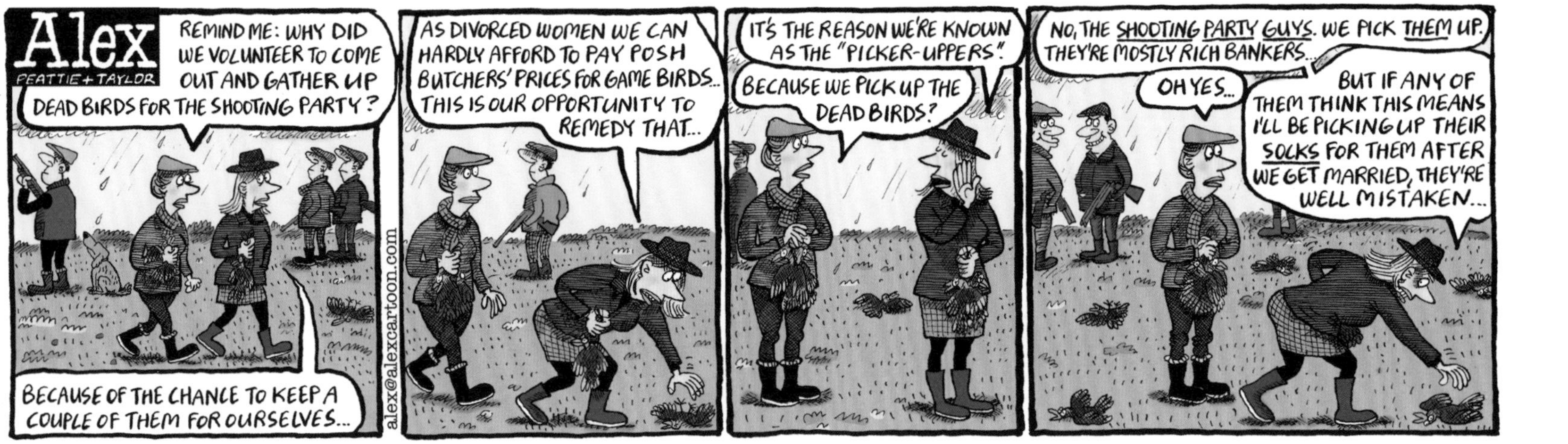
Alex
PEATTIE + TAYLOR
REMIND ME: WHY DID WE VOLUNTEER TO COME OUT AND GATHER UP DEAD BIRDS FOR THE SHOOTING PARTY?
BECAUSE OF THE CHANCE TO KEEP A COUPLE OF THEM FOR OURSELVES...
alex@alexcartoon.com
AS DIVORCED WOMEN WE CAN HARDLY AFFORD TO PAY POSH BUTCHERS' PRICES FOR GAME BIRDS... THIS IS OUR OPPORTUNITY TO REMEDY THAT...
IT'S THE REASON WE'RE KNOWN AS THE "PICKER-UPPERS".
BECAUSE WE PICK UP THE DEAD BIRDS?
NO, THE SHOOTING PARTY GUYS. WE PICK THEM UP. THEY'RE MOSTLY RICH BANKERS...
OH YES...
BUT IF ANY OF THEM THINK THIS MEANS I'LL BE PICKING UP THEIR SOCKS FOR THEM AFTER WE GET MARRIED, THEY'RE WELL MISTAKEN...

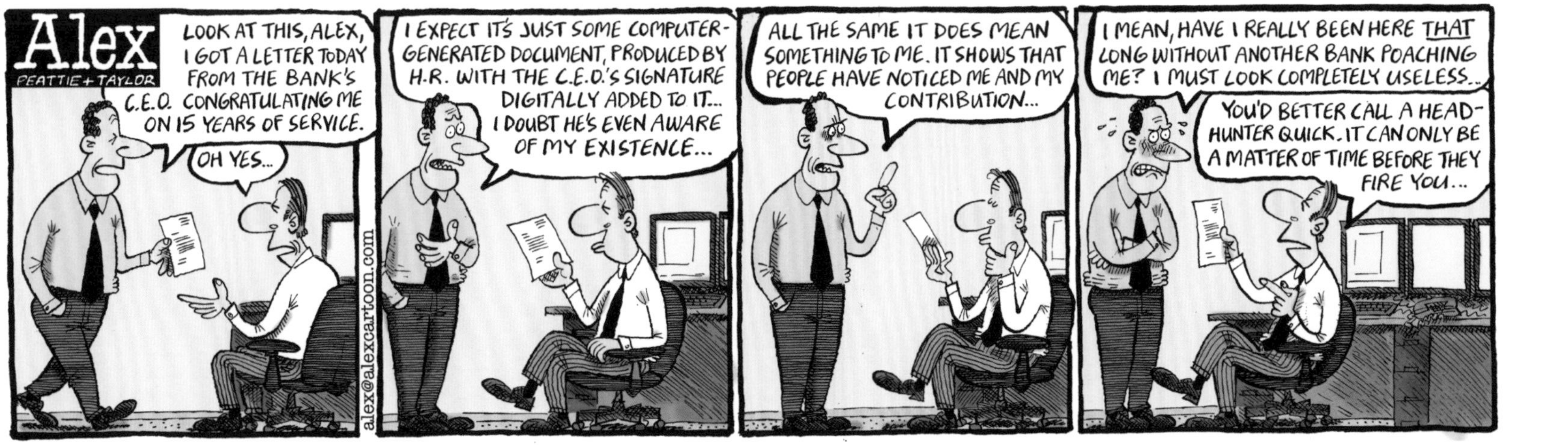
Alex
PEATTIE + TAYLOR
LOOK AT THIS, ALEX, I GOT A LETTER TODAY FROM THE BANK'S C.E.O. CONGRATULATING ME ON 15 YEARS OF SERVICE.
OH YES...
alex@alexcartoon.com
I EXPECT IT'S JUST SOME COMPUTER-GENERATED DOCUMENT, PRODUCED BY H.R. WITH THE C.E.O.'S SIGNATURE DIGITALLY ADDED TO IT... I DOUBT HE'S EVEN AWARE OF MY EXISTENCE...
ALL THE SAME IT DOES MEAN SOMETHING TO ME. IT SHOWS THAT PEOPLE HAVE NOTICED ME AND MY CONTRIBUTION...
I MEAN, HAVE I REALLY BEEN HERE THAT LONG WITHOUT ANOTHER BANK POACHING ME? I MUST LOOK COMPLETELY USELESS...
YOU'D BETTER CALL A HEAD-HUNTER QUICK. IT CAN ONLY BE A MATTER OF TIME BEFORE THEY FIRE YOU...

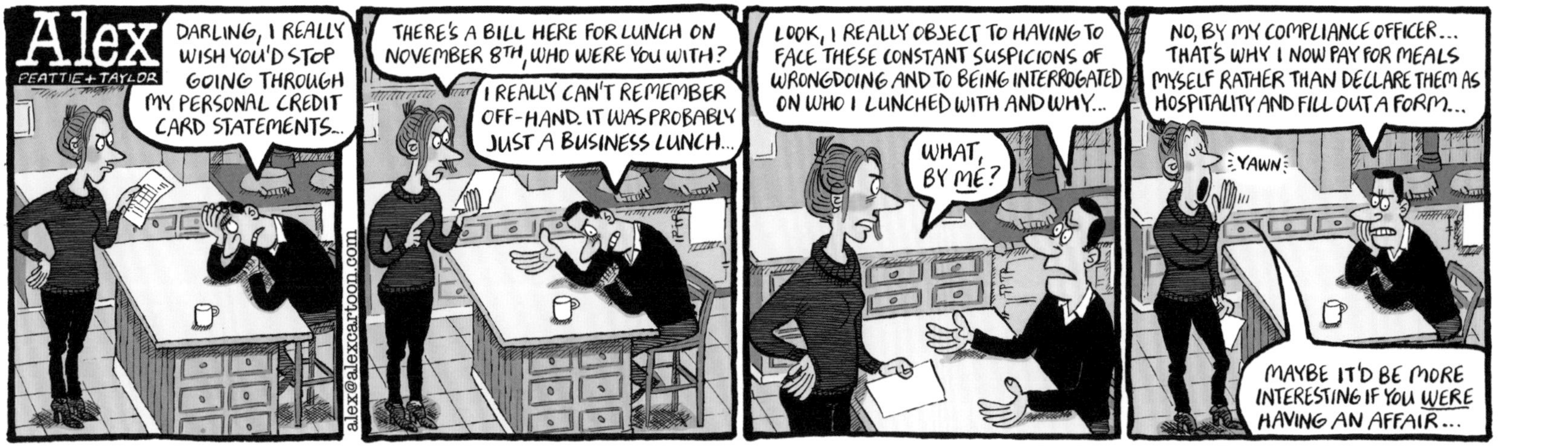
Alex
PEATTIE + TAYLOR
DARLING, I REALLY WISH YOU'D STOP GOING THROUGH MY PERSONAL CREDIT CARD STATEMENTS...
alex@alexcartoon.com
THERE'S A BILL HERE FOR LUNCH ON NOVEMBER 8TH, WHO WERE YOU WITH?
I REALLY CAN'T REMEMBER OFF-HAND. IT WAS PROBABLY JUST A BUSINESS LUNCH...
LOOK, I REALLY OBJECT TO HAVING TO FACE THESE CONSTANT SUSPICIONS OF WRONGDOING AND TO BEING INTERROGATED ON WHO I LUNCHED WITH AND WHY...
WHAT, BY ME?
NO, BY MY COMPLIANCE OFFICER... THAT'S WHY I NOW PAY FOR MEALS MYSELF RATHER THAN DECLARE THEM AS HOSPITALITY AND FILL OUT A FORM...
YAWN
MAYBE IT'D BE MORE INTERESTING IF YOU WERE HAVING AN AFFAIR...

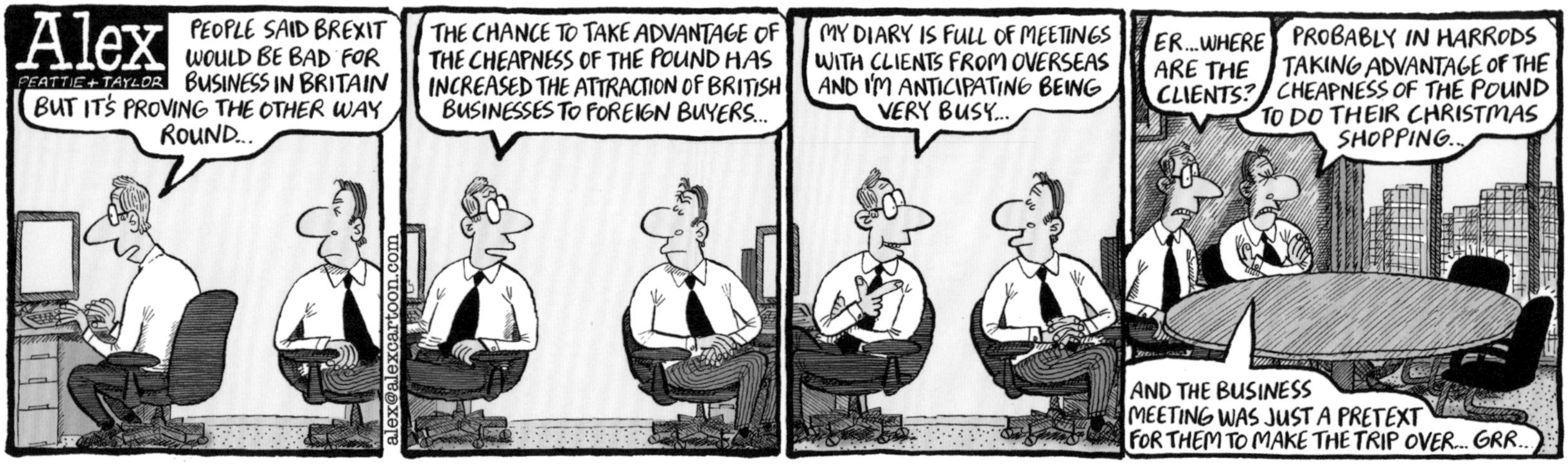
Alex
PEATTIE + TAYLOR
PEOPLE SAID BREXIT WOULD BE BAD FOR BUSINESS IN BRITAIN BUT IT'S PROVING THE OTHER WAY ROUND...
alex@alexcartoon.com
THE CHANCE TO TAKE ADVANTAGE OF THE CHEAPNESS OF THE POUND HAS INCREASED THE ATTRACTION OF BRITISH BUSINESSES TO FOREIGN BUYERS...
MY DIARY IS FULL OF MEETINGS WITH CLIENTS FROM OVERSEAS AND I'M ANTICIPATING BEING VERY BUSY...
ER... WHERE ARE THE CLIENTS?
PROBABLY IN HARRODS TAKING ADVANTAGE OF THE CHEAPNESS OF THE POUND TO DO THEIR CHRISTMAS SHOPPING...
AND THE BUSINESS MEETING WAS JUST A PRETEXT FOR THEM TO MAKE THE TRIP OVER... GRR...

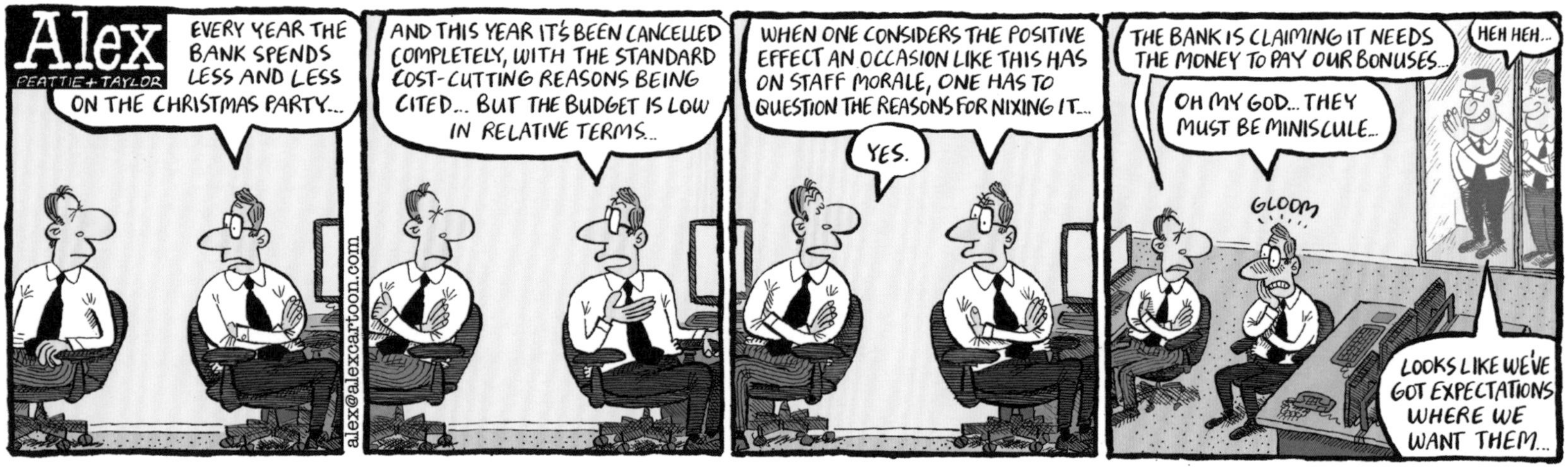
Alex
PEATTIE + TAYLOR
EVERY YEAR THE BANK SPENDS LESS AND LESS ON THE CHRISTMAS PARTY...
alex@alexcartoon.com
AND THIS YEAR IT'S BEEN CANCELLED COMPLETELY, WITH THE STANDARD COST-CUTTING REASONS BEING CITED... BUT THE BUDGET IS LOW IN RELATIVE TERMS...
WHEN ONE CONSIDERS THE POSITIVE EFFECT AN OCCASION LIKE THIS HAS ON STAFF MORALE, ONE HAS TO QUESTION THE REASONS FOR NIXING IT...
YES.
THE BANK IS CLAIMING IT NEEDS THE MONEY TO PAY OUR BONUSES...
HEH HEH...
OH MY GOD... THEY MUST BE MINISCULE...
GLOOM
LOOKS LIKE WE'VE GOT EXPECTATIONS WHERE WE WANT THEM...

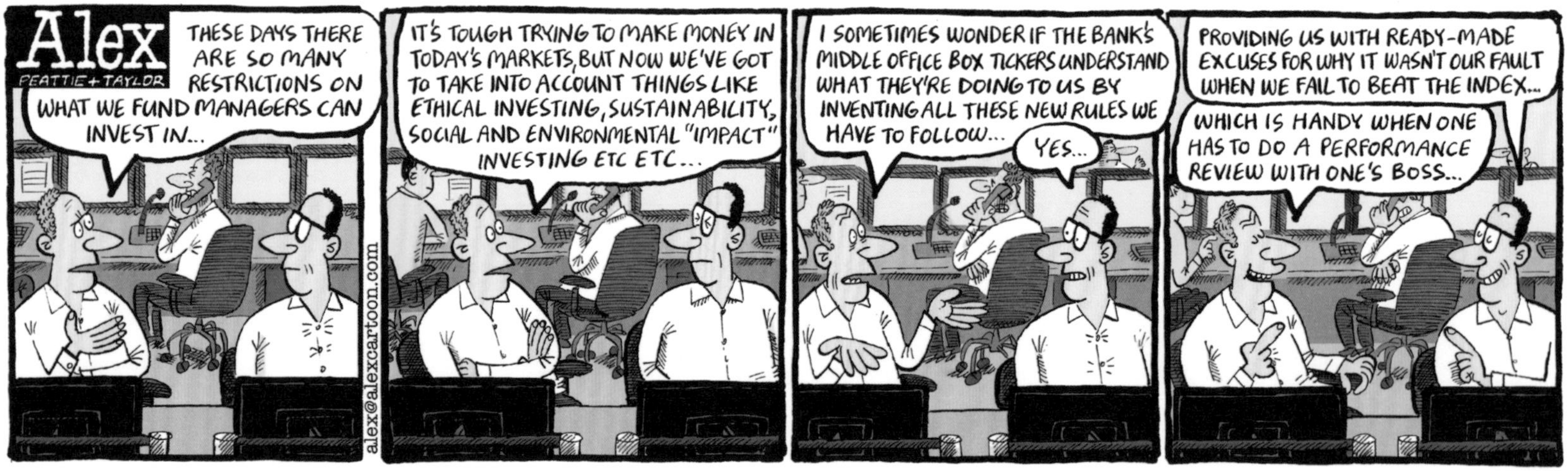
Alex
PEATTIE + TAYLOR
THESE DAYS THERE ARE SO MANY RESTRICTIONS ON WHAT WE FUND MANAGERS CAN INVEST IN...
alex@alexcartoon.com
IT'S TOUGH TRYING TO MAKE MONEY IN TODAY'S MARKETS, BUT NOW WE'VE GOT TO TAKE INTO ACCOUNT THINGS LIKE ETHICAL INVESTING, SUSTAINABILITY, SOCIAL AND ENVIRONMENTAL "IMPACT" INVESTING ETC ETC...
I SOMETIMES WONDER IF THE BANK'S MIDDLE OFFICE BOX TICKERS UNDERSTAND WHAT THEY'RE DOING TO US BY INVENTING ALL THESE NEW RULES WE HAVE TO FOLLOW...
YES...
PROVIDING US WITH READY-MADE EXCUSES FOR WHY IT WASN'T OUR FAULT WHEN WE FAIL TO BEAT THE INDEX...
WHICH IS HANDY WHEN ONE HAS TO DO A PERFORMANCE REVIEW WITH ONE'S BOSS...

Alex — PEATTIE + TAYLOR

Panel 1: CUSTOMERS PAY £25,000 FOR A DAY'S SHOOTING ON OUR LAND... IT'S A GOOD BUSINESS FOR US...

Panel 2: THEY GET A DAY OUT WITH ALL THE TRIMMINGS, TRANSPORT AND THE CHANCE TO SHOOT DOWN 400 BIRDS... OUR JOB IS TO SEE IT RUNS SMOOTHLY...

Panel 3: THAT MEANS HAVING THE BIRDS FLY OVER AT THE RIGHT TIMES AND MAKING SURE THE GUNS ARE PROPERLY LOADED...

DON'T WORRY ABOUT THAT...

Panel 4: WITH WHAT I PUT IN THEIR HIP FLASKS THEY'LL BE WELL SQUIFFY... AND THEN THEY'LL BE HAPPY TO SHOOT DOWN SOME EXTRA BIRDS... AT £35 EACH!

I MEANT: "LOADED" = "RICH"...

OH YES THEY'RE ALL SENIOR BANKERS AT MEGA BANK... THEY CAN EASILY AFFORD THE 'OVERAGE'...

TAP — GLUG

PHEW! THANKS, BILL...

Alex — PEATTIE + TAYLOR

Panel 1: ON OUR SHOOTS, THE IDEA IS TO PLY THE GUESTS WITH DRINK SO THEY'RE RELAXED ABOUT SPENDING MORE MONEY...

Panel 2: THEY CONTRACT TO SHOOT 400 BIRDS, BUT AFTER THEY'VE INDULGED IN THE HOSPITALITY THEY OFTEN WANT TO SHOOT MORE THAN THAT, EVEN AT AN EXTRA £45 A BIRD... IT'S CALLED "OVERAGE"...

I KNOW...

Panel 3: BUT OBVIOUSLY IT'S UP TO US TO KEEP A MONITOR ON WHEN THEY'VE REACHED THE MAXIMUM AMOUNT OF WHAT THEY'RE SUPPOSED TO GET...

I KNOW... I'M SORRY... I THINK I SORT OF LOST COUNT...

Panel 4: I JUST CARRIED ON GIVING THEM REFILLS...

YOU TWIT! THEY AGREED TO SHOOT UP TO 100 EXTRA BIRDS BUT THEY'RE ALL SO P*SSED NONE OF THEM CAN HIT ANYTHING...

SORRY...

BLAM — BOTHER. — HIC — BLAM

Alex — PEATTIE + TAYLOR

Panel 1: MANY OF OUR CLIENTS ARE NOW BARRED FROM COMING TO THE BANK'S CHRISTMAS DRINKS PARTY BY THEIR INTERNAL COMPLIANCE RULES...

MEGA BANK CLIENT PARTY

Panel 2: AND THE FEW OF THEM THAT CAN ATTEND USUALLY HAVE A LIMIT IMPOSED ON THE VALUE OF THE HOSPITALITY THEY CAN ACCEPT... LIKE ONLY £10...

Panel 3: IT MEANS WE CAN'T EVEN GET THEM SOZZLED. FRANKLY IT UNDERMINES THE WHOLE RELATIONSHIP-ENHANCING FUNCTION OF THE PARTY...

IT DOES...

Panel 4: BECAUSE UNFORTUNATELY THE SAME RULES DON'T APPLY TO US HOSTS... AND YOU HAVEN'T GIVEN ME ANY BUSINESS ALL YEAR, YOU SCROOGE...

SOMEONE TAKE CLIVE'S GLASS OFF HIM...

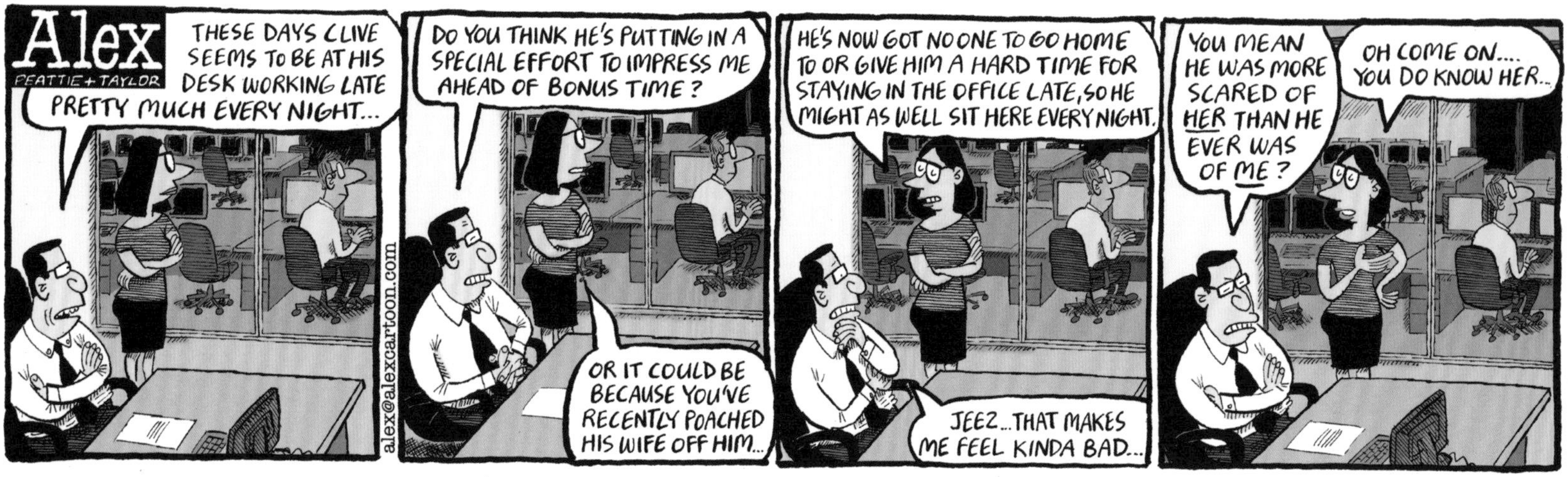
Alex
PEATTIE+TAYLOR
THESE DAYS CLIVE SEEMS TO BE AT HIS DESK WORKING LATE PRETTY MUCH EVERY NIGHT...
DO YOU THINK HE'S PUTTING IN A SPECIAL EFFORT TO IMPRESS ME AHEAD OF BONUS TIME?
OR IT COULD BE BECAUSE YOU'VE RECENTLY POACHED HIS WIFE OFF HIM...
alex@alexcartoon.com
HE'S NOW GOT NO ONE TO GO HOME TO OR GIVE HIM A HARD TIME FOR STAYING IN THE OFFICE LATE, SO HE MIGHT AS WELL SIT HERE EVERY NIGHT.
JEEZ... THAT MAKES ME FEEL KINDA BAD...
YOU MEAN HE WAS MORE SCARED OF HER THAN HE EVER WAS OF ME?
OH COME ON.... YOU DO KNOW HER...

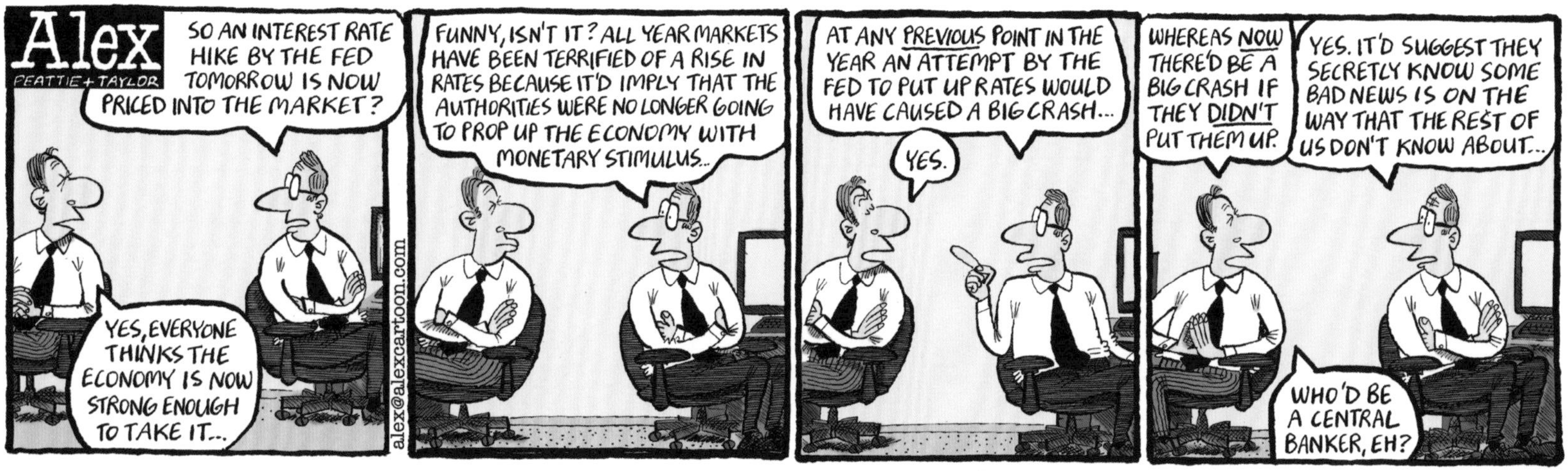
Alex
PEATTIE+TAYLOR
SO AN INTEREST RATE HIKE BY THE FED TOMORROW IS NOW PRICED INTO THE MARKET?
YES, EVERYONE THINKS THE ECONOMY IS NOW STRONG ENOUGH TO TAKE IT...
alex@alexcartoon.com
FUNNY, ISN'T IT? ALL YEAR MARKETS HAVE BEEN TERRIFIED OF A RISE IN RATES BECAUSE IT'D IMPLY THAT THE AUTHORITIES WERE NO LONGER GOING TO PROP UP THE ECONOMY WITH MONETARY STIMULUS...
AT ANY PREVIOUS POINT IN THE YEAR AN ATTEMPT BY THE FED TO PUT UP RATES WOULD HAVE CAUSED A BIG CRASH...
YES.
WHEREAS NOW THERE'D BE A BIG CRASH IF THEY DIDN'T PUT THEM UP.
YES. IT'D SUGGEST THEY SECRETLY KNOW SOME BAD NEWS IS ON THE WAY THAT THE REST OF US DON'T KNOW ABOUT...
WHO'D BE A CENTRAL BANKER, EH?

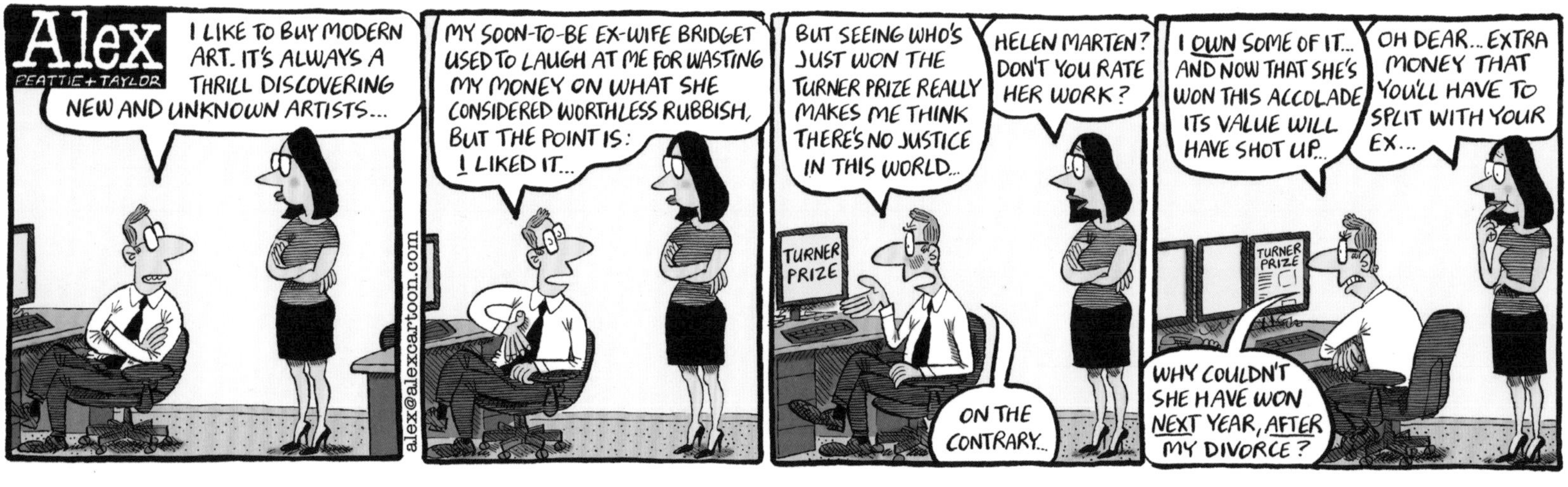
Alex
PEATTIE+TAYLOR
I LIKE TO BUY MODERN ART. IT'S ALWAYS A THRILL DISCOVERING NEW AND UNKNOWN ARTISTS...
alex@alexcartoon.com
MY SOON-TO-BE EX-WIFE BRIDGET USED TO LAUGH AT ME FOR WASTING MY MONEY ON WHAT SHE CONSIDERED WORTHLESS RUBBISH, BUT THE POINT IS: I LIKED IT...
BUT SEEING WHO'S JUST WON THE TURNER PRIZE REALLY MAKES ME THINK THERE'S NO JUSTICE IN THIS WORLD...
HELEN MARTEN? DON'T YOU RATE HER WORK?
TURNER PRIZE
ON THE CONTRARY...
I OWN SOME OF IT... AND NOW THAT SHE'S WON THIS ACCOLADE ITS VALUE WILL HAVE SHOT UP...
OH DEAR... EXTRA MONEY THAT YOU'LL HAVE TO SPLIT WITH YOUR EX...
TURNER PRIZE
WHY COULDN'T SHE HAVE WON NEXT YEAR, AFTER MY DIVORCE?

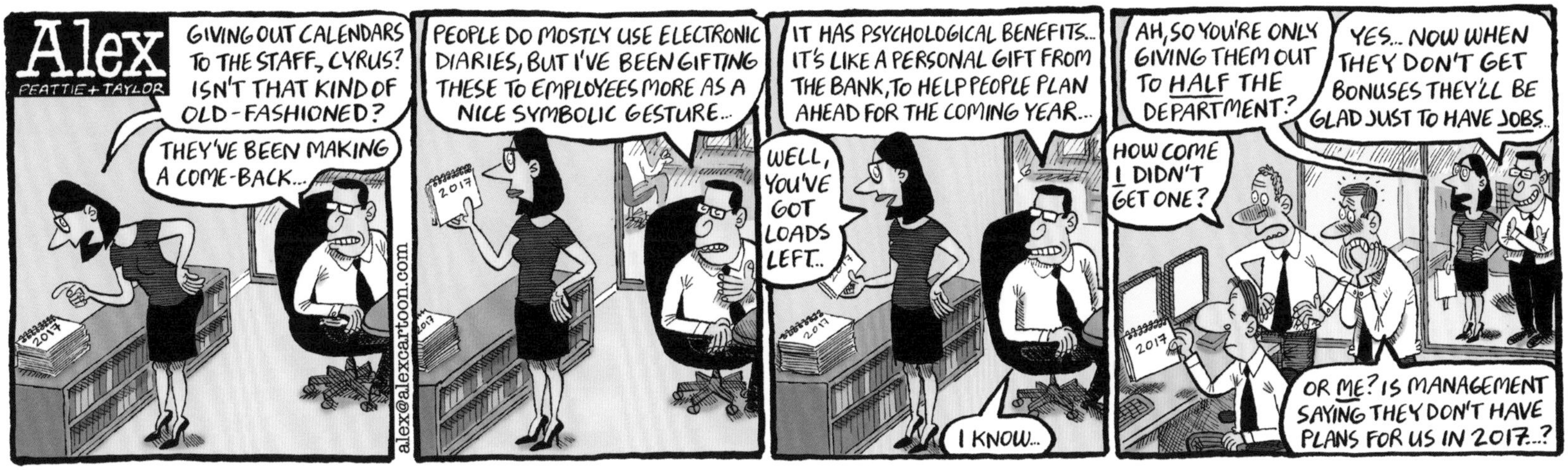
Alex
PEATTIE + TAYLOR
GIVING OUT CALENDARS TO THE STAFF, CYRUS? ISN'T THAT KIND OF OLD-FASHIONED?
THEY'VE BEEN MAKING A COME-BACK...
PEOPLE DO MOSTLY USE ELECTRONIC DIARIES, BUT I'VE BEEN GIFTING THESE TO EMPLOYEES MORE AS A NICE SYMBOLIC GESTURE...
IT HAS PSYCHOLOGICAL BENEFITS... IT'S LIKE A PERSONAL GIFT FROM THE BANK, TO HELP PEOPLE PLAN AHEAD FOR THE COMING YEAR...
WELL, YOU'VE GOT LOADS LEFT...
I KNOW...
AH, SO YOU'RE ONLY GIVING THEM OUT TO HALF THE DEPARTMENT?
YES... NOW WHEN THEY DON'T GET BONUSES THEY'LL BE GLAD JUST TO HAVE JOBS...
HOW COME I DIDN'T GET ONE?
OR ME? IS MANAGEMENT SAYING THEY DON'T HAVE PLANS FOR US IN 2017...?
alex@alexcartoon.com

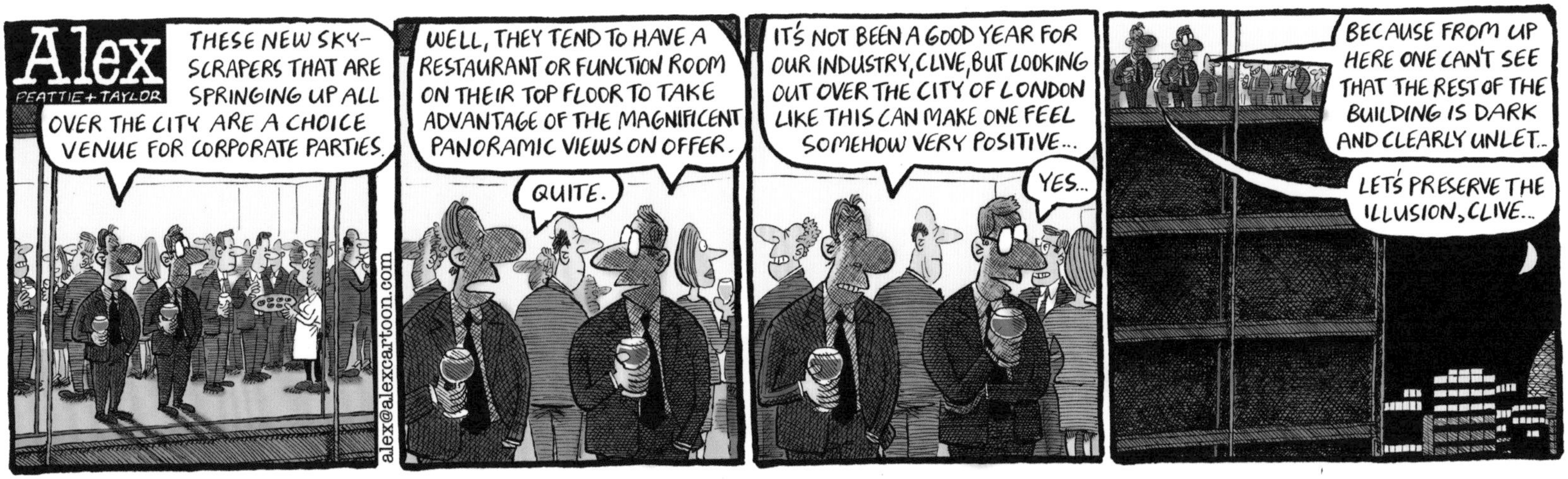
Alex
PEATTIE + TAYLOR
THESE NEW SKY-SCRAPERS THAT ARE SPRINGING UP ALL OVER THE CITY ARE A CHOICE VENUE FOR CORPORATE PARTIES.
WELL, THEY TEND TO HAVE A RESTAURANT OR FUNCTION ROOM ON THEIR TOP FLOOR TO TAKE ADVANTAGE OF THE MAGNIFICENT PANORAMIC VIEWS ON OFFER.
QUITE.
IT'S NOT BEEN A GOOD YEAR FOR OUR INDUSTRY, CLIVE, BUT LOOKING OUT OVER THE CITY OF LONDON LIKE THIS CAN MAKE ONE FEEL SOMEHOW VERY POSITIVE...
YES...
BECAUSE FROM UP HERE ONE CAN'T SEE THAT THE REST OF THE BUILDING IS DARK AND CLEARLY UNLET...
LET'S PRESERVE THE ILLUSION, CLIVE...
alex@alexcartoon.com

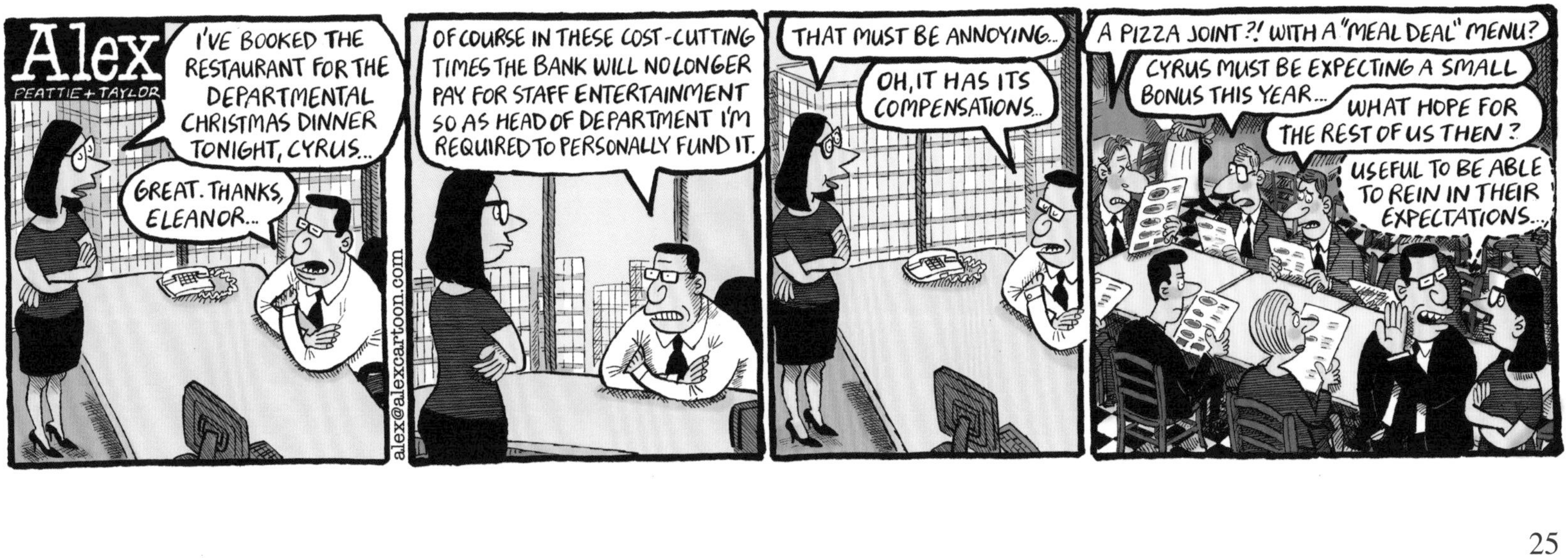
Alex
PEATTIE + TAYLOR
I'VE BOOKED THE RESTAURANT FOR THE DEPARTMENTAL CHRISTMAS DINNER TONIGHT, CYRUS...
GREAT. THANKS, ELEANOR...
OF COURSE IN THESE COST-CUTTING TIMES THE BANK WILL NO LONGER PAY FOR STAFF ENTERTAINMENT SO AS HEAD OF DEPARTMENT I'M REQUIRED TO PERSONALLY FUND IT.
THAT MUST BE ANNOYING...
OH, IT HAS ITS COMPENSATIONS...
A PIZZA JOINT?! WITH A "MEAL DEAL" MENU?
CYRUS MUST BE EXPECTING A SMALL BONUS THIS YEAR...
WHAT HOPE FOR THE REST OF US THEN?
USEFUL TO BE ABLE TO REIN IN THEIR EXPECTATIONS...
alex@alexcartoon.com

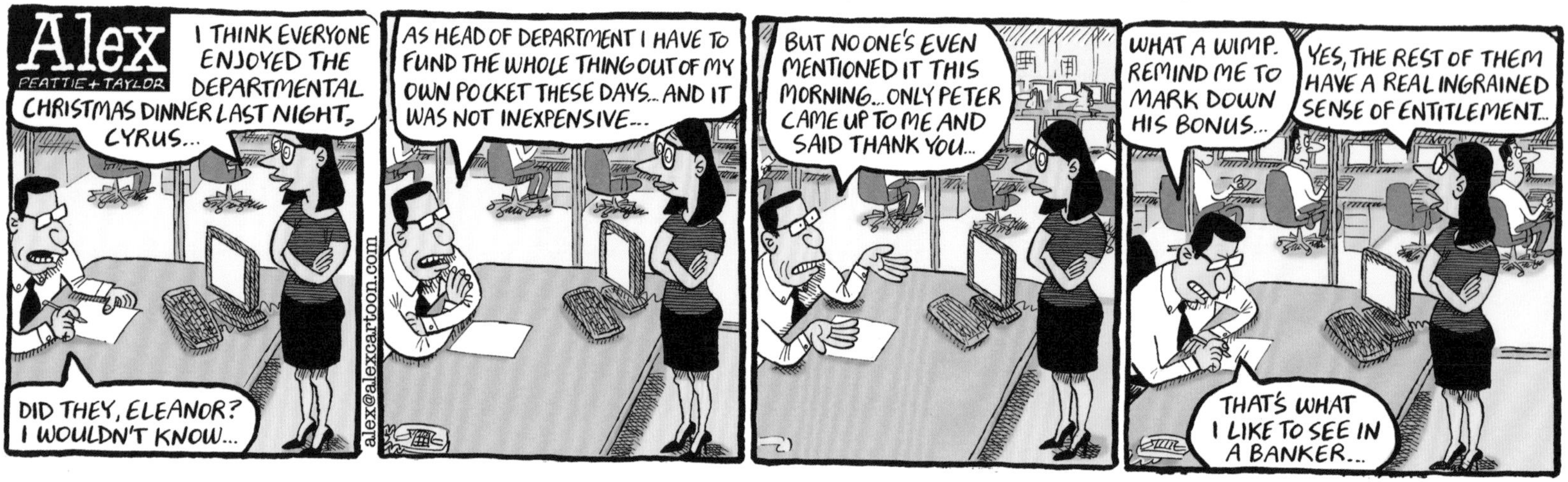
Alex
PEATTIE+TAYLOR
I THINK EVERYONE ENJOYED THE DEPARTMENTAL CHRISTMAS DINNER LAST NIGHT, CYRUS...
DID THEY, ELEANOR? I WOULDN'T KNOW...
AS HEAD OF DEPARTMENT I HAVE TO FUND THE WHOLE THING OUT OF MY OWN POCKET THESE DAYS... AND IT WAS NOT INEXPENSIVE...
alex@alexcartoon.com
BUT NO ONE'S EVEN MENTIONED IT THIS MORNING... ONLY PETER CAME UP TO ME AND SAID THANK YOU...
WHAT A WIMP. REMIND ME TO MARK DOWN HIS BONUS...
YES, THE REST OF THEM HAVE A REAL INGRAINED SENSE OF ENTITLEMENT...
THAT'S WHAT I LIKE TO SEE IN A BANKER...

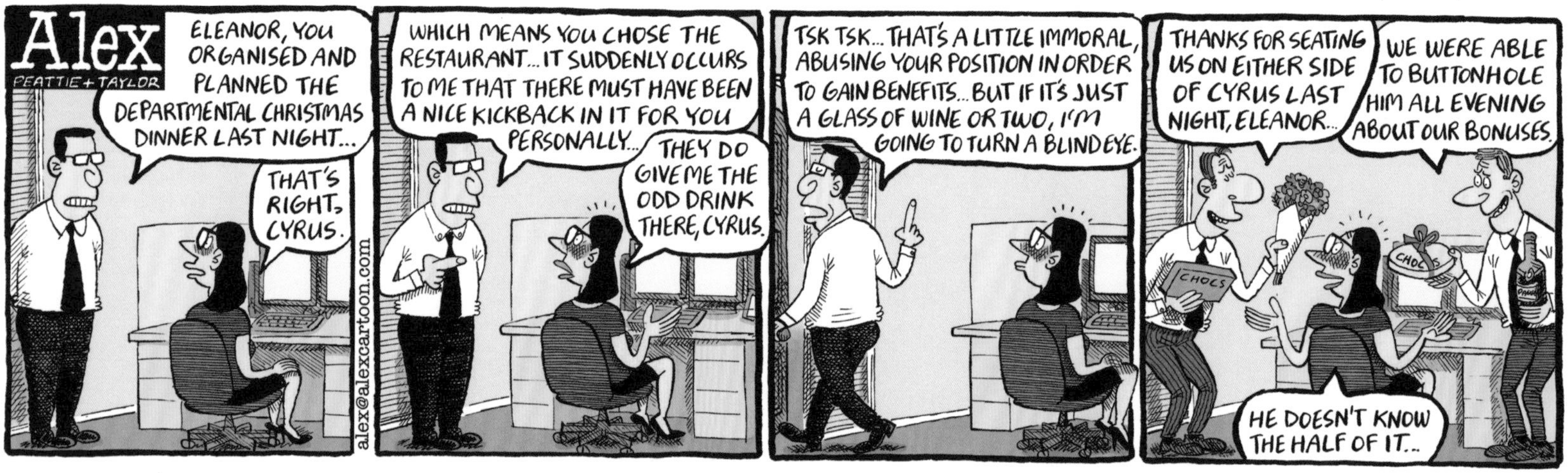
Alex
PEATTIE+TAYLOR
ELEANOR, YOU ORGANISED AND PLANNED THE DEPARTMENTAL CHRISTMAS DINNER LAST NIGHT...
THAT'S RIGHT, CYRUS.
alex@alexcartoon.com
WHICH MEANS YOU CHOSE THE RESTAURANT... IT SUDDENLY OCCURS TO ME THAT THERE MUST HAVE BEEN A NICE KICKBACK IN IT FOR YOU PERSONALLY...
THEY DO GIVE ME THE ODD DRINK THERE, CYRUS.
TSK TSK... THAT'S A LITTLE IMMORAL, ABUSING YOUR POSITION IN ORDER TO GAIN BENEFITS... BUT IF IT'S JUST A GLASS OF WINE OR TWO, I'M GOING TO TURN A BLIND EYE.
THANKS FOR SEATING US ON EITHER SIDE OF CYRUS LAST NIGHT, ELEANOR...
WE WERE ABLE TO BUTTONHOLE HIM ALL EVENING ABOUT OUR BONUSES.
CHOCS
CHOCS
HE DOESN'T KNOW THE HALF OF IT...

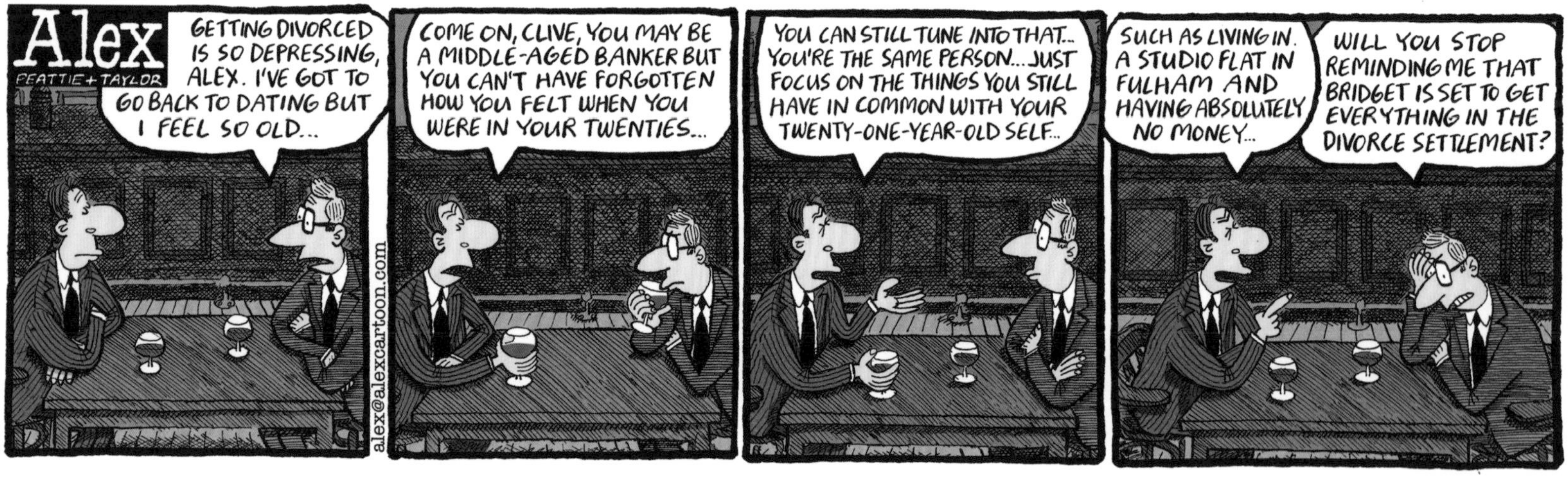
Alex
PEATTIE+TAYLOR
GETTING DIVORCED IS SO DEPRESSING, ALEX. I'VE GOT TO GO BACK TO DATING BUT I FEEL SO OLD...
alex@alexcartoon.com
COME ON, CLIVE, YOU MAY BE A MIDDLE-AGED BANKER BUT YOU CAN'T HAVE FORGOTTEN HOW YOU FELT WHEN YOU WERE IN YOUR TWENTIES...
YOU CAN STILL TUNE INTO THAT... YOU'RE THE SAME PERSON... JUST FOCUS ON THE THINGS YOU STILL HAVE IN COMMON WITH YOUR TWENTY-ONE-YEAR-OLD SELF...
SUCH AS LIVING IN A STUDIO FLAT IN FULHAM AND HAVING ABSOLUTELY NO MONEY...
WILL YOU STOP REMINDING ME THAT BRIDGET IS SET TO GET EVERYTHING IN THE DIVORCE SETTLEMENT?

ALEX WAS ON CHRISTMAS PHONE DUTY

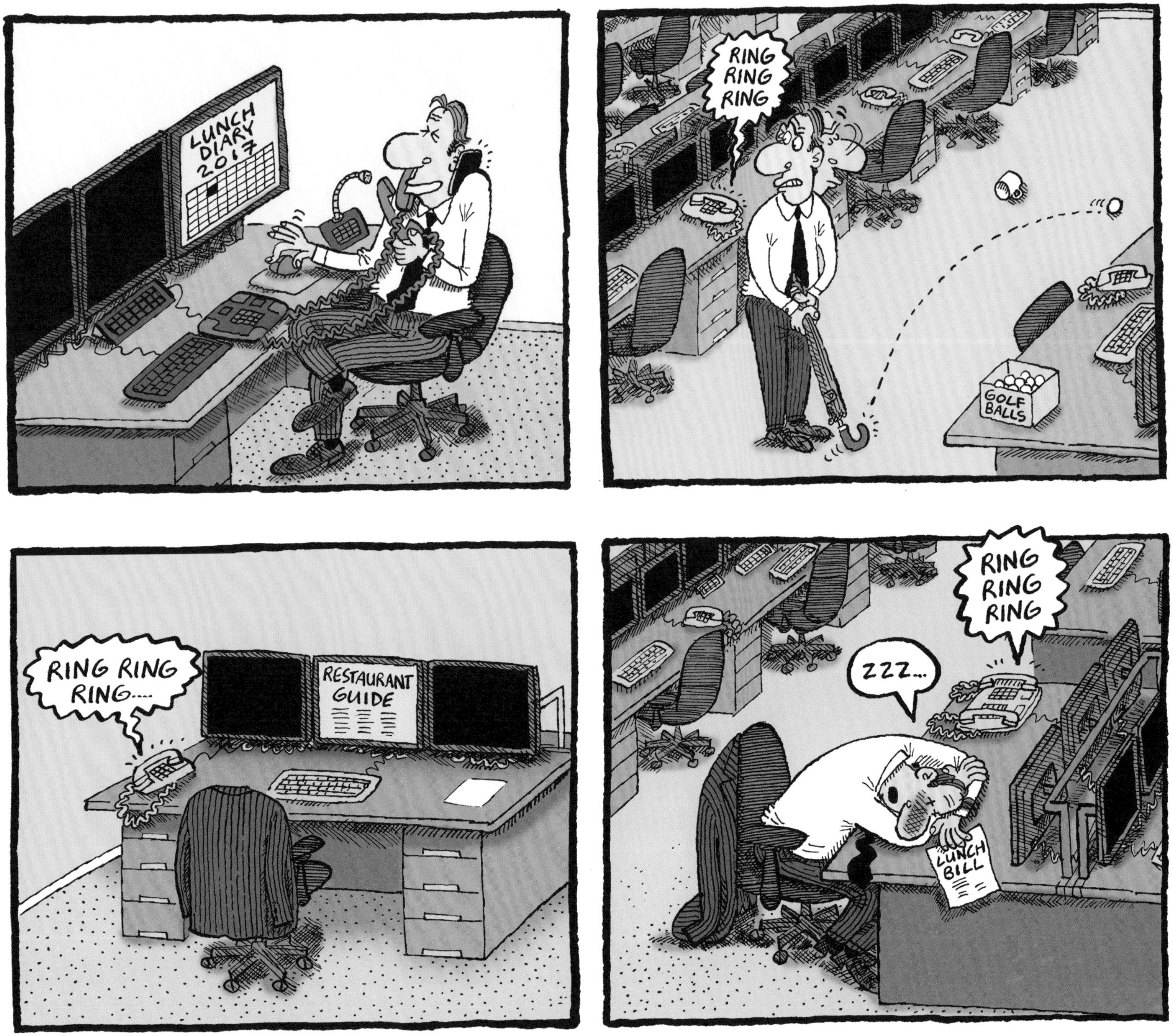
LUNCH DIARY 2017
RING RING RING
GOLF BALLS
RING RING RING....
RESTAURANT GUIDE
RING RING RING
ZZZ...
LUNCH BILL

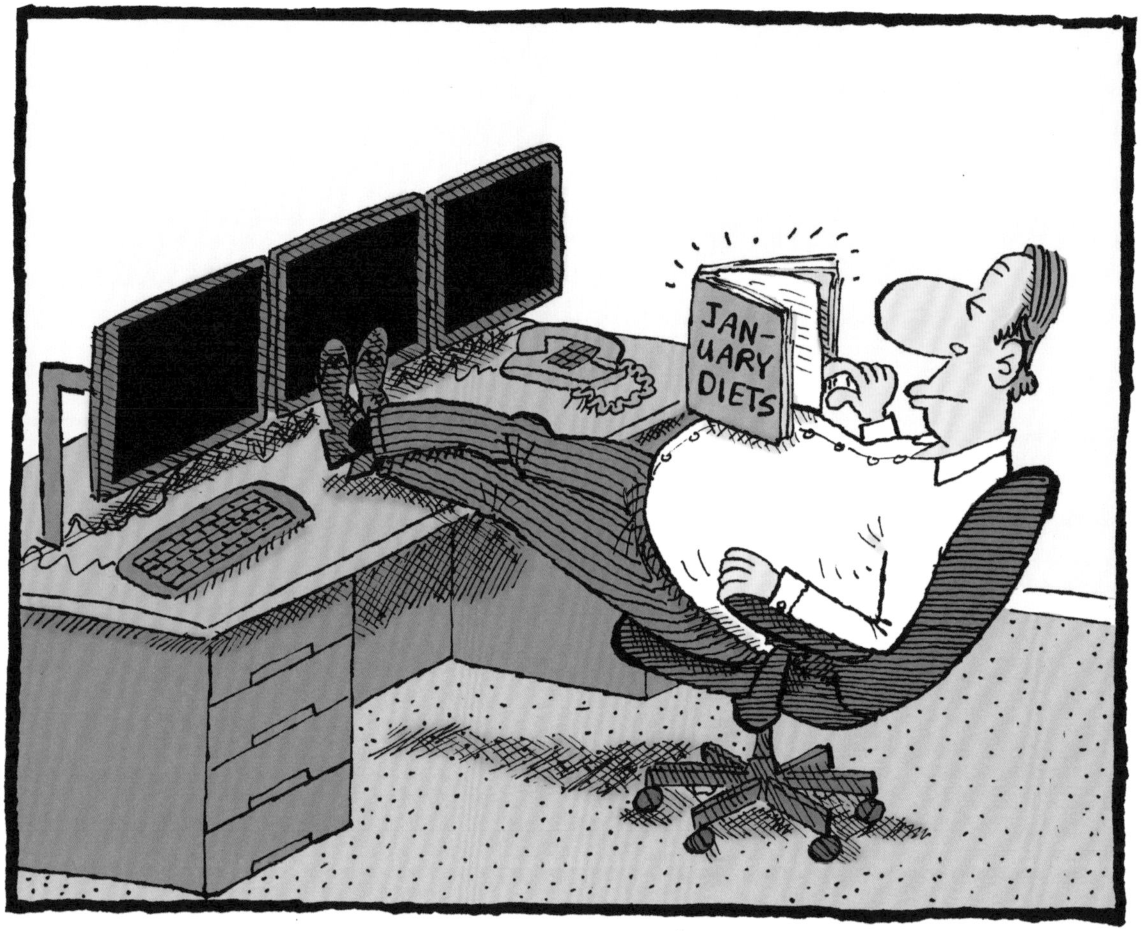

JAN-
UARY
DIETS

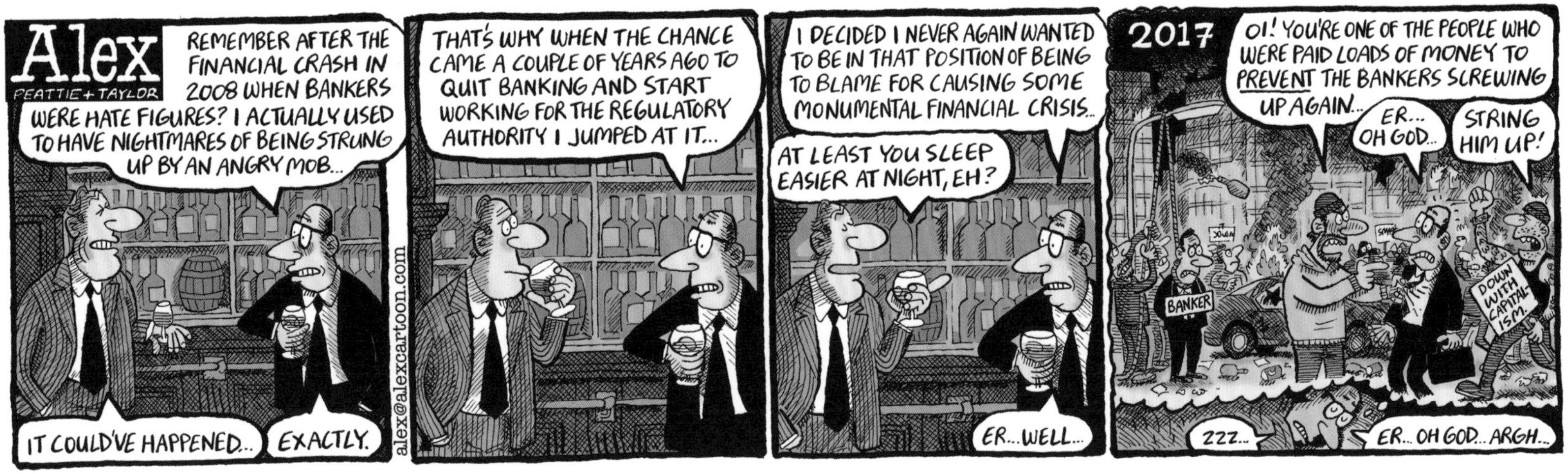
Alex
PEATTIE + TAYLOR
REMEMBER AFTER THE FINANCIAL CRASH IN 2008 WHEN BANKERS WERE HATE FIGURES? I ACTUALLY USED TO HAVE NIGHTMARES OF BEING STRUNG UP BY AN ANGRY MOB...
IT COULD'VE HAPPENED...
EXACTLY.
alex@alexcartoon.com
THAT'S WHY WHEN THE CHANCE CAME A COUPLE OF YEARS AGO TO QUIT BANKING AND START WORKING FOR THE REGULATORY AUTHORITY I JUMPED AT IT...
I DECIDED I NEVER AGAIN WANTED TO BE IN THAT POSITION OF BEING TO BLAME FOR CAUSING SOME MONUMENTAL FINANCIAL CRISIS...
AT LEAST YOU SLEEP EASIER AT NIGHT, EH?
ER... WELL...
2017
OI! YOU'RE ONE OF THE PEOPLE WHO WERE PAID LOADS OF MONEY TO PREVENT THE BANKERS SCREWING UP AGAIN...
ER... OH GOD...
STRING HIM UP!
BANKER
DOWN WITH CAPITAL-ISM.
ZZZ...
ER... OH GOD... ARGH...

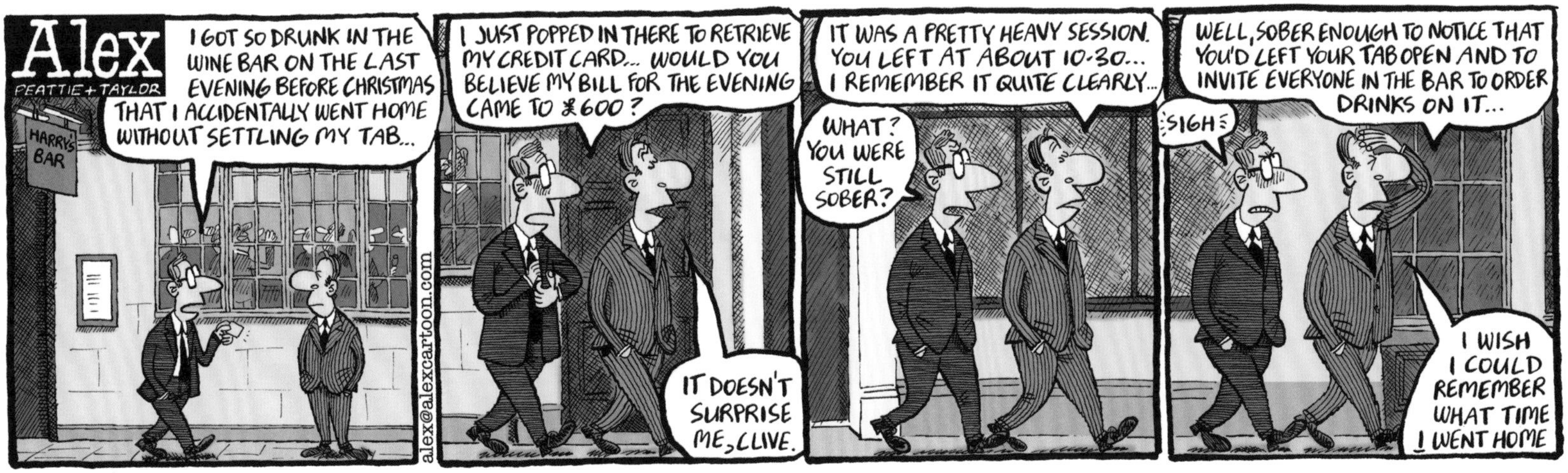
Alex
PEATTIE + TAYLOR
I GOT SO DRUNK IN THE WINE BAR ON THE LAST EVENING BEFORE CHRISTMAS THAT I ACCIDENTALLY WENT HOME WITHOUT SETTLING MY TAB...
HARRY'S BAR
alex@alexcartoon.com
I JUST POPPED IN THERE TO RETRIEVE MY CREDIT CARD... WOULD YOU BELIEVE MY BILL FOR THE EVENING CAME TO £600?
IT DOESN'T SURPRISE ME, CLIVE.
IT WAS A PRETTY HEAVY SESSION. YOU LEFT AT ABOUT 10-30... I REMEMBER IT QUITE CLEARLY...
WHAT? YOU WERE STILL SOBER?
WELL, SOBER ENOUGH TO NOTICE THAT YOU'D LEFT YOUR TAB OPEN AND TO INVITE EVERYONE IN THE BAR TO ORDER DRINKS ON IT...
SIGH
I WISH I COULD REMEMBER WHAT TIME I WENT HOME

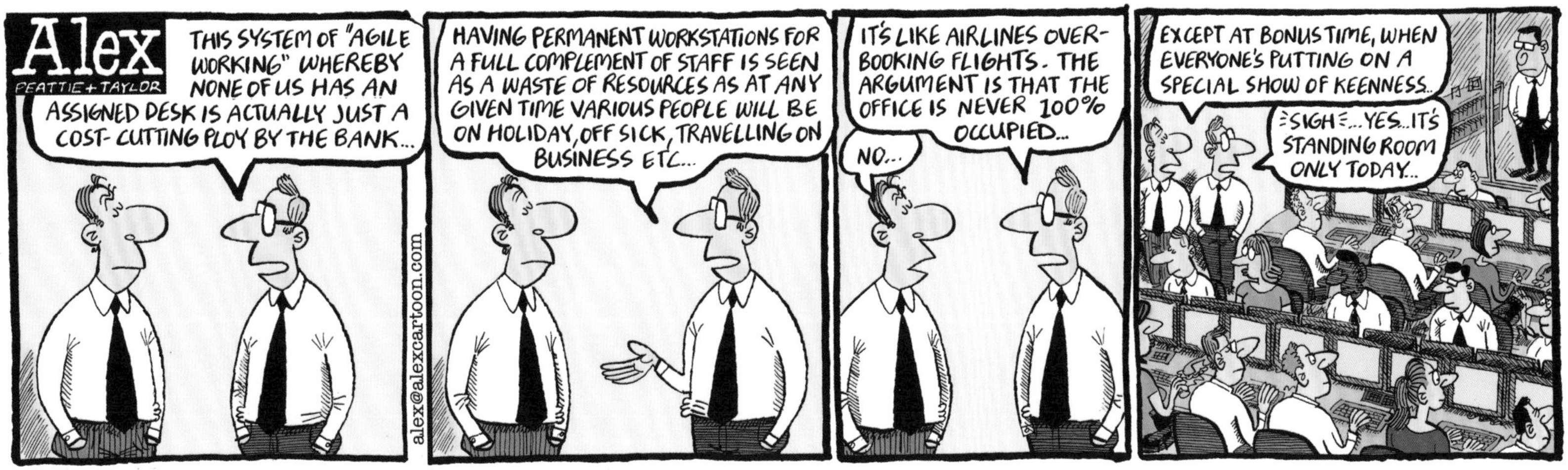
Alex
PEATTIE + TAYLOR
THIS SYSTEM OF "AGILE WORKING" WHEREBY NONE OF US HAS AN ASSIGNED DESK IS ACTUALLY JUST A COST-CUTTING PLOY BY THE BANK...
alex@alexcartoon.com
HAVING PERMANENT WORKSTATIONS FOR A FULL COMPLEMENT OF STAFF IS SEEN AS A WASTE OF RESOURCES AS AT ANY GIVEN TIME VARIOUS PEOPLE WILL BE ON HOLIDAY, OFF SICK, TRAVELLING ON BUSINESS ETC...
IT'S LIKE AIRLINES OVER-BOOKING FLIGHTS. THE ARGUMENT IS THAT THE OFFICE IS NEVER 100% OCCUPIED...
NO...
EXCEPT AT BONUS TIME, WHEN EVERYONE'S PUTTING ON A SPECIAL SHOW OF KEENNESS...
SIGH... YES... IT'S STANDING ROOM ONLY TODAY...

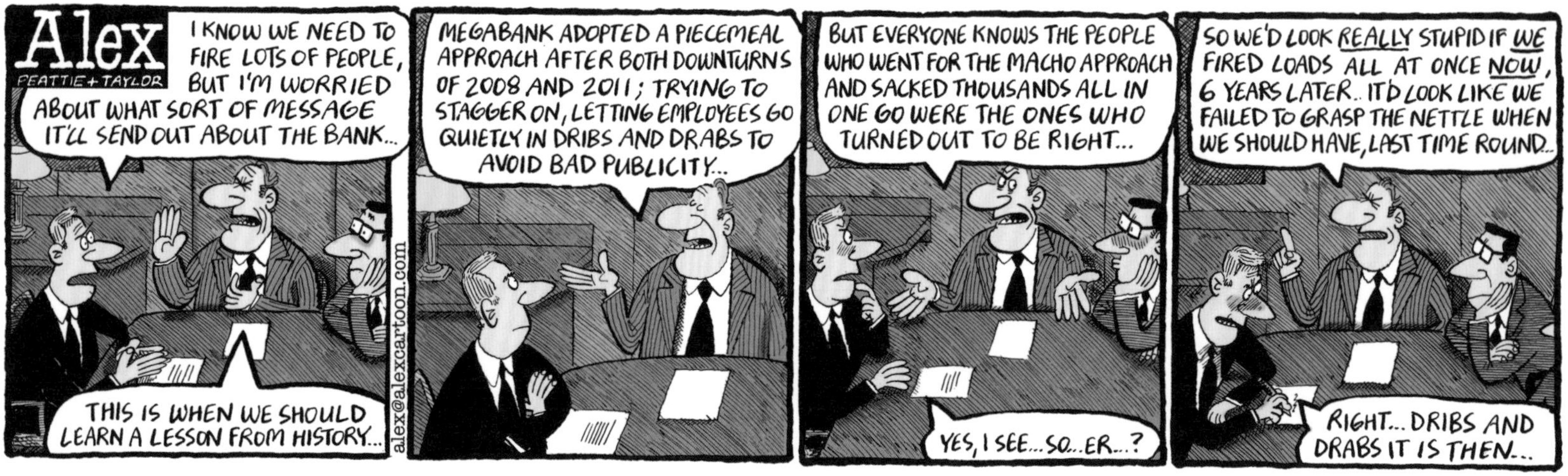
Alex
PEATTIE + TAYLOR
I KNOW WE NEED TO FIRE LOTS OF PEOPLE, BUT I'M WORRIED ABOUT WHAT SORT OF MESSAGE IT'LL SEND OUT ABOUT THE BANK...
THIS IS WHEN WE SHOULD LEARN A LESSON FROM HISTORY...
alex@alexcartoon.com
MEGABANK ADOPTED A PIECEMEAL APPROACH AFTER BOTH DOWNTURNS OF 2008 AND 2011; TRYING TO STAGGER ON, LETTING EMPLOYEES GO QUIETLY IN DRIBS AND DRABS TO AVOID BAD PUBLICITY...
BUT EVERYONE KNOWS THE PEOPLE WHO WENT FOR THE MACHO APPROACH AND SACKED THOUSANDS ALL IN ONE GO WERE THE ONES WHO TURNED OUT TO BE RIGHT...
YES, I SEE... SO...ER...?
SO WE'D LOOK REALLY STUPID IF WE FIRED LOADS ALL AT ONCE NOW, 6 YEARS LATER.. IT'D LOOK LIKE WE FAILED TO GRASP THE NETTLE WHEN WE SHOULD HAVE, LAST TIME ROUND...
RIGHT... DRIBS AND DRABS IT IS THEN...

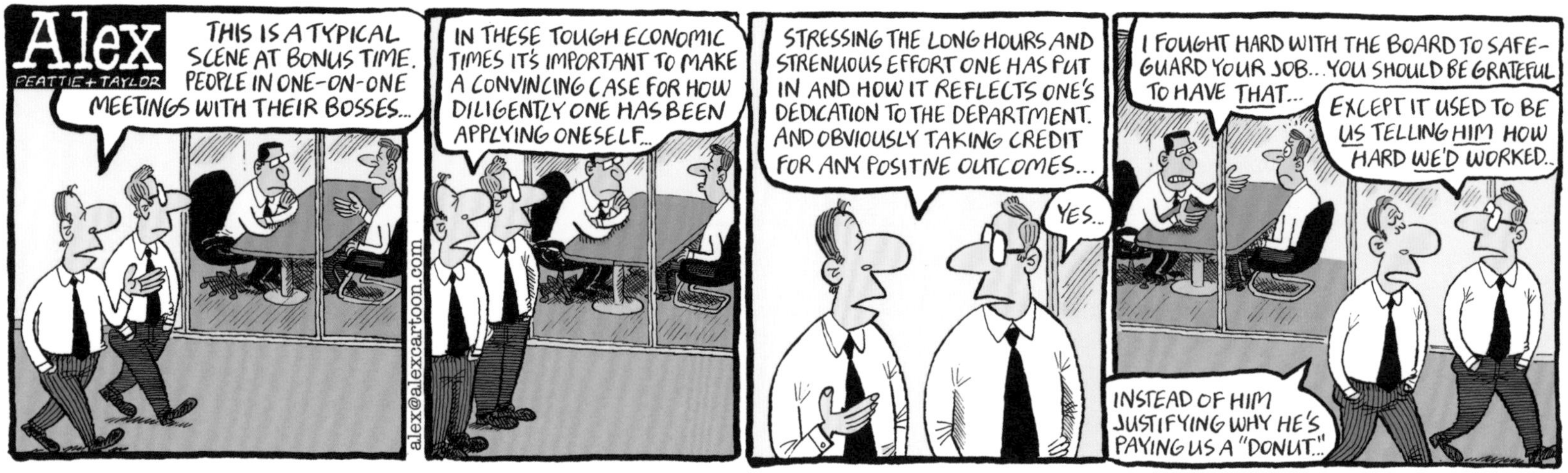
Alex
PEATTIE + TAYLOR
THIS IS A TYPICAL SCENE AT BONUS TIME. PEOPLE IN ONE-ON-ONE MEETINGS WITH THEIR BOSSES...
alex@alexcartoon.com
IN THESE TOUGH ECONOMIC TIMES IT'S IMPORTANT TO MAKE A CONVINCING CASE FOR HOW DILIGENTLY ONE HAS BEEN APPLYING ONESELF...
STRESSING THE LONG HOURS AND STRENUOUS EFFORT ONE HAS PUT IN AND HOW IT REFLECTS ONE'S DEDICATION TO THE DEPARTMENT. AND OBVIOUSLY TAKING CREDIT FOR ANY POSITIVE OUTCOMES...
YES...
I FOUGHT HARD WITH THE BOARD TO SAFE-GUARD YOUR JOB... YOU SHOULD BE GRATEFUL TO HAVE THAT...
EXCEPT IT USED TO BE US TELLING HIM HOW HARD WE'D WORKED...
INSTEAD OF HIM JUSTIFYING WHY HE'S PAYING US A "DONUT."

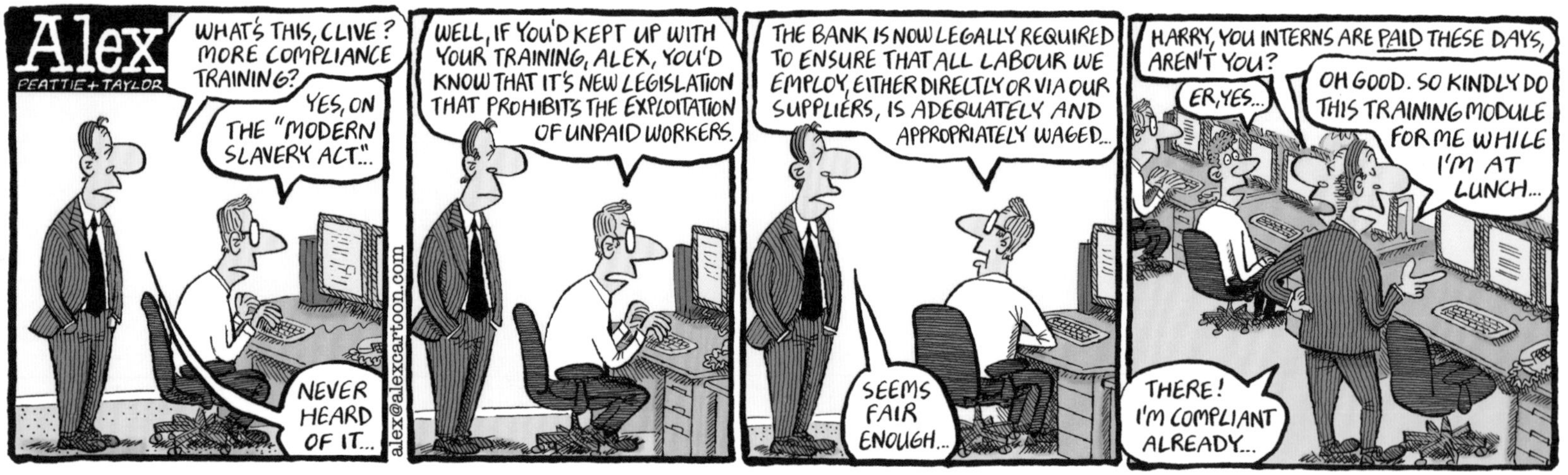
Alex
PEATTIE + TAYLOR
WHAT'S THIS, CLIVE? MORE COMPLIANCE TRAINING?
YES, ON THE "MODERN SLAVERY ACT."
NEVER HEARD OF IT...
alex@alexcartoon.com
WELL, IF YOU'D KEPT UP WITH YOUR TRAINING, ALEX, YOU'D KNOW THAT IT'S NEW LEGISLATION THAT PROHIBITS THE EXPLOITATION OF UNPAID WORKERS.
THE BANK IS NOW LEGALLY REQUIRED TO ENSURE THAT ALL LABOUR WE EMPLOY, EITHER DIRECTLY OR VIA OUR SUPPLIERS, IS ADEQUATELY AND APPROPRIATELY WAGED...
SEEMS FAIR ENOUGH...
HARRY, YOU INTERNS ARE PAID THESE DAYS, AREN'T YOU?
ER, YES...
OH GOOD. SO KINDLY DO THIS TRAINING MODULE FOR ME WHILE I'M AT LUNCH...
THERE! I'M COMPLIANT ALREADY...

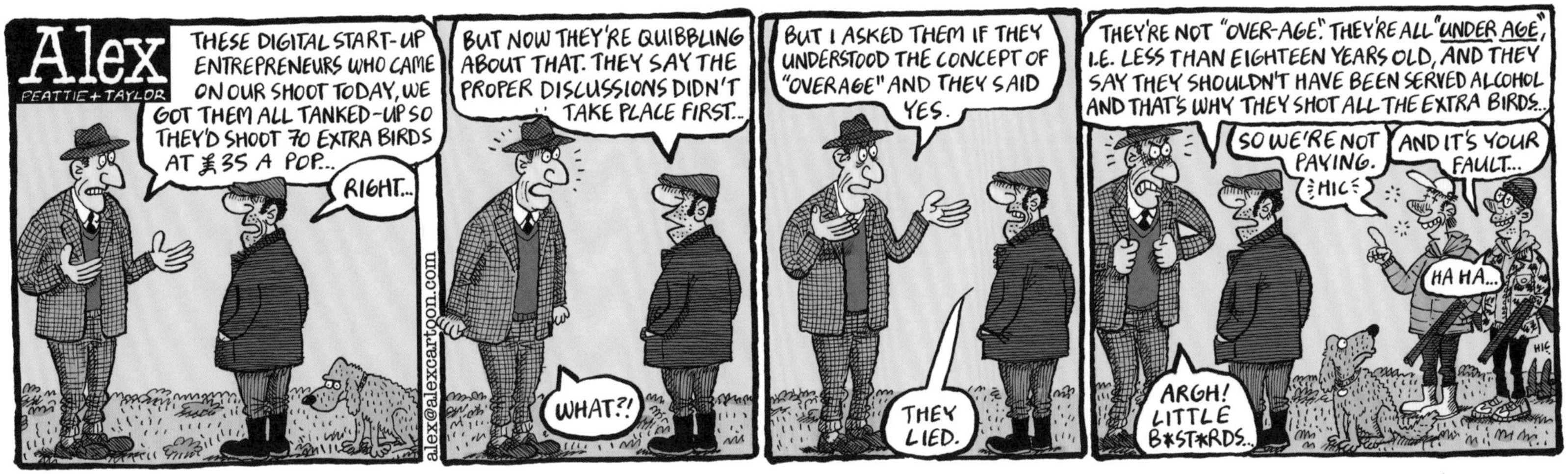
Alex
PEATTIE+TAYLOR
THESE DIGITAL START-UP ENTREPRENEURS WHO CAME ON OUR SHOOT TODAY, WE GOT THEM ALL TANKED-UP SO THEY'D SHOOT 70 EXTRA BIRDS AT £35 A POP...
RIGHT...
BUT NOW THEY'RE QUIBBLING ABOUT THAT. THEY SAY THE PROPER DISCUSSIONS DIDN'T TAKE PLACE FIRST...
WHAT?!
alex@alexcartoon.com
BUT I ASKED THEM IF THEY UNDERSTOOD THE CONCEPT OF "OVERAGE" AND THEY SAID YES.
THEY LIED.
THEY'RE NOT "OVER-AGE". THEY'RE ALL "UNDER AGE", I.E. LESS THAN EIGHTEEN YEARS OLD, AND THEY SAY THEY SHOULDN'T HAVE BEEN SERVED ALCOHOL AND THAT'S WHY THEY SHOT ALL THE EXTRA BIRDS...
SO WE'RE NOT PAYING.. HIC
AND IT'S YOUR FAULT...
HA HA...
HIC
ARGH! LITTLE B*ST*RDS...

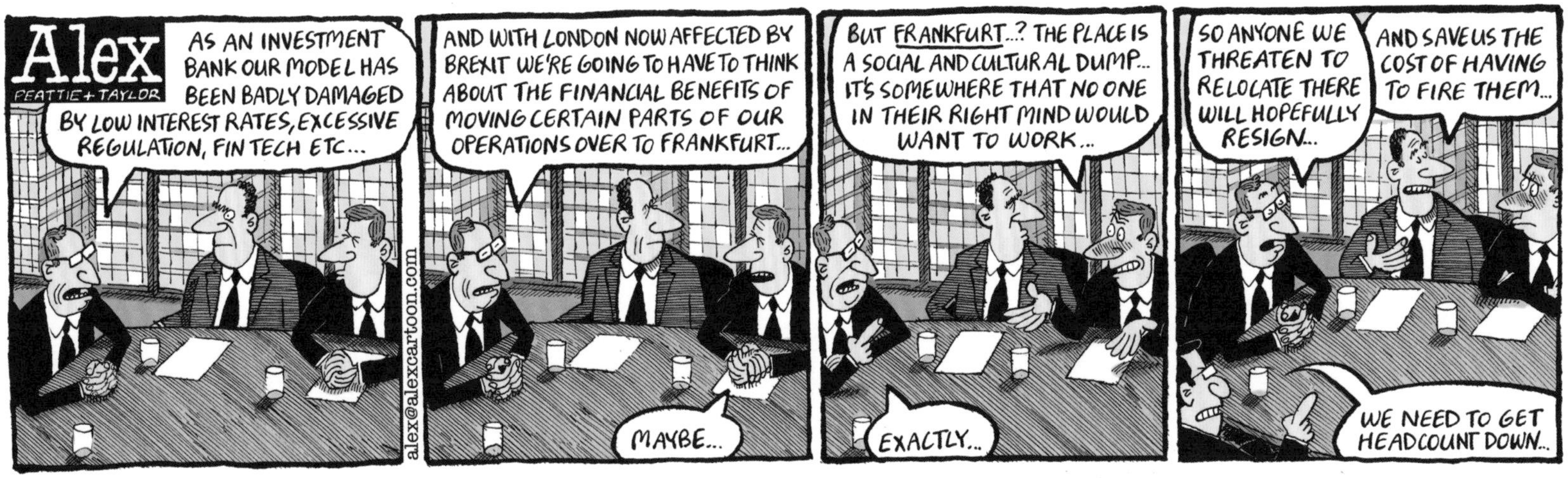
Alex
PEATTIE+TAYLOR
AS AN INVESTMENT BANK OUR MODEL HAS BEEN BADLY DAMAGED BY LOW INTEREST RATES, EXCESSIVE REGULATION, FIN TECH ETC...
AND WITH LONDON NOW AFFECTED BY BREXIT WE'RE GOING TO HAVE TO THINK ABOUT THE FINANCIAL BENEFITS OF MOVING CERTAIN PARTS OF OUR OPERATIONS OVER TO FRANKFURT...
MAYBE...
alex@alexcartoon.com
BUT FRANKFURT...? THE PLACE IS A SOCIAL AND CULTURAL DUMP... IT'S SOMEWHERE THAT NO ONE IN THEIR RIGHT MIND WOULD WANT TO WORK...
EXACTLY...
SO ANYONE WE THREATEN TO RELOCATE THERE WILL HOPEFULLY RESIGN...
AND SAVE US THE COST OF HAVING TO FIRE THEM...
WE NEED TO GET HEADCOUNT DOWN...

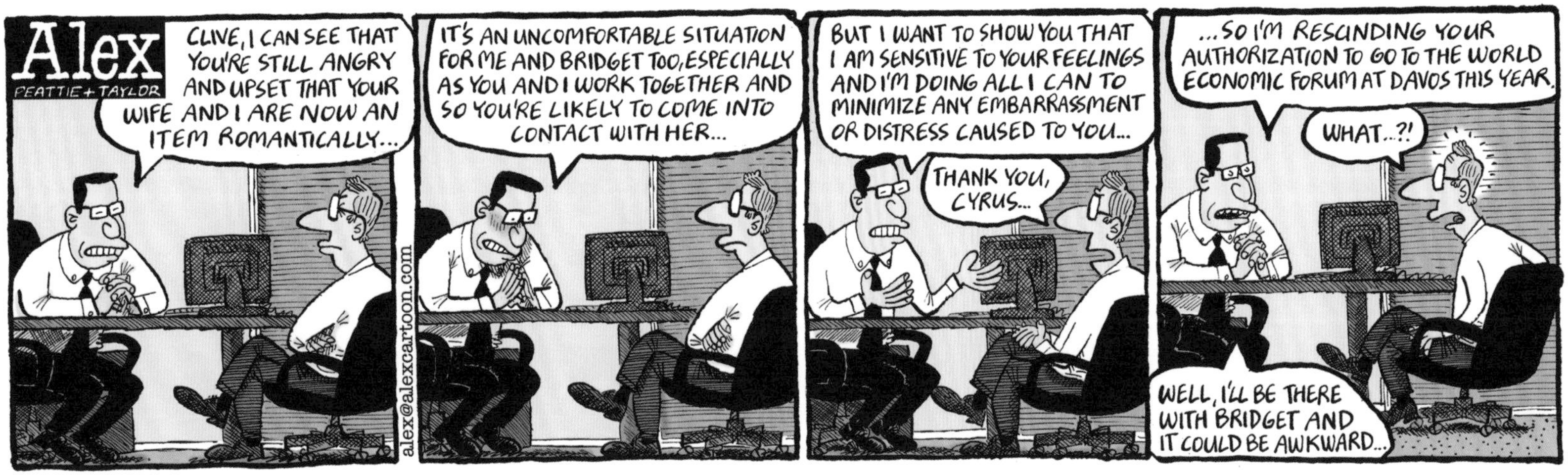
Alex
PEATTIE+TAYLOR
CLIVE, I CAN SEE THAT YOU'RE STILL ANGRY AND UPSET THAT YOUR WIFE AND I ARE NOW AN ITEM ROMANTICALLY...
IT'S AN UNCOMFORTABLE SITUATION FOR ME AND BRIDGET TOO, ESPECIALLY AS YOU AND I WORK TOGETHER AND SO YOU'RE LIKELY TO COME INTO CONTACT WITH HER...
alex@alexcartoon.com
BUT I WANT TO SHOW YOU THAT I AM SENSITIVE TO YOUR FEELINGS AND I'M DOING ALL I CAN TO MINIMIZE ANY EMBARRASSMENT OR DISTRESS CAUSED TO YOU...
THANK YOU, CYRUS...
...SO I'M RESCINDING YOUR AUTHORIZATION TO GO TO THE WORLD ECONOMIC FORUM AT DAVOS THIS YEAR.
WHAT...?!
WELL, I'LL BE THERE WITH BRIDGET AND IT COULD BE AWKWARD...

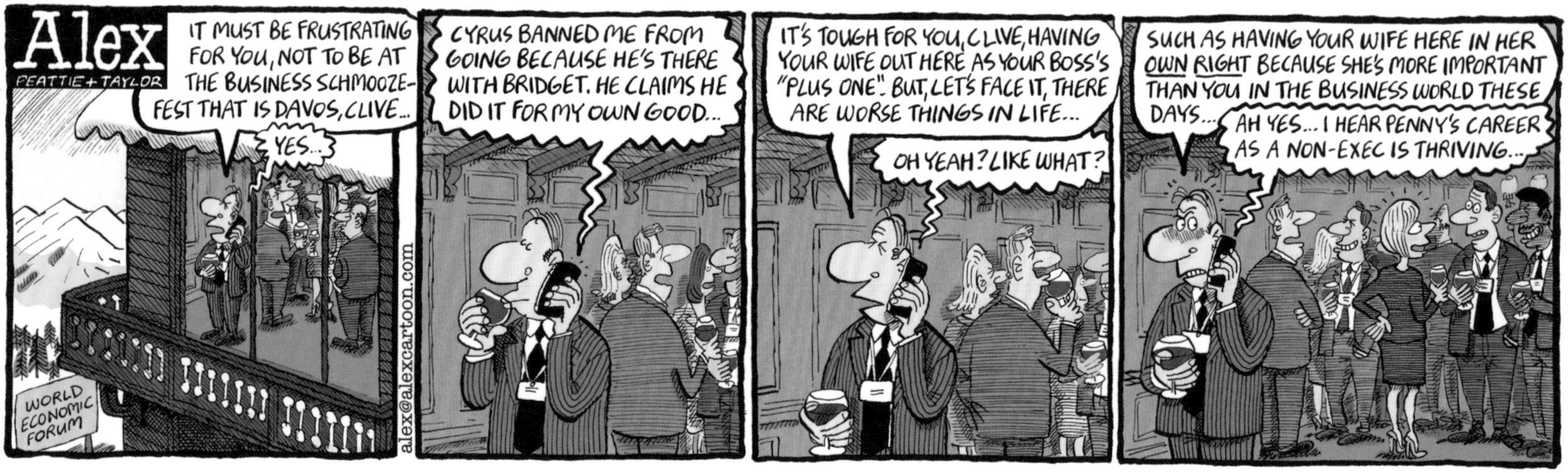
Alex
PEATTIE+TAYLOR
IT MUST BE FRUSTRATING FOR YOU, NOT TO BE AT THE BUSINESS SCHMOOZE-FEST THAT IS DAVOS, CLIVE...
YES...
WORLD ECONOMIC FORUM
alex@alexcartoon.com
CYRUS BANNED ME FROM GOING BECAUSE HE'S THERE WITH BRIDGET. HE CLAIMS HE DID IT FOR MY OWN GOOD...
IT'S TOUGH FOR YOU, CLIVE, HAVING YOUR WIFE OUT HERE AS YOUR BOSS'S "PLUS ONE". BUT, LET'S FACE IT, THERE ARE WORSE THINGS IN LIFE...
OH YEAH? LIKE WHAT?
SUCH AS HAVING YOUR WIFE HERE IN HER OWN RIGHT BECAUSE SHE'S MORE IMPORTANT THAN YOU IN THE BUSINESS WORLD THESE DAYS...
AH YES... I HEAR PENNY'S CAREER AS A NON-EXEC IS THRIVING...

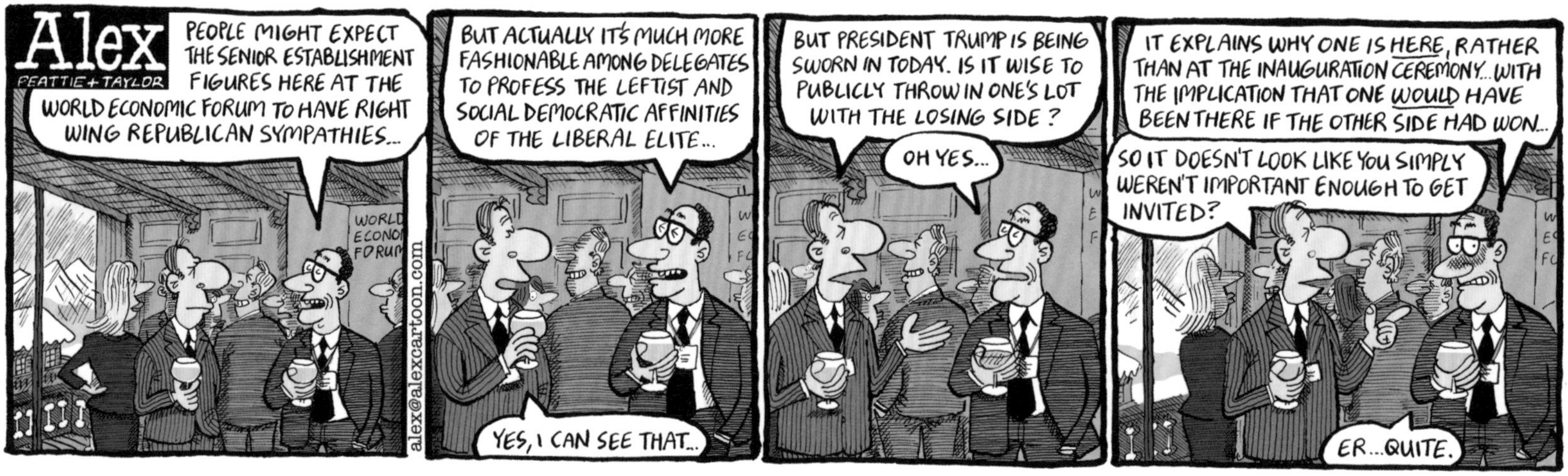
Alex
PEATTIE+TAYLOR
PEOPLE MIGHT EXPECT THE SENIOR ESTABLISHMENT FIGURES HERE AT THE WORLD ECONOMIC FORUM TO HAVE RIGHT WING REPUBLICAN SYMPATHIES...
WORLD ECONOMIC FORUM
alex@alexcartoon.com
BUT ACTUALLY IT'S MUCH MORE FASHIONABLE AMONG DELEGATES TO PROFESS THE LEFTIST AND SOCIAL DEMOCRATIC AFFINITIES OF THE LIBERAL ELITE...
YES, I CAN SEE THAT...
BUT PRESIDENT TRUMP IS BEING SWORN IN TODAY. IS IT WISE TO PUBLICLY THROW IN ONE'S LOT WITH THE LOSING SIDE?
OH YES...
IT EXPLAINS WHY ONE IS HERE, RATHER THAN AT THE INAUGURATION CEREMONY... WITH THE IMPLICATION THAT ONE WOULD HAVE BEEN THERE IF THE OTHER SIDE HAD WON...
SO IT DOESN'T LOOK LIKE YOU SIMPLY WEREN'T IMPORTANT ENOUGH TO GET INVITED?
ER...QUITE.

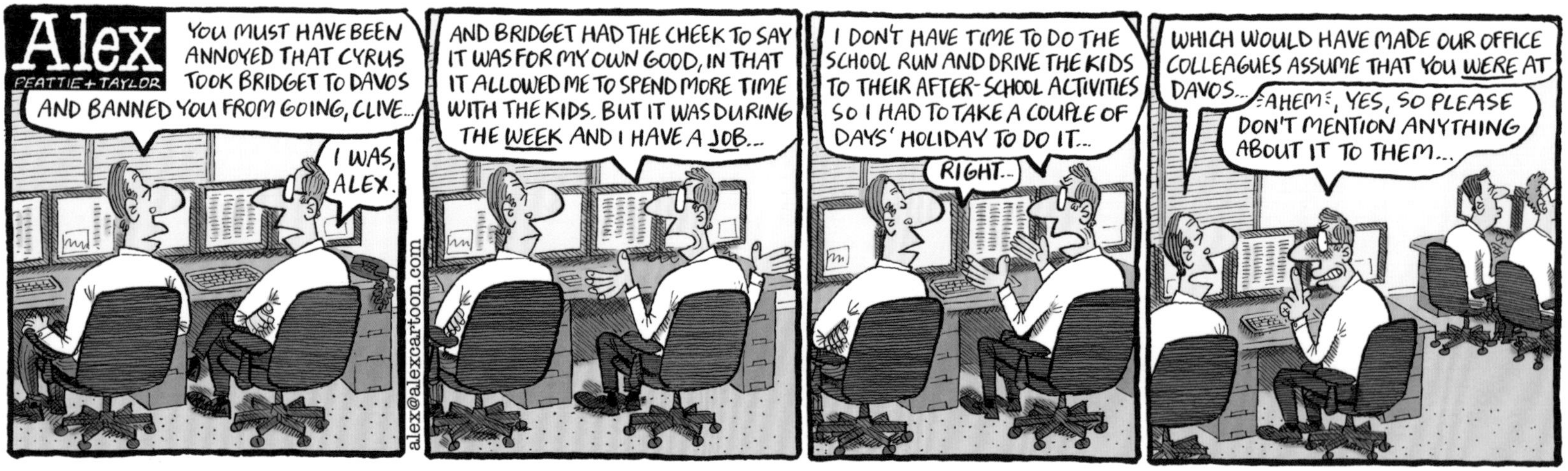
Alex
PEATTIE+TAYLOR
YOU MUST HAVE BEEN ANNOYED THAT CYRUS TOOK BRIDGET TO DAVOS AND BANNED YOU FROM GOING, CLIVE...
I WAS, ALEX.
alex@alexcartoon.com
AND BRIDGET HAD THE CHEEK TO SAY IT WAS FOR MY OWN GOOD, IN THAT IT ALLOWED ME TO SPEND MORE TIME WITH THE KIDS. BUT IT WAS DURING THE WEEK AND I HAVE A JOB...
I DON'T HAVE TIME TO DO THE SCHOOL RUN AND DRIVE THE KIDS TO THEIR AFTER-SCHOOL ACTIVITIES SO I HAD TO TAKE A COUPLE OF DAYS' HOLIDAY TO DO IT...
RIGHT...
WHICH WOULD HAVE MADE OUR OFFICE COLLEAGUES ASSUME THAT YOU WERE AT DAVOS...
AHEM, YES, SO PLEASE DON'T MENTION ANYTHING ABOUT IT TO THEM...

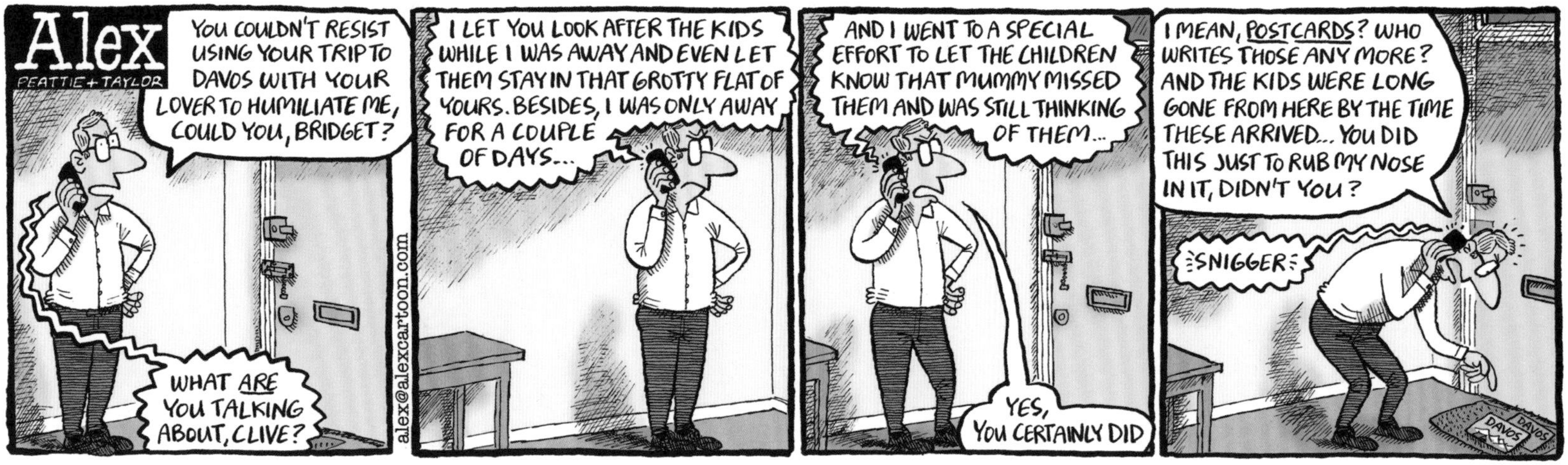
Alex
PEATTIE+TAYLOR
YOU COULDN'T RESIST USING YOUR TRIP TO DAVOS WITH YOUR LOVER TO HUMILIATE ME, COULD YOU, BRIDGET?
WHAT ARE YOU TALKING ABOUT, CLIVE?
alex@alexcartoon.com
I LET YOU LOOK AFTER THE KIDS WHILE I WAS AWAY AND EVEN LET THEM STAY IN THAT GROTTY FLAT OF YOURS. BESIDES, I WAS ONLY AWAY FOR A COUPLE OF DAYS...
AND I WENT TO A SPECIAL EFFORT TO LET THE CHILDREN KNOW THAT MUMMY MISSED THEM AND WAS STILL THINKING OF THEM...
YES, YOU CERTAINLY DID
I MEAN, POSTCARDS? WHO WRITES THOSE ANY MORE? AND THE KIDS WERE LONG GONE FROM HERE BY THE TIME THESE ARRIVED... YOU DID THIS JUST TO RUB MY NOSE IN IT, DIDN'T YOU?
SNIGGER
DAVOS
DAVOS
DAVOS

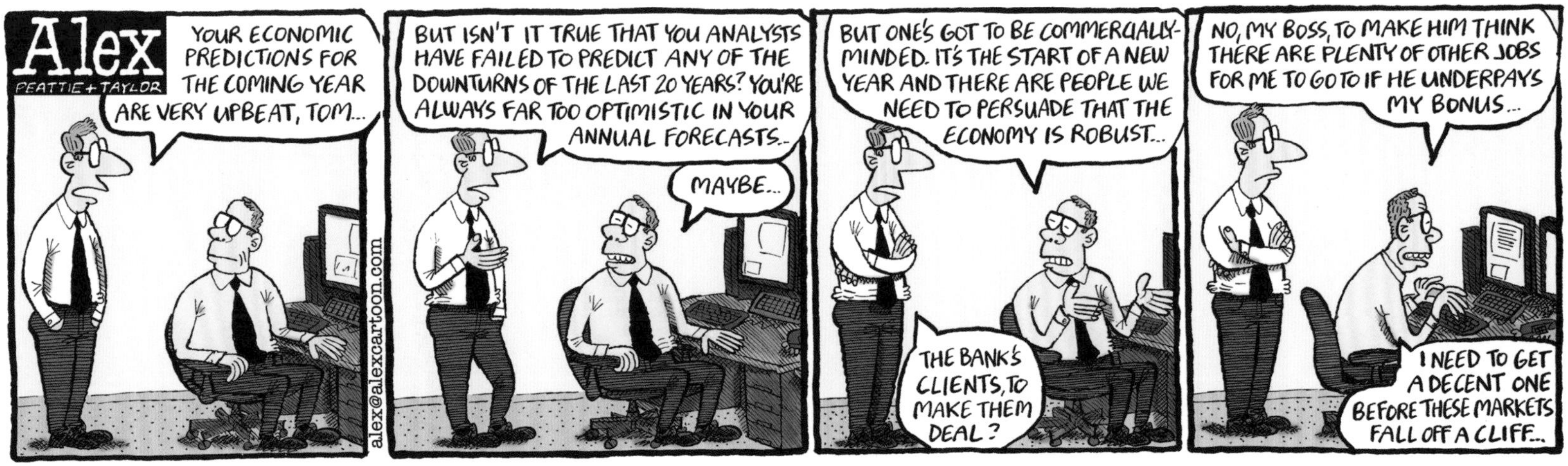
Alex
PEATTIE+TAYLOR
YOUR ECONOMIC PREDICTIONS FOR THE COMING YEAR ARE VERY UPBEAT, TOM...
alex@alexcartoon.com
BUT ISN'T IT TRUE THAT YOU ANALYSTS HAVE FAILED TO PREDICT ANY OF THE DOWNTURNS OF THE LAST 20 YEARS? YOU'RE ALWAYS FAR TOO OPTIMISTIC IN YOUR ANNUAL FORECASTS...
MAYBE...
BUT ONE'S GOT TO BE COMMERCIALLY-MINDED. IT'S THE START OF A NEW YEAR AND THERE ARE PEOPLE WE NEED TO PERSUADE THAT THE ECONOMY IS ROBUST...
THE BANK'S CLIENTS, TO MAKE THEM DEAL?
NO, MY BOSS, TO MAKE HIM THINK THERE ARE PLENTY OF OTHER JOBS FOR ME TO GO TO IF HE UNDERPAYS MY BONUS...
I NEED TO GET A DECENT ONE BEFORE THESE MARKETS FALL OFF A CLIFF...

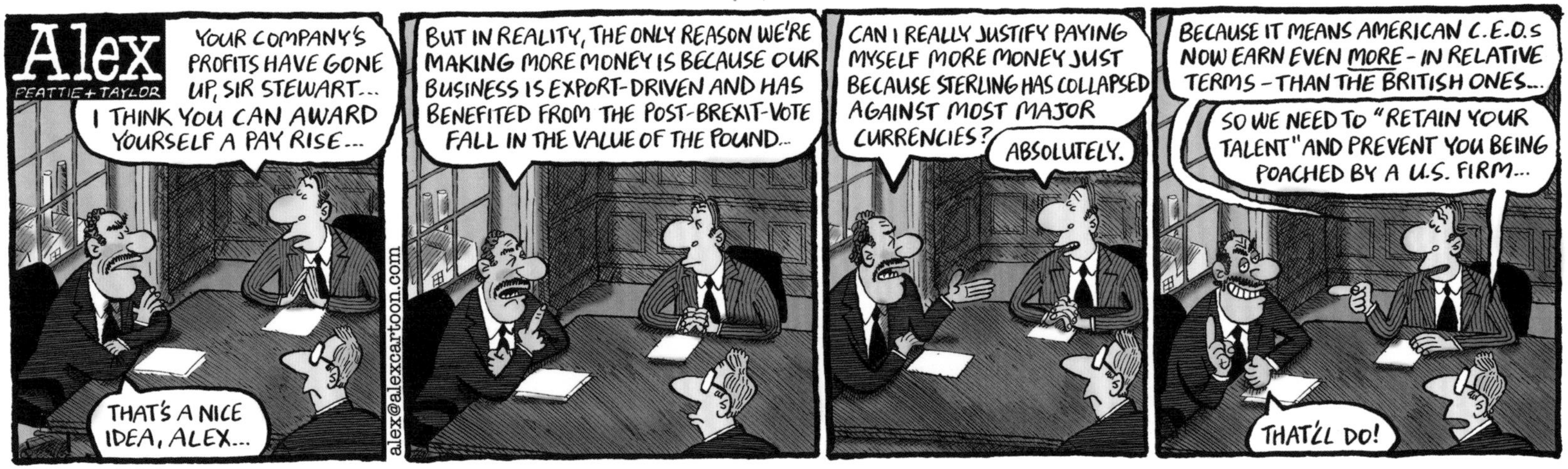
Alex
PEATTIE+TAYLOR
YOUR COMPANY'S PROFITS HAVE GONE UP, SIR STEWART... I THINK YOU CAN AWARD YOURSELF A PAY RISE...
THAT'S A NICE IDEA, ALEX...
alex@alexcartoon.com
BUT IN REALITY, THE ONLY REASON WE'RE MAKING MORE MONEY IS BECAUSE OUR BUSINESS IS EXPORT-DRIVEN AND HAS BENEFITED FROM THE POST-BREXIT-VOTE FALL IN THE VALUE OF THE POUND...
CAN I REALLY JUSTIFY PAYING MYSELF MORE MONEY JUST BECAUSE STERLING HAS COLLAPSED AGAINST MOST MAJOR CURRENCIES?
ABSOLUTELY.
BECAUSE IT MEANS AMERICAN C.E.O.s NOW EARN EVEN MORE - IN RELATIVE TERMS - THAN THE BRITISH ONES...
SO WE NEED TO "RETAIN YOUR TALENT" AND PREVENT YOU BEING POACHED BY A U.S. FIRM...
THAT'LL DO!

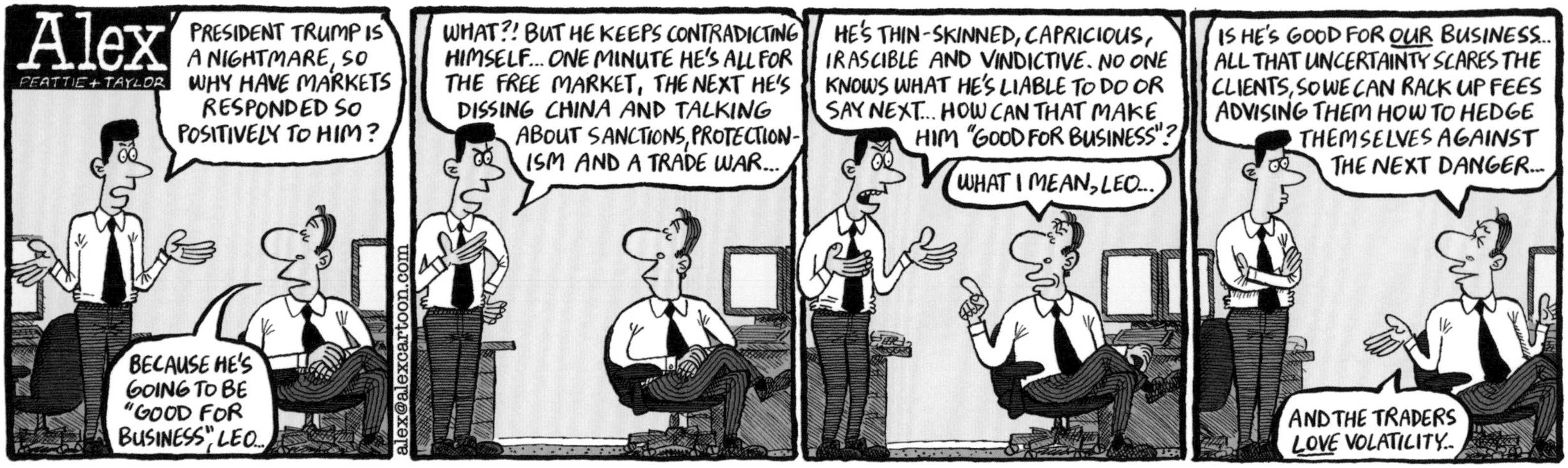
Alex
PEATTIE + TAYLOR
PRESIDENT TRUMP IS A NIGHTMARE, SO WHY HAVE MARKETS RESPONDED SO POSITIVELY TO HIM?
BECAUSE HE'S GOING TO BE "GOOD FOR BUSINESS", LEO...
alex@alexcartoon.com
WHAT?! BUT HE KEEPS CONTRADICTING HIMSELF... ONE MINUTE HE'S ALL FOR THE FREE MARKET, THE NEXT HE'S DISSING CHINA AND TALKING ABOUT SANCTIONS, PROTECTION-ISM AND A TRADE WAR...
HE'S THIN-SKINNED, CAPRICIOUS, IRASCIBLE AND VINDICTIVE. NO ONE KNOWS WHAT HE'S LIABLE TO DO OR SAY NEXT... HOW CAN THAT MAKE HIM "GOOD FOR BUSINESS"?
WHAT I MEAN, LEO...
IS HE'S GOOD FOR OUR BUSINESS... ALL THAT UNCERTAINTY SCARES THE CLIENTS, SO WE CAN RACK UP FEES ADVISING THEM HOW TO HEDGE THEMSELVES AGAINST THE NEXT DANGER...
AND THE TRADERS LOVE VOLATILITY...

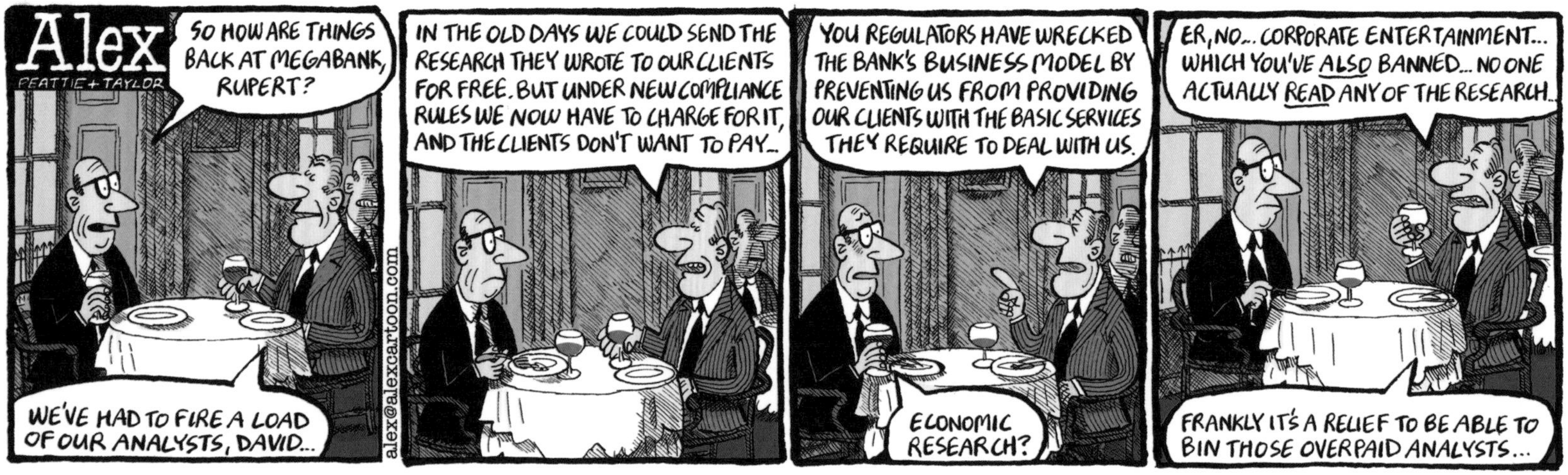
Alex
PEATTIE + TAYLOR
SO HOW ARE THINGS BACK AT MEGABANK, RUPERT?
WE'VE HAD TO FIRE A LOAD OF OUR ANALYSTS, DAVID...
alex@alexcartoon.com
IN THE OLD DAYS WE COULD SEND THE RESEARCH THEY WROTE TO OUR CLIENTS FOR FREE. BUT UNDER NEW COMPLIANCE RULES WE NOW HAVE TO CHARGE FOR IT, AND THE CLIENTS DON'T WANT TO PAY...
YOU REGULATORS HAVE WRECKED THE BANK'S BUSINESS MODEL BY PREVENTING US FROM PROVIDING OUR CLIENTS WITH THE BASIC SERVICES THEY REQUIRE TO DEAL WITH US.
ECONOMIC RESEARCH?
ER, NO... CORPORATE ENTERTAINMENT... WHICH YOU'VE ALSO BANNED... NO ONE ACTUALLY READ ANY OF THE RESEARCH...
FRANKLY IT'S A RELIEF TO BE ABLE TO BIN THOSE OVERPAID ANALYSTS...

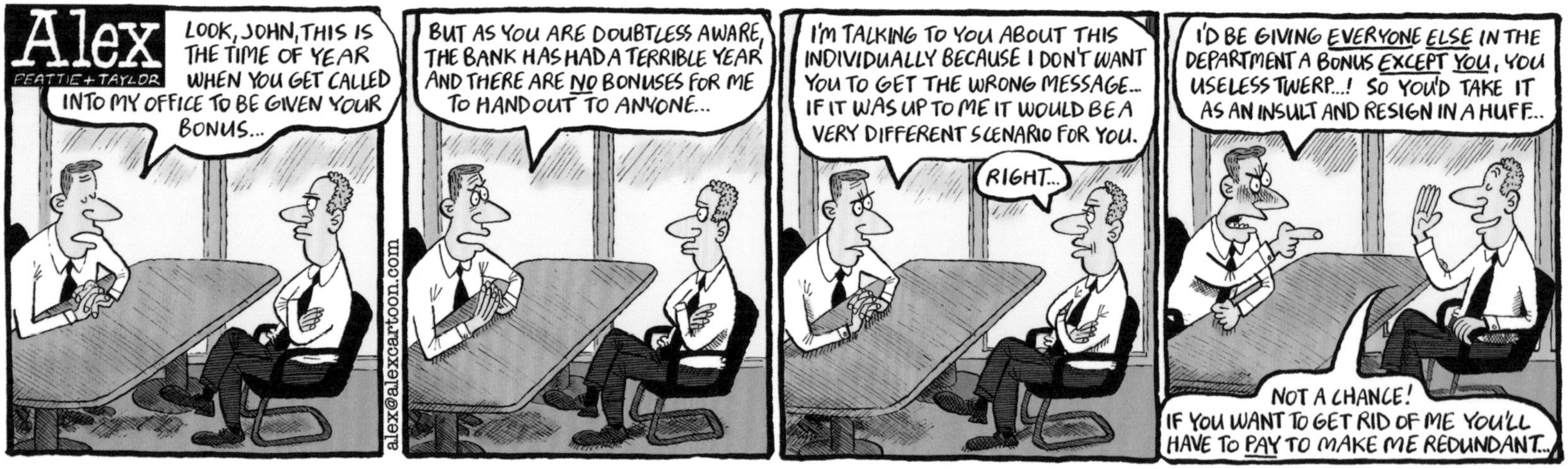
Alex
PEATTIE + TAYLOR
LOOK, JOHN, THIS IS THE TIME OF YEAR WHEN YOU GET CALLED INTO MY OFFICE TO BE GIVEN YOUR BONUS...
alex@alexcartoon.com
BUT AS YOU ARE DOUBTLESS AWARE, THE BANK HAS HAD A TERRIBLE YEAR AND THERE ARE NO BONUSES FOR ME TO HAND OUT TO ANYONE...
I'M TALKING TO YOU ABOUT THIS INDIVIDUALLY BECAUSE I DON'T WANT YOU TO GET THE WRONG MESSAGE... IF IT WAS UP TO ME IT WOULD BE A VERY DIFFERENT SCENARIO FOR YOU.
RIGHT...
I'D BE GIVING EVERYONE ELSE IN THE DEPARTMENT A BONUS EXCEPT YOU, YOU USELESS TWERP...! SO YOU'D TAKE IT AS AN INSULT AND RESIGN IN A HUFF...
NOT A CHANCE! IF YOU WANT TO GET RID OF ME YOU'LL HAVE TO PAY TO MAKE ME REDUNDANT...

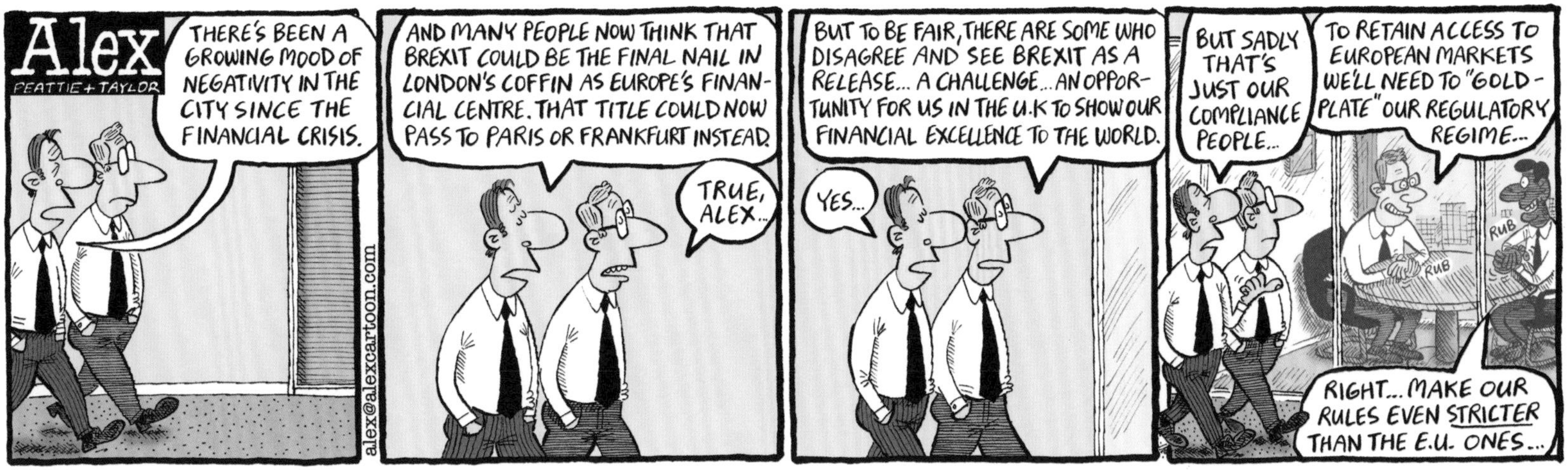
Alex
PEATTIE + TAYLOR
THERE'S BEEN A GROWING MOOD OF NEGATIVITY IN THE CITY SINCE THE FINANCIAL CRISIS.
AND MANY PEOPLE NOW THINK THAT BREXIT COULD BE THE FINAL NAIL IN LONDON'S COFFIN AS EUROPE'S FINANCIAL CENTRE. THAT TITLE COULD NOW PASS TO PARIS OR FRANKFURT INSTEAD.
TRUE, ALEX...
BUT TO BE FAIR, THERE ARE SOME WHO DISAGREE AND SEE BREXIT AS A RELEASE... A CHALLENGE... AN OPPORTUNITY FOR US IN THE U.K TO SHOW OUR FINANCIAL EXCELLENCE TO THE WORLD.
YES...
BUT SADLY THAT'S JUST OUR COMPLIANCE PEOPLE...
TO RETAIN ACCESS TO EUROPEAN MARKETS WE'LL NEED TO "GOLD-PLATE" OUR REGULATORY REGIME...
RUB
RUB
RIGHT... MAKE OUR RULES EVEN STRICTER THAN THE E.U. ONES...
alex@alexcartoon.com

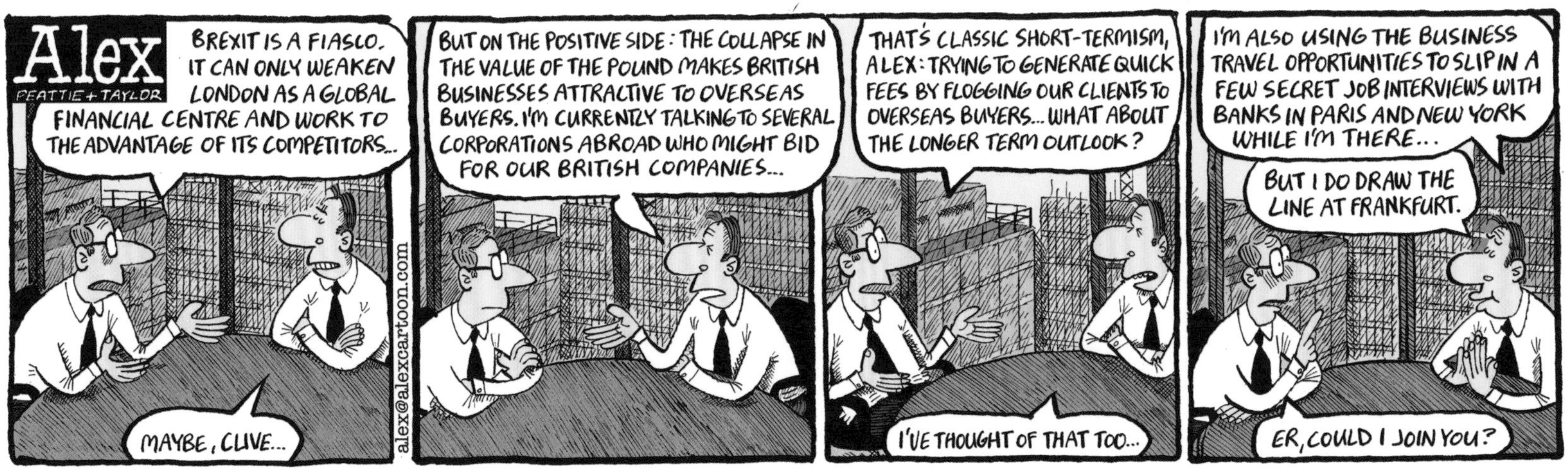
Alex
PEATTIE + TAYLOR
BREXIT IS A FIASCO. IT CAN ONLY WEAKEN LONDON AS A GLOBAL FINANCIAL CENTRE AND WORK TO THE ADVANTAGE OF ITS COMPETITORS...
MAYBE, CLIVE...
BUT ON THE POSITIVE SIDE: THE COLLAPSE IN THE VALUE OF THE POUND MAKES BRITISH BUSINESSES ATTRACTIVE TO OVERSEAS BUYERS. I'M CURRENTLY TALKING TO SEVERAL CORPORATIONS ABROAD WHO MIGHT BID FOR OUR BRITISH COMPANIES...
THAT'S CLASSIC SHORT-TERMISM, ALEX: TRYING TO GENERATE QUICK FEES BY FLOGGING OUR CLIENTS TO OVERSEAS BUYERS... WHAT ABOUT THE LONGER TERM OUTLOOK?
I'VE THOUGHT OF THAT TOO...
I'M ALSO USING THE BUSINESS TRAVEL OPPORTUNITIES TO SLIP IN A FEW SECRET JOB INTERVIEWS WITH BANKS IN PARIS AND NEW YORK WHILE I'M THERE...
BUT I DO DRAW THE LINE AT FRANKFURT.
ER, COULD I JOIN YOU?
alex@alexcartoon.com

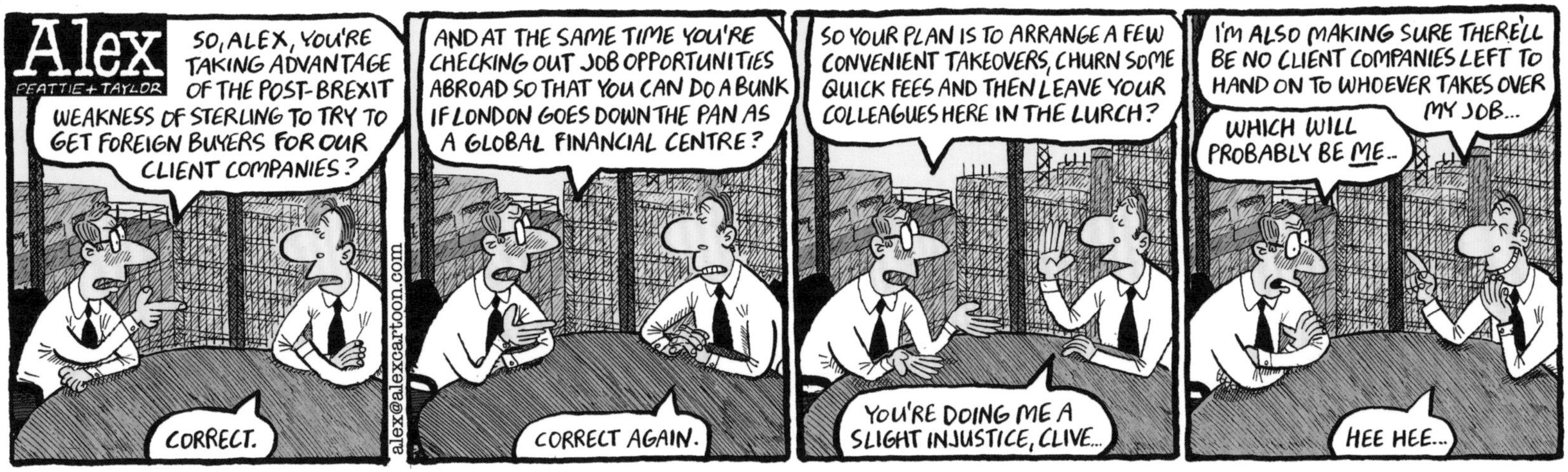
Alex
PEATTIE + TAYLOR
SO, ALEX, YOU'RE TAKING ADVANTAGE OF THE POST-BREXIT WEAKNESS OF STERLING TO TRY TO GET FOREIGN BUYERS FOR OUR CLIENT COMPANIES?
CORRECT.
AND AT THE SAME TIME YOU'RE CHECKING OUT JOB OPPORTUNITIES ABROAD SO THAT YOU CAN DO A BUNK IF LONDON GOES DOWN THE PAN AS A GLOBAL FINANCIAL CENTRE?
CORRECT AGAIN.
SO YOUR PLAN IS TO ARRANGE A FEW CONVENIENT TAKEOVERS, CHURN SOME QUICK FEES AND THEN LEAVE YOUR COLLEAGUES HERE IN THE LURCH?
YOU'RE DOING ME A SLIGHT INJUSTICE, CLIVE...
I'M ALSO MAKING SURE THERE'LL BE NO CLIENT COMPANIES LEFT TO HAND ON TO WHOEVER TAKES OVER MY JOB...
WHICH WILL PROBABLY BE ME...
HEE HEE...
alex@alexcartoon.com

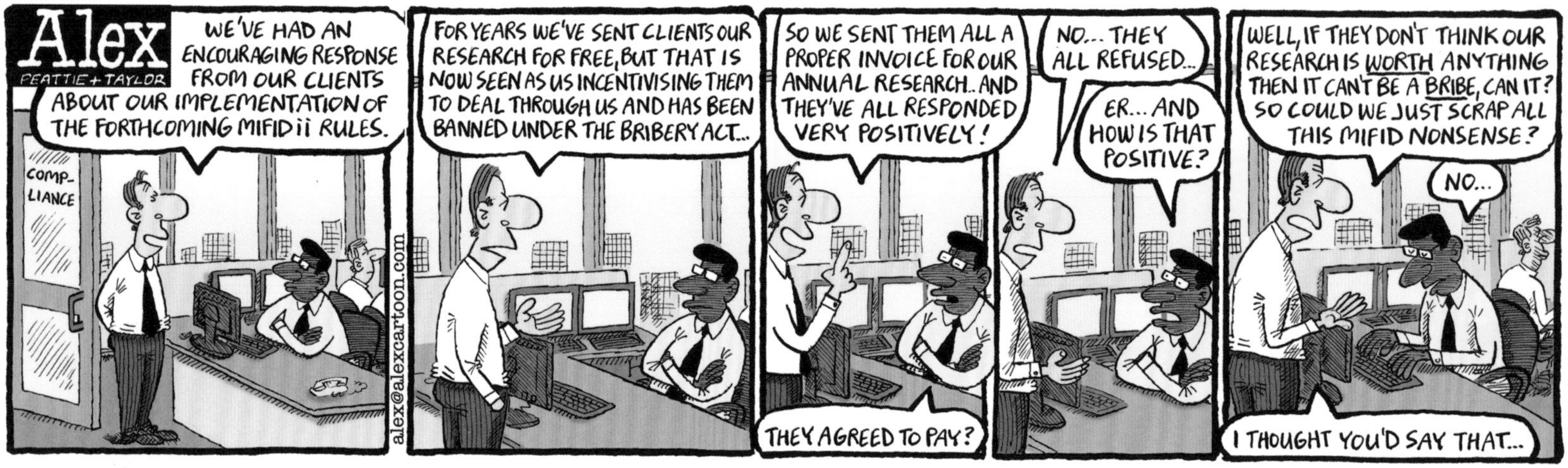
Alex
PEATTIE + TAYLOR
WE'VE HAD AN ENCOURAGING RESPONSE FROM OUR CLIENTS ABOUT OUR IMPLEMENTATION OF THE FORTHCOMING MIFID ii RULES.
COMP_LIANCE
FOR YEARS WE'VE SENT CLIENTS OUR RESEARCH FOR FREE, BUT THAT IS NOW SEEN AS US INCENTIVISING THEM TO DEAL THROUGH US AND HAS BEEN BANNED UNDER THE BRIBERY ACT...
alex@alexcartoon.com
SO WE SENT THEM ALL A PROPER INVOICE FOR OUR ANNUAL RESEARCH... AND THEY'VE ALL RESPONDED VERY POSITIVELY!
THEY AGREED TO PAY?
NO... THEY ALL REFUSED...
ER... AND HOW IS THAT POSITIVE?
WELL, IF THEY DON'T THINK OUR RESEARCH IS WORTH ANYTHING THEN IT CAN'T BE A BRIBE, CAN IT? SO COULD WE JUST SCRAP ALL THIS MIFID NONSENSE?
NO...
I THOUGHT YOU'D SAY THAT...

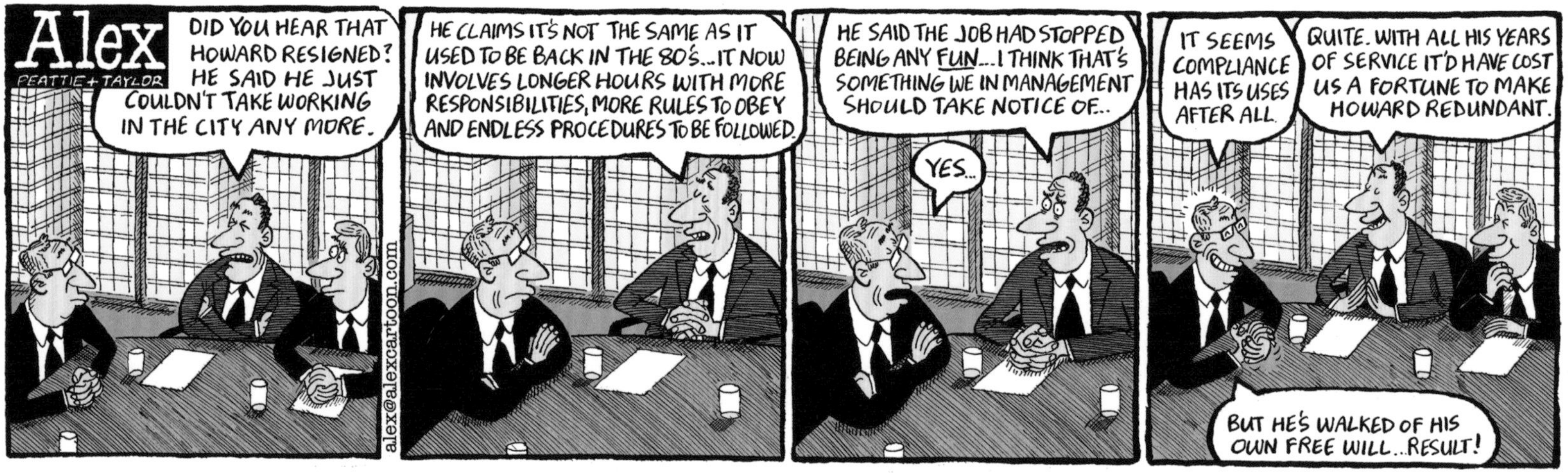
Alex
PEATTIE + TAYLOR
DID YOU HEAR THAT HOWARD RESIGNED? HE SAID HE JUST COULDN'T TAKE WORKING IN THE CITY ANY MORE.
HE CLAIMS IT'S NOT THE SAME AS IT USED TO BE BACK IN THE 80'S... IT NOW INVOLVES LONGER HOURS WITH MORE RESPONSIBILITIES, MORE RULES TO OBEY AND ENDLESS PROCEDURES TO BE FOLLOWED.
alex@alexcartoon.com
HE SAID THE JOB HAD STOPPED BEING ANY FUN... I THINK THAT'S SOMETHING WE IN MANAGEMENT SHOULD TAKE NOTICE OF...
YES...
IT SEEMS COMPLIANCE HAS ITS USES AFTER ALL.
QUITE. WITH ALL HIS YEARS OF SERVICE IT'D HAVE COST US A FORTUNE TO MAKE HOWARD REDUNDANT.
BUT HE'S WALKED OF HIS OWN FREE WILL... RESULT!

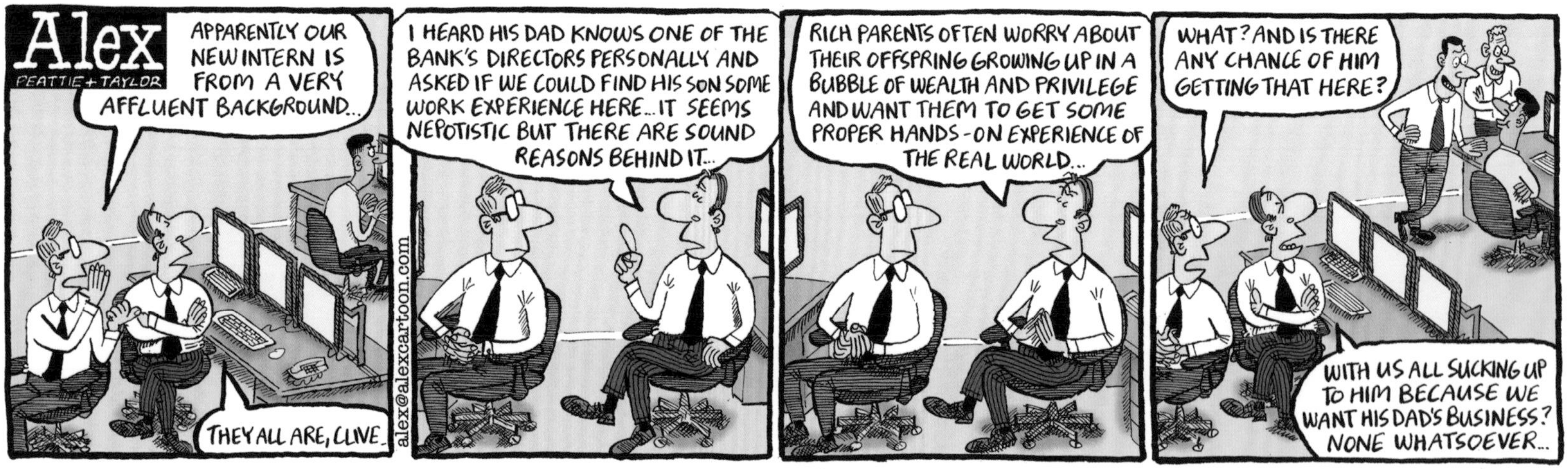
Alex
PEATTIE + TAYLOR
APPARENTLY OUR NEW INTERN IS FROM A VERY AFFLUENT BACKGROUND...
THEY ALL ARE, CLIVE.
I HEARD HIS DAD KNOWS ONE OF THE BANK'S DIRECTORS PERSONALLY AND ASKED IF WE COULD FIND HIS SON SOME WORK EXPERIENCE HERE... IT SEEMS NEPOTISTIC BUT THERE ARE SOUND REASONS BEHIND IT...
alex@alexcartoon.com
RICH PARENTS OFTEN WORRY ABOUT THEIR OFFSPRING GROWING UP IN A BUBBLE OF WEALTH AND PRIVILEGE AND WANT THEM TO GET SOME PROPER HANDS-ON EXPERIENCE OF THE REAL WORLD...
WHAT? AND IS THERE ANY CHANCE OF HIM GETTING THAT HERE?
WITH US ALL SUCKING UP TO HIM BECAUSE WE WANT HIS DAD'S BUSINESS? NONE WHATSOEVER...

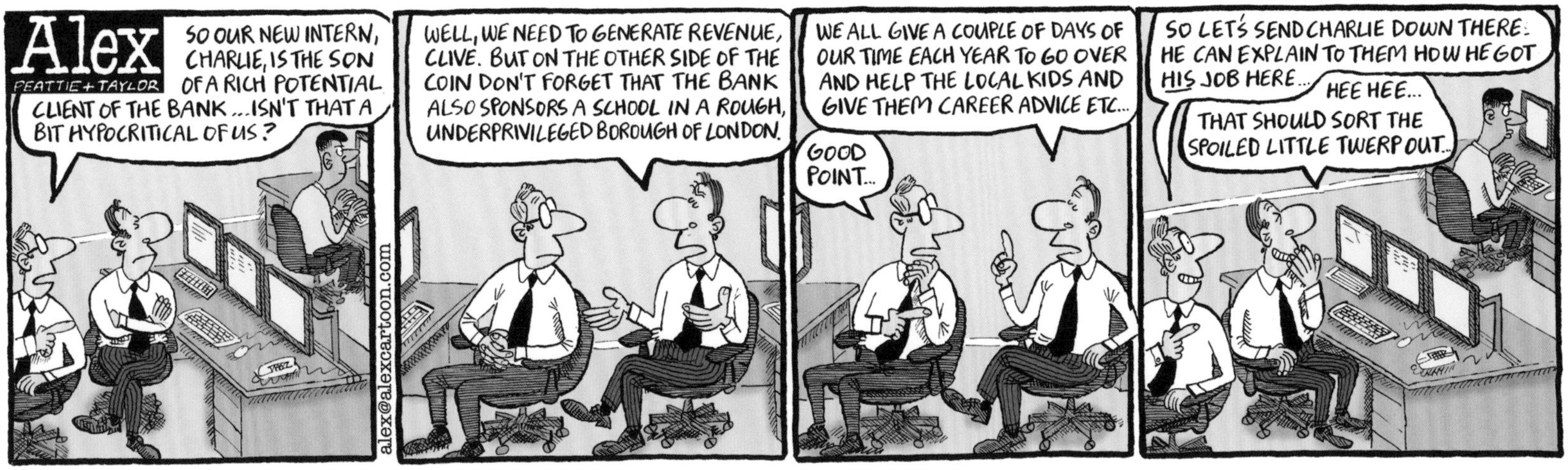
Alex
PEATTIE+TAYLOR
SO OUR NEW INTERN, CHARLIE, IS THE SON OF A RICH POTENTIAL CLIENT OF THE BANK ... ISN'T THAT A BIT HYPOCRITICAL OF US?
alex@alexcartoon.com
WELL, WE NEED TO GENERATE REVENUE, CLIVE. BUT ON THE OTHER SIDE OF THE COIN DON'T FORGET THAT THE BANK ALSO SPONSORS A SCHOOL IN A ROUGH, UNDERPRIVILEGED BOROUGH OF LONDON.
WE ALL GIVE A COUPLE OF DAYS OF OUR TIME EACH YEAR TO GO OVER AND HELP THE LOCAL KIDS AND GIVE THEM CAREER ADVICE ETC...
GOOD POINT...
SO LET'S SEND CHARLIE DOWN THERE: HE CAN EXPLAIN TO THEM HOW HE GOT HIS JOB HERE...
HEE HEE... THAT SHOULD SORT THE SPOILED LITTLE TWERP OUT...

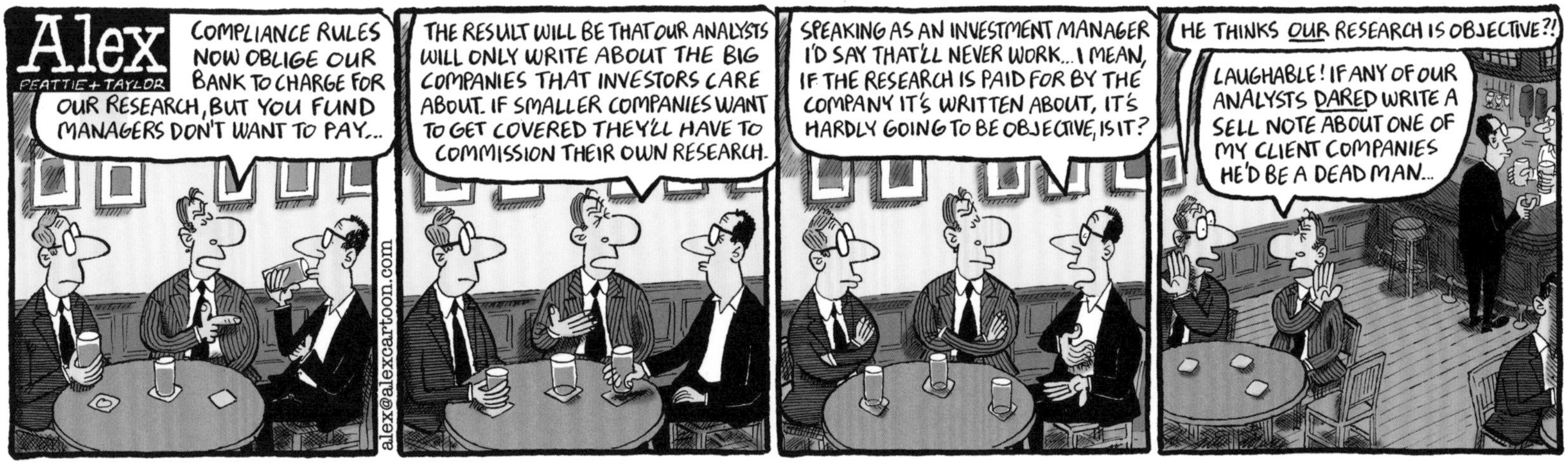
Alex
PEATTIE+TAYLOR
COMPLIANCE RULES NOW OBLIGE OUR BANK TO CHARGE FOR OUR RESEARCH, BUT YOU FUND MANAGERS DON'T WANT TO PAY...
alex@alexcartoon.com
THE RESULT WILL BE THAT OUR ANALYSTS WILL ONLY WRITE ABOUT THE BIG COMPANIES THAT INVESTORS CARE ABOUT. IF SMALLER COMPANIES WANT TO GET COVERED THEY'LL HAVE TO COMMISSION THEIR OWN RESEARCH.
SPEAKING AS AN INVESTMENT MANAGER I'D SAY THAT'LL NEVER WORK... I MEAN, IF THE RESEARCH IS PAID FOR BY THE COMPANY IT'S WRITTEN ABOUT, IT'S HARDLY GOING TO BE OBJECTIVE, IS IT?
HE THINKS OUR RESEARCH IS OBJECTIVE?!
LAUGHABLE! IF ANY OF OUR ANALYSTS DARED WRITE A SELL NOTE ABOUT ONE OF MY CLIENT COMPANIES HE'D BE A DEAD MAN...

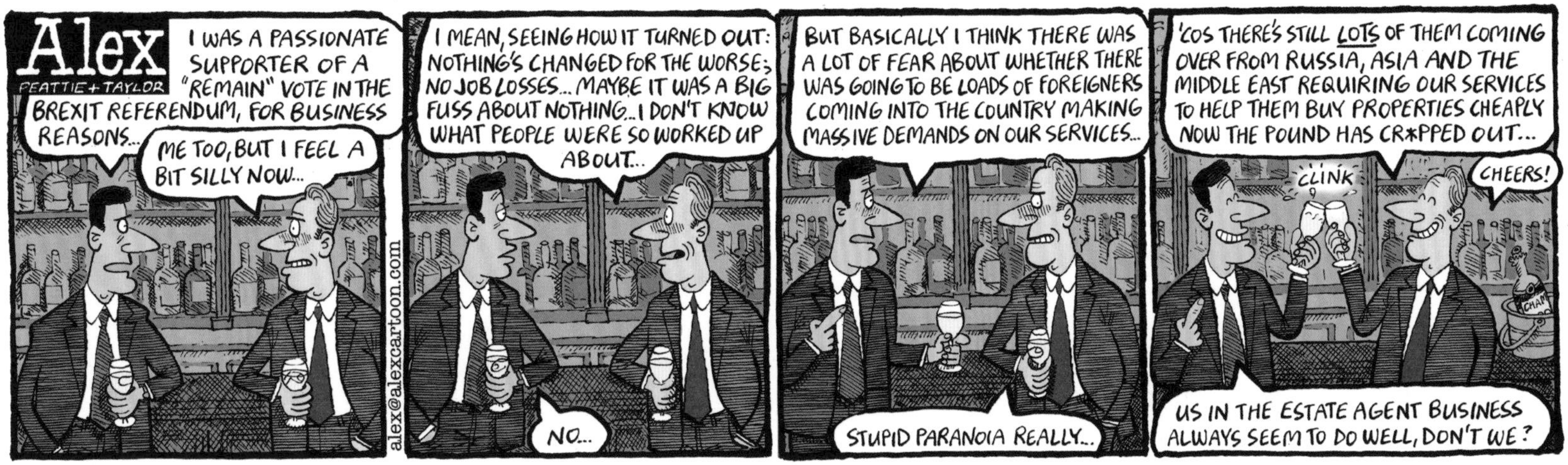
Alex
PEATTIE+TAYLOR
I WAS A PASSIONATE SUPPORTER OF A "REMAIN" VOTE IN THE BREXIT REFERENDUM, FOR BUSINESS REASONS...
ME TOO, BUT I FEEL A BIT SILLY NOW...
alex@alexcartoon.com
I MEAN, SEEING HOW IT TURNED OUT: NOTHING'S CHANGED FOR THE WORSE; NO JOB LOSSES... MAYBE IT WAS A BIG FUSS ABOUT NOTHING... I DON'T KNOW WHAT PEOPLE WERE SO WORKED UP ABOUT...
NO...
BUT BASICALLY I THINK THERE WAS A LOT OF FEAR ABOUT WHETHER THERE WAS GOING TO BE LOADS OF FOREIGNERS COMING INTO THE COUNTRY MAKING MASSIVE DEMANDS ON OUR SERVICES...
STUPID PARANOIA REALLY...
'COS THERE'S STILL LOTS OF THEM COMING OVER FROM RUSSIA, ASIA AND THE MIDDLE EAST REQUIRING OUR SERVICES TO HELP THEM BUY PROPERTIES CHEAPLY NOW THE POUND HAS CR*PPED OUT...
CLINK
CHEERS!
US IN THE ESTATE AGENT BUSINESS ALWAYS SEEM TO DO WELL, DON'T WE?

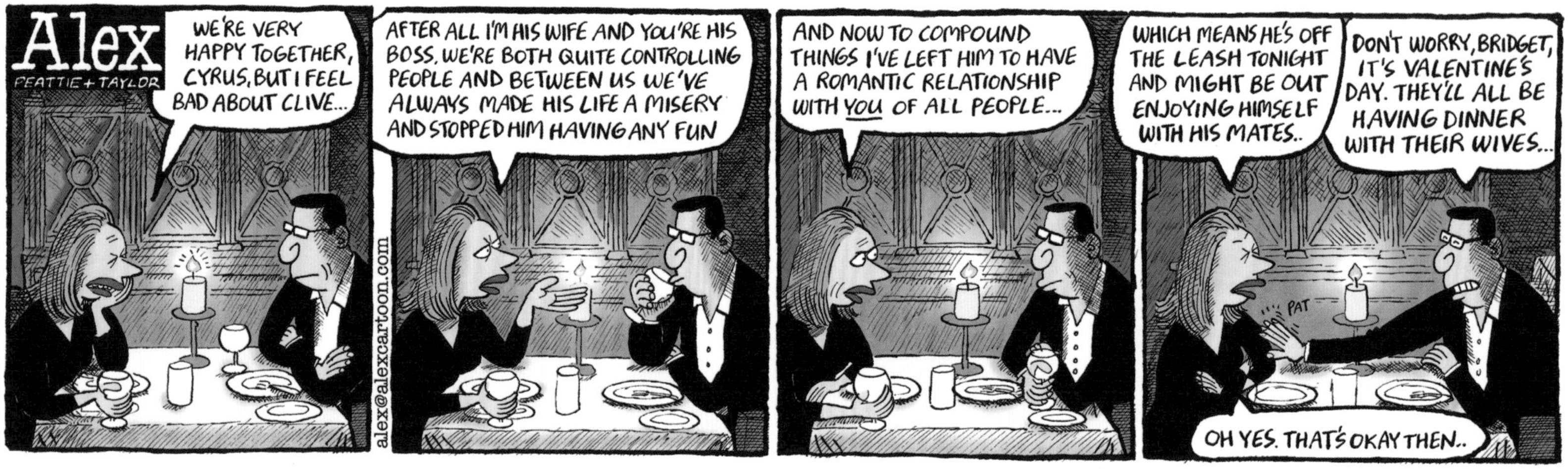
Alex
PEATTIE + TAYLOR
WE'RE VERY HAPPY TOGETHER, CYRUS, BUT I FEEL BAD ABOUT CLIVE...
AFTER ALL I'M HIS WIFE AND YOU'RE HIS BOSS. WE'RE BOTH QUITE CONTROLLING PEOPLE AND BETWEEN US WE'VE ALWAYS MADE HIS LIFE A MISERY AND STOPPED HIM HAVING ANY FUN
alex@alexcartoon.com
AND NOW TO COMPOUND THINGS I'VE LEFT HIM TO HAVE A ROMANTIC RELATIONSHIP WITH YOU OF ALL PEOPLE...
WHICH MEANS HE'S OFF THE LEASH TONIGHT AND MIGHT BE OUT ENJOYING HIMSELF WITH HIS MATES..
DON'T WORRY, BRIDGET, IT'S VALENTINE'S DAY. THEY'LL ALL BE HAVING DINNER WITH THEIR WIVES...
PAT
OH YES. THAT'S OKAY THEN..

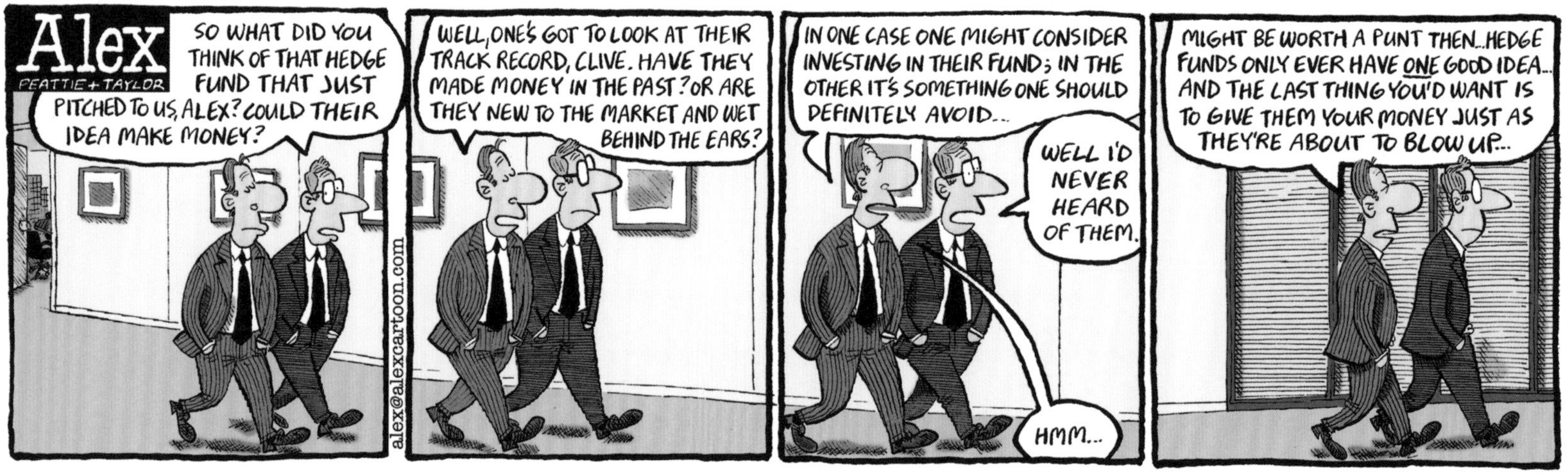
Alex
PEATTIE + TAYLOR
SO WHAT DID YOU THINK OF THAT HEDGE FUND THAT JUST PITCHED TO US, ALEX? COULD THEIR IDEA MAKE MONEY?
WELL, ONE'S GOT TO LOOK AT THEIR TRACK RECORD, CLIVE. HAVE THEY MADE MONEY IN THE PAST? OR ARE THEY NEW TO THE MARKET AND WET BEHIND THE EARS?
alex@alexcartoon.com
IN ONE CASE ONE MIGHT CONSIDER INVESTING IN THEIR FUND; IN THE OTHER IT'S SOMETHING ONE SHOULD DEFINITELY AVOID...
WELL I'D NEVER HEARD OF THEM.
HMM...
MIGHT BE WORTH A PUNT THEN...HEDGE FUNDS ONLY EVER HAVE ONE GOOD IDEA... AND THE LAST THING YOU'D WANT IS TO GIVE THEM YOUR MONEY JUST AS THEY'RE ABOUT TO BLOW UP...

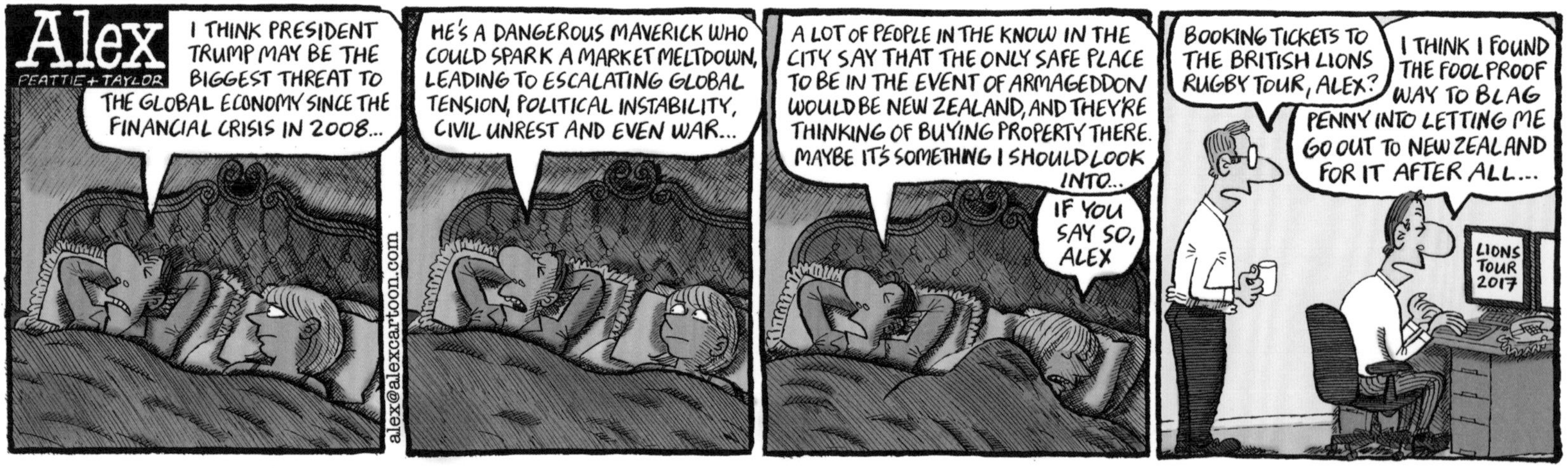
Alex
PEATTIE + TAYLOR
I THINK PRESIDENT TRUMP MAY BE THE BIGGEST THREAT TO THE GLOBAL ECONOMY SINCE THE FINANCIAL CRISIS IN 2008...
HE'S A DANGEROUS MAVERICK WHO COULD SPARK A MARKET MELTDOWN, LEADING TO ESCALATING GLOBAL TENSION, POLITICAL INSTABILITY, CIVIL UNREST AND EVEN WAR...
alex@alexcartoon.com
A LOT OF PEOPLE IN THE KNOW IN THE CITY SAY THAT THE ONLY SAFE PLACE TO BE IN THE EVENT OF ARMAGEDDON WOULD BE NEW ZEALAND, AND THEY'RE THINKING OF BUYING PROPERTY THERE. MAYBE IT'S SOMETHING I SHOULD LOOK INTO...
IF YOU SAY SO, ALEX
BOOKING TICKETS TO THE BRITISH LIONS RUGBY TOUR, ALEX?
I THINK I FOUND THE FOOLPROOF WAY TO BLAG PENNY INTO LETTING ME GO OUT TO NEW ZEALAND FOR IT AFTER ALL...
LIONS TOUR 2017

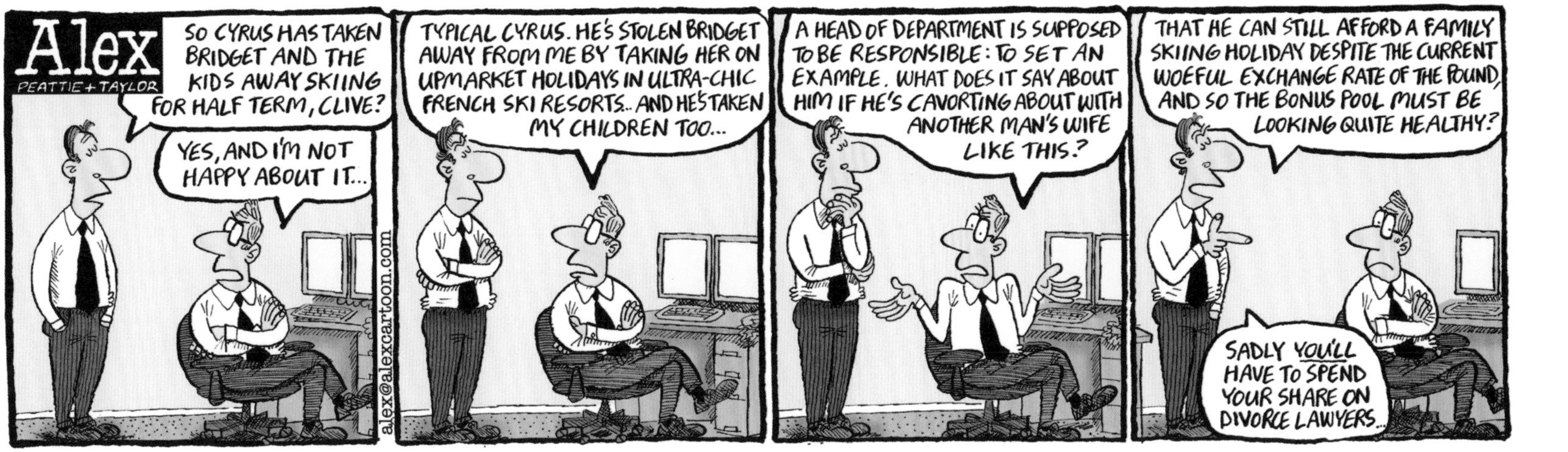
Alex
PEATTIE + TAYLOR
SO CYRUS HAS TAKEN BRIDGET AND THE KIDS AWAY SKIING FOR HALF TERM, CLIVE?
YES, AND I'M NOT HAPPY ABOUT IT...
TYPICAL CYRUS. HE'S STOLEN BRIDGET AWAY FROM ME BY TAKING HER ON UPMARKET HOLIDAYS IN ULTRA-CHIC FRENCH SKI RESORTS.. AND HE'S TAKEN MY CHILDREN TOO...
A HEAD OF DEPARTMENT IS SUPPOSED TO BE RESPONSIBLE: TO SET AN EXAMPLE. WHAT DOES IT SAY ABOUT HIM IF HE'S CAVORTING ABOUT WITH ANOTHER MAN'S WIFE LIKE THIS?
THAT HE CAN STILL AFFORD A FAMILY SKIING HOLIDAY DESPITE THE CURRENT WOEFUL EXCHANGE RATE OF THE POUND, AND SO THE BONUS POOL MUST BE LOOKING QUITE HEALTHY?
SADLY YOU'LL HAVE TO SPEND YOUR SHARE ON DIVORCE LAWYERS...
alex@alexcartoon.com

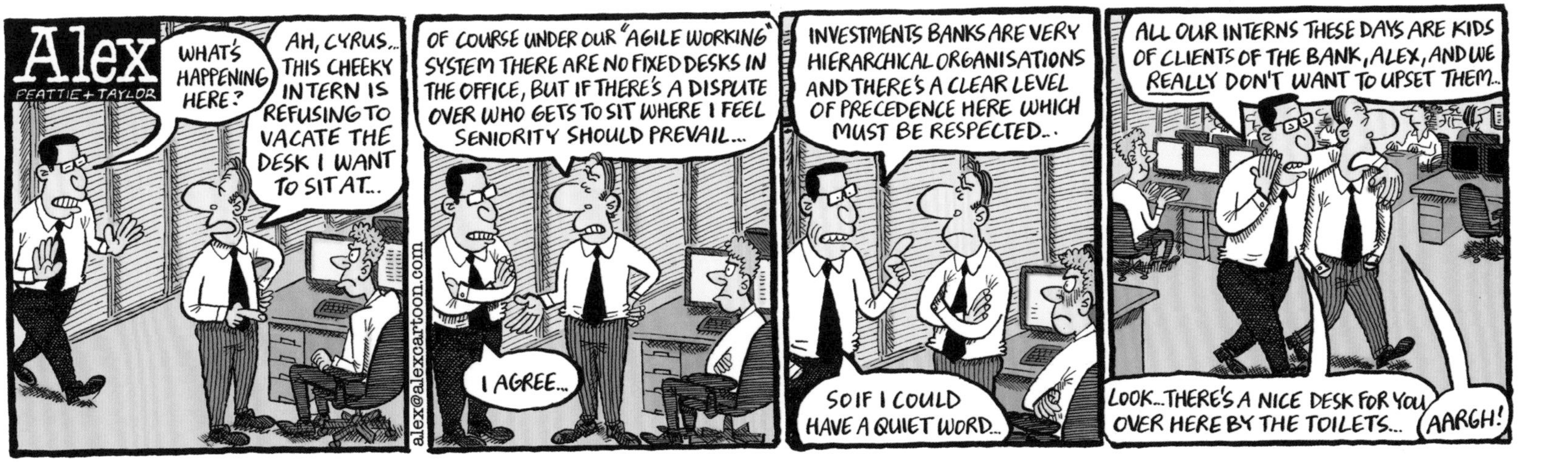
Alex
PEATTIE + TAYLOR
WHAT'S HAPPENING HERE?
AH, CYRUS... THIS CHEEKY INTERN IS REFUSING TO VACATE THE DESK I WANT TO SIT AT...
OF COURSE UNDER OUR "AGILE WORKING" SYSTEM THERE ARE NO FIXED DESKS IN THE OFFICE, BUT IF THERE'S A DISPUTE OVER WHO GETS TO SIT WHERE I FEEL SENIORITY SHOULD PREVAIL...
I AGREE...
INVESTMENTS BANKS ARE VERY HIERARCHICAL ORGANISATIONS AND THERE'S A CLEAR LEVEL OF PRECEDENCE HERE WHICH MUST BE RESPECTED...
SO IF I COULD HAVE A QUIET WORD...
ALL OUR INTERNS THESE DAYS ARE KIDS OF CLIENTS OF THE BANK, ALEX, AND WE REALLY DON'T WANT TO UPSET THEM...
LOOK... THERE'S A NICE DESK FOR YOU OVER HERE BY THE TOILETS...
AARGH!
alex@alexcartoon.com

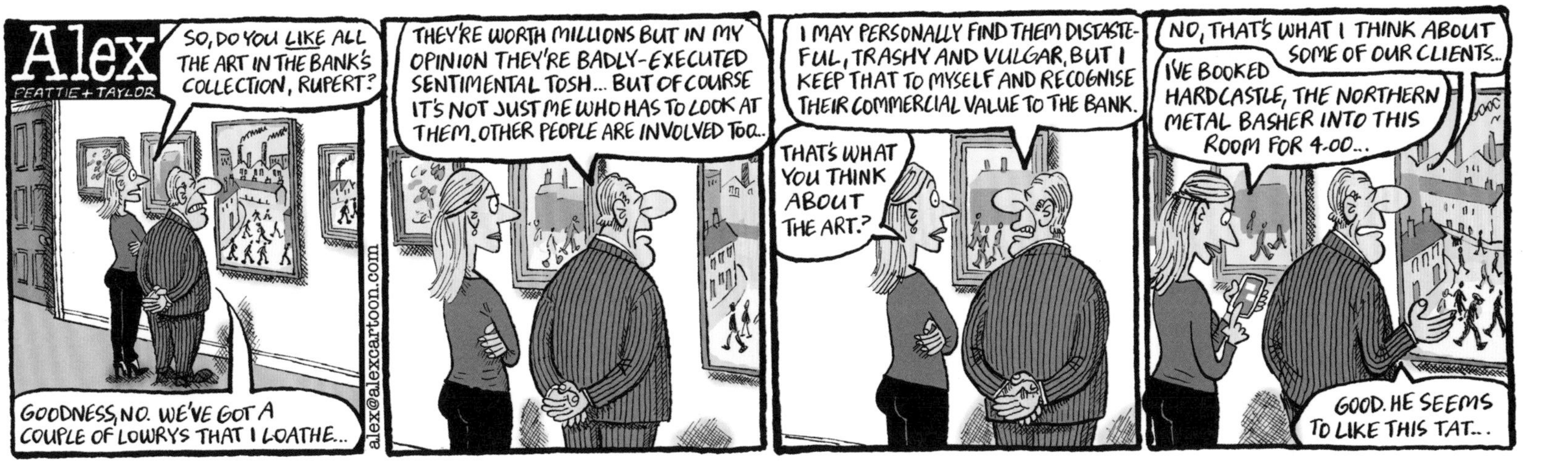
Alex
PEATTIE + TAYLOR
SO, DO YOU LIKE ALL THE ART IN THE BANK'S COLLECTION, RUPERT?
GOODNESS, NO. WE'VE GOT A COUPLE OF LOWRYS THAT I LOATHE...
THEY'RE WORTH MILLIONS BUT IN MY OPINION THEY'RE BADLY-EXECUTED SENTIMENTAL TOSH... BUT OF COURSE IT'S NOT JUST ME WHO HAS TO LOOK AT THEM. OTHER PEOPLE ARE INVOLVED TOO...
I MAY PERSONALLY FIND THEM DISTASTEFUL, TRASHY AND VULGAR, BUT I KEEP THAT TO MYSELF AND RECOGNISE THEIR COMMERCIAL VALUE TO THE BANK.
THAT'S WHAT YOU THINK ABOUT THE ART?
NO, THAT'S WHAT I THINK ABOUT SOME OF OUR CLIENTS...
I'VE BOOKED HARDCASTLE, THE NORTHERN METAL BASHER INTO THIS ROOM FOR 4.00...
GOOD. HE SEEMS TO LIKE THIS TAT...
alex@alexcartoon.com

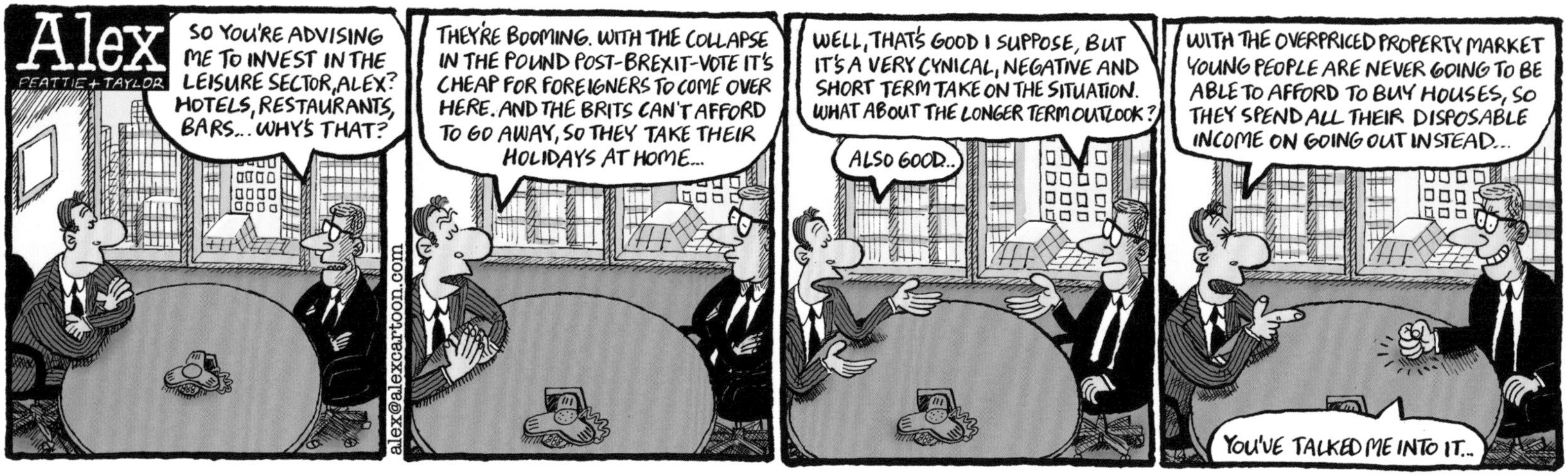
Alex
PEATTIE + TAYLOR
SO YOU'RE ADVISING ME TO INVEST IN THE LEISURE SECTOR, ALEX? HOTELS, RESTAURANTS, BARS... WHY'S THAT?
alex@alexcartoon.com
THEY'RE BOOMING. WITH THE COLLAPSE IN THE POUND POST-BREXIT-VOTE IT'S CHEAP FOR FOREIGNERS TO COME OVER HERE. AND THE BRITS CAN'T AFFORD TO GO AWAY, SO THEY TAKE THEIR HOLIDAYS AT HOME...
WELL, THAT'S GOOD I SUPPOSE, BUT IT'S A VERY CYNICAL, NEGATIVE AND SHORT TERM TAKE ON THE SITUATION. WHAT ABOUT THE LONGER TERM OUTLOOK?
ALSO GOOD...
WITH THE OVERPRICED PROPERTY MARKET YOUNG PEOPLE ARE NEVER GOING TO BE ABLE TO AFFORD TO BUY HOUSES, SO THEY SPEND ALL THEIR DISPOSABLE INCOME ON GOING OUT INSTEAD...
YOU'VE TALKED ME INTO IT...

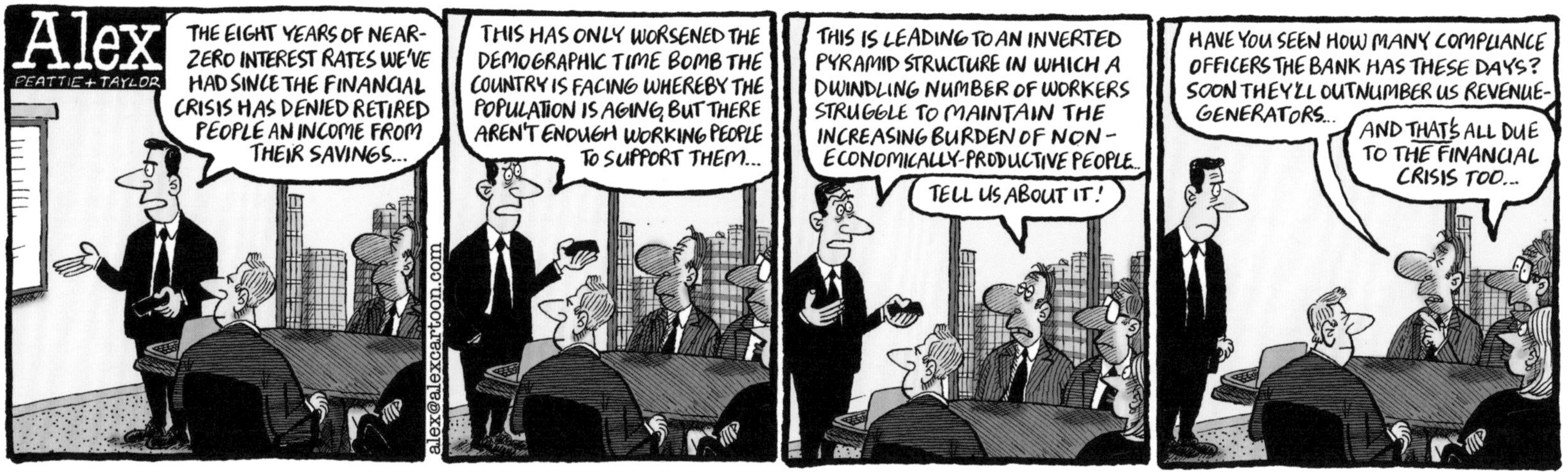
Alex
PEATTIE + TAYLOR
THE EIGHT YEARS OF NEAR-ZERO INTEREST RATES WE'VE HAD SINCE THE FINANCIAL CRISIS HAS DENIED RETIRED PEOPLE AN INCOME FROM THEIR SAVINGS...
alex@alexcartoon.com
THIS HAS ONLY WORSENED THE DEMOGRAPHIC TIME BOMB THE COUNTRY IS FACING WHEREBY THE POPULATION IS AGING, BUT THERE AREN'T ENOUGH WORKING PEOPLE TO SUPPORT THEM...
THIS IS LEADING TO AN INVERTED PYRAMID STRUCTURE IN WHICH A DWINDLING NUMBER OF WORKERS STRUGGLE TO MAINTAIN THE INCREASING BURDEN OF NON-ECONOMICALLY-PRODUCTIVE PEOPLE...
TELL US ABOUT IT!
HAVE YOU SEEN HOW MANY COMPLIANCE OFFICERS THE BANK HAS THESE DAYS? SOON THEY'LL OUTNUMBER US REVENUE-GENERATORS...
AND THAT'S ALL DUE TO THE FINANCIAL CRISIS TOO...

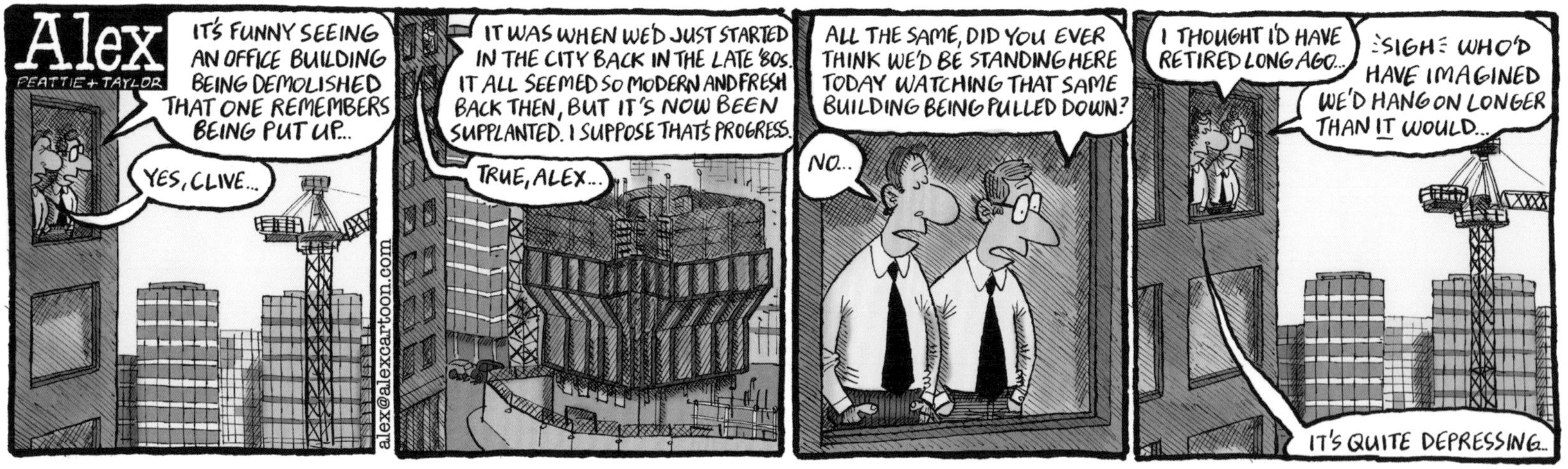
Alex
PEATTIE + TAYLOR
IT'S FUNNY SEEING AN OFFICE BUILDING BEING DEMOLISHED THAT ONE REMEMBERS BEING PUT UP...
YES, CLIVE...
alex@alexcartoon.com
IT WAS WHEN WE'D JUST STARTED IN THE CITY BACK IN THE LATE '80S. IT ALL SEEMED SO MODERN AND FRESH BACK THEN, BUT IT'S NOW BEEN SUPPLANTED. I SUPPOSE THAT'S PROGRESS.
TRUE, ALEX...
ALL THE SAME, DID YOU EVER THINK WE'D BE STANDING HERE TODAY WATCHING THAT SAME BUILDING BEING PULLED DOWN?
NO...
I THOUGHT I'D HAVE RETIRED LONG AGO...
SIGH WHO'D HAVE IMAGINED WE'D HANG ON LONGER THAN IT WOULD...
IT'S QUITE DEPRESSING...

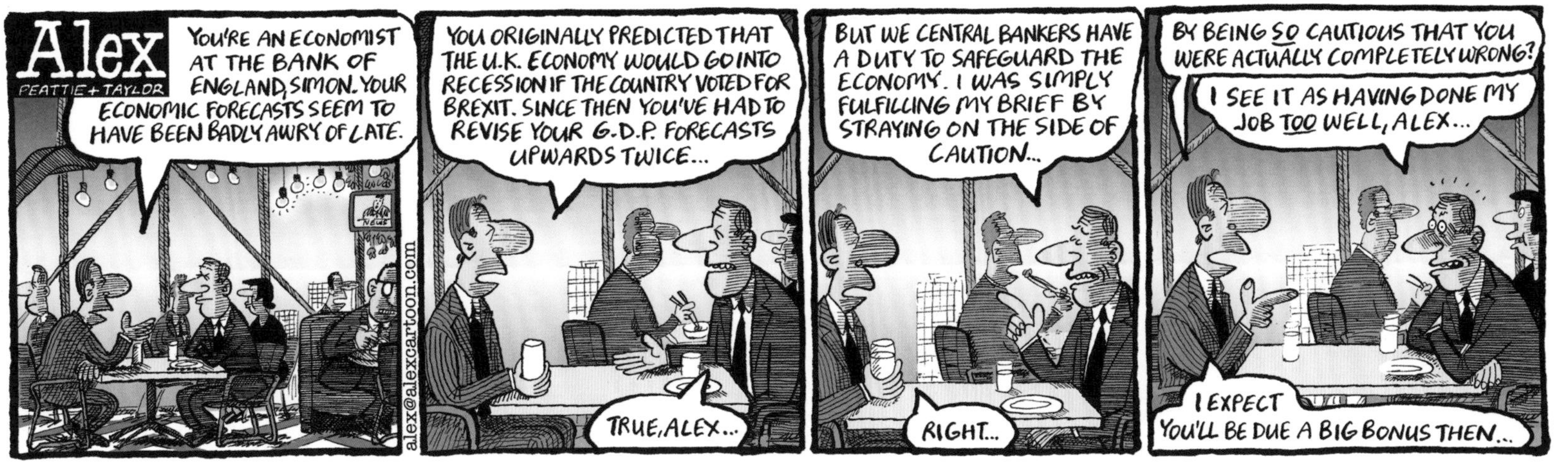
Alex
PEATTIE + TAYLOR
YOU'RE AN ECONOMIST AT THE BANK OF ENGLAND, SIMON. YOUR ECONOMIC FORECASTS SEEM TO HAVE BEEN BADLY AWRY OF LATE.
YOU ORIGINALLY PREDICTED THAT THE U.K. ECONOMY WOULD GO INTO RECESSION IF THE COUNTRY VOTED FOR BREXIT. SINCE THEN YOU'VE HAD TO REVISE YOUR G.D.P. FORECASTS UPWARDS TWICE...
TRUE, ALEX...
alex@alexcartoon.com
BUT WE CENTRAL BANKERS HAVE A DUTY TO SAFEGUARD THE ECONOMY. I WAS SIMPLY FULFILLING MY BRIEF BY STRAYING ON THE SIDE OF CAUTION...
RIGHT...
BY BEING SO CAUTIOUS THAT YOU WERE ACTUALLY COMPLETELY WRONG?
I SEE IT AS HAVING DONE MY JOB TOO WELL, ALEX...
I EXPECT YOU'LL BE DUE A BIG BONUS THEN...

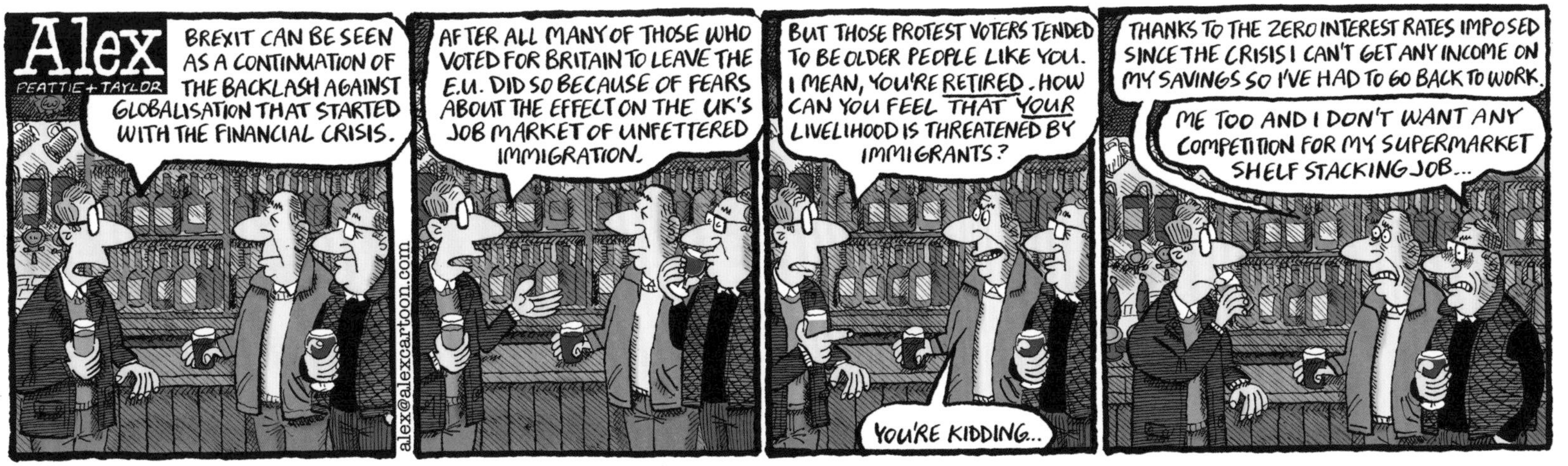
Alex
PEATTIE + TAYLOR
BREXIT CAN BE SEEN AS A CONTINUATION OF THE BACKLASH AGAINST GLOBALISATION THAT STARTED WITH THE FINANCIAL CRISIS.
AFTER ALL MANY OF THOSE WHO VOTED FOR BRITAIN TO LEAVE THE E.U. DID SO BECAUSE OF FEARS ABOUT THE EFFECT ON THE UK'S JOB MARKET OF UNFETTERED IMMIGRATION.
alex@alexcartoon.com
BUT THOSE PROTEST VOTERS TENDED TO BE OLDER PEOPLE LIKE YOU. I MEAN, YOU'RE RETIRED. HOW CAN YOU FEEL THAT YOUR LIVELIHOOD IS THREATENED BY IMMIGRANTS?
YOU'RE KIDDING...
THANKS TO THE ZERO INTEREST RATES IMPOSED SINCE THE CRISIS I CAN'T GET ANY INCOME ON MY SAVINGS SO I'VE HAD TO GO BACK TO WORK.
ME TOO AND I DON'T WANT ANY COMPETITION FOR MY SUPERMARKET SHELF STACKING JOB...

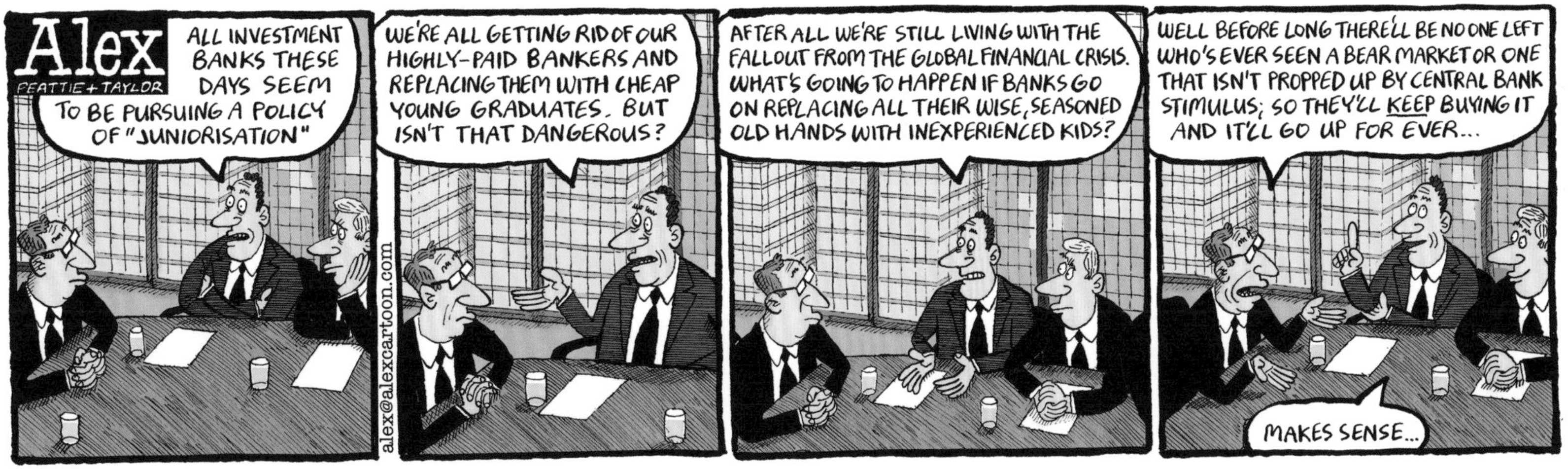
Alex
PEATTIE + TAYLOR
ALL INVESTMENT BANKS THESE DAYS SEEM TO BE PURSUING A POLICY OF "JUNIORISATION"
alex@alexcartoon.com
WE'RE ALL GETTING RID OF OUR HIGHLY-PAID BANKERS AND REPLACING THEM WITH CHEAP YOUNG GRADUATES. BUT ISN'T THAT DANGEROUS?
AFTER ALL WE'RE STILL LIVING WITH THE FALLOUT FROM THE GLOBAL FINANCIAL CRISIS. WHAT'S GOING TO HAPPEN IF BANKS GO ON REPLACING ALL THEIR WISE, SEASONED OLD HANDS WITH INEXPERIENCED KIDS?
WELL BEFORE LONG THERE'LL BE NO ONE LEFT WHO'S EVER SEEN A BEAR MARKET OR ONE THAT ISN'T PROPPED UP BY CENTRAL BANK STIMULUS; SO THEY'LL KEEP BUYING IT AND IT'LL GO UP FOR EVER...
MAKES SENSE...

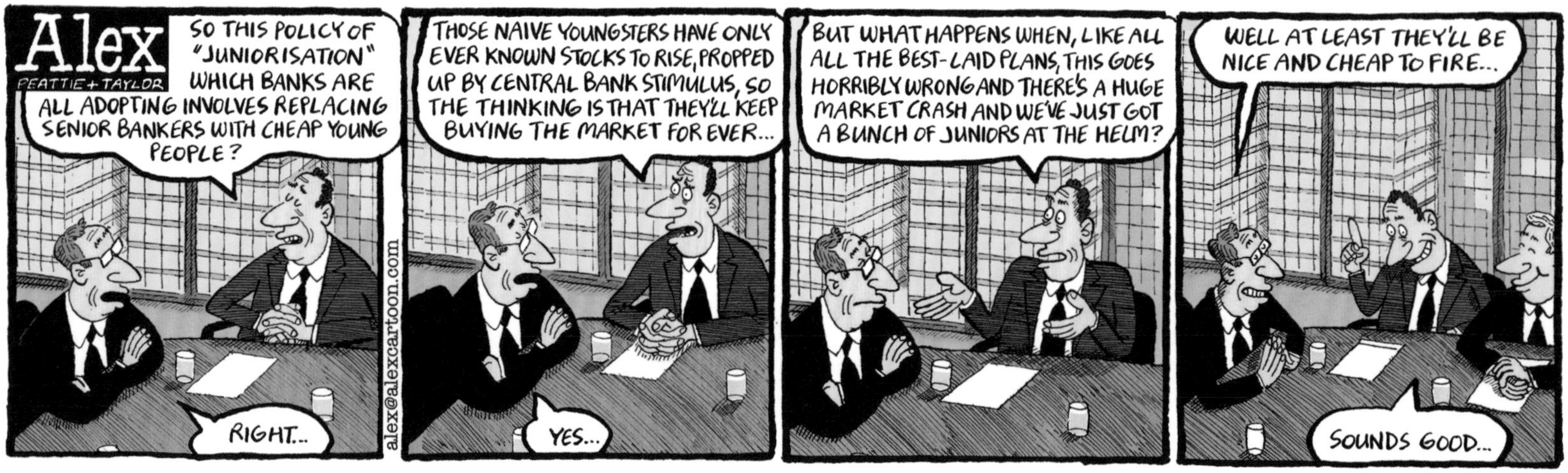
Alex
PEATTIE + TAYLOR
SO THIS POLICY OF "JUNIORISATION" WHICH BANKS ARE ALL ADOPTING INVOLVES REPLACING SENIOR BANKERS WITH CHEAP YOUNG PEOPLE?
RIGHT...
alex@alexcartoon.com
THOSE NAIVE YOUNGSTERS HAVE ONLY EVER KNOWN STOCKS TO RISE, PROPPED UP BY CENTRAL BANK STIMULUS, SO THE THINKING IS THAT THEY'LL KEEP BUYING THE MARKET FOR EVER...
YES...
BUT WHAT HAPPENS WHEN, LIKE ALL ALL THE BEST-LAID PLANS, THIS GOES HORRIBLY WRONG AND THERE'S A HUGE MARKET CRASH AND WE'VE JUST GOT A BUNCH OF JUNIORS AT THE HELM?
WELL AT LEAST THEY'LL BE NICE AND CHEAP TO FIRE...
SOUNDS GOOD...

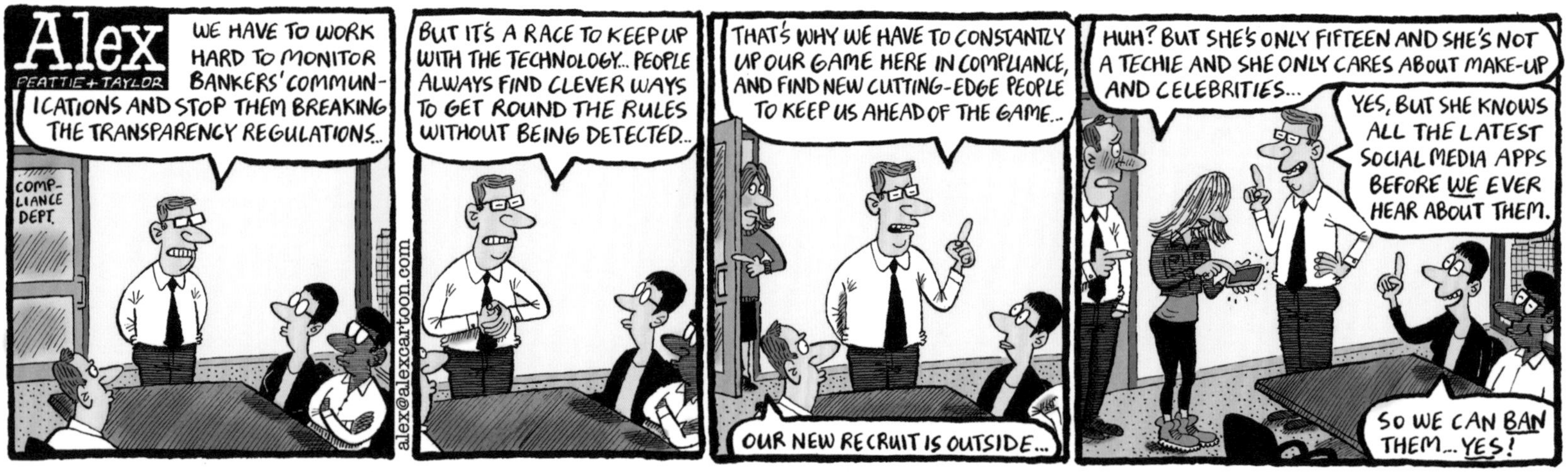
Alex
PEATTIE + TAYLOR
WE HAVE TO WORK HARD TO MONITOR BANKERS' COMMUNICATIONS AND STOP THEM BREAKING THE TRANSPARENCY REGULATIONS...
COMPLIANCE DEPT.
alex@alexcartoon.com
BUT IT'S A RACE TO KEEP UP WITH THE TECHNOLOGY... PEOPLE ALWAYS FIND CLEVER WAYS TO GET ROUND THE RULES WITHOUT BEING DETECTED...
THAT'S WHY WE HAVE TO CONSTANTLY UP OUR GAME HERE IN COMPLIANCE, AND FIND NEW CUTTING-EDGE PEOPLE TO KEEP US AHEAD OF THE GAME...
OUR NEW RECRUIT IS OUTSIDE...
HUH? BUT SHE'S ONLY FIFTEEN AND SHE'S NOT A TECHIE AND SHE ONLY CARES ABOUT MAKE-UP AND CELEBRITIES...
YES, BUT SHE KNOWS ALL THE LATEST SOCIAL MEDIA APPS BEFORE WE EVER HEAR ABOUT THEM.
SO WE CAN BAN THEM... YES!

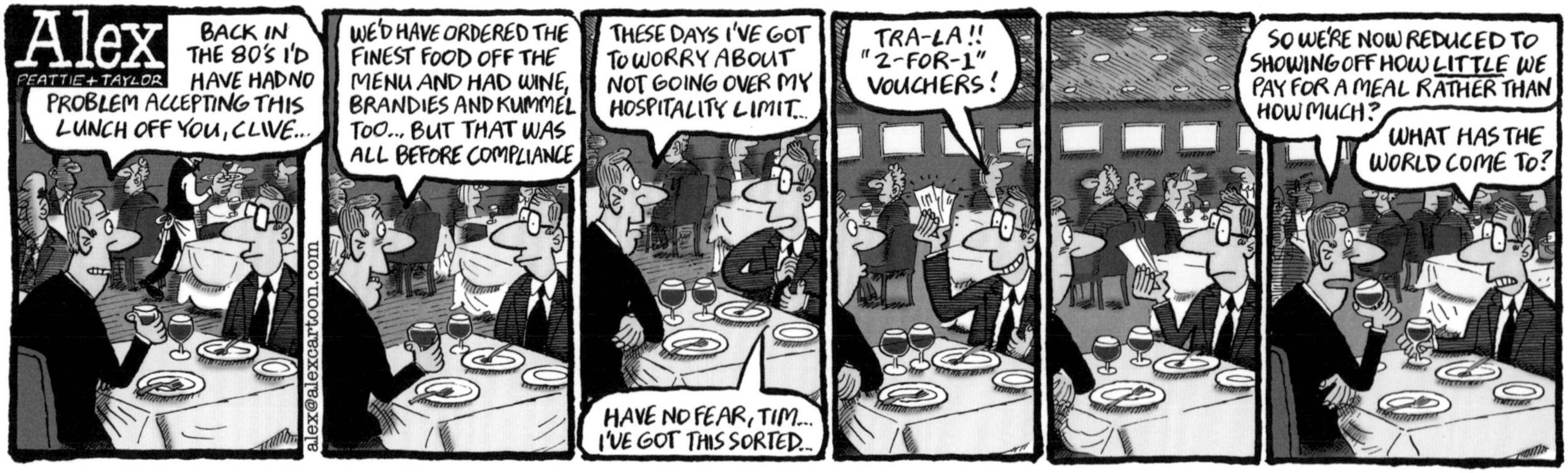
Alex
PEATTIE + TAYLOR
BACK IN THE 80'S I'D HAVE HAD NO PROBLEM ACCEPTING THIS LUNCH OFF YOU, CLIVE...
alex@alexcartoon.com
WE'D HAVE ORDERED THE FINEST FOOD OFF THE MENU AND HAD WINE, BRANDIES AND KUMMEL TOO... BUT THAT WAS ALL BEFORE COMPLIANCE
THESE DAYS I'VE GOT TO WORRY ABOUT NOT GOING OVER MY HOSPITALITY LIMIT...
HAVE NO FEAR, TIM... I'VE GOT THIS SORTED...
TRA-LA!! "2-FOR-1" VOUCHERS!
SO WE'RE NOW REDUCED TO SHOWING OFF HOW LITTLE WE PAY FOR A MEAL RATHER THAN HOW MUCH?
WHAT HAS THE WORLD COME TO?

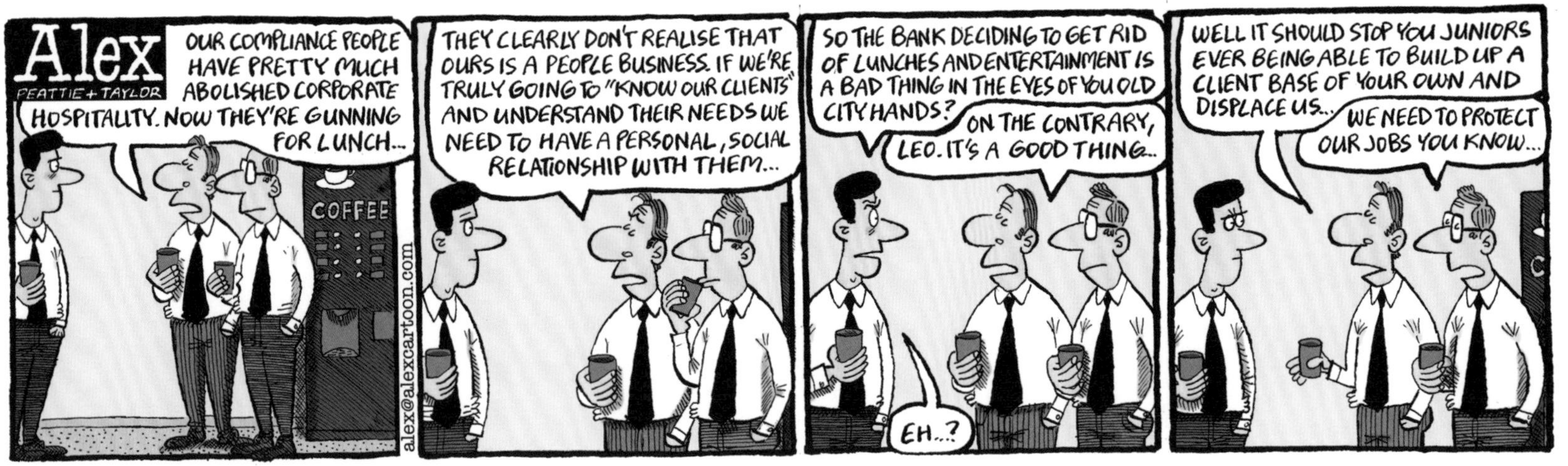
Alex
PEATTIE + TAYLOR
OUR COMPLIANCE PEOPLE HAVE PRETTY MUCH ABOLISHED CORPORATE HOSPITALITY. NOW THEY'RE GUNNING FOR LUNCH...
COFFEE
alex@alexcartoon.com
THEY CLEARLY DON'T REALISE THAT OURS IS A PEOPLE BUSINESS. IF WE'RE TRULY GOING TO "KNOW OUR CLIENTS" AND UNDERSTAND THEIR NEEDS WE NEED TO HAVE A PERSONAL, SOCIAL RELATIONSHIP WITH THEM...
SO THE BANK DECIDING TO GET RID OF LUNCHES AND ENTERTAINMENT IS A BAD THING IN THE EYES OF YOU OLD CITY HANDS?
ON THE CONTRARY, LEO. IT'S A GOOD THING...
EH...?
WELL IT SHOULD STOP YOU JUNIORS EVER BEING ABLE TO BUILD UP A CLIENT BASE OF YOUR OWN AND DISPLACE US...
WE NEED TO PROTECT OUR JOBS YOU KNOW...

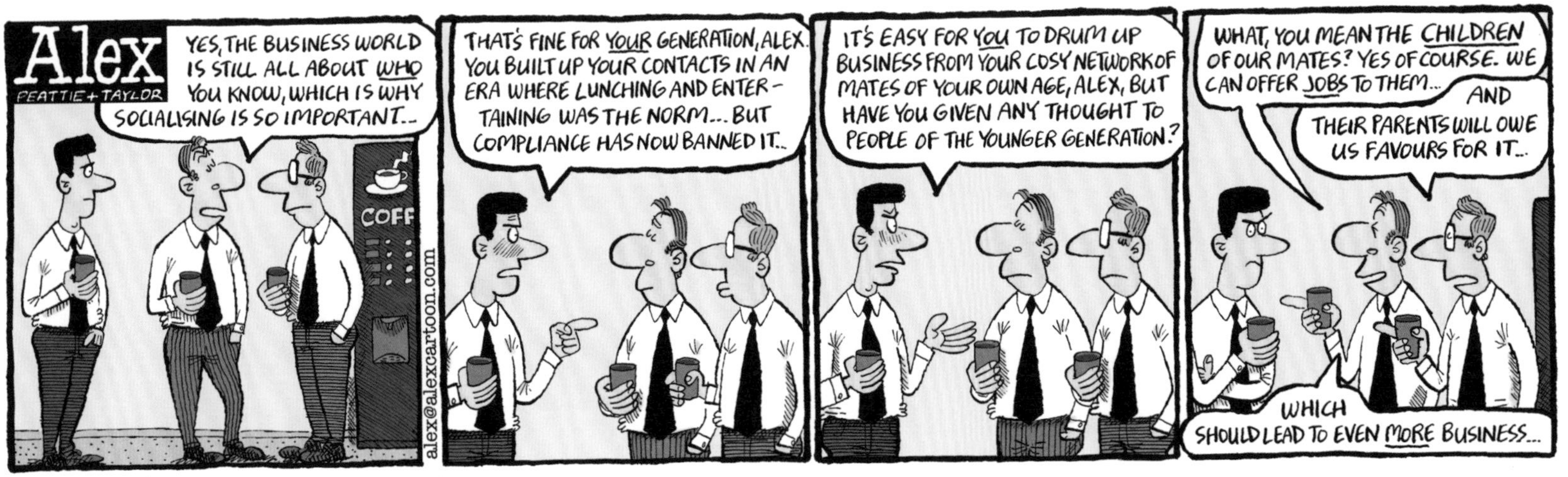
Alex
PEATTIE + TAYLOR
YES, THE BUSINESS WORLD IS STILL ALL ABOUT WHO YOU KNOW, WHICH IS WHY SOCIALISING IS SO IMPORTANT...
COFF
alex@alexcartoon.com
THAT'S FINE FOR YOUR GENERATION, ALEX. YOU BUILT UP YOUR CONTACTS IN AN ERA WHERE LUNCHING AND ENTERTAINING WAS THE NORM... BUT COMPLIANCE HAS NOW BANNED IT...
IT'S EASY FOR YOU TO DRUM UP BUSINESS FROM YOUR COSY NETWORK OF MATES OF YOUR OWN AGE, ALEX, BUT HAVE YOU GIVEN ANY THOUGHT TO PEOPLE OF THE YOUNGER GENERATION?
WHAT, YOU MEAN THE CHILDREN OF OUR MATES? YES OF COURSE. WE CAN OFFER JOBS TO THEM...
AND THEIR PARENTS WILL OWE US FAVOURS FOR IT...
WHICH SHOULD LEAD TO EVEN MORE BUSINESS...

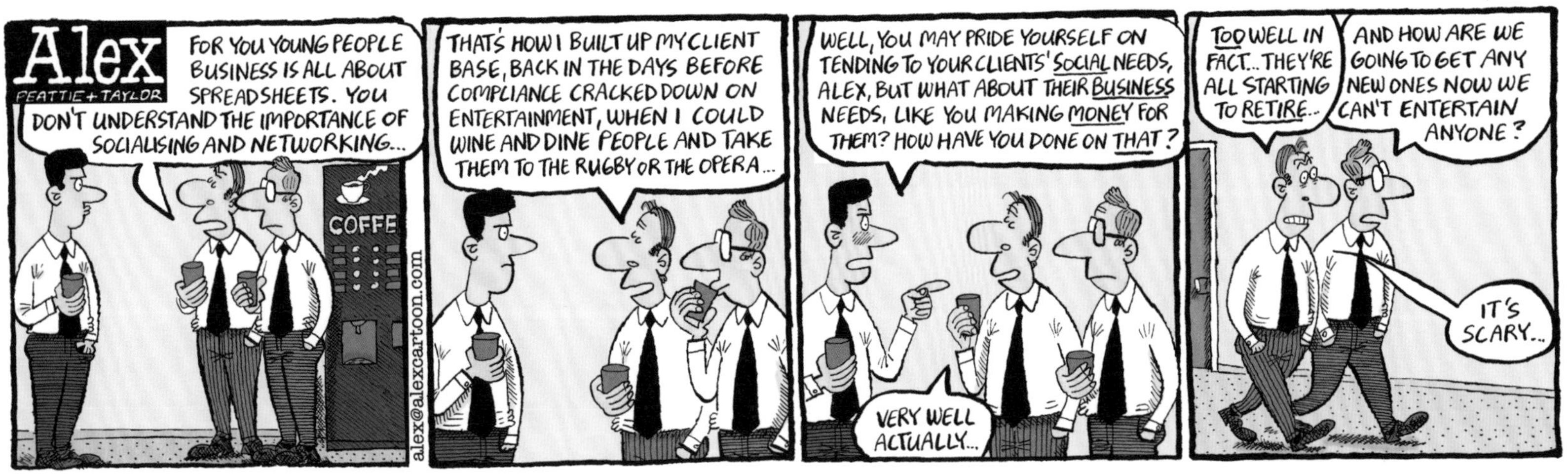
Alex
PEATTIE + TAYLOR
FOR YOU YOUNG PEOPLE BUSINESS IS ALL ABOUT SPREADSHEETS. YOU DON'T UNDERSTAND THE IMPORTANCE OF SOCIALISING AND NETWORKING...
COFFE
alex@alexcartoon.com
THAT'S HOW I BUILT UP MY CLIENT BASE, BACK IN THE DAYS BEFORE COMPLIANCE CRACKED DOWN ON ENTERTAINMENT, WHEN I COULD WINE AND DINE PEOPLE AND TAKE THEM TO THE RUGBY OR THE OPERA...
WELL, YOU MAY PRIDE YOURSELF ON TENDING TO YOUR CLIENTS' SOCIAL NEEDS, ALEX, BUT WHAT ABOUT THEIR BUSINESS NEEDS, LIKE YOU MAKING MONEY FOR THEM? HOW HAVE YOU DONE ON THAT?
VERY WELL ACTUALLY...
TOO WELL IN FACT... THEY'RE ALL STARTING TO RETIRE...
AND HOW ARE WE GOING TO GET ANY NEW ONES NOW WE CAN'T ENTERTAIN ANYONE?
IT'S SCARY...

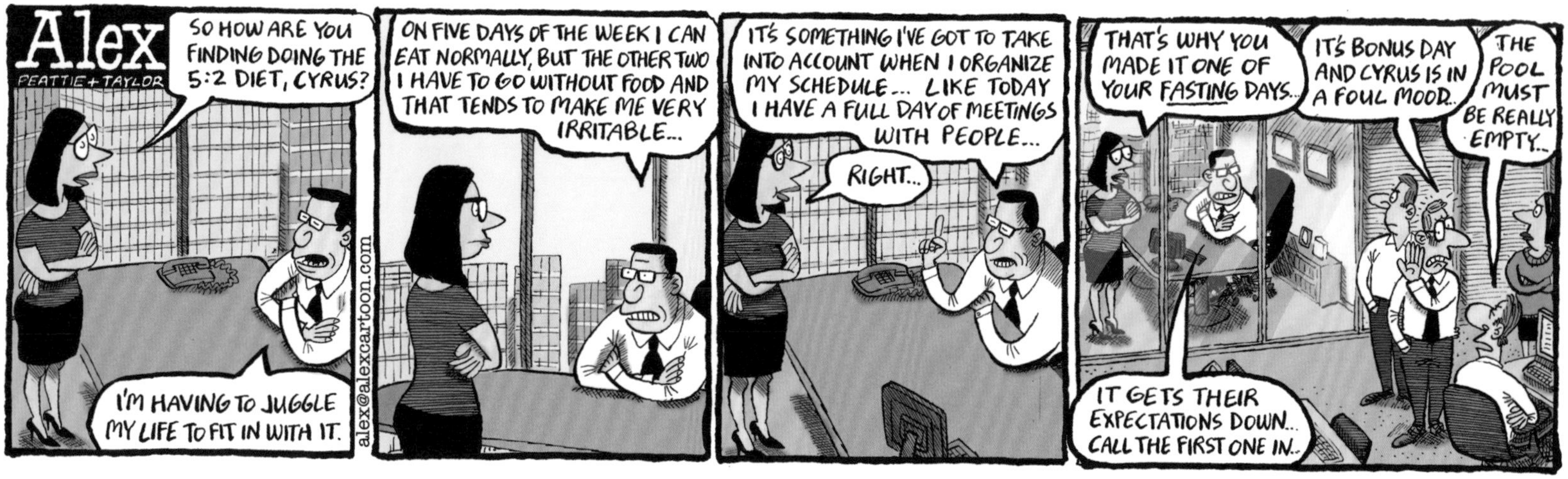
Alex
PEATTIE+TAYLOR
SO HOW ARE YOU FINDING DOING THE 5:2 DIET, CYRUS?
I'M HAVING TO JUGGLE MY LIFE TO FIT IN WITH IT.
alex@alexcartoon.com
ON FIVE DAYS OF THE WEEK I CAN EAT NORMALLY, BUT THE OTHER TWO I HAVE TO GO WITHOUT FOOD AND THAT TENDS TO MAKE ME VERY IRRITABLE...
IT'S SOMETHING I'VE GOT TO TAKE INTO ACCOUNT WHEN I ORGANIZE MY SCHEDULE... LIKE TODAY I HAVE A FULL DAY OF MEETINGS WITH PEOPLE...
RIGHT...
THAT'S WHY YOU MADE IT ONE OF YOUR FASTING DAYS...
IT GETS THEIR EXPECTATIONS DOWN... CALL THE FIRST ONE IN...
IT'S BONUS DAY AND CYRUS IS IN A FOUL MOOD...
THE POOL MUST BE REALLY EMPTY...

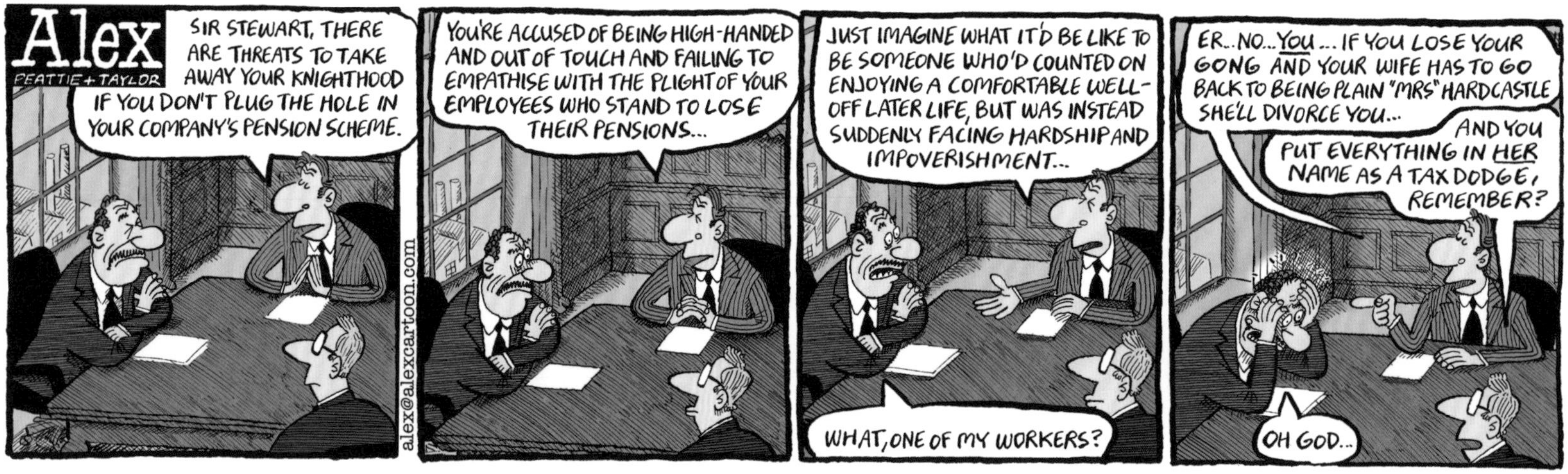
Alex
PEATTIE+TAYLOR
SIR STEWART, THERE ARE THREATS TO TAKE AWAY YOUR KNIGHTHOOD IF YOU DON'T PLUG THE HOLE IN YOUR COMPANY'S PENSION SCHEME.
alex@alexcartoon.com
YOU'RE ACCUSED OF BEING HIGH-HANDED AND OUT OF TOUCH AND FAILING TO EMPATHISE WITH THE PLIGHT OF YOUR EMPLOYEES WHO STAND TO LOSE THEIR PENSIONS...
JUST IMAGINE WHAT IT'D BE LIKE TO BE SOMEONE WHO'D COUNTED ON ENJOYING A COMFORTABLE WELL-OFF LATER LIFE, BUT WAS INSTEAD SUDDENLY FACING HARDSHIP AND IMPOVERISHMENT...
WHAT, ONE OF MY WORKERS?
ER... NO... YOU... IF YOU LOSE YOUR GONG AND YOUR WIFE HAS TO GO BACK TO BEING PLAIN "MRS" HARDCASTLE SHE'LL DIVORCE YOU...
AND YOU PUT EVERYTHING IN HER NAME AS A TAX DODGE, REMEMBER?
OH GOD...

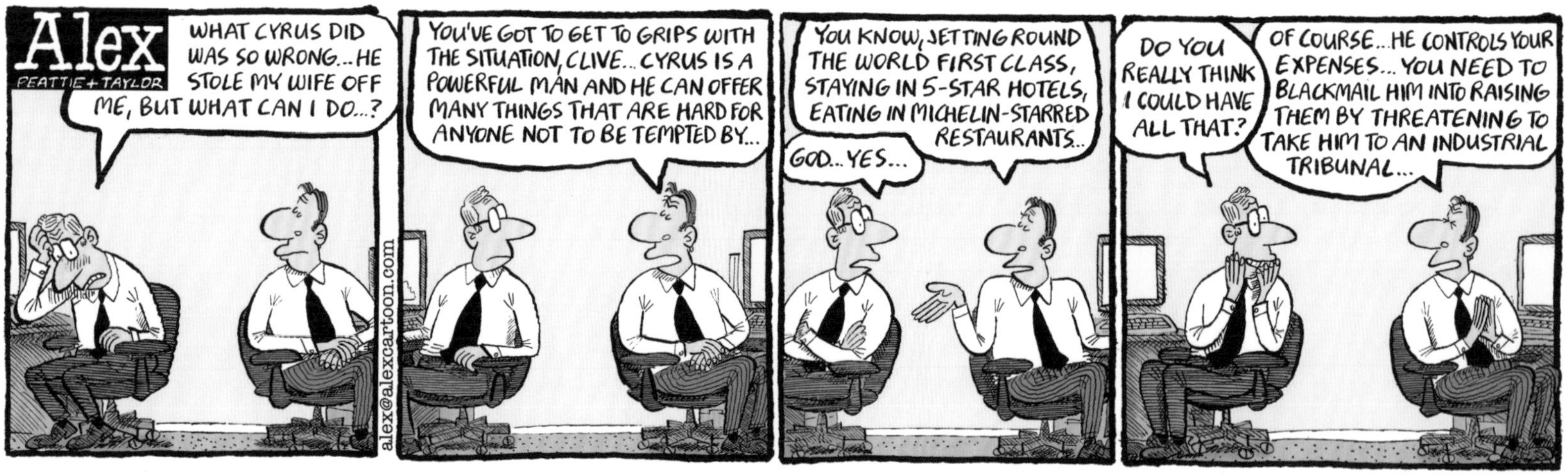
Alex
PEATTIE+TAYLOR
WHAT CYRUS DID WAS SO WRONG... HE STOLE MY WIFE OFF ME, BUT WHAT CAN I DO...?
alex@alexcartoon.com
YOU'VE GOT TO GET TO GRIPS WITH THE SITUATION, CLIVE... CYRUS IS A POWERFUL MAN AND HE CAN OFFER MANY THINGS THAT ARE HARD FOR ANYONE NOT TO BE TEMPTED BY...
YOU KNOW, JETTING ROUND THE WORLD FIRST CLASS, STAYING IN 5-STAR HOTELS, EATING IN MICHELIN-STARRED RESTAURANTS...
GOD... YES...
DO YOU REALLY THINK I COULD HAVE ALL THAT?
OF COURSE... HE CONTROLS YOUR EXPENSES... YOU NEED TO BLACKMAIL HIM INTO RAISING THEM BY THREATENING TO TAKE HIM TO AN INDUSTRIAL TRIBUNAL...

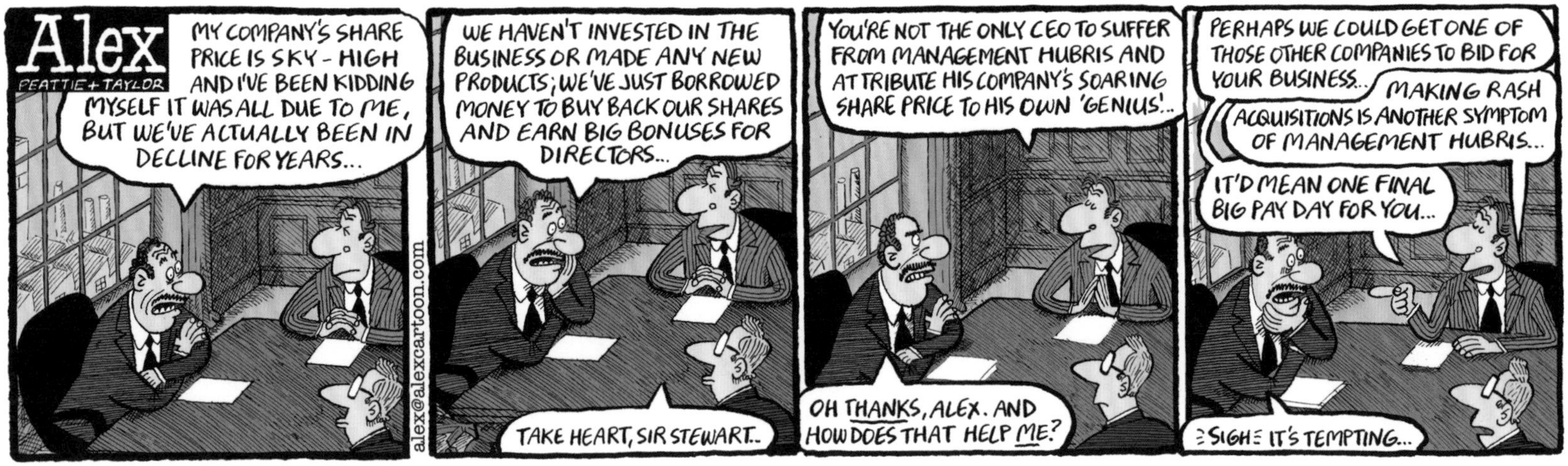
Alex
PEATTIE+TAYLOR
MY COMPANY'S SHARE PRICE IS SKY-HIGH AND I'VE BEEN KIDDING MYSELF IT WAS ALL DUE TO ME, BUT WE'VE ACTUALLY BEEN IN DECLINE FOR YEARS...
alex@alexcartoon.com
WE HAVEN'T INVESTED IN THE BUSINESS OR MADE ANY NEW PRODUCTS; WE'VE JUST BORROWED MONEY TO BUY BACK OUR SHARES AND EARN BIG BONUSES FOR DIRECTORS...
TAKE HEART, SIR STEWART..
YOU'RE NOT THE ONLY CEO TO SUFFER FROM MANAGEMENT HUBRIS AND ATTRIBUTE HIS COMPANY'S SOARING SHARE PRICE TO HIS OWN 'GENIUS'...
OH THANKS, ALEX. AND HOW DOES THAT HELP ME?
PERHAPS WE COULD GET ONE OF THOSE OTHER COMPANIES TO BID FOR YOUR BUSINESS...
MAKING RASH ACQUISITIONS IS ANOTHER SYMPTOM OF MANAGEMENT HUBRIS...
IT'D MEAN ONE FINAL BIG PAY DAY FOR YOU...
=SIGH= IT'S TEMPTING...

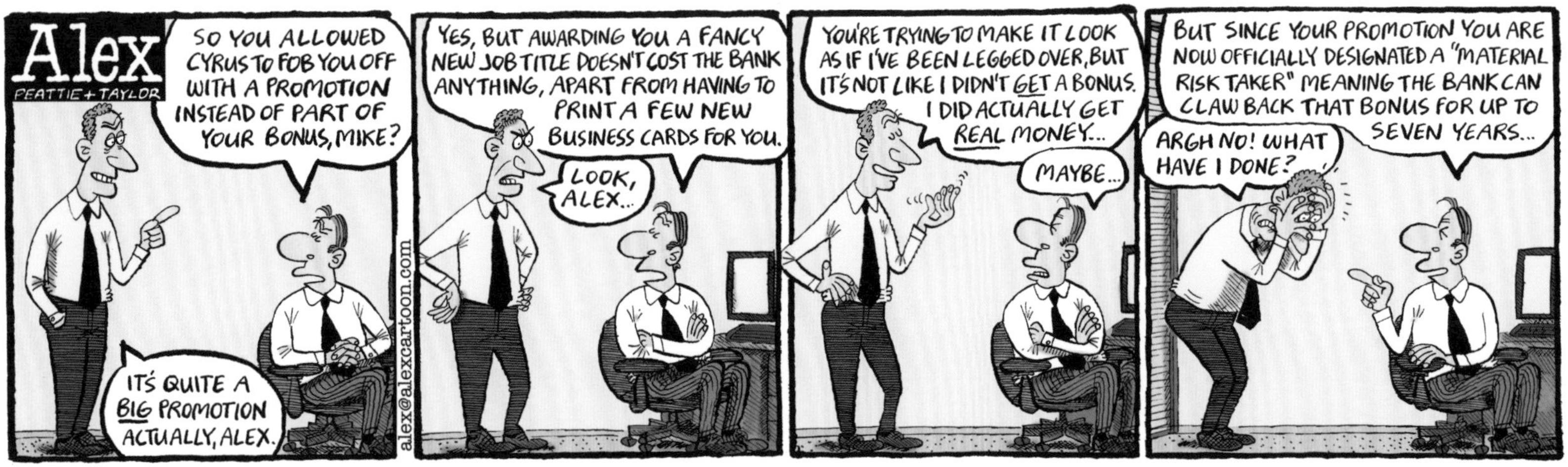
Alex
PEATTIE+TAYLOR
SO YOU ALLOWED CYRUS TO FOB YOU OFF WITH A PROMOTION INSTEAD OF PART OF YOUR BONUS, MIKE?
IT'S QUITE A BIG PROMOTION ACTUALLY, ALEX.
alex@alexcartoon.com
YES, BUT AWARDING YOU A FANCY NEW JOB TITLE DOESN'T COST THE BANK ANYTHING, APART FROM HAVING TO PRINT A FEW NEW BUSINESS CARDS FOR YOU.
LOOK, ALEX...
YOU'RE TRYING TO MAKE IT LOOK AS IF I'VE BEEN LEGGED OVER, BUT IT'S NOT LIKE I DIDN'T GET A BONUS. I DID ACTUALLY GET REAL MONEY...
MAYBE...
BUT SINCE YOUR PROMOTION YOU ARE NOW OFFICIALLY DESIGNATED A "MATERIAL RISK TAKER" MEANING THE BANK CAN CLAW BACK THAT BONUS FOR UP TO SEVEN YEARS...
ARGH NO! WHAT HAVE I DONE?

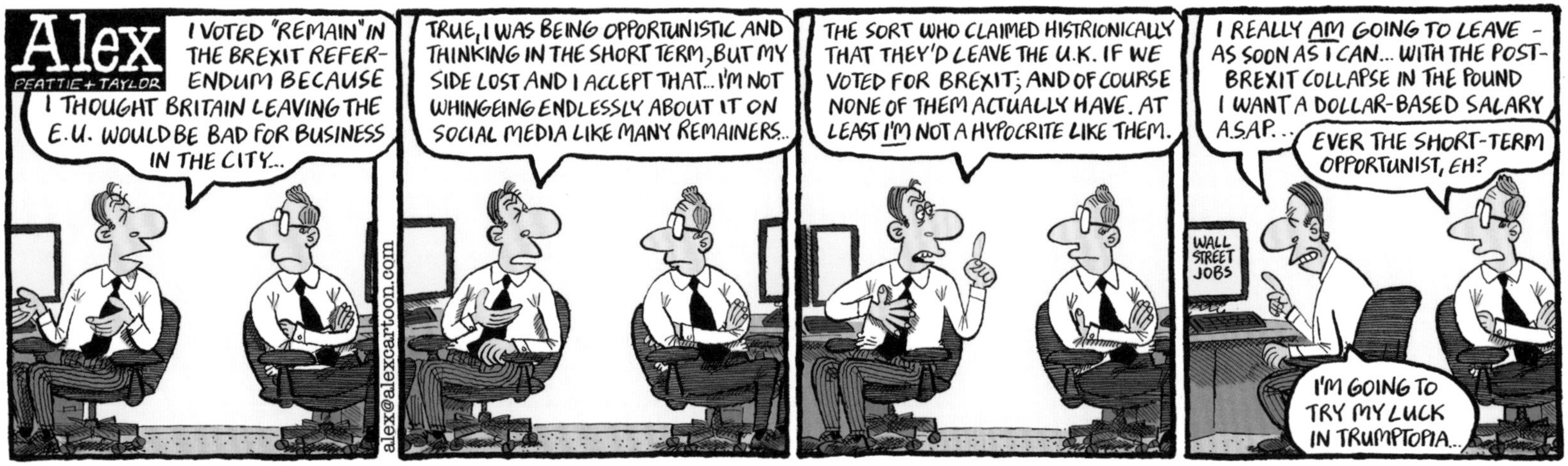
Alex
PEATTIE+TAYLOR
I VOTED "REMAIN" IN THE BREXIT REFERENDUM BECAUSE I THOUGHT BRITAIN LEAVING THE E.U. WOULD BE BAD FOR BUSINESS IN THE CITY...
alex@alexcartoon.com
TRUE, I WAS BEING OPPORTUNISTIC AND THINKING IN THE SHORT TERM, BUT MY SIDE LOST AND I ACCEPT THAT... I'M NOT WHINGEING ENDLESSLY ABOUT IT ON SOCIAL MEDIA LIKE MANY REMAINERS...
THE SORT WHO CLAIMED HISTRIONICALLY THAT THEY'D LEAVE THE U.K. IF WE VOTED FOR BREXIT; AND OF COURSE NONE OF THEM ACTUALLY HAVE. AT LEAST I'M NOT A HYPOCRITE LIKE THEM.
I REALLY AM GOING TO LEAVE - AS SOON AS I CAN... WITH THE POST-BREXIT COLLAPSE IN THE POUND I WANT A DOLLAR-BASED SALARY A.S.A.P...
EVER THE SHORT-TERM OPPORTUNIST, EH?
WALL STREET JOBS
I'M GOING TO TRY MY LUCK IN TRUMPTOPIA...

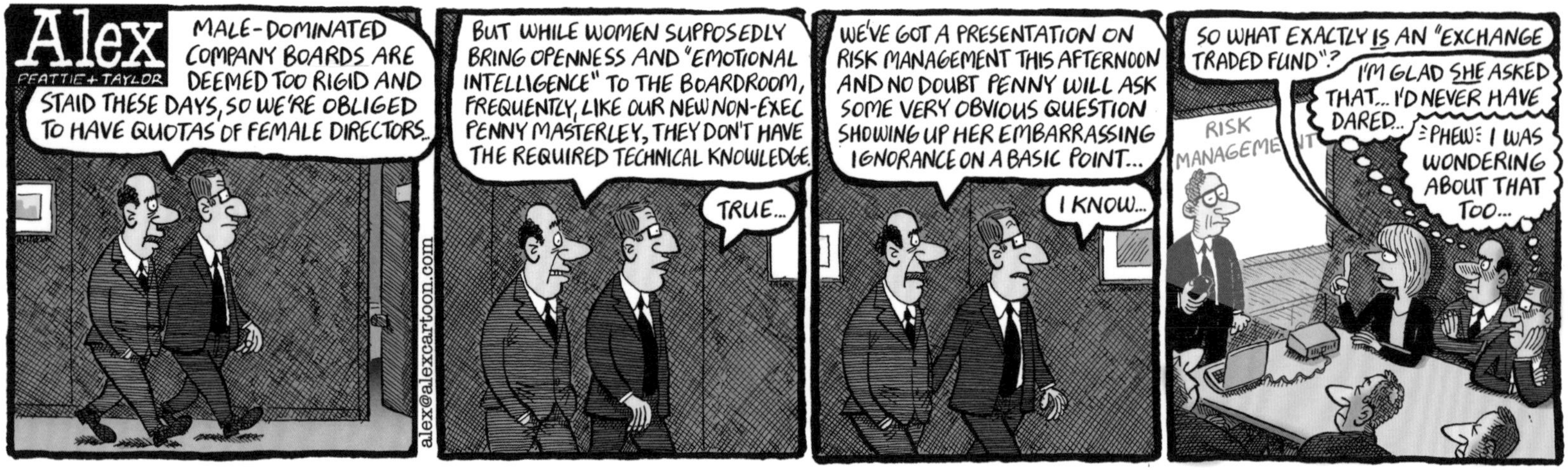
Alex
PEATTIE + TAYLOR
MALE-DOMINATED COMPANY BOARDS ARE DEEMED TOO RIGID AND STAID THESE DAYS, SO WE'RE OBLIGED TO HAVE QUOTAS OF FEMALE DIRECTORS...
BUT WHILE WOMEN SUPPOSEDLY BRING OPENNESS AND "EMOTIONAL INTELLIGENCE" TO THE BOARDROOM, FREQUENTLY, LIKE OUR NEW NON-EXEC PENNY MASTERLEY, THEY DON'T HAVE THE REQUIRED TECHNICAL KNOWLEDGE.
TRUE...
alex@alexcartoon.com
WE'VE GOT A PRESENTATION ON RISK MANAGEMENT THIS AFTERNOON AND NO DOUBT PENNY WILL ASK SOME VERY OBVIOUS QUESTION SHOWING UP HER EMBARRASSING IGNORANCE ON A BASIC POINT...
I KNOW...
SO WHAT EXACTLY IS AN "EXCHANGE TRADED FUND"?
I'M GLAD SHE ASKED THAT... I'D NEVER HAVE DARED...
PHEW! I WAS WONDERING ABOUT THAT TOO...

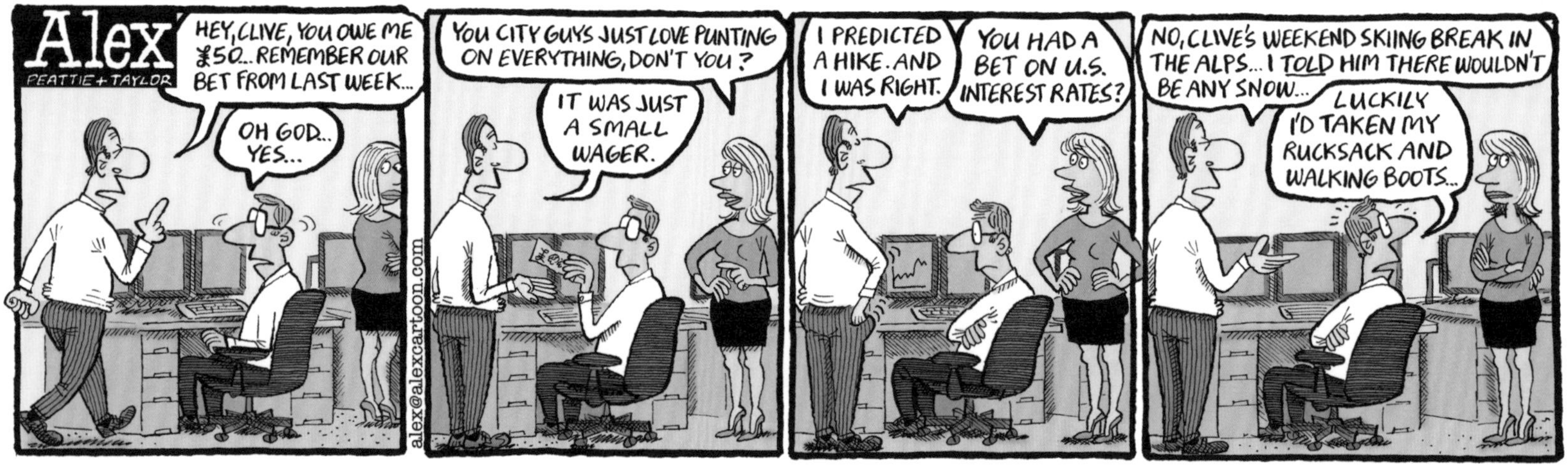
Alex
PEATTIE + TAYLOR
HEY, CLIVE, YOU OWE ME £50... REMEMBER OUR BET FROM LAST WEEK...
OH GOD... YES...
alex@alexcartoon.com
YOU CITY GUYS JUST LOVE PUNTING ON EVERYTHING, DON'T YOU?
IT WAS JUST A SMALL WAGER.
I PREDICTED A HIKE. AND I WAS RIGHT.
YOU HAD A BET ON U.S. INTEREST RATES?
NO, CLIVE'S WEEKEND SKIING BREAK IN THE ALPS... I TOLD HIM THERE WOULDN'T BE ANY SNOW...
LUCKILY I'D TAKEN MY RUCKSACK AND WALKING BOOTS...

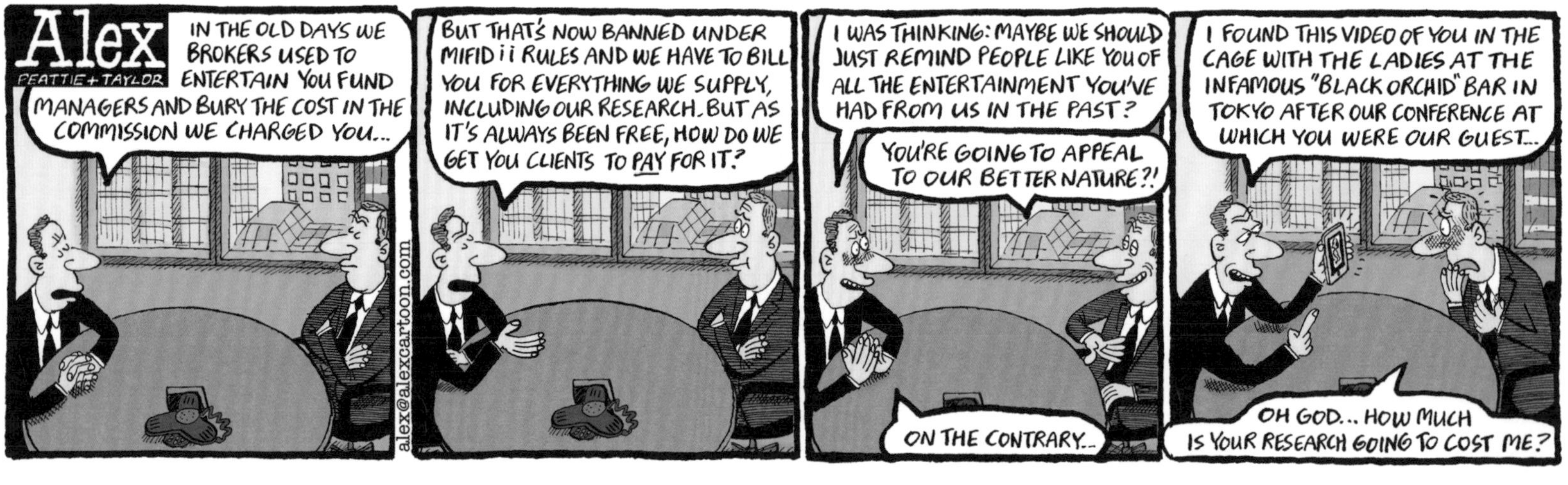
Alex
PEATTIE + TAYLOR
IN THE OLD DAYS WE BROKERS USED TO ENTERTAIN YOU FUND MANAGERS AND BURY THE COST IN THE COMMISSION WE CHARGED YOU...
alex@alexcartoon.com
BUT THAT'S NOW BANNED UNDER MIFID II RULES AND WE HAVE TO BILL YOU FOR EVERYTHING WE SUPPLY, INCLUDING OUR RESEARCH. BUT AS IT'S ALWAYS BEEN FREE, HOW DO WE GET YOU CLIENTS TO PAY FOR IT?
I WAS THINKING: MAYBE WE SHOULD JUST REMIND PEOPLE LIKE YOU OF ALL THE ENTERTAINMENT YOU'VE HAD FROM US IN THE PAST?
YOU'RE GOING TO APPEAL TO OUR BETTER NATURE?!
ON THE CONTRARY...
I FOUND THIS VIDEO OF YOU IN THE CAGE WITH THE LADIES AT THE INFAMOUS "BLACK ORCHID" BAR IN TOKYO AFTER OUR CONFERENCE AT WHICH YOU WERE OUR GUEST...
OH GOD... HOW MUCH IS YOUR RESEARCH GOING TO COST ME?

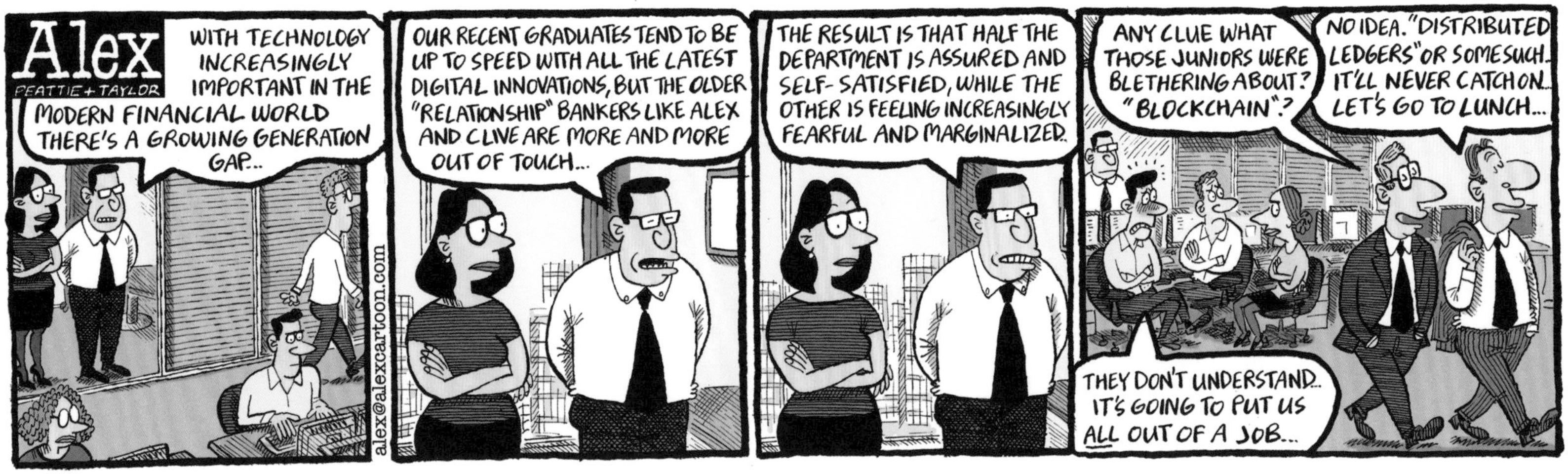
Alex
PEATTIE+TAYLOR
WITH TECHNOLOGY INCREASINGLY IMPORTANT IN THE MODERN FINANCIAL WORLD THERE'S A GROWING GENERATION GAP...
alex@alexcartoon.com
OUR RECENT GRADUATES TEND TO BE UP TO SPEED WITH ALL THE LATEST DIGITAL INNOVATIONS, BUT THE OLDER "RELATIONSHIP" BANKERS LIKE ALEX AND CLIVE ARE MORE AND MORE OUT OF TOUCH...
THE RESULT IS THAT HALF THE DEPARTMENT IS ASSURED AND SELF-SATISFIED, WHILE THE OTHER IS FEELING INCREASINGLY FEARFUL AND MARGINALIZED.
ANY CLUE WHAT THOSE JUNIORS WERE BLETHERING ABOUT? "BLOCKCHAIN"?
NO IDEA. "DISTRIBUTED LEDGERS" OR SOMESUCH.. IT'LL NEVER CATCH ON.. LET'S GO TO LUNCH...
THEY DON'T UNDERSTAND... IT'S GOING TO PUT US ALL OUT OF A JOB...

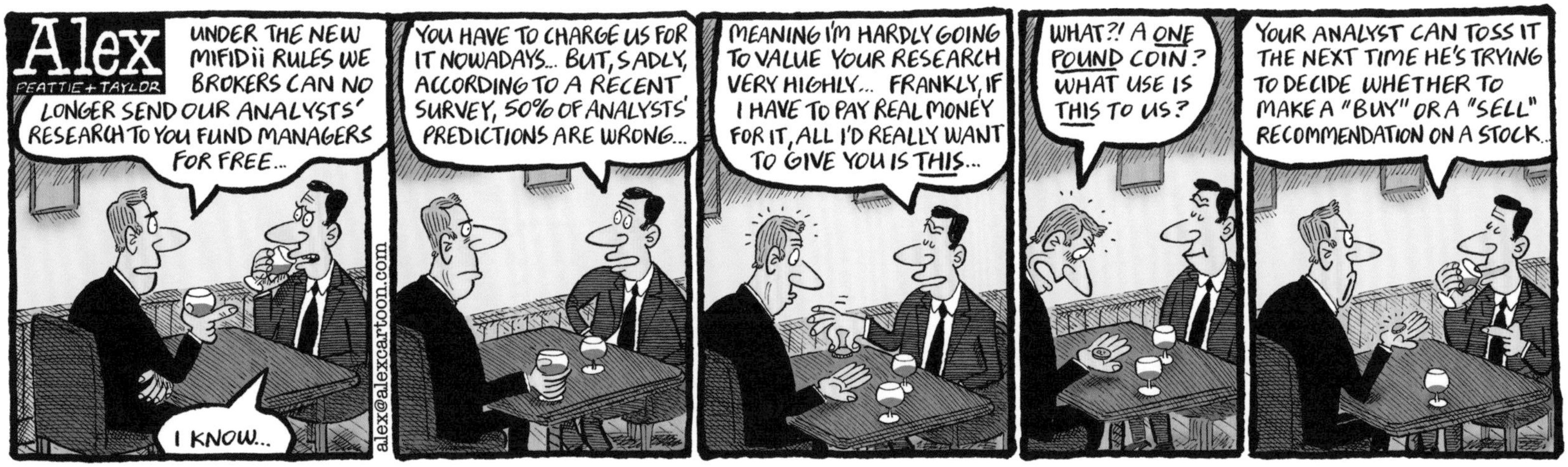
Alex
PEATTIE+TAYLOR
UNDER THE NEW MIFIDii RULES WE BROKERS CAN NO LONGER SEND OUR ANALYSTS' RESEARCH TO YOU FUND MANAGERS FOR FREE...
I KNOW...
alex@alexcartoon.com
YOU HAVE TO CHARGE US FOR IT NOWADAYS... BUT, SADLY, ACCORDING TO A RECENT SURVEY, 50% OF ANALYSTS' PREDICTIONS ARE WRONG...
MEANING I'M HARDLY GOING TO VALUE YOUR RESEARCH VERY HIGHLY... FRANKLY, IF I HAVE TO PAY REAL MONEY FOR IT, ALL I'D REALLY WANT TO GIVE YOU IS THIS...
WHAT?! A ONE POUND COIN? WHAT USE IS THIS TO US?
YOUR ANALYST CAN TOSS IT THE NEXT TIME HE'S TRYING TO DECIDE WHETHER TO MAKE A "BUY" OR A "SELL" RECOMMENDATION ON A STOCK...

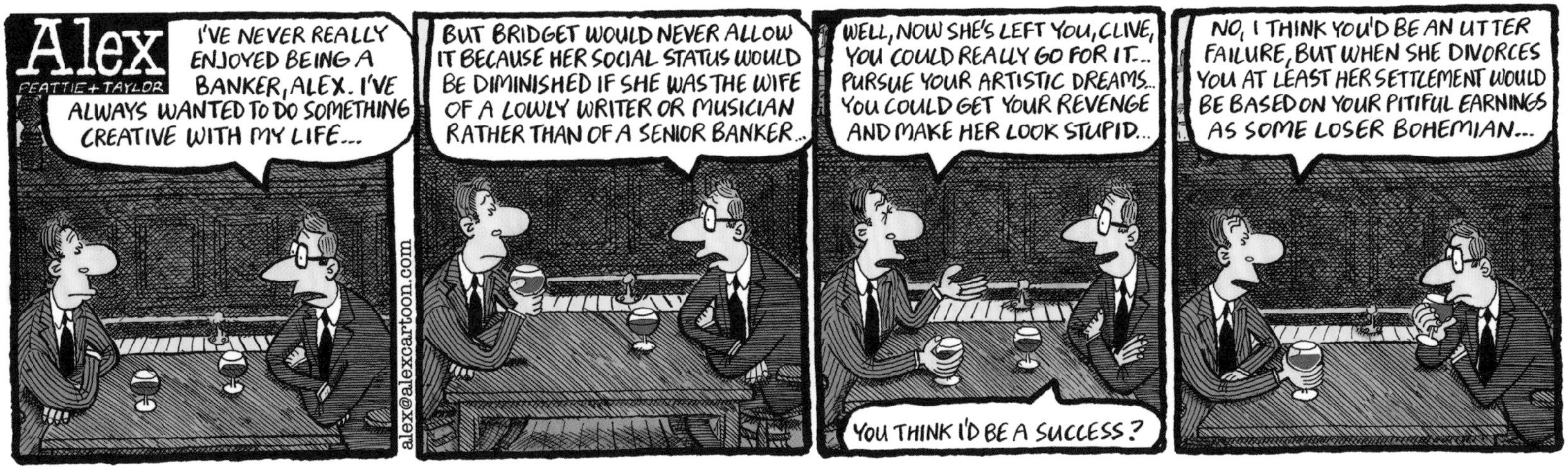
Alex
PEATTIE+TAYLOR
I'VE NEVER REALLY ENJOYED BEING A BANKER, ALEX. I'VE ALWAYS WANTED TO DO SOMETHING CREATIVE WITH MY LIFE...
alex@alexcartoon.com
BUT BRIDGET WOULD NEVER ALLOW IT BECAUSE HER SOCIAL STATUS WOULD BE DIMINISHED IF SHE WAS THE WIFE OF A LOWLY WRITER OR MUSICIAN RATHER THAN OF A SENIOR BANKER...
WELL, NOW SHE'S LEFT YOU, CLIVE, YOU COULD REALLY GO FOR IT... PURSUE YOUR ARTISTIC DREAMS... YOU COULD GET YOUR REVENGE AND MAKE HER LOOK STUPID...
YOU THINK I'D BE A SUCCESS?
NO, I THINK YOU'D BE AN UTTER FAILURE, BUT WHEN SHE DIVORCES YOU AT LEAST HER SETTLEMENT WOULD BE BASED ON YOUR PITIFUL EARNINGS AS SOME LOSER BOHEMIAN...

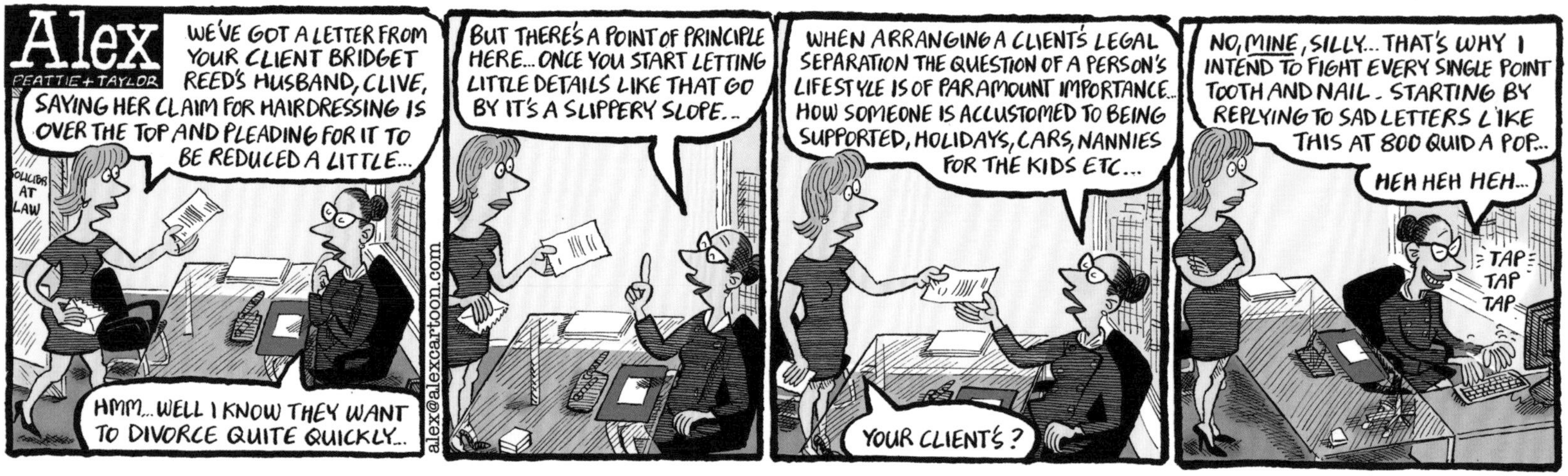
Alex
PEATTIE+TAYLOR
WE'VE GOT A LETTER FROM YOUR CLIENT BRIDGET REED'S HUSBAND, CLIVE, SAYING HER CLAIM FOR HAIRDRESSING IS OVER THE TOP AND PLEADING FOR IT TO BE REDUCED A LITTLE...
HMM... WELL I KNOW THEY WANT TO DIVORCE QUITE QUICKLY...
alex@alexcartoon.com
BUT THERE'S A POINT OF PRINCIPLE HERE... ONCE YOU START LETTING LITTLE DETAILS LIKE THAT GO BY IT'S A SLIPPERY SLOPE...
WHEN ARRANGING A CLIENT'S LEGAL SEPARATION THE QUESTION OF A PERSON'S LIFESTYLE IS OF PARAMOUNT IMPORTANCE... HOW SOMEONE IS ACCUSTOMED TO BEING SUPPORTED, HOLIDAYS, CARS, NANNIES FOR THE KIDS ETC...
YOUR CLIENT'S?
NO, MINE, SILLY... THAT'S WHY I INTEND TO FIGHT EVERY SINGLE POINT TOOTH AND NAIL - STARTING BY REPLYING TO SAD LETTERS LIKE THIS AT 800 QUID A POP...
HEH HEH HEH...
TAP TAP TAP

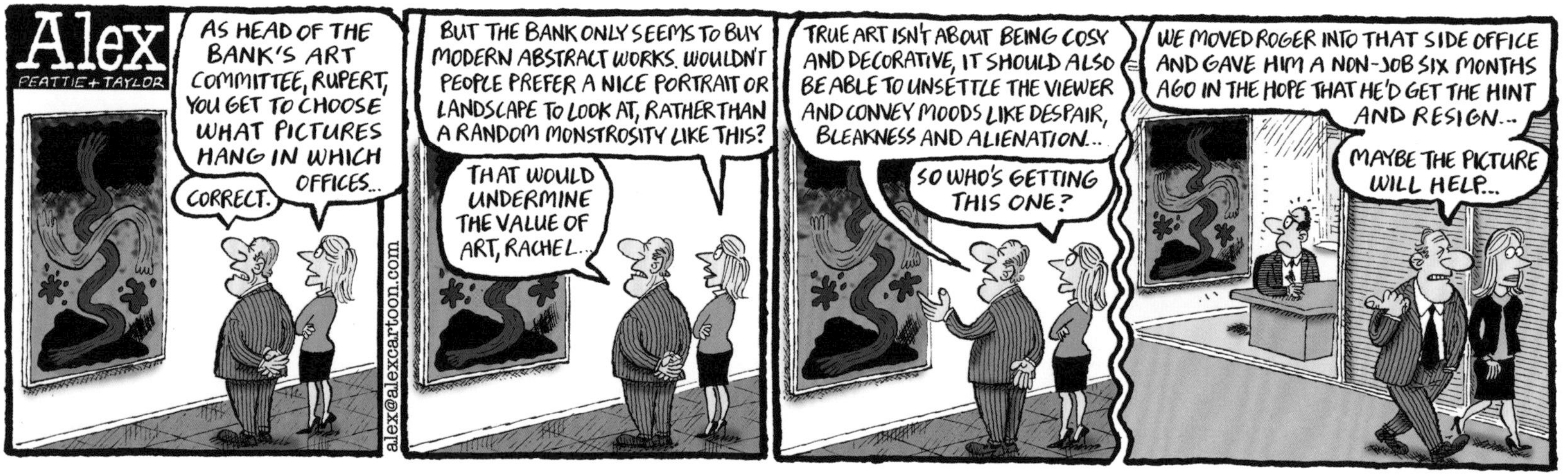
Alex
PEATTIE+TAYLOR
AS HEAD OF THE BANK'S ART COMMITTEE, RUPERT, YOU GET TO CHOOSE WHAT PICTURES HANG IN WHICH OFFICES...
CORRECT.
alex@alexcartoon.com
BUT THE BANK ONLY SEEMS TO BUY MODERN ABSTRACT WORKS. WOULDN'T PEOPLE PREFER A NICE PORTRAIT OR LANDSCAPE TO LOOK AT, RATHER THAN A RANDOM MONSTROSITY LIKE THIS?
THAT WOULD UNDERMINE THE VALUE OF ART, RACHEL...
TRUE ART ISN'T ABOUT BEING COSY AND DECORATIVE, IT SHOULD ALSO BE ABLE TO UNSETTLE THE VIEWER AND CONVEY MOODS LIKE DESPAIR, BLEAKNESS AND ALIENATION...
SO WHO'S GETTING THIS ONE?
WE MOVED ROGER INTO THAT SIDE OFFICE AND GAVE HIM A NON-JOB SIX MONTHS AGO IN THE HOPE THAT HE'D GET THE HINT AND RESIGN...
MAYBE THE PICTURE WILL HELP...

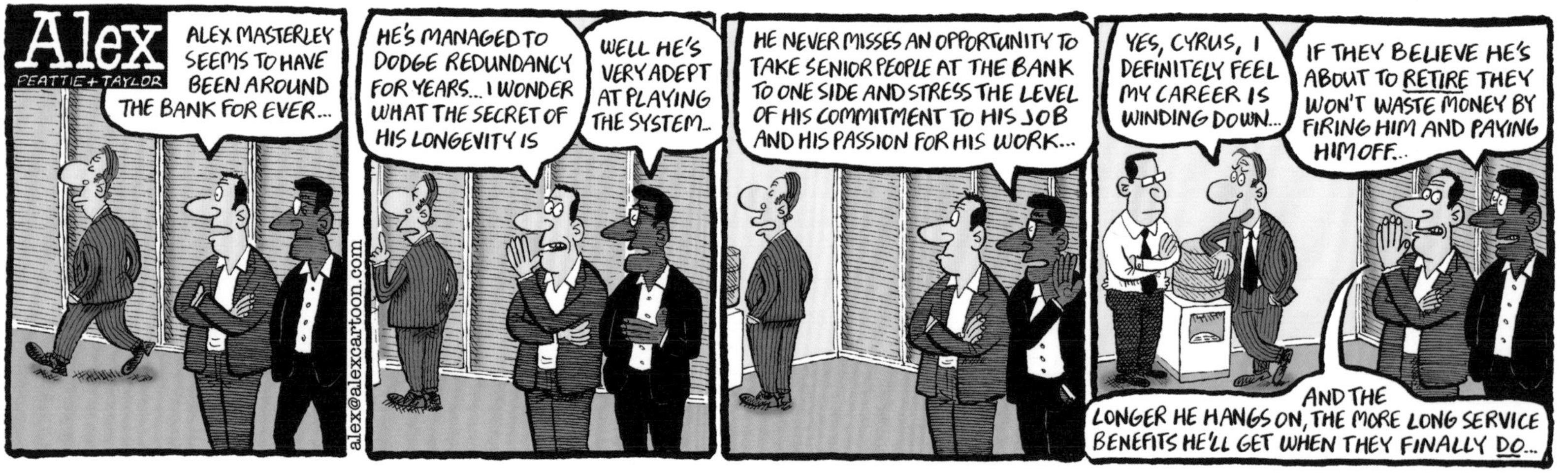
Alex
PEATTIE+TAYLOR
ALEX MASTERLEY SEEMS TO HAVE BEEN AROUND THE BANK FOR EVER...
alex@alexcartoon.com
HE'S MANAGED TO DODGE REDUNDANCY FOR YEARS... I WONDER WHAT THE SECRET OF HIS LONGEVITY IS
WELL HE'S VERY ADEPT AT PLAYING THE SYSTEM...
HE NEVER MISSES AN OPPORTUNITY TO TAKE SENIOR PEOPLE AT THE BANK TO ONE SIDE AND STRESS THE LEVEL OF HIS COMMITMENT TO HIS JOB AND HIS PASSION FOR HIS WORK...
YES, CYRUS, I DEFINITELY FEEL MY CAREER IS WINDING DOWN...
IF THEY BELIEVE HE'S ABOUT TO RETIRE THEY WON'T WASTE MONEY BY FIRING HIM AND PAYING HIM OFF...
AND THE LONGER HE HANGS ON, THE MORE LONG SERVICE BENEFITS HE'LL GET WHEN THEY FINALLY DO...

Alex
PEATTIE + TAYLOR

Panel 1: I'VE GOT OUR EASTER HOLIDAY BOOKED, CYRUS... I'M LOOKING FORWARD TO IT ALREADY...

Panel 2: BUT VACATIONS ARE WEIRD FOR ME, BRIDGET... I'VE ALWAYS BEEN SUCH A WORKAHOLIC...

YOU MAY NEED TO ADJUST TO SOME NEW LIFESTYLE EXPERIENCES, CYRUS...

Panel 3: YOU KNOW WHAT I'M TALKING ABOUT: RELAXING... ENJOYING FINE CUISINE, DRINKING GOOD WINE, PUTTING YOUR FEET UP, READING A BOOK...

OH MY GOSH...

Panel 4: ON THE <u>FLIGHT</u>, YOU MEAN? BECAUSE NORMALLY I'D <u>WORK</u> ON IT... YOU THINK THE AIRLINES ARE SERIOUS ABOUT THIS LAPTOP BAN?

LET'S HOPE SO. THAT'S WHY I USED YOUR AIR MILES TO BOOK US INTO FIRST CLASS...

Alex
PEATTIE + TAYLOR

Panel 5: HONESTLY, SINCE CLIVE DISCOVERED I WAS CHEATING ON HIM WITH HIS BOSS HIS REACTION HAS BEEN A DISAPPOINTMENT...

Panel 6: IT'S ONE OF THE THINGS I'VE ALWAYS DESPISED ABOUT MY HUSBAND: THE WAY HE TENDS TO WIMP OUT OF ANY CONFLICT...

Panel 7: THERE'S A SIDE OF ME THAT WISHES HE WOULD MAN UP... MAYBE <u>FIGHT</u> A LITTLE...≥SIGH≤ PEOPLE ARE ALWAYS SO KEEN TO APPEASE, AREN'T THEY? TO MAINTAIN THE STATUS QUO...

WHO? PEOPLE LIKE CLIVE?

Panel 8: NO, PEOPLE LIKE <u>EMPLOYERS</u>... IF CLIVE HAD THE BALLS TO THREATEN TO TAKE HIS BANK TO AN INDUSTRIAL TRIBUNAL THEN THEY'D PROBABLY CAVE IN AND PAY HIM OFF TO AVOID GOING TO COURT...

AND HALF OF ANY HUSH MONEY HE GOT WOULD GO TO <u>ME</u> IN MY DIVORCE SETTLEMENT...

Alex
PEATTIE + TAYLOR

Panel 9: IF CLIVE TOOK HIS BANK TO AN INDUSTRIAL TRIBUNAL OVER CYRUS HAVING AN AFFAIR WITH ME, HE MIGHT GET AWARDED A BIG SUM...

SOLICITORS AT LAW

Panel 10: AND THEN <u>I</u> COULD CLAIM HALF OF IT IN MY DIVORCE SETTLEMENT, RIGHT?

DON'T THINK LIKE THAT, BRIDGET...

Panel 11: IF IT WENT TO A TRIBUNAL YOU'D BE CALLED AS WITNESS AND HAVE TO TESTIFY IN OPEN COURT THAT YOU'D HAD AN AFFAIR WITH YOUR HUSBAND'S BOSS...

WHY?

Panel 12: YOU'D BE ASKED TO ATTEST THAT THE RELATIONSHIP STARTED BEFORE YOUR MARITAL SPLIT... YOUR EVIDENCE WOULD BE A VITAL PART OF CLIVE'S CASE.

AH... I SEE WHAT YOU MEAN...

Panel 13: SO I COULD THREATEN NOT TO CO-OPERATE AND TO DENY THE WHOLE THING UNLESS HE AGREED TO GIVE ME A BIGGER SHARE OF HIS WINNINGS?

EXACTLY. <u>HALF</u>?! YOU CAN DO BETTER THAN THAT! 60% AT LEAST...

alex@alexcartoon.com

49

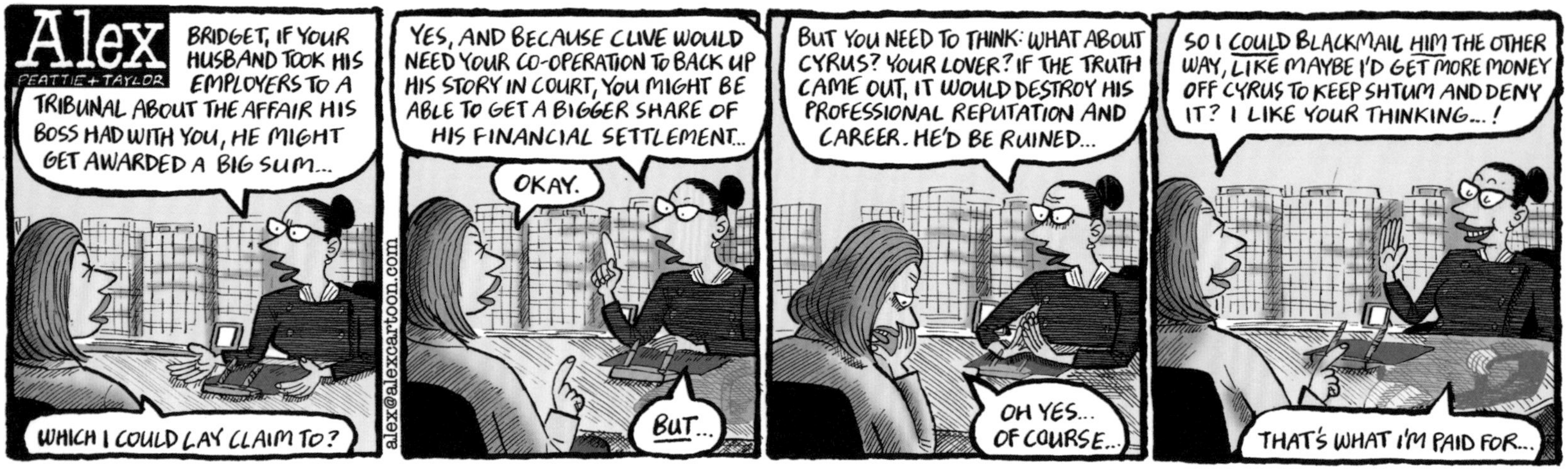
Alex
PEATTIE+TAYLOR
BRIDGET, IF YOUR HUSBAND TOOK HIS EMPLOYERS TO A TRIBUNAL ABOUT THE AFFAIR HIS BOSS HAD WITH YOU, HE MIGHT GET AWARDED A BIG SUM...
WHICH I COULD LAY CLAIM TO?
alex@alexcartoon.com
YES, AND BECAUSE CLIVE WOULD NEED YOUR CO-OPERATION TO BACK UP HIS STORY IN COURT, YOU MIGHT BE ABLE TO GET A BIGGER SHARE OF HIS FINANCIAL SETTLEMENT...
OKAY.
BUT...
BUT YOU NEED TO THINK: WHAT ABOUT CYRUS? YOUR LOVER? IF THE TRUTH CAME OUT, IT WOULD DESTROY HIS PROFESSIONAL REPUTATION AND CAREER. HE'D BE RUINED...
OH YES... OF COURSE...
SO I COULD BLACKMAIL HIM THE OTHER WAY, LIKE MAYBE I'D GET MORE MONEY OFF CYRUS TO KEEP SHTUM AND DENY IT? I LIKE YOUR THINKING...!
THAT'S WHAT I'M PAID FOR...

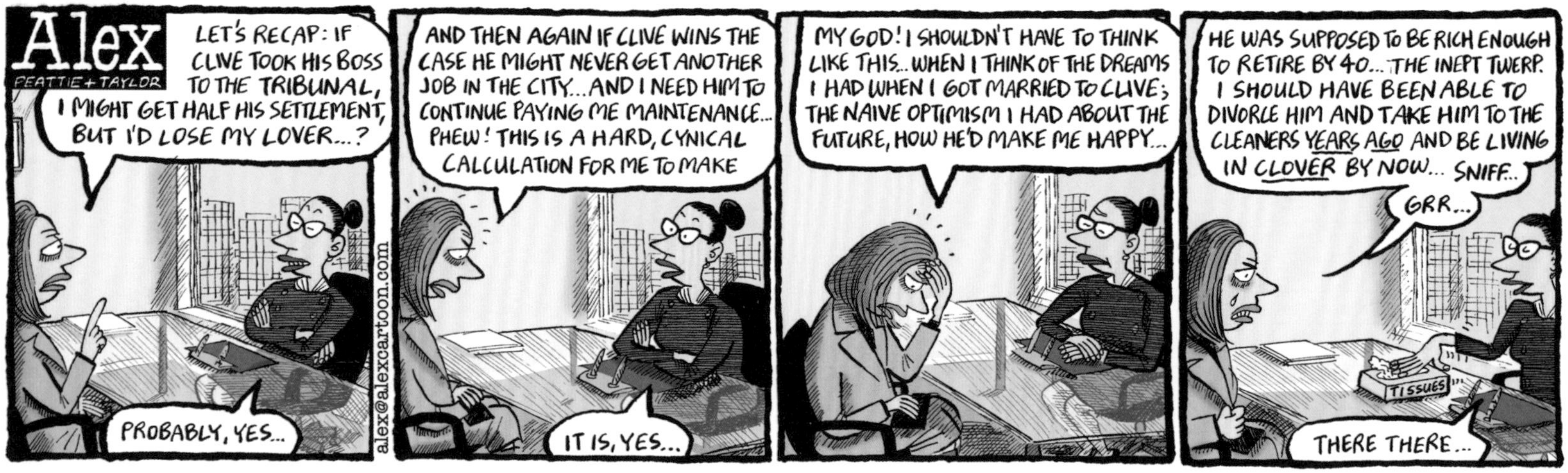
Alex
PEATTIE+TAYLOR
LET'S RECAP: IF CLIVE TOOK HIS BOSS TO THE TRIBUNAL, I MIGHT GET HALF HIS SETTLEMENT, BUT I'D LOSE MY LOVER...?
PROBABLY, YES...
alex@alexcartoon.com
AND THEN AGAIN IF CLIVE WINS THE CASE HE MIGHT NEVER GET ANOTHER JOB IN THE CITY... AND I NEED HIM TO CONTINUE PAYING ME MAINTENANCE... PHEW! THIS IS A HARD, CYNICAL CALCULATION FOR ME TO MAKE
IT IS, YES...
MY GOD! I SHOULDN'T HAVE TO THINK LIKE THIS... WHEN I THINK OF THE DREAMS I HAD WHEN I GOT MARRIED TO CLIVE; THE NAIVE OPTIMISM I HAD ABOUT THE FUTURE, HOW HE'D MAKE ME HAPPY...
HE WAS SUPPOSED TO BE RICH ENOUGH TO RETIRE BY 40... THE INEPT TWERP. I SHOULD HAVE BEEN ABLE TO DIVORCE HIM AND TAKE HIM TO THE CLEANERS YEARS AGO AND BE LIVING IN CLOVER BY NOW... SNIFF...
GRR...
TISSUES
THERE THERE...

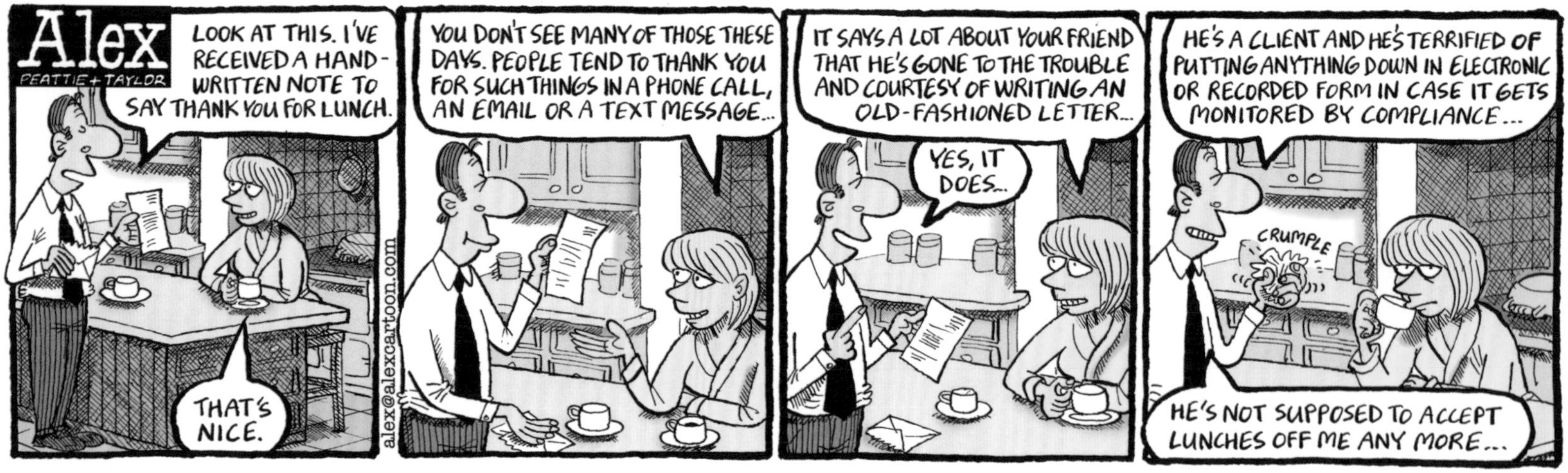
Alex
PEATTIE+TAYLOR
LOOK AT THIS. I'VE RECEIVED A HAND-WRITTEN NOTE TO SAY THANK YOU FOR LUNCH.
THAT'S NICE.
alex@alexcartoon.com
YOU DON'T SEE MANY OF THOSE THESE DAYS. PEOPLE TEND TO THANK YOU FOR SUCH THINGS IN A PHONE CALL, AN EMAIL OR A TEXT MESSAGE...
IT SAYS A LOT ABOUT YOUR FRIEND THAT HE'S GONE TO THE TROUBLE AND COURTESY OF WRITING AN OLD-FASHIONED LETTER...
YES, IT DOES...
HE'S A CLIENT AND HE'S TERRIFIED OF PUTTING ANYTHING DOWN IN ELECTRONIC OR RECORDED FORM IN CASE IT GETS MONITORED BY COMPLIANCE...
CRUMPLE
HE'S NOT SUPPOSED TO ACCEPT LUNCHES OFF ME ANY MORE...

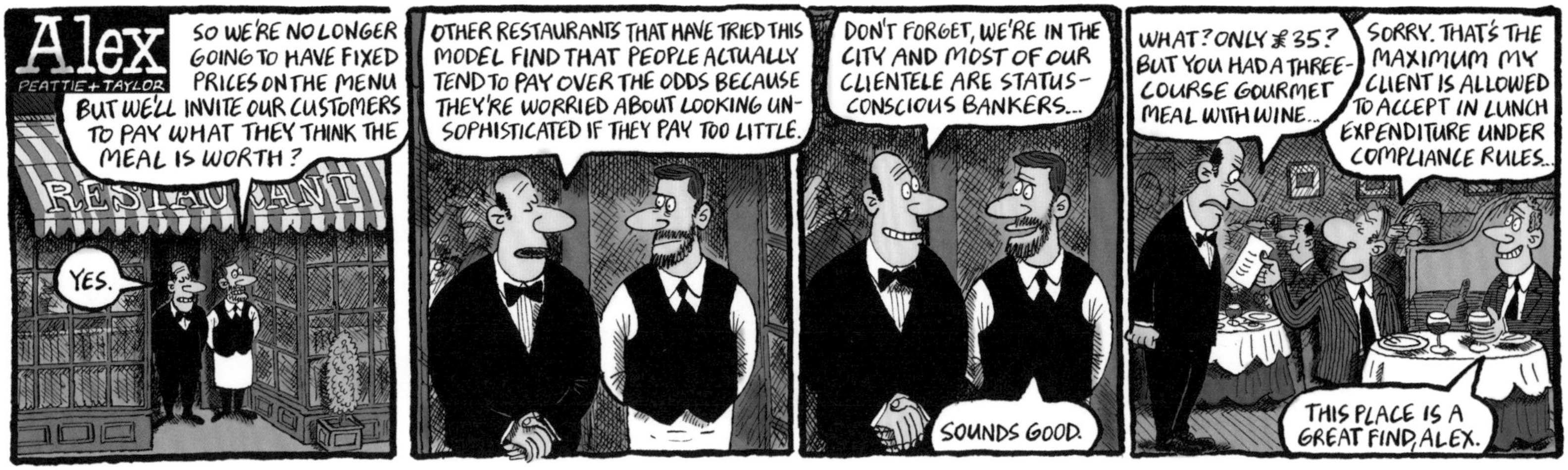
Alex
PEATTIE + TAYLOR
SO WE'RE NO LONGER GOING TO HAVE FIXED PRICES ON THE MENU BUT WE'LL INVITE OUR CUSTOMERS TO PAY WHAT THEY THINK THE MEAL IS WORTH?
RESTAURANT
YES.
OTHER RESTAURANTS THAT HAVE TRIED THIS MODEL FIND THAT PEOPLE ACTUALLY TEND TO PAY OVER THE ODDS BECAUSE THEY'RE WORRIED ABOUT LOOKING UNSOPHISTICATED IF THEY PAY TOO LITTLE.
DON'T FORGET, WE'RE IN THE CITY AND MOST OF OUR CLIENTELE ARE STATUS-CONSCIOUS BANKERS...
SOUNDS GOOD.
WHAT? ONLY £35? BUT YOU HAD A THREE-COURSE GOURMET MEAL WITH WINE...
SORRY. THAT'S THE MAXIMUM MY CLIENT IS ALLOWED TO ACCEPT IN LUNCH EXPENDITURE UNDER COMPLIANCE RULES...
THIS PLACE IS A GREAT FIND, ALEX.

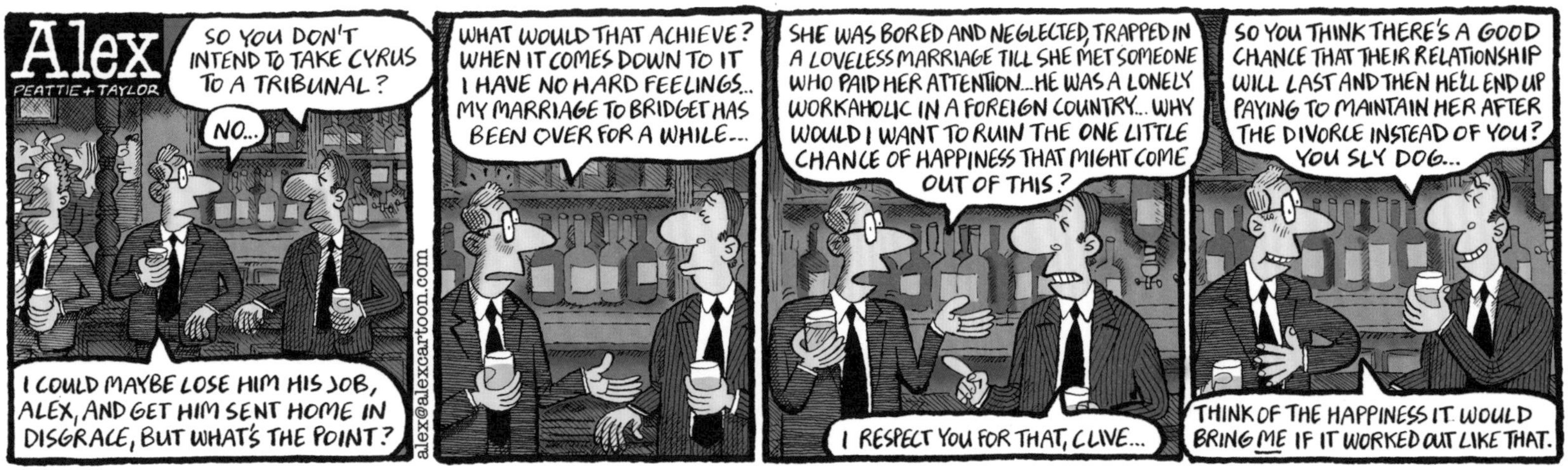
Alex
PEATTIE + TAYLOR
SO YOU DON'T INTEND TO TAKE CYRUS TO A TRIBUNAL?
NO...
I COULD MAYBE LOSE HIM HIS JOB, ALEX, AND GET HIM SENT HOME IN DISGRACE, BUT WHAT'S THE POINT?
alex@alexcartoon.com
WHAT WOULD THAT ACHIEVE? WHEN IT COMES DOWN TO IT I HAVE NO HARD FEELINGS... MY MARRIAGE TO BRIDGET HAS BEEN OVER FOR A WHILE...
SHE WAS BORED AND NEGLECTED, TRAPPED IN A LOVELESS MARRIAGE TILL SHE MET SOMEONE WHO PAID HER ATTENTION... HE WAS A LONELY WORKAHOLIC IN A FOREIGN COUNTRY... WHY WOULD I WANT TO RUIN THE ONE LITTLE CHANCE OF HAPPINESS THAT MIGHT COME OUT OF THIS?
I RESPECT YOU FOR THAT, CLIVE...
SO YOU THINK THERE'S A GOOD CHANCE THAT THEIR RELATIONSHIP WILL LAST AND THEN HE'LL END UP PAYING TO MAINTAIN HER AFTER THE DIVORCE INSTEAD OF YOU? YOU SLY DOG...
THINK OF THE HAPPINESS IT WOULD BRING ME IF IT WORKED OUT LIKE THAT.

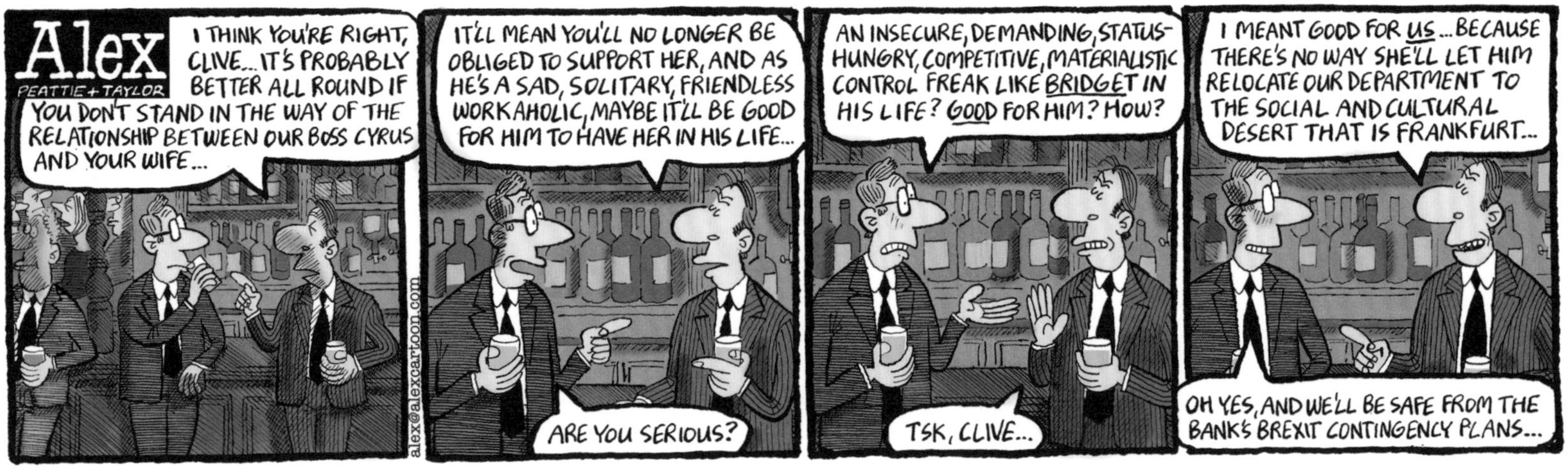
Alex
PEATTIE + TAYLOR
I THINK YOU'RE RIGHT, CLIVE... IT'S PROBABLY BETTER ALL ROUND IF YOU DON'T STAND IN THE WAY OF THE RELATIONSHIP BETWEEN OUR BOSS CYRUS AND YOUR WIFE...
alex@alexcartoon.com
IT'LL MEAN YOU'LL NO LONGER BE OBLIGED TO SUPPORT HER, AND AS HE'S A SAD, SOLITARY, FRIENDLESS WORKAHOLIC, MAYBE IT'LL BE GOOD FOR HIM TO HAVE HER IN HIS LIFE...
ARE YOU SERIOUS?
AN INSECURE, DEMANDING, STATUS-HUNGRY, COMPETITIVE, MATERIALISTIC CONTROL FREAK LIKE BRIDGET IN HIS LIFE? GOOD FOR HIM? HOW?
TSK, CLIVE...
I MEANT GOOD FOR US... BECAUSE THERE'S NO WAY SHE'LL LET HIM RELOCATE OUR DEPARTMENT TO THE SOCIAL AND CULTURAL DESERT THAT IS FRANKFURT...
OH YES, AND WE'LL BE SAFE FROM THE BANK'S BREXIT CONTINGENCY PLANS...

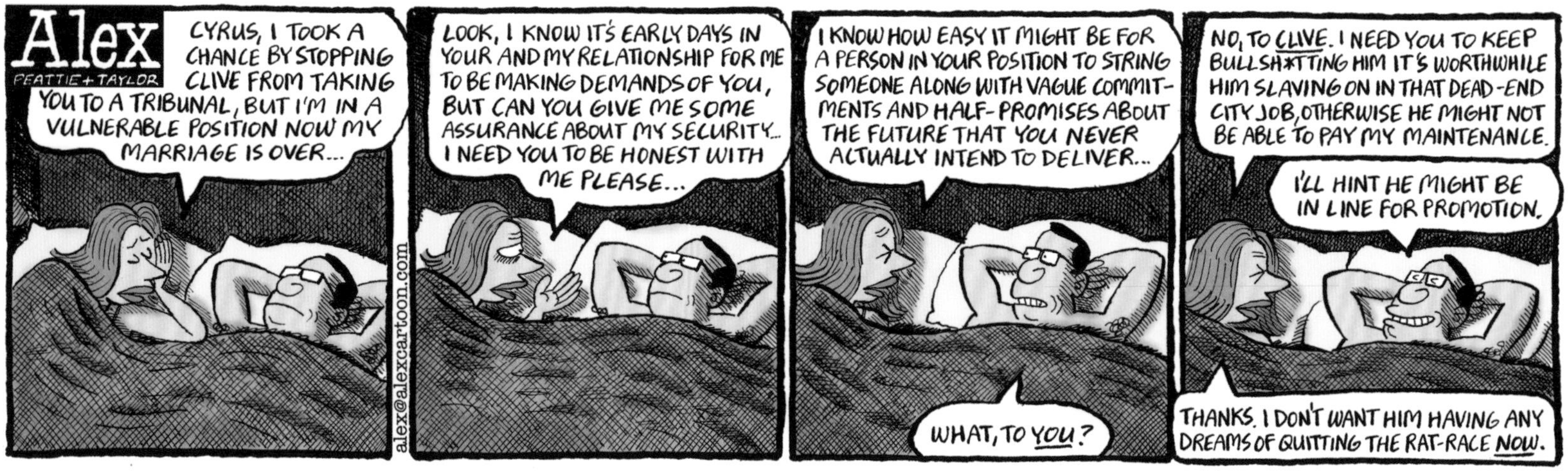
Alex
PEATTIE + TAYLOR
CYRUS, I TOOK A CHANCE BY STOPPING CLIVE FROM TAKING YOU TO A TRIBUNAL, BUT I'M IN A VULNERABLE POSITION NOW MY MARRIAGE IS OVER...
alex@alexcartoon.com
LOOK, I KNOW IT'S EARLY DAYS IN YOUR AND MY RELATIONSHIP FOR ME TO BE MAKING DEMANDS OF YOU, BUT CAN YOU GIVE ME SOME ASSURANCE ABOUT MY SECURITY... I NEED YOU TO BE HONEST WITH ME PLEASE...
I KNOW HOW EASY IT MIGHT BE FOR A PERSON IN YOUR POSITION TO STRING SOMEONE ALONG WITH VAGUE COMMITMENTS AND HALF-PROMISES ABOUT THE FUTURE THAT YOU NEVER ACTUALLY INTEND TO DELIVER...
WHAT, TO YOU?
NO, TO CLIVE. I NEED YOU TO KEEP BULLSH*TTING HIM IT'S WORTHWHILE HIM SLAVING ON IN THAT DEAD-END CITY JOB, OTHERWISE HE MIGHT NOT BE ABLE TO PAY MY MAINTENANCE.
I'LL HINT HE MIGHT BE IN LINE FOR PROMOTION.
THANKS. I DON'T WANT HIM HAVING ANY DREAMS OF QUITTING THE RAT-RACE NOW.

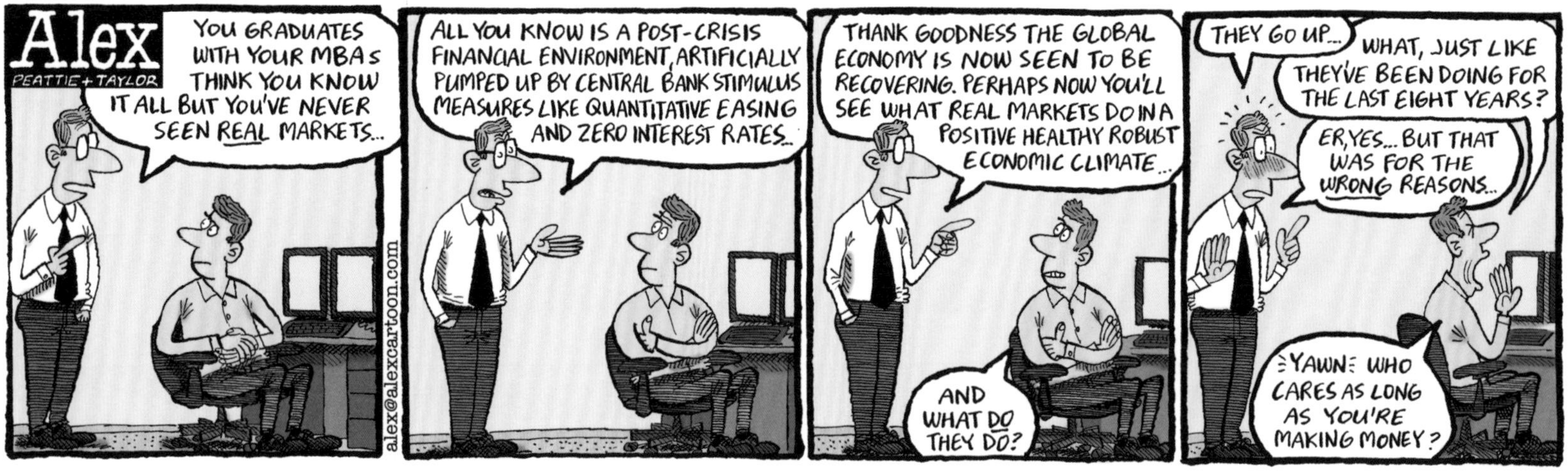
Alex
PEATTIE + TAYLOR
YOU GRADUATES WITH YOUR MBAs THINK YOU KNOW IT ALL BUT YOU'VE NEVER SEEN REAL MARKETS...
alex@alexcartoon.com
ALL YOU KNOW IS A POST-CRISIS FINANCIAL ENVIRONMENT, ARTIFICIALLY PUMPED UP BY CENTRAL BANK STIMULUS MEASURES LIKE QUANTITATIVE EASING AND ZERO INTEREST RATES...
THANK GOODNESS THE GLOBAL ECONOMY IS NOW SEEN TO BE RECOVERING. PERHAPS NOW YOU'LL SEE WHAT REAL MARKETS DO IN A POSITIVE HEALTHY ROBUST ECONOMIC CLIMATE...
AND WHAT DO THEY DO?
THEY GO UP...
WHAT, JUST LIKE THEY'VE BEEN DOING FOR THE LAST EIGHT YEARS?
ER, YES... BUT THAT WAS FOR THE WRONG REASONS...
YAWN WHO CARES AS LONG AS YOU'RE MAKING MONEY?

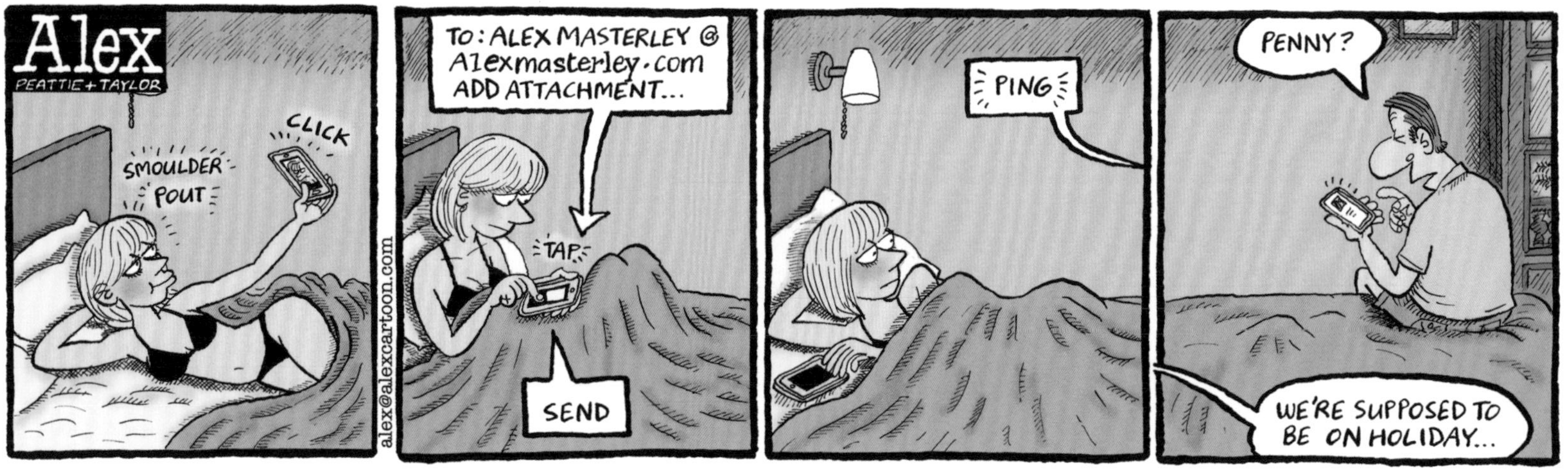
Alex
PEATTIE + TAYLOR
SMOULDER
POUT
CLICK
alex@alexcartoon.com
TO: ALEX MASTERLEY @ Alexmasterley.com ADD ATTACHMENT...
TAP
SEND
PING
PENNY?
WE'RE SUPPOSED TO BE ON HOLIDAY...

ALEX WAS ON A POST BREXIT HOLIDAY IN FRANCE

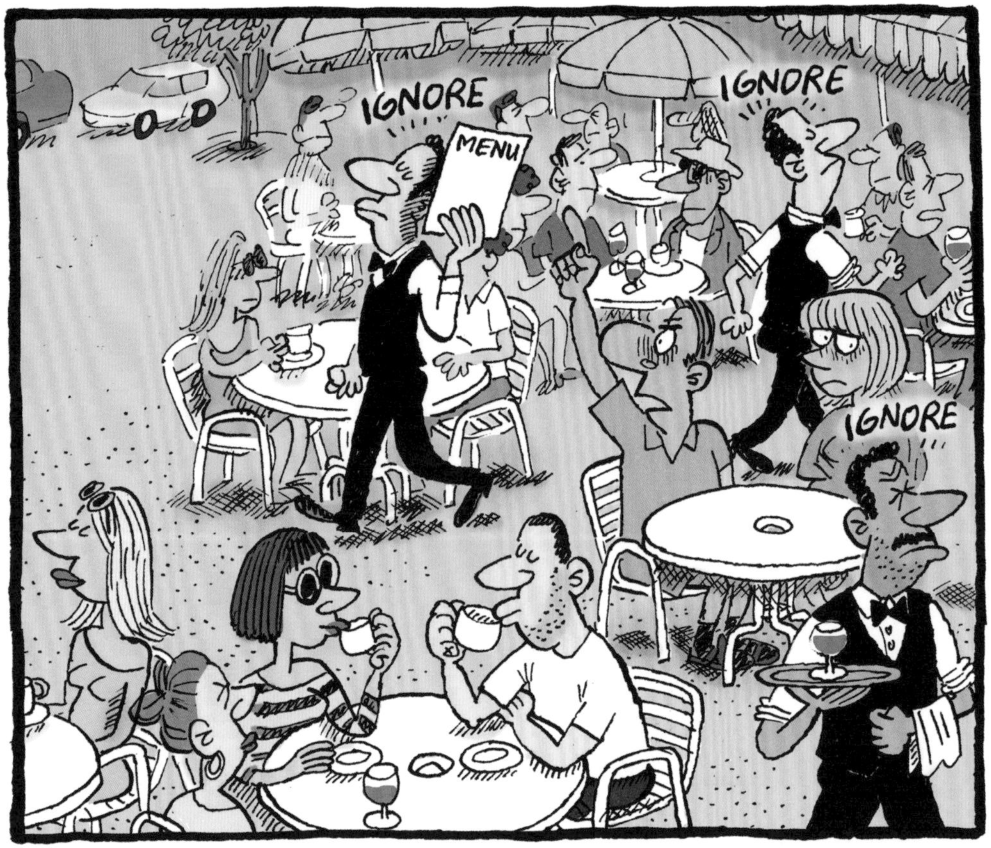
IGNORE
MENU
IGNORE
IGNORE

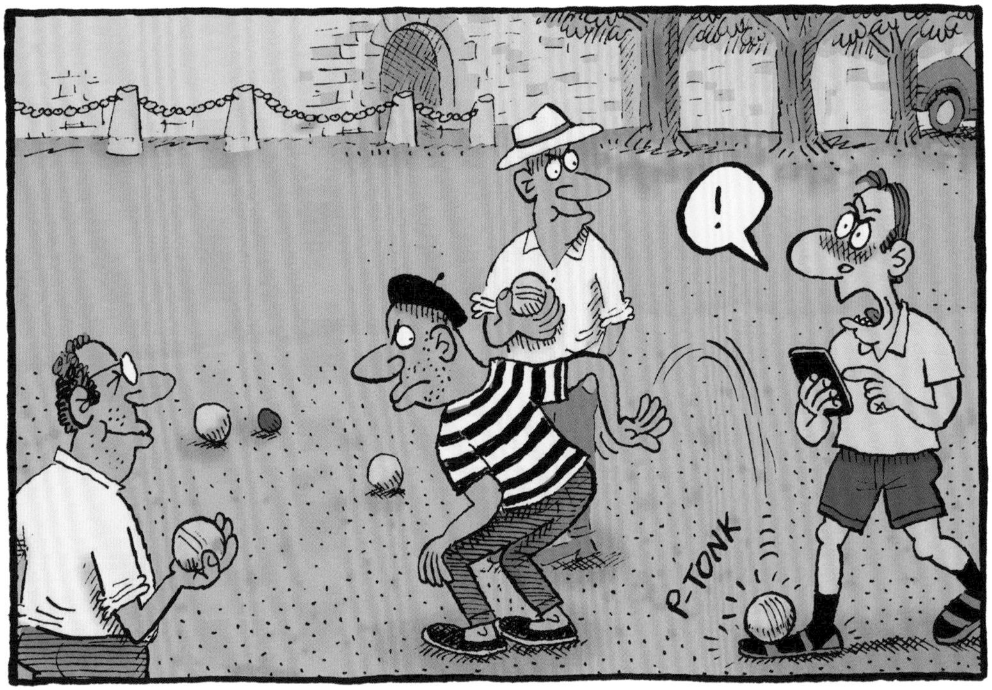
!
P-TONK

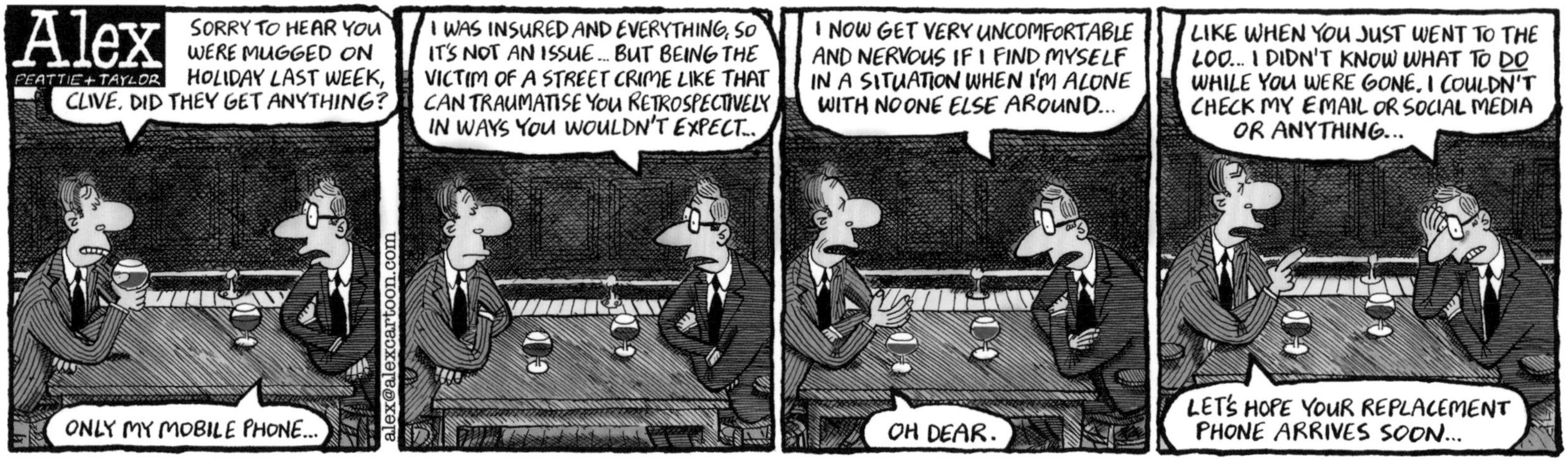
Alex
PEATTIE + TAYLOR
SORRY TO HEAR YOU WERE MUGGED ON HOLIDAY LAST WEEK, CLIVE. DID THEY GET ANYTHING?
ONLY MY MOBILE PHONE...
alex@alexcartoon.com
I WAS INSURED AND EVERYTHING, SO IT'S NOT AN ISSUE... BUT BEING THE VICTIM OF A STREET CRIME LIKE THAT CAN TRAUMATISE YOU RETROSPECTIVELY IN WAYS YOU WOULDN'T EXPECT...
I NOW GET VERY UNCOMFORTABLE AND NERVOUS IF I FIND MYSELF IN A SITUATION WHEN I'M ALONE WITH NO ONE ELSE AROUND...
OH DEAR.
LIKE WHEN YOU JUST WENT TO THE LOO... I DIDN'T KNOW WHAT TO DO WHILE YOU WERE GONE. I COULDN'T CHECK MY EMAIL OR SOCIAL MEDIA OR ANYTHING...
LET'S HOPE YOUR REPLACEMENT PHONE ARRIVES SOON...

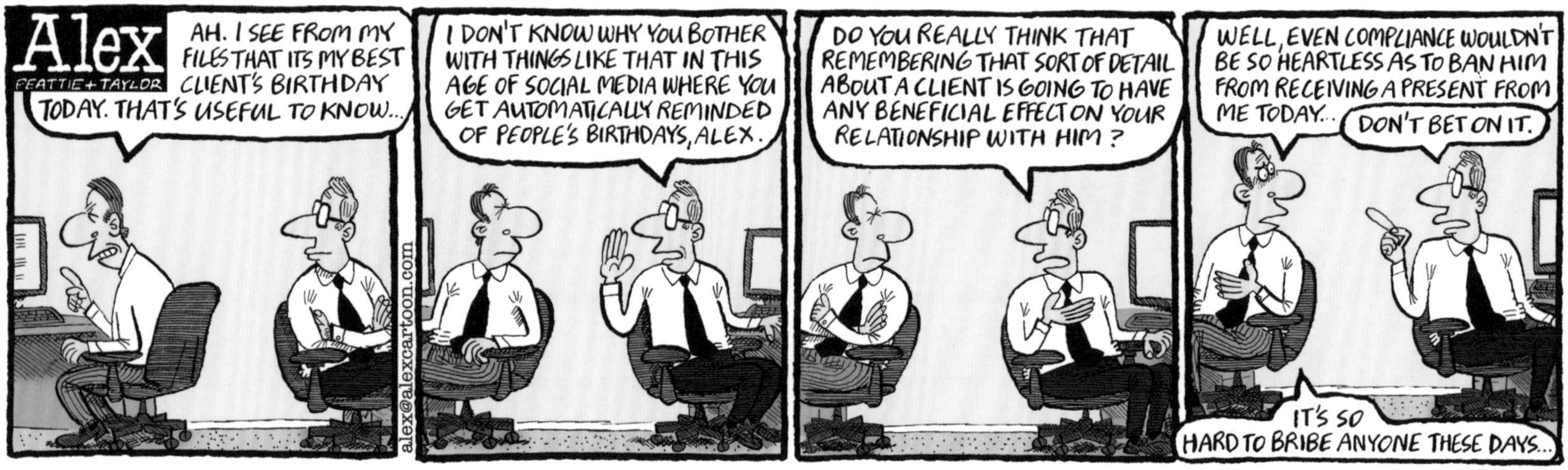
Alex
PEATTIE + TAYLOR
AH. I SEE FROM MY FILES THAT ITS MY BEST CLIENT'S BIRTHDAY TODAY. THAT'S USEFUL TO KNOW...
alex@alexcartoon.com
I DON'T KNOW WHY YOU BOTHER WITH THINGS LIKE THAT IN THIS AGE OF SOCIAL MEDIA WHERE YOU GET AUTOMATICALLY REMINDED OF PEOPLE'S BIRTHDAYS, ALEX.
DO YOU REALLY THINK THAT REMEMBERING THAT SORT OF DETAIL ABOUT A CLIENT IS GOING TO HAVE ANY BENEFICIAL EFFECT ON YOUR RELATIONSHIP WITH HIM?
WELL, EVEN COMPLIANCE WOULDN'T BE SO HEARTLESS AS TO BAN HIM FROM RECEIVING A PRESENT FROM ME TODAY...
DON'T BET ON IT.
IT'S SO HARD TO BRIBE ANYONE THESE DAYS...

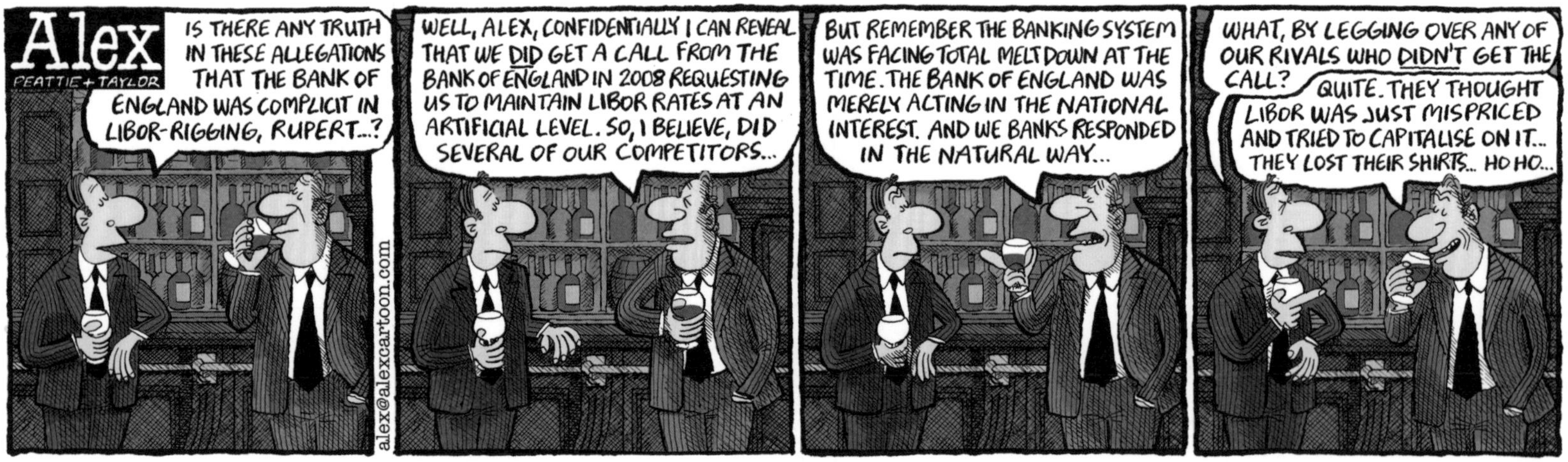
Alex
PEATTIE + TAYLOR
IS THERE ANY TRUTH IN THESE ALLEGATIONS THAT THE BANK OF ENGLAND WAS COMPLICIT IN LIBOR-RIGGING, RUPERT...?
alex@alexcartoon.com
WELL, ALEX, CONFIDENTIALLY I CAN REVEAL THAT WE DID GET A CALL FROM THE BANK OF ENGLAND IN 2008 REQUESTING US TO MAINTAIN LIBOR RATES AT AN ARTIFICIAL LEVEL. SO, I BELIEVE, DID SEVERAL OF OUR COMPETITORS...
BUT REMEMBER THE BANKING SYSTEM WAS FACING TOTAL MELTDOWN AT THE TIME. THE BANK OF ENGLAND WAS MERELY ACTING IN THE NATIONAL INTEREST. AND WE BANKS RESPONDED IN THE NATURAL WAY...
WHAT, BY LEGGING OVER ANY OF OUR RIVALS WHO DIDN'T GET THE CALL?
QUITE. THEY THOUGHT LIBOR WAS JUST MISPRICED AND TRIED TO CAPITALISE ON IT... THEY LOST THEIR SHIRTS... HO HO...

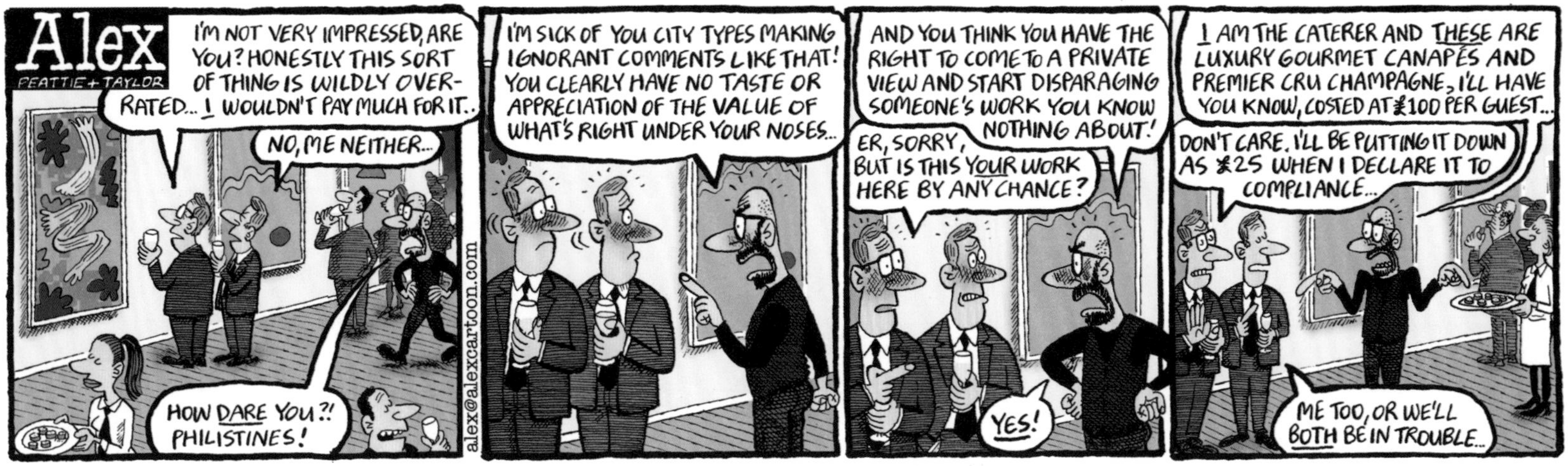
Alex
PEATTIE + TAYLOR
I'M NOT VERY IMPRESSED, ARE YOU? HONESTLY THIS SORT OF THING IS WILDLY OVER-RATED... I WOULDN'T PAY MUCH FOR IT..
NO, ME NEITHER...
HOW DARE YOU?! PHILISTINES!
alex@alexcartoon.com
I'M SICK OF YOU CITY TYPES MAKING IGNORANT COMMENTS LIKE THAT! YOU CLEARLY HAVE NO TASTE OR APPRECIATION OF THE VALUE OF WHAT'S RIGHT UNDER YOUR NOSES...
AND YOU THINK YOU HAVE THE RIGHT TO COME TO A PRIVATE VIEW AND START DISPARAGING SOMEONE'S WORK YOU KNOW NOTHING ABOUT!
ER, SORRY, BUT IS THIS YOUR WORK HERE BY ANY CHANCE?
YES!
I AM THE CATERER AND THESE ARE LUXURY GOURMET CANAPÉS AND PREMIER CRU CHAMPAGNE, I'LL HAVE YOU KNOW, COSTED AT £100 PER GUEST...
DON'T CARE. I'LL BE PUTTING IT DOWN AS £25 WHEN I DECLARE IT TO COMPLIANCE...
ME TOO, OR WE'LL BOTH BE IN TROUBLE...

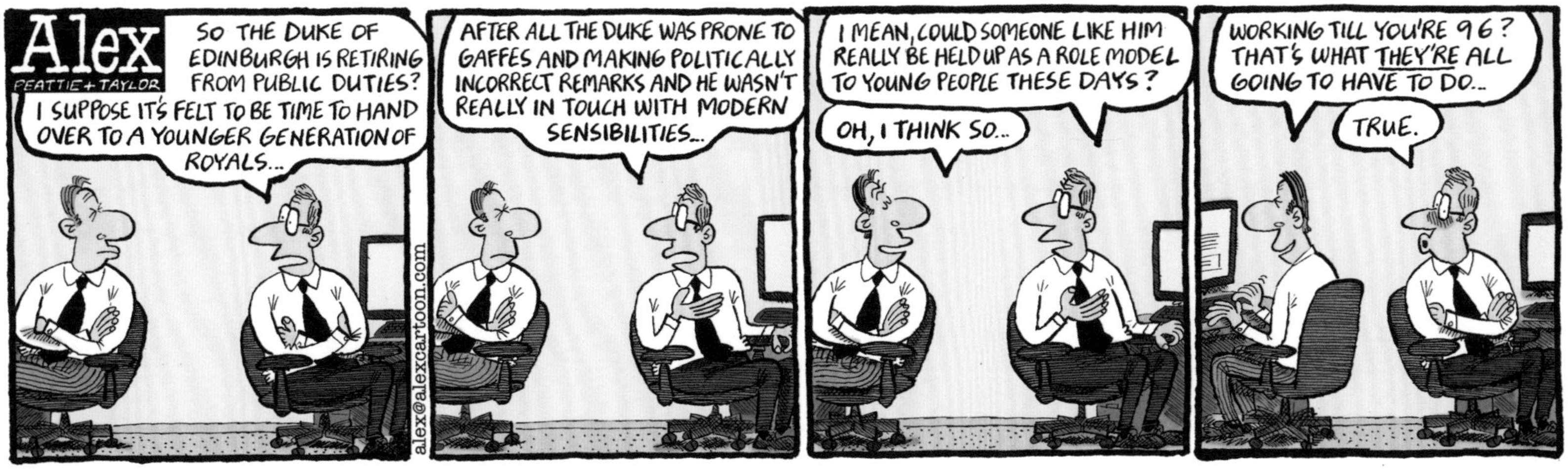
Alex
PEATTIE + TAYLOR
SO THE DUKE OF EDINBURGH IS RETIRING FROM PUBLIC DUTIES?
I SUPPOSE IT'S FELT TO BE TIME TO HAND OVER TO A YOUNGER GENERATION OF ROYALS...
alex@alexcartoon.com
AFTER ALL THE DUKE WAS PRONE TO GAFFES AND MAKING POLITICALLY INCORRECT REMARKS AND HE WASN'T REALLY IN TOUCH WITH MODERN SENSIBILITIES...
I MEAN, COULD SOMEONE LIKE HIM REALLY BE HELD UP AS A ROLE MODEL TO YOUNG PEOPLE THESE DAYS?
OH, I THINK SO...
WORKING TILL YOU'RE 96? THAT'S WHAT THEY'RE ALL GOING TO HAVE TO DO...
TRUE.

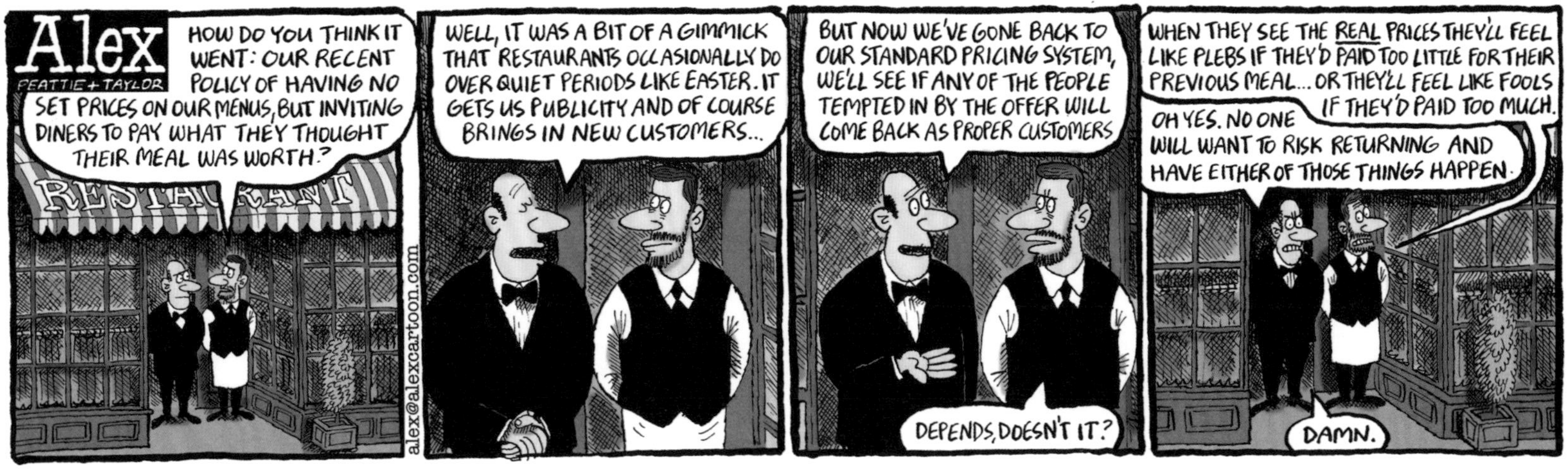
Alex
PEATTIE + TAYLOR
HOW DO YOU THINK IT WENT: OUR RECENT POLICY OF HAVING NO SET PRICES ON OUR MENUS, BUT INVITING DINERS TO PAY WHAT THEY THOUGHT THEIR MEAL WAS WORTH?
RESTAURANT
alex@alexcartoon.com
WELL, IT WAS A BIT OF A GIMMICK THAT RESTAURANTS OCCASIONALLY DO OVER QUIET PERIODS LIKE EASTER. IT GETS US PUBLICITY AND OF COURSE BRINGS IN NEW CUSTOMERS...
BUT NOW WE'VE GONE BACK TO OUR STANDARD PRICING SYSTEM, WE'LL SEE IF ANY OF THE PEOPLE TEMPTED IN BY THE OFFER WILL COME BACK AS PROPER CUSTOMERS
DEPENDS, DOESN'T IT?
WHEN THEY SEE THE REAL PRICES THEY'LL FEEL LIKE PLEBS IF THEY'D PAID TOO LITTLE FOR THEIR PREVIOUS MEAL... OR THEY'LL FEEL LIKE FOOLS IF THEY'D PAID TOO MUCH.
OH YES. NO ONE WILL WANT TO RISK RETURNING AND HAVE EITHER OF THOSE THINGS HAPPEN.
DAMN.

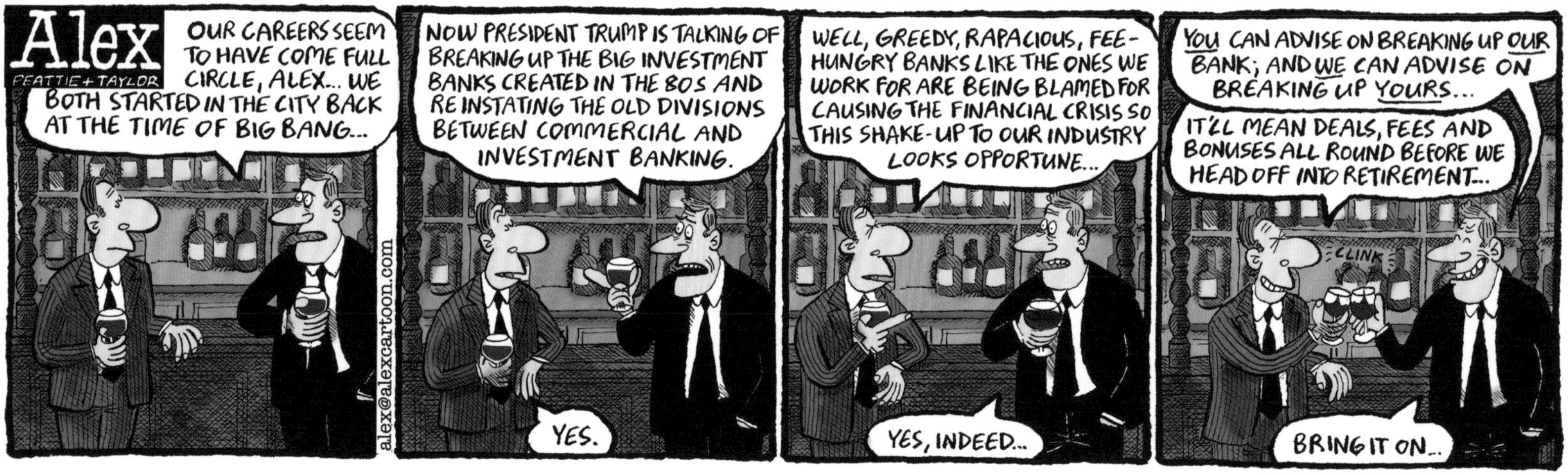
Alex
PEATTIE + TAYLOR
OUR CAREERS SEEM TO HAVE COME FULL CIRCLE, ALEX... WE BOTH STARTED IN THE CITY BACK AT THE TIME OF BIG BANG...
NOW PRESIDENT TRUMP IS TALKING OF BREAKING UP THE BIG INVESTMENT BANKS CREATED IN THE 80S AND REINSTATING THE OLD DIVISIONS BETWEEN COMMERCIAL AND INVESTMENT BANKING.
YES.
WELL, GREEDY, RAPACIOUS, FEE-HUNGRY BANKS LIKE THE ONES WE WORK FOR ARE BEING BLAMED FOR CAUSING THE FINANCIAL CRISIS SO THIS SHAKE-UP TO OUR INDUSTRY LOOKS OPPORTUNE...
YES, INDEED...
YOU CAN ADVISE ON BREAKING UP OUR BANK; AND WE CAN ADVISE ON BREAKING UP YOURS...
IT'LL MEAN DEALS, FEES AND BONUSES ALL ROUND BEFORE WE HEAD OFF INTO RETIREMENT...
CLINK
BRING IT ON...
alex@alexcartoon.com

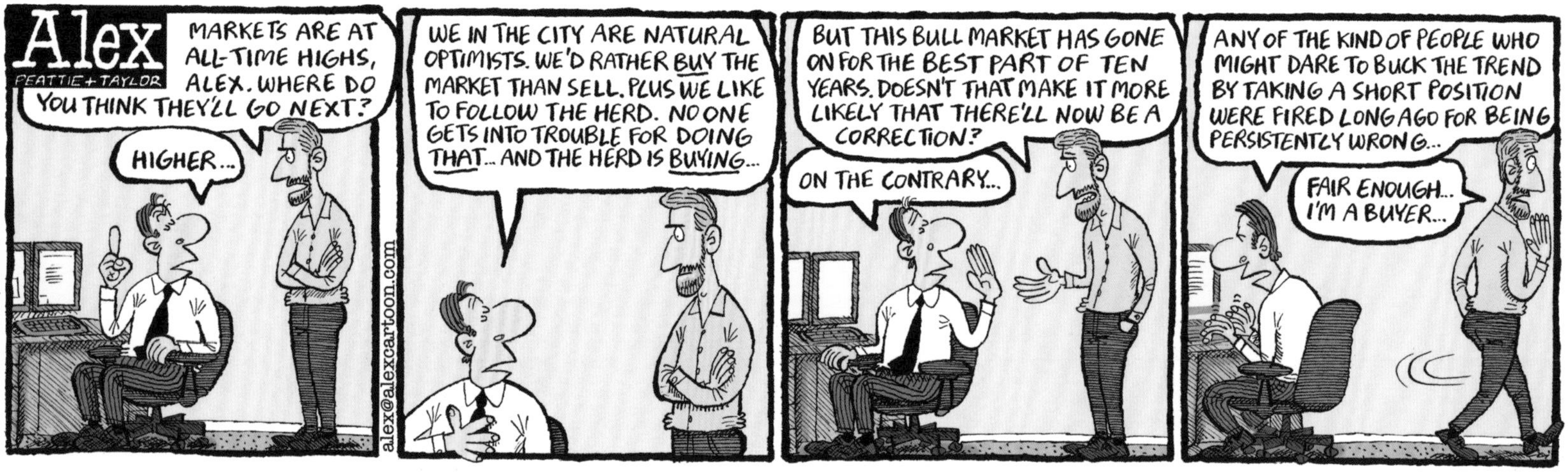
Alex
PEATTIE + TAYLOR
MARKETS ARE AT ALL-TIME HIGHS, ALEX. WHERE DO YOU THINK THEY'LL GO NEXT?
HIGHER...
WE IN THE CITY ARE NATURAL OPTIMISTS. WE'D RATHER BUY THE MARKET THAN SELL. PLUS WE LIKE TO FOLLOW THE HERD. NO ONE GETS INTO TROUBLE FOR DOING THAT... AND THE HERD IS BUYING...
BUT THIS BULL MARKET HAS GONE ON FOR THE BEST PART OF TEN YEARS. DOESN'T THAT MAKE IT MORE LIKELY THAT THERE'LL NOW BE A CORRECTION?
ON THE CONTRARY...
ANY OF THE KIND OF PEOPLE WHO MIGHT DARE TO BUCK THE TREND BY TAKING A SHORT POSITION WERE FIRED LONG AGO FOR BEING PERSISTENTLY WRONG...
FAIR ENOUGH... I'M A BUYER...
alex@alexcartoon.com

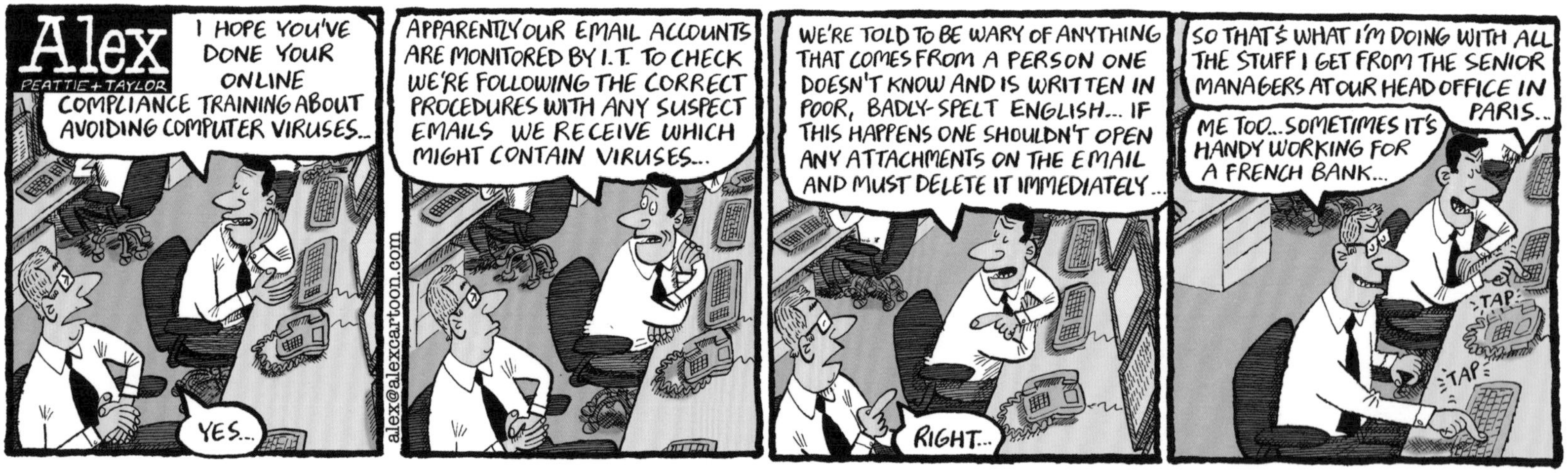
Alex
PEATTIE + TAYLOR
I HOPE YOU'VE DONE YOUR ONLINE COMPLIANCE TRAINING ABOUT AVOIDING COMPUTER VIRUSES...
YES...
APPARENTLY OUR EMAIL ACCOUNTS ARE MONITORED BY I.T. TO CHECK WE'RE FOLLOWING THE CORRECT PROCEDURES WITH ANY SUSPECT EMAILS WE RECEIVE WHICH MIGHT CONTAIN VIRUSES...
WE'RE TOLD TO BE WARY OF ANYTHING THAT COMES FROM A PERSON ONE DOESN'T KNOW AND IS WRITTEN IN POOR, BADLY-SPELT ENGLISH... IF THIS HAPPENS ONE SHOULDN'T OPEN ANY ATTACHMENTS ON THE EMAIL AND MUST DELETE IT IMMEDIATELY...
RIGHT...
SO THAT'S WHAT I'M DOING WITH ALL THE STUFF I GET FROM THE SENIOR MANAGERS AT OUR HEAD OFFICE IN PARIS...
ME TOO... SOMETIMES IT'S HANDY WORKING FOR A FRENCH BANK...
TAP
TAP
alex@alexcartoon.com

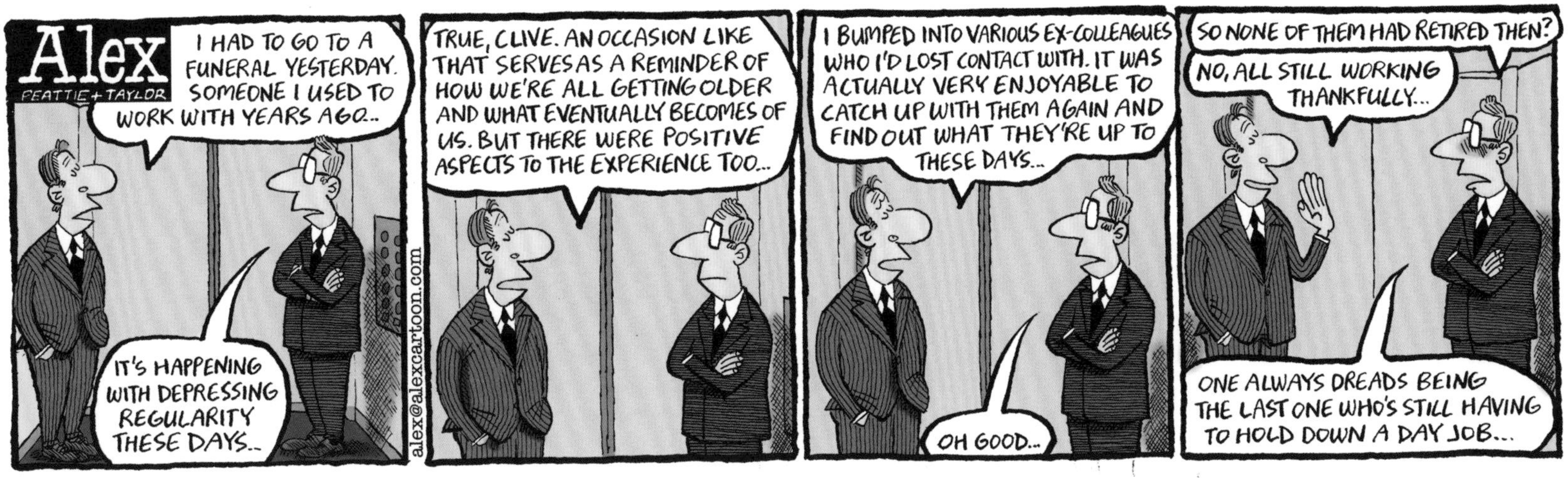
Alex
PEATTIE + TAYLOR
I HAD TO GO TO A FUNERAL YESTERDAY. SOMEONE I USED TO WORK WITH YEARS AGO...
IT'S HAPPENING WITH DEPRESSING REGULARITY THESE DAYS...
alex@alexcartoon.com
TRUE, CLIVE. AN OCCASION LIKE THAT SERVES AS A REMINDER OF HOW WE'RE ALL GETTING OLDER AND WHAT EVENTUALLY BECOMES OF US. BUT THERE WERE POSITIVE ASPECTS TO THE EXPERIENCE TOO...
I BUMPED INTO VARIOUS EX-COLLEAGUES WHO I'D LOST CONTACT WITH. IT WAS ACTUALLY VERY ENJOYABLE TO CATCH UP WITH THEM AGAIN AND FIND OUT WHAT THEY'RE UP TO THESE DAYS...
OH GOOD...
SO NONE OF THEM HAD RETIRED THEN?
NO, ALL STILL WORKING THANKFULLY...
ONE ALWAYS DREADS BEING THE LAST ONE WHO'S STILL HAVING TO HOLD DOWN A DAY JOB...

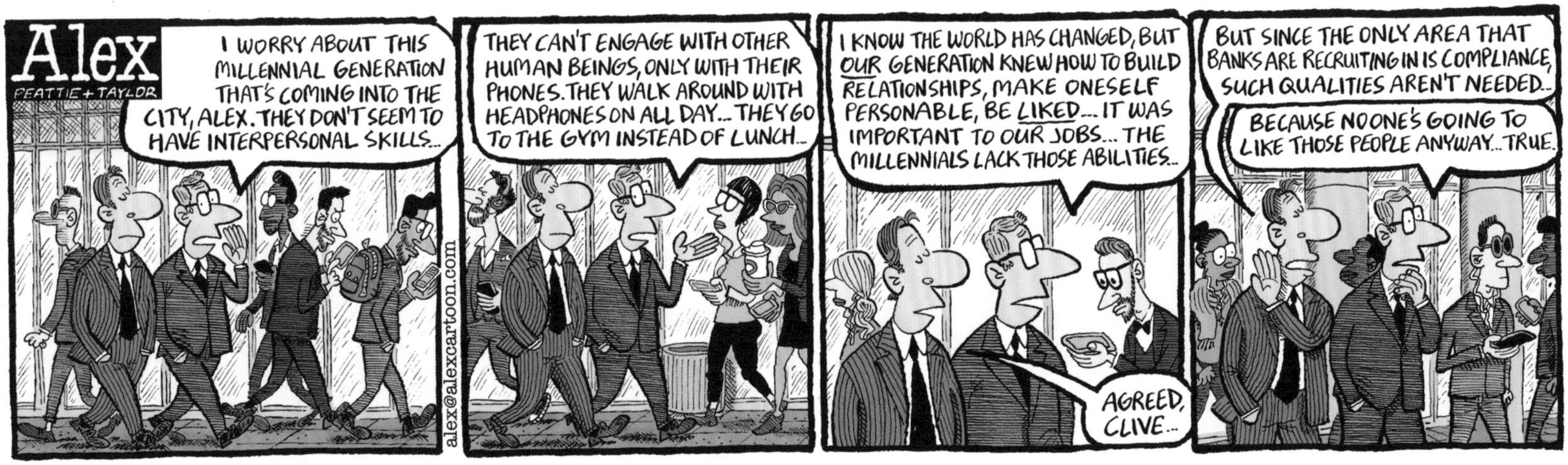
Alex
PEATTIE + TAYLOR
I WORRY ABOUT THIS MILLENNIAL GENERATION THAT'S COMING INTO THE CITY, ALEX. THEY DON'T SEEM TO HAVE INTERPERSONAL SKILLS...
alex@alexcartoon.com
THEY CAN'T ENGAGE WITH OTHER HUMAN BEINGS, ONLY WITH THEIR PHONES. THEY WALK AROUND WITH HEADPHONES ON ALL DAY... THEY GO TO THE GYM INSTEAD OF LUNCH...
I KNOW THE WORLD HAS CHANGED, BUT OUR GENERATION KNEW HOW TO BUILD RELATIONSHIPS, MAKE ONESELF PERSONABLE, BE LIKED... IT WAS IMPORTANT TO OUR JOBS... THE MILLENNIALS LACK THOSE ABILITIES...
AGREED, CLIVE...
BUT SINCE THE ONLY AREA THAT BANKS ARE RECRUITING IN IS COMPLIANCE, SUCH QUALITIES AREN'T NEEDED...
BECAUSE NO ONE'S GOING TO LIKE THOSE PEOPLE ANYWAY... TRUE.

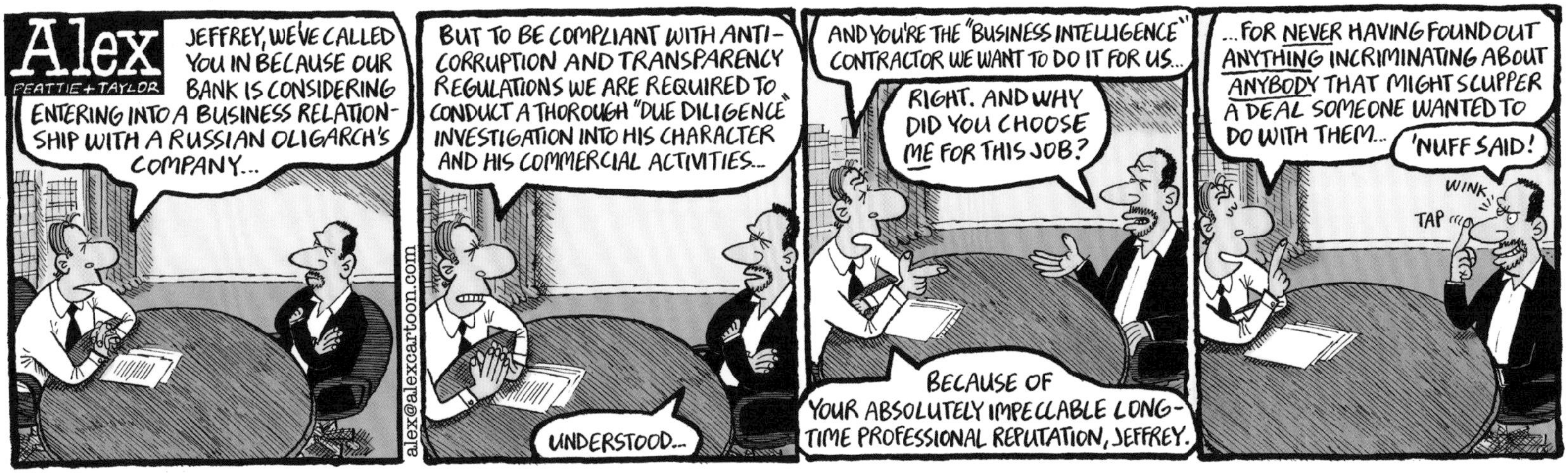
Alex
PEATTIE + TAYLOR
JEFFREY, WE'VE CALLED YOU IN BECAUSE OUR BANK IS CONSIDERING ENTERING INTO A BUSINESS RELATIONSHIP WITH A RUSSIAN OLIGARCH'S COMPANY...
alex@alexcartoon.com
BUT TO BE COMPLIANT WITH ANTI-CORRUPTION AND TRANSPARENCY REGULATIONS WE ARE REQUIRED TO CONDUCT A THOROUGH "DUE DILIGENCE" INVESTIGATION INTO HIS CHARACTER AND HIS COMMERCIAL ACTIVITIES...
UNDERSTOOD...
AND YOU'RE THE "BUSINESS INTELLIGENCE" CONTRACTOR WE WANT TO DO IT FOR US...
RIGHT. AND WHY DID YOU CHOOSE ME FOR THIS JOB?
BECAUSE OF YOUR ABSOLUTELY IMPECCABLE LONG-TIME PROFESSIONAL REPUTATION, JEFFREY.
...FOR NEVER HAVING FOUND OUT ANYTHING INCRIMINATING ABOUT ANYBODY THAT MIGHT SCUPPER A DEAL SOMEONE WANTED TO DO WITH THEM...
'NUFF SAID!
WINK
TAP

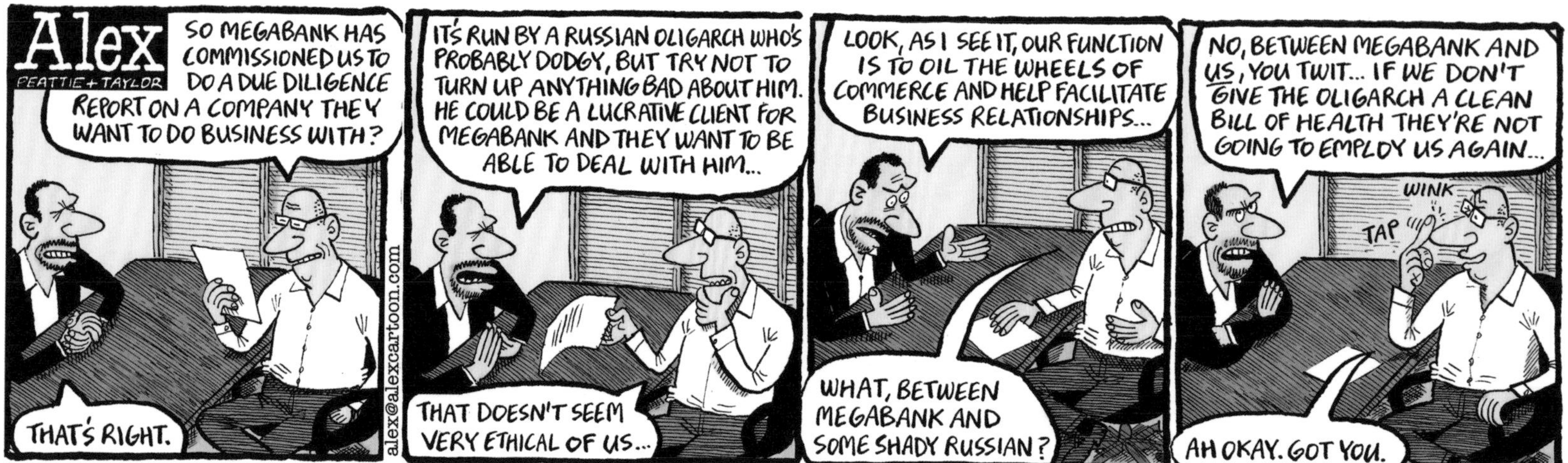
Alex
PEATTIE + TAYLOR
SO MEGABANK HAS COMMISSIONED US TO DO A DUE DILIGENCE REPORT ON A COMPANY THEY WANT TO DO BUSINESS WITH?
THAT'S RIGHT.
IT'S RUN BY A RUSSIAN OLIGARCH WHO'S PROBABLY DODGY, BUT TRY NOT TO TURN UP ANYTHING BAD ABOUT HIM. HE COULD BE A LUCRATIVE CLIENT FOR MEGABANK AND THEY WANT TO BE ABLE TO DEAL WITH HIM...
THAT DOESN'T SEEM VERY ETHICAL OF US...
alex@alexcartoon.com
LOOK, AS I SEE IT, OUR FUNCTION IS TO OIL THE WHEELS OF COMMERCE AND HELP FACILITATE BUSINESS RELATIONSHIPS...
WHAT, BETWEEN MEGABANK AND SOME SHADY RUSSIAN?
NO, BETWEEN MEGABANK AND US, YOU TWIT... IF WE DON'T GIVE THE OLIGARCH A CLEAN BILL OF HEALTH THEY'RE NOT GOING TO EMPLOY US AGAIN...
WINK
TAP
AH OKAY. GOT YOU.

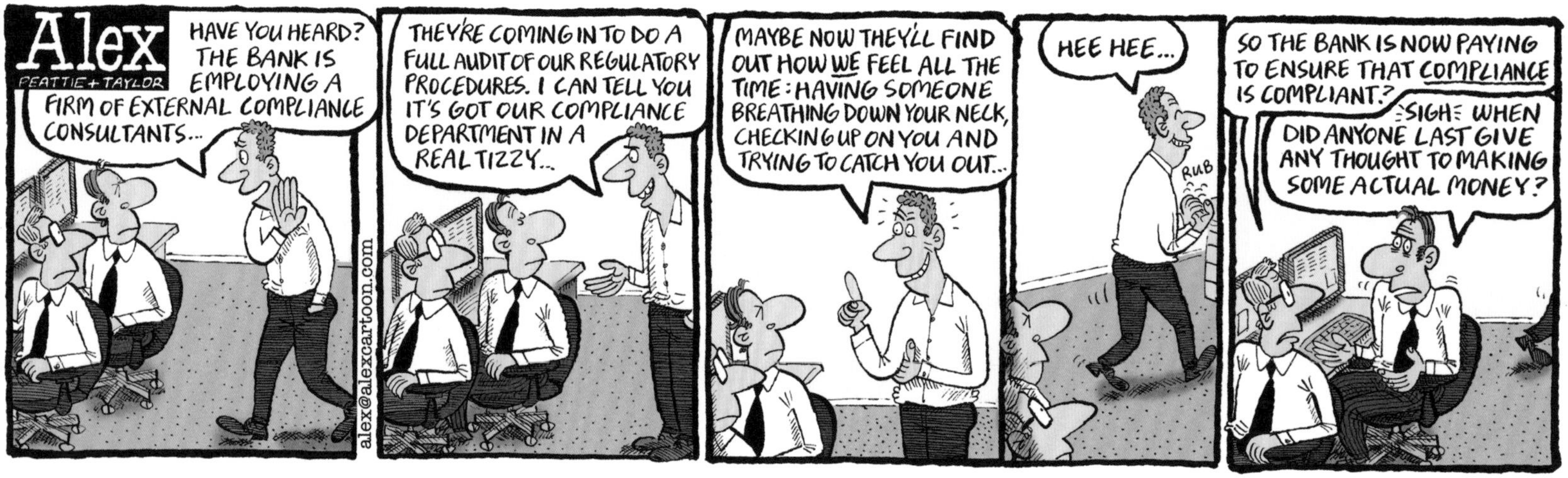
Alex
PEATTIE + TAYLOR
HAVE YOU HEARD? THE BANK IS EMPLOYING A FIRM OF EXTERNAL COMPLIANCE CONSULTANTS...
THEY'RE COMING IN TO DO A FULL AUDIT OF OUR REGULATORY PROCEDURES. I CAN TELL YOU IT'S GOT OUR COMPLIANCE DEPARTMENT IN A REAL TIZZY...
alex@alexcartoon.com
MAYBE NOW THEY'LL FIND OUT HOW WE FEEL ALL THE TIME: HAVING SOMEONE BREATHING DOWN YOUR NECK, CHECKING UP ON YOU AND TRYING TO CATCH YOU OUT...
HEE HEE...
RUB
SO THE BANK IS NOW PAYING TO ENSURE THAT COMPLIANCE IS COMPLIANT?
SIGH
WHEN DID ANYONE LAST GIVE ANY THOUGHT TO MAKING SOME ACTUAL MONEY?

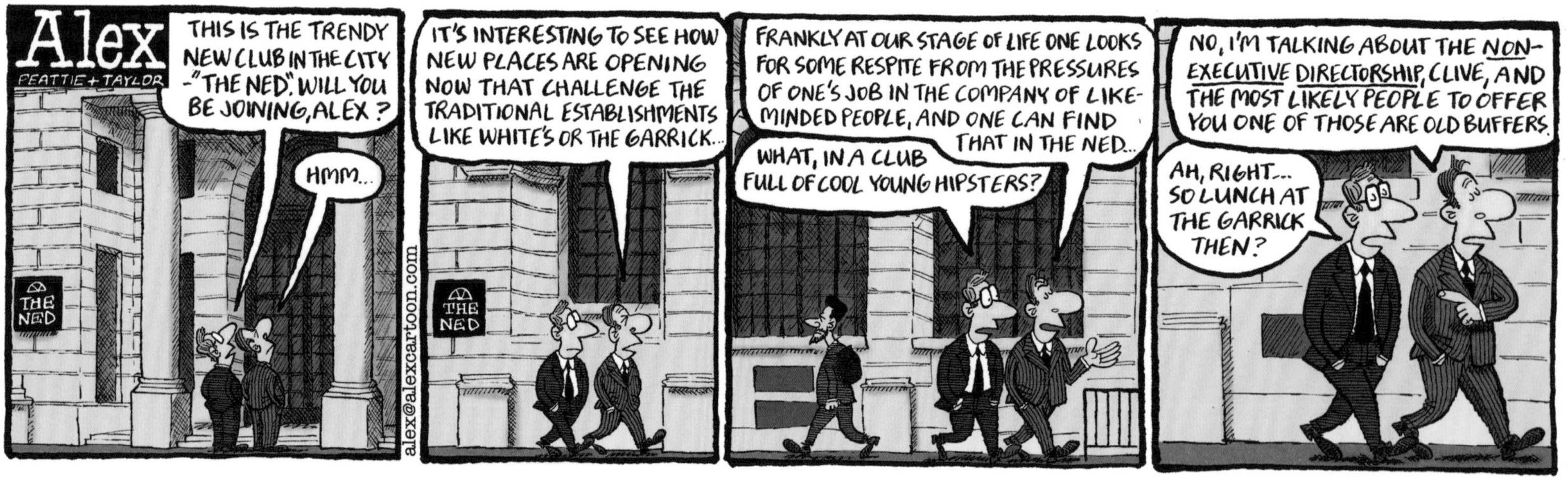
Alex
PEATTIE + TAYLOR
THIS IS THE TRENDY NEW CLUB IN THE CITY - "THE NED". WILL YOU BE JOINING, ALEX?
HMM...
THE NED
IT'S INTERESTING TO SEE HOW NEW PLACES ARE OPENING NOW THAT CHALLENGE THE TRADITIONAL ESTABLISHMENTS LIKE WHITE'S OR THE GARRICK...
THE NED
alex@alexcartoon.com
FRANKLY AT OUR STAGE OF LIFE ONE LOOKS FOR SOME RESPITE FROM THE PRESSURES OF ONE'S JOB IN THE COMPANY OF LIKE-MINDED PEOPLE, AND ONE CAN FIND THAT IN THE NED...
WHAT, IN A CLUB FULL OF COOL YOUNG HIPSTERS?
NO, I'M TALKING ABOUT THE NON-EXECUTIVE DIRECTORSHIP, CLIVE, AND THE MOST LIKELY PEOPLE TO OFFER YOU ONE OF THOSE ARE OLD BUFFERS.
AH, RIGHT... SO LUNCH AT THE GARRICK THEN?

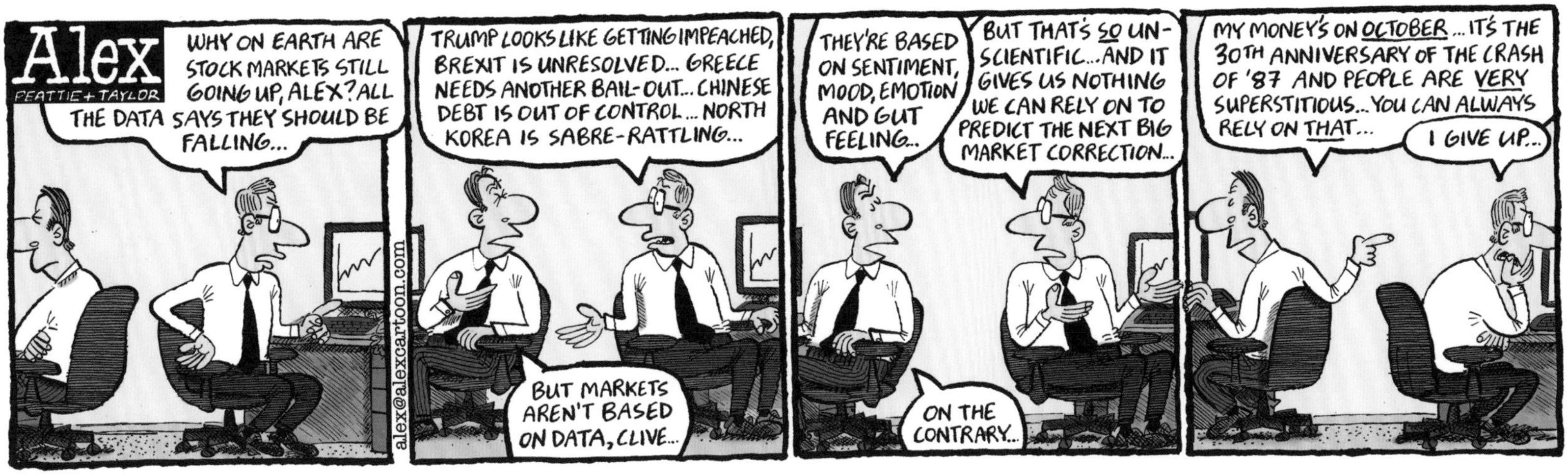
Alex
PEATTIE + TAYLOR
WHY ON EARTH ARE STOCK MARKETS STILL GOING UP, ALEX? ALL THE DATA SAYS THEY SHOULD BE FALLING...
alex@alexcartoon.com
TRUMP LOOKS LIKE GETTING IMPEACHED, BREXIT IS UNRESOLVED... GREECE NEEDS ANOTHER BAIL-OUT... CHINESE DEBT IS OUT OF CONTROL... NORTH KOREA IS SABRE-RATTLING...
BUT MARKETS AREN'T BASED ON DATA, CLIVE...
THEY'RE BASED ON SENTIMENT, MOOD, EMOTION AND GUT FEELING...
BUT THAT'S SO UN-SCIENTIFIC... AND IT GIVES US NOTHING WE CAN RELY ON TO PREDICT THE NEXT BIG MARKET CORRECTION...
ON THE CONTRARY...
MY MONEY'S ON OCTOBER... IT'S THE 30TH ANNIVERSARY OF THE CRASH OF '87 AND PEOPLE ARE VERY SUPERSTITIOUS... YOU CAN ALWAYS RELY ON THAT...
I GIVE UP...

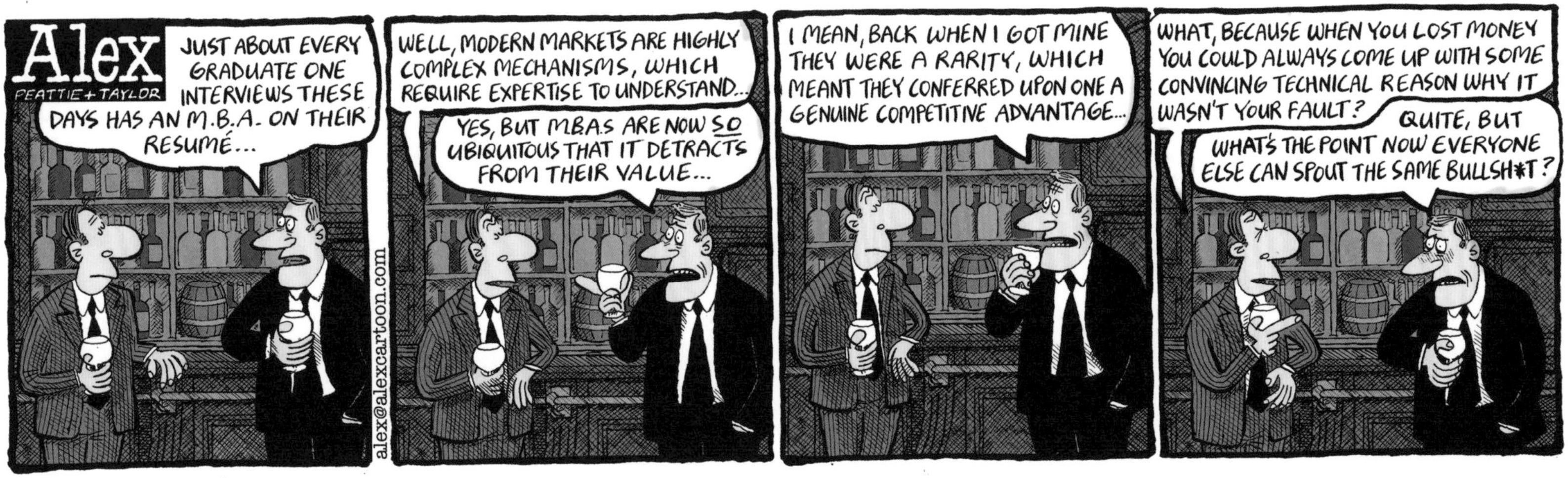
Alex
PEATTIE + TAYLOR
JUST ABOUT EVERY GRADUATE ONE INTERVIEWS THESE DAYS HAS AN M.B.A. ON THEIR RESUMÉ...
alex@alexcartoon.com
WELL, MODERN MARKETS ARE HIGHLY COMPLEX MECHANISMS, WHICH REQUIRE EXPERTISE TO UNDERSTAND...
YES, BUT MBAS ARE NOW SO UBIQUITOUS THAT IT DETRACTS FROM THEIR VALUE...
I MEAN, BACK WHEN I GOT MINE THEY WERE A RARITY, WHICH MEANT THEY CONFERRED UPON ONE A GENUINE COMPETITIVE ADVANTAGE...
WHAT, BECAUSE WHEN YOU LOST MONEY YOU COULD ALWAYS COME UP WITH SOME CONVINCING TECHNICAL REASON WHY IT WASN'T YOUR FAULT?
QUITE, BUT WHAT'S THE POINT NOW EVERYONE ELSE CAN SPOUT THE SAME BULLSH*T?

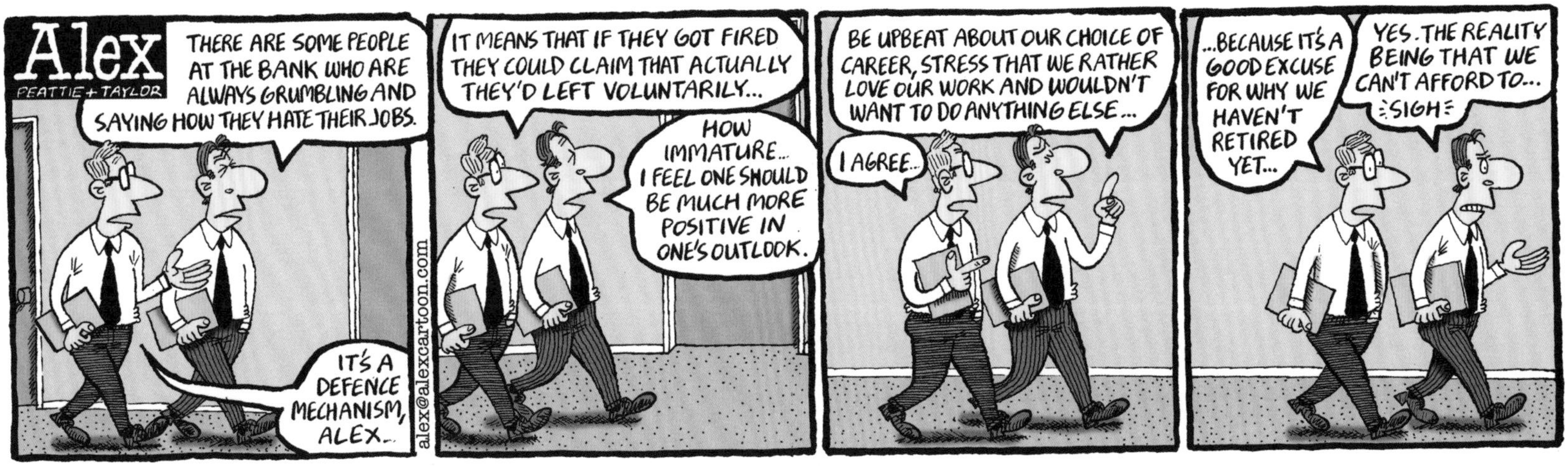
Alex
PEATTIE + TAYLOR
THERE ARE SOME PEOPLE AT THE BANK WHO ARE ALWAYS GRUMBLING AND SAYING HOW THEY HATE THEIR JOBS.
IT'S A DEFENCE MECHANISM, ALEX...
alex@alexcartoon.com
IT MEANS THAT IF THEY GOT FIRED THEY COULD CLAIM THAT ACTUALLY THEY'D LEFT VOLUNTARILY...
HOW IMMATURE... I FEEL ONE SHOULD BE MUCH MORE POSITIVE IN ONE'S OUTLOOK.
BE UPBEAT ABOUT OUR CHOICE OF CAREER, STRESS THAT WE RATHER LOVE OUR WORK AND WOULDN'T WANT TO DO ANYTHING ELSE...
I AGREE...
...BECAUSE IT'S A GOOD EXCUSE FOR WHY WE HAVEN'T RETIRED YET...
YES. THE REALITY BEING THAT WE CAN'T AFFORD TO...
SIGH

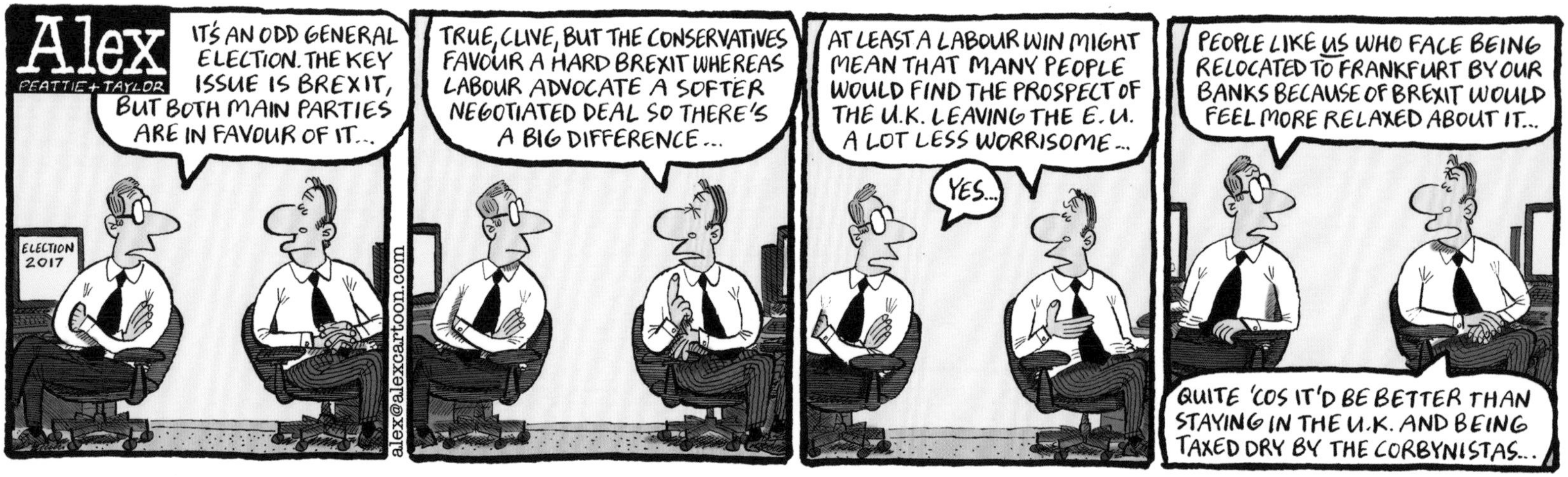
Alex
PEATTIE + TAYLOR
IT'S AN ODD GENERAL ELECTION. THE KEY ISSUE IS BREXIT, BUT BOTH MAIN PARTIES ARE IN FAVOUR OF IT...
ELECTION 2017
alex@alexcartoon.com
TRUE, CLIVE, BUT THE CONSERVATIVES FAVOUR A HARD BREXIT WHEREAS LABOUR ADVOCATE A SOFTER NEGOTIATED DEAL SO THERE'S A BIG DIFFERENCE...
AT LEAST A LABOUR WIN MIGHT MEAN THAT MANY PEOPLE WOULD FIND THE PROSPECT OF THE U.K. LEAVING THE E.U. A LOT LESS WORRISOME...
YES...
PEOPLE LIKE US WHO FACE BEING RELOCATED TO FRANKFURT BY OUR BANKS BECAUSE OF BREXIT WOULD FEEL MORE RELAXED ABOUT IT...
QUITE 'COS IT'D BE BETTER THAN STAYING IN THE U.K. AND BEING TAXED DRY BY THE CORBYNISTAS...

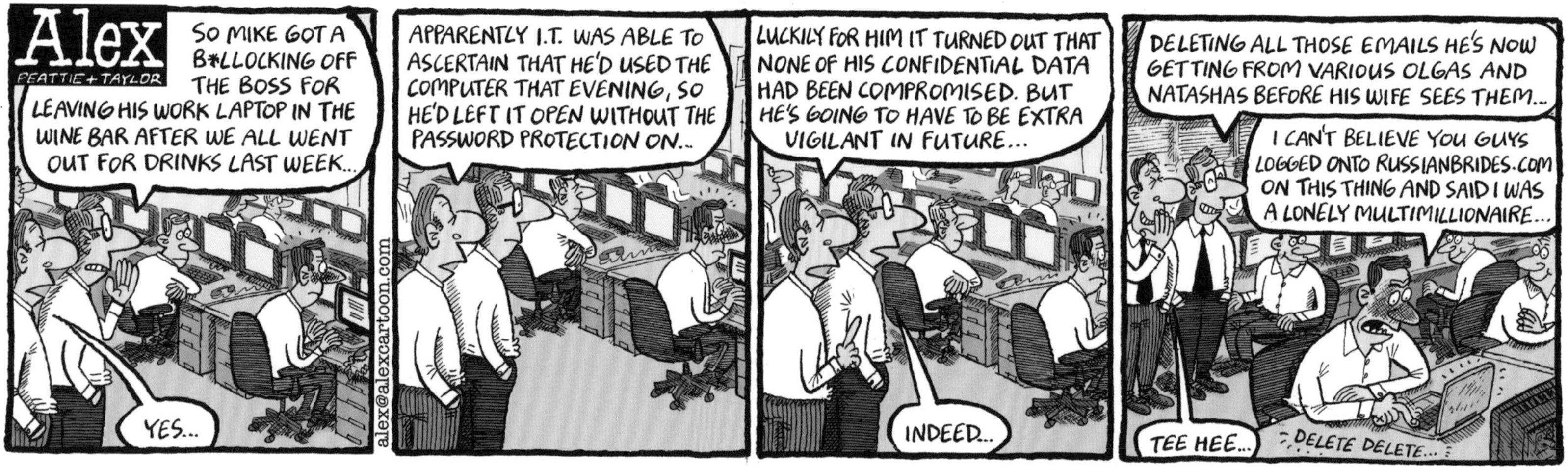
Alex
PEATTIE + TAYLOR
SO MIKE GOT A B*LLOCKING OFF THE BOSS FOR LEAVING HIS WORK LAPTOP IN THE WINE BAR AFTER WE ALL WENT OUT FOR DRINKS LAST WEEK...
YES...
alex@alexcartoon.com
APPARENTLY I.T. WAS ABLE TO ASCERTAIN THAT HE'D USED THE COMPUTER THAT EVENING, SO HE'D LEFT IT OPEN WITHOUT THE PASSWORD PROTECTION ON...
LUCKILY FOR HIM IT TURNED OUT THAT NONE OF HIS CONFIDENTIAL DATA HAD BEEN COMPROMISED. BUT HE'S GOING TO HAVE TO BE EXTRA VIGILANT IN FUTURE...
INDEED...
DELETING ALL THOSE EMAILS HE'S NOW GETTING FROM VARIOUS OLGAS AND NATASHAS BEFORE HIS WIFE SEES THEM...
I CAN'T BELIEVE YOU GUYS LOGGED ONTO RUSSIANBRIDES.COM ON THIS THING AND SAID I WAS A LONELY MULTIMILLIONAIRE...
TEE HEE...
DELETE DELETE...

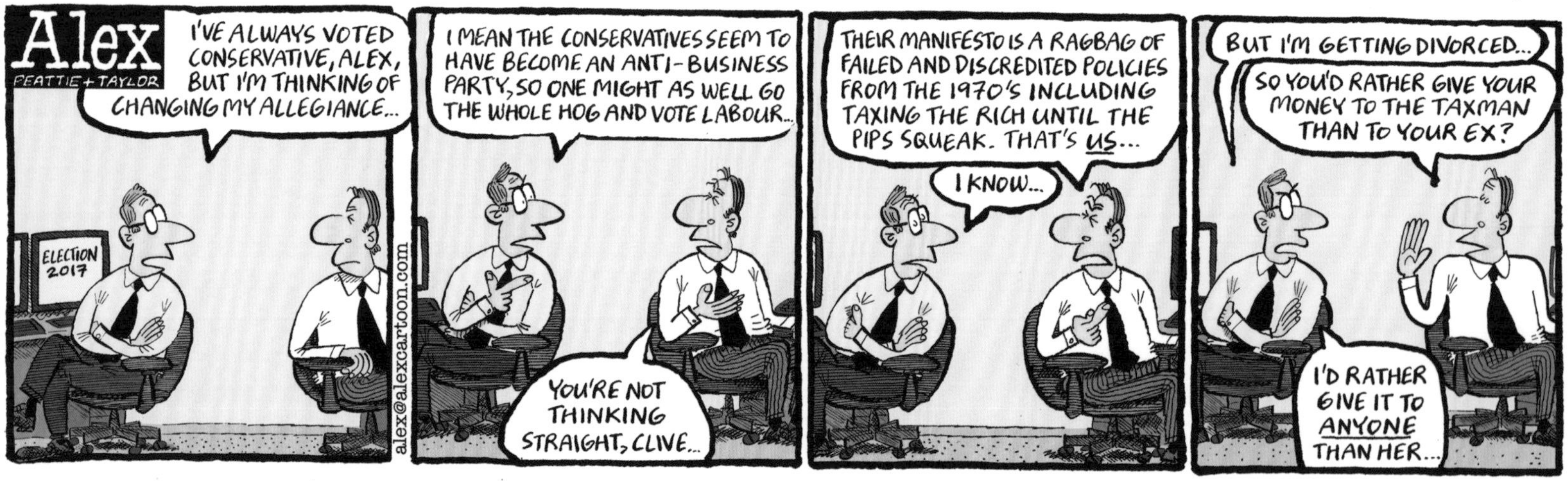
Alex
PEATTIE + TAYLOR
I'VE ALWAYS VOTED CONSERVATIVE, ALEX, BUT I'M THINKING OF CHANGING MY ALLEGIANCE...
ELECTION 2017
alex@alexcartoon.com
I MEAN THE CONSERVATIVES SEEM TO HAVE BECOME AN ANTI-BUSINESS PARTY, SO ONE MIGHT AS WELL GO THE WHOLE HOG AND VOTE LABOUR...
YOU'RE NOT THINKING STRAIGHT, CLIVE...
THEIR MANIFESTO IS A RAGBAG OF FAILED AND DISCREDITED POLICIES FROM THE 1970'S INCLUDING TAXING THE RICH UNTIL THE PIPS SQUEAK. THAT'S US...
I KNOW...
BUT I'M GETTING DIVORCED...
SO YOU'D RATHER GIVE YOUR MONEY TO THE TAXMAN THAN TO YOUR EX?
I'D RATHER GIVE IT TO ANYONE THAN HER...

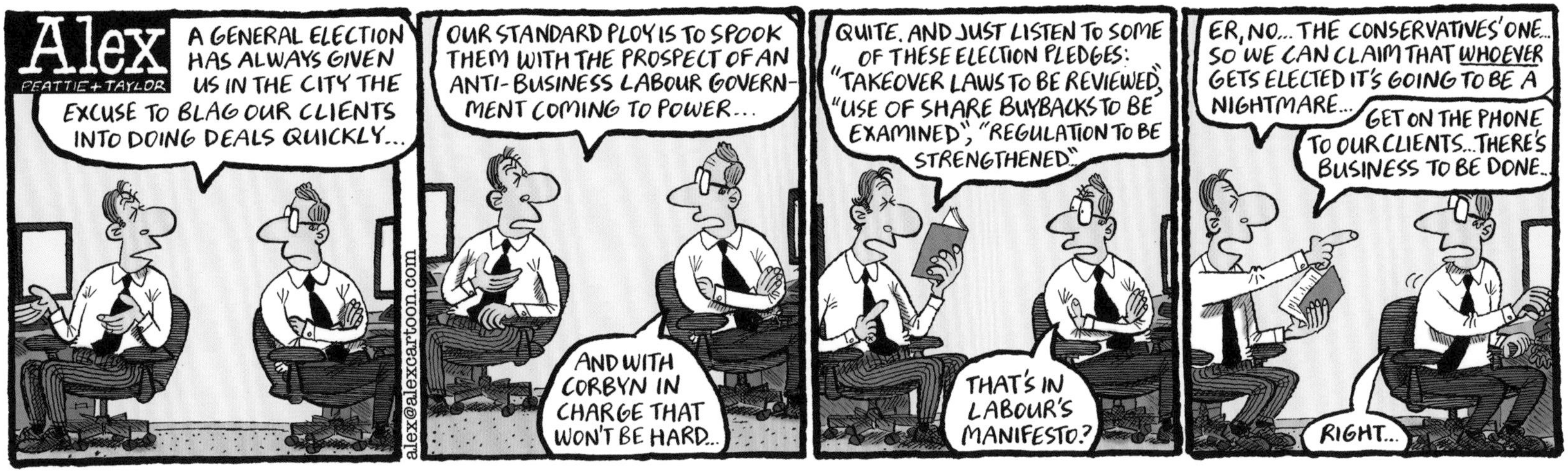
Alex
PEATTIE + TAYLOR
A GENERAL ELECTION HAS ALWAYS GIVEN US IN THE CITY THE EXCUSE TO BLAG OUR CLIENTS INTO DOING DEALS QUICKLY...
OUR STANDARD PLOY IS TO SPOOK THEM WITH THE PROSPECT OF AN ANTI-BUSINESS LABOUR GOVERNMENT COMING TO POWER...
AND WITH CORBYN IN CHARGE THAT WON'T BE HARD...
QUITE. AND JUST LISTEN TO SOME OF THESE ELECTION PLEDGES: "TAKEOVER LAWS TO BE REVIEWED", "USE OF SHARE BUYBACKS TO BE EXAMINED", "REGULATION TO BE STRENGTHENED"...
THAT'S IN LABOUR'S MANIFESTO?
ER, NO... THE CONSERVATIVES' ONE... SO WE CAN CLAIM THAT WHOEVER GETS ELECTED IT'S GOING TO BE A NIGHTMARE...
GET ON THE PHONE TO OUR CLIENTS... THERE'S BUSINESS TO BE DONE...
RIGHT...
alex@alexcartoon.com

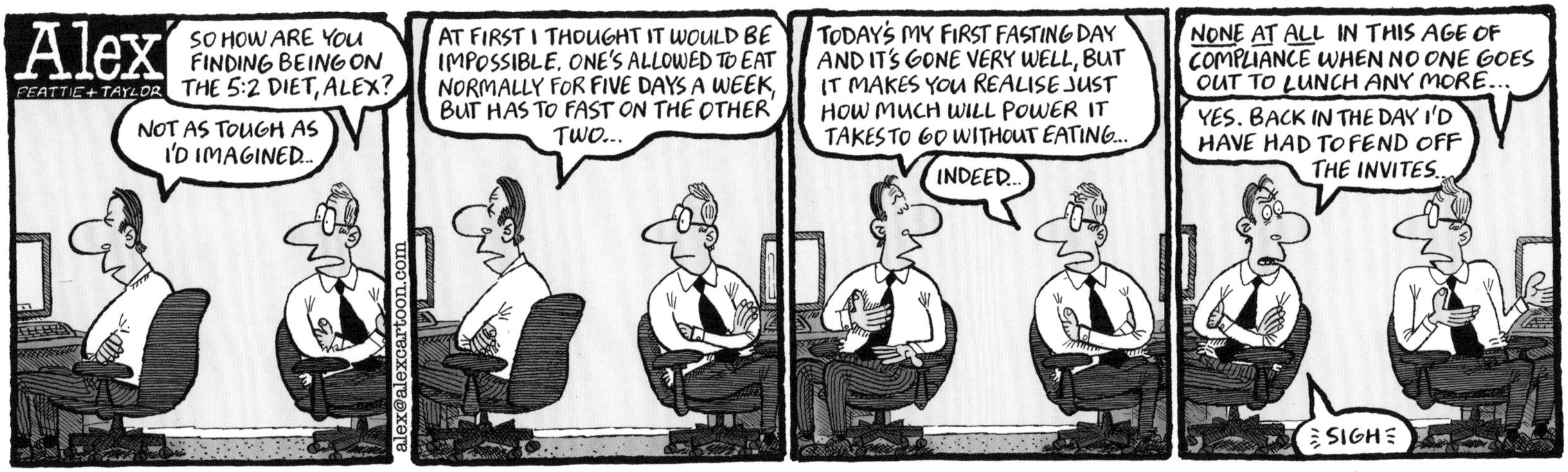
Alex
PEATTIE + TAYLOR
SO HOW ARE YOU FINDING BEING ON THE 5:2 DIET, ALEX?
NOT AS TOUGH AS I'D IMAGINED...
AT FIRST I THOUGHT IT WOULD BE IMPOSSIBLE. ONE'S ALLOWED TO EAT NORMALLY FOR FIVE DAYS A WEEK, BUT HAS TO FAST ON THE OTHER TWO...
TODAY'S MY FIRST FASTING DAY AND IT'S GONE VERY WELL, BUT IT MAKES YOU REALISE JUST HOW MUCH WILL POWER IT TAKES TO GO WITHOUT EATING...
INDEED...
NONE AT ALL IN THIS AGE OF COMPLIANCE WHEN NO ONE GOES OUT TO LUNCH ANY MORE...
YES. BACK IN THE DAY I'D HAVE HAD TO FEND OFF THE INVITES...
SIGH
alex@alexcartoon.com

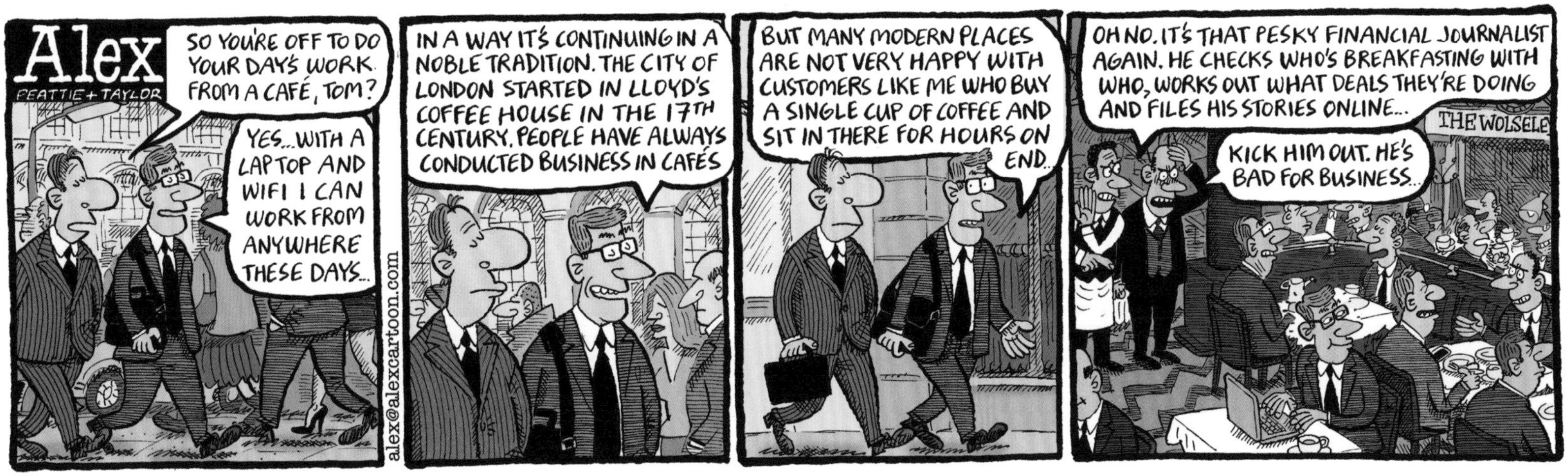
Alex
PEATTIE + TAYLOR
SO YOU'RE OFF TO DO YOUR DAY'S WORK FROM A CAFÉ, TOM?
YES... WITH A LAPTOP AND WIFI I CAN WORK FROM ANYWHERE THESE DAYS...
IN A WAY IT'S CONTINUING IN A NOBLE TRADITION. THE CITY OF LONDON STARTED IN LLOYD'S COFFEE HOUSE IN THE 17TH CENTURY. PEOPLE HAVE ALWAYS CONDUCTED BUSINESS IN CAFÉS
BUT MANY MODERN PLACES ARE NOT VERY HAPPY WITH CUSTOMERS LIKE ME WHO BUY A SINGLE CUP OF COFFEE AND SIT IN THERE FOR HOURS ON END...
OH NO. IT'S THAT PESKY FINANCIAL JOURNALIST AGAIN. HE CHECKS WHO'S BREAKFASTING WITH WHO, WORKS OUT WHAT DEALS THEY'RE DOING AND FILES HIS STORIES ONLINE...
KICK HIM OUT. HE'S BAD FOR BUSINESS...
alex@alexcartoon.com

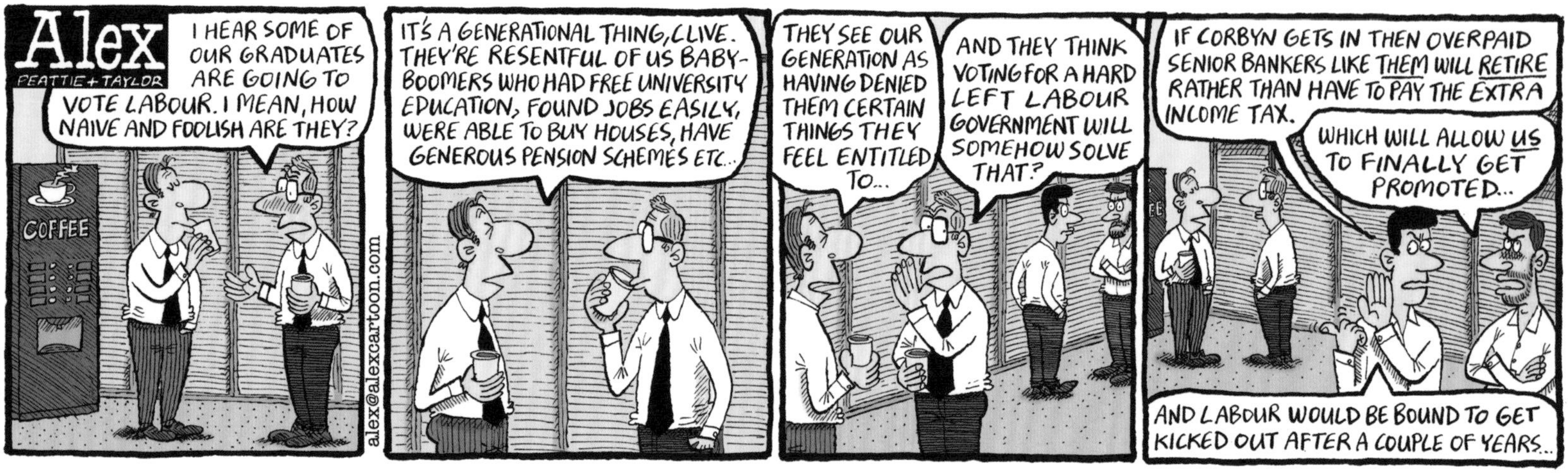
Alex
PEATTIE + TAYLOR
I HEAR SOME OF OUR GRADUATES ARE GOING TO VOTE LABOUR. I MEAN, HOW NAIVE AND FOOLISH ARE THEY?
COFFEE
alex@alexcartoon.com
IT'S A GENERATIONAL THING, CLIVE. THEY'RE RESENTFUL OF US BABY-BOOMERS WHO HAD FREE UNIVERSITY EDUCATION, FOUND JOBS EASILY, WERE ABLE TO BUY HOUSES, HAVE GENEROUS PENSION SCHEMES ETC...
THEY SEE OUR GENERATION AS HAVING DENIED THEM CERTAIN THINGS THEY FEEL ENTITLED TO...
AND THEY THINK VOTING FOR A HARD LEFT LABOUR GOVERNMENT WILL SOMEHOW SOLVE THAT?
IF CORBYN GETS IN THEN OVERPAID SENIOR BANKERS LIKE THEM WILL RETIRE RATHER THAN HAVE TO PAY THE EXTRA INCOME TAX.
WHICH WILL ALLOW US TO FINALLY GET PROMOTED...
AND LABOUR WOULD BE BOUND TO GET KICKED OUT AFTER A COUPLE OF YEARS...

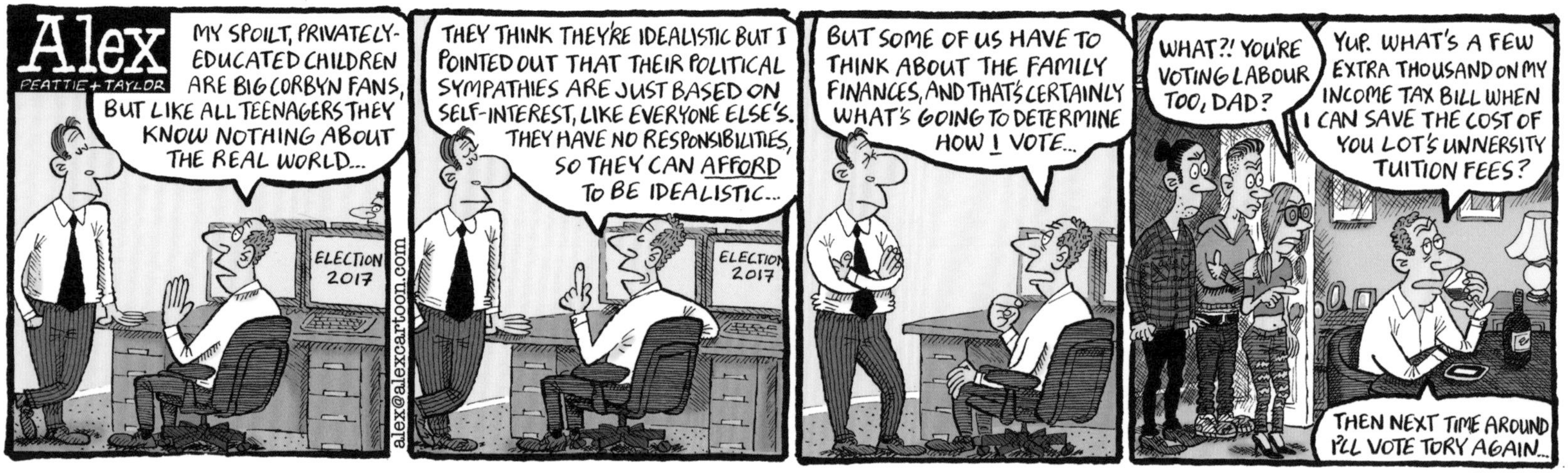
Alex
PEATTIE + TAYLOR
MY SPOILT, PRIVATELY-EDUCATED CHILDREN ARE BIG CORBYN FANS, BUT LIKE ALL TEENAGERS THEY KNOW NOTHING ABOUT THE REAL WORLD...
ELECTION 2017
alex@alexcartoon.com
THEY THINK THEY'RE IDEALISTIC BUT I POINTED OUT THAT THEIR POLITICAL SYMPATHIES ARE JUST BASED ON SELF-INTEREST, LIKE EVERYONE ELSE'S. THEY HAVE NO RESPONSIBILITIES, SO THEY CAN AFFORD TO BE IDEALISTIC...
ELECTION 2017
BUT SOME OF US HAVE TO THINK ABOUT THE FAMILY FINANCES, AND THAT'S CERTAINLY WHAT'S GOING TO DETERMINE HOW I VOTE...
WHAT?! YOU'RE VOTING LABOUR TOO, DAD?
YUP. WHAT'S A FEW EXTRA THOUSAND ON MY INCOME TAX BILL WHEN I CAN SAVE THE COST OF YOU LOT'S UNIVERSITY TUITION FEES?
THEN NEXT TIME AROUND I'LL VOTE TORY AGAIN...

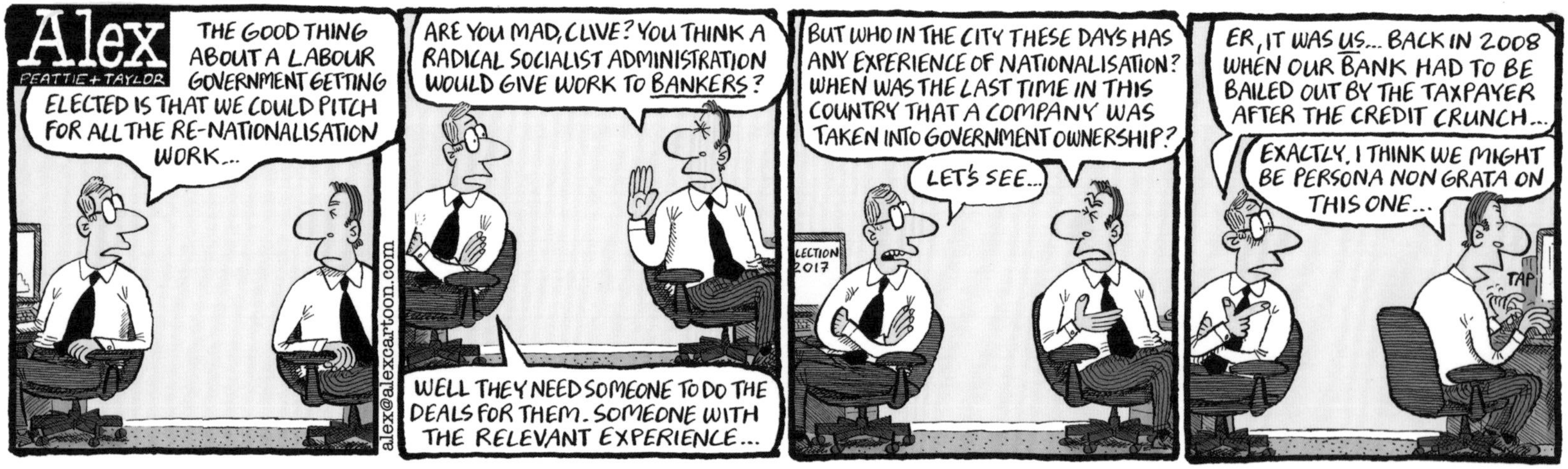
Alex
PEATTIE + TAYLOR
THE GOOD THING ABOUT A LABOUR GOVERNMENT GETTING ELECTED IS THAT WE COULD PITCH FOR ALL THE RE-NATIONALISATION WORK...
ARE YOU MAD, CLIVE? YOU THINK A RADICAL SOCIALIST ADMINISTRATION WOULD GIVE WORK TO BANKERS?
alex@alexcartoon.com
WELL THEY NEED SOMEONE TO DO THE DEALS FOR THEM. SOMEONE WITH THE RELEVANT EXPERIENCE...
BUT WHO IN THE CITY THESE DAYS HAS ANY EXPERIENCE OF NATIONALISATION? WHEN WAS THE LAST TIME IN THIS COUNTRY THAT A COMPANY WAS TAKEN INTO GOVERNMENT OWNERSHIP?
LET'S SEE...
ER, IT WAS US... BACK IN 2008 WHEN OUR BANK HAD TO BE BAILED OUT BY THE TAXPAYER AFTER THE CREDIT CRUNCH...
EXACTLY. I THINK WE MIGHT BE PERSONA NON GRATA ON THIS ONE...
TAP

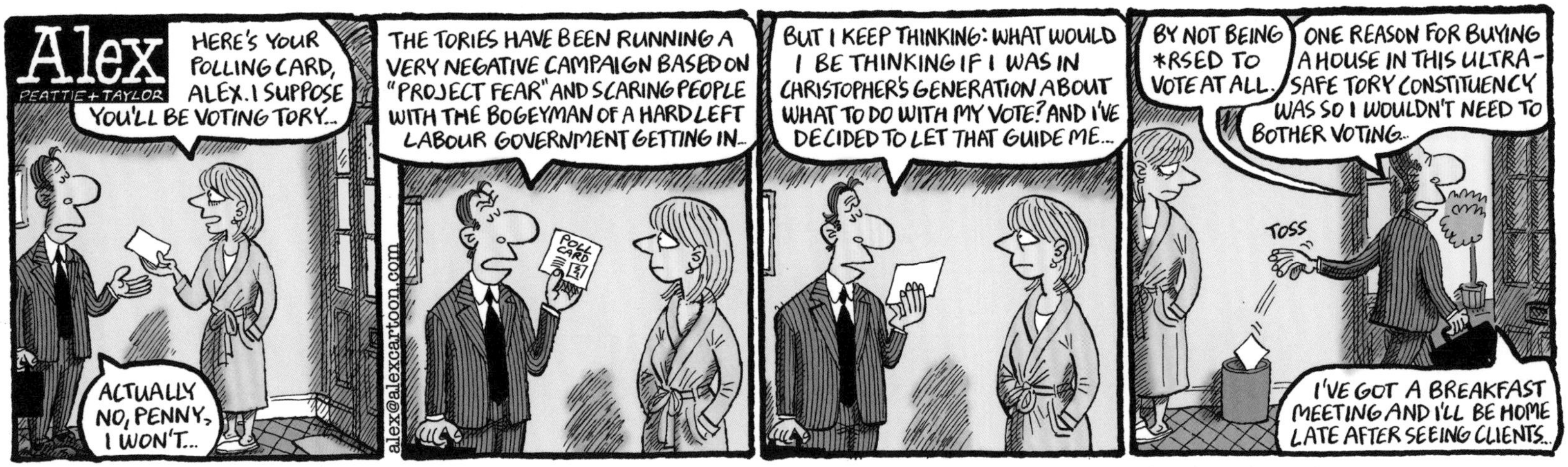
Alex
PEATTIE + TAYLOR
HERE'S YOUR POLLING CARD, ALEX. I SUPPOSE YOU'LL BE VOTING TORY...
ACTUALLY NO, PENNY, I WON'T...
alex@alexcartoon.com
THE TORIES HAVE BEEN RUNNING A VERY NEGATIVE CAMPAIGN BASED ON "PROJECT FEAR" AND SCARING PEOPLE WITH THE BOGEYMAN OF A HARD LEFT LABOUR GOVERNMENT GETTING IN...
POLL CARD
BUT I KEEP THINKING: WHAT WOULD I BE THINKING IF I WAS IN CHRISTOPHER'S GENERATION ABOUT WHAT TO DO WITH MY VOTE? AND I'VE DECIDED TO LET THAT GUIDE ME...
ONE REASON FOR BUYING A HOUSE IN THIS ULTRA-SAFE TORY CONSTITUENCY WAS SO I WOULDN'T NEED TO BOTHER VOTING...
BY NOT BEING *RSED TO VOTE AT ALL.
TOSS
I'VE GOT A BREAKFAST MEETING AND I'LL BE HOME LATE AFTER SEEING CLIENTS...

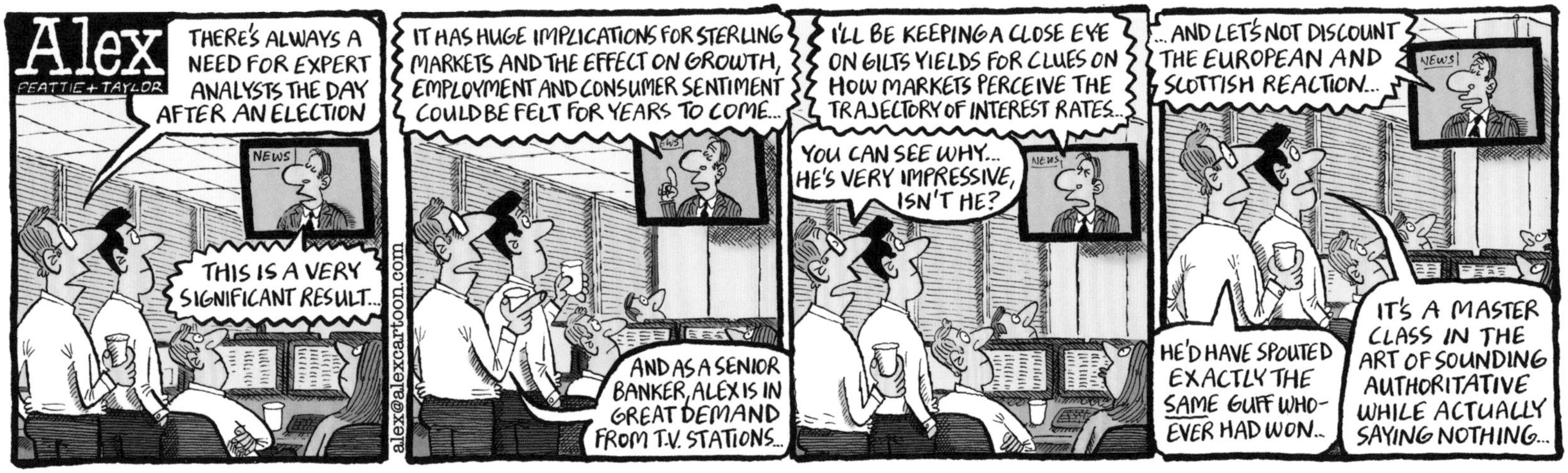
Alex
PEATTIE + TAYLOR
THERE'S ALWAYS A NEED FOR EXPERT ANALYSTS THE DAY AFTER AN ELECTION
NEWS
THIS IS A VERY SIGNIFICANT RESULT...
alex@alexcartoon.com
IT HAS HUGE IMPLICATIONS FOR STERLING MARKETS AND THE EFFECT ON GROWTH, EMPLOYMENT AND CONSUMER SENTIMENT COULD BE FELT FOR YEARS TO COME...
AND AS A SENIOR BANKER, ALEX IS IN GREAT DEMAND FROM T.V. STATIONS...
I'LL BE KEEPING A CLOSE EYE ON GILTS YIELDS FOR CLUES ON HOW MARKETS PERCEIVE THE TRAJECTORY OF INTEREST RATES...
YOU CAN SEE WHY... HE'S VERY IMPRESSIVE, ISN'T HE?
NEWS
...AND LET'S NOT DISCOUNT THE EUROPEAN AND SCOTTISH REACTION...
NEWS
HE'D HAVE SPOUTED EXACTLY THE SAME GUFF WHO-EVER HAD WON...
IT'S A MASTER CLASS IN THE ART OF SOUNDING AUTHORITATIVE WHILE ACTUALLY SAYING NOTHING...

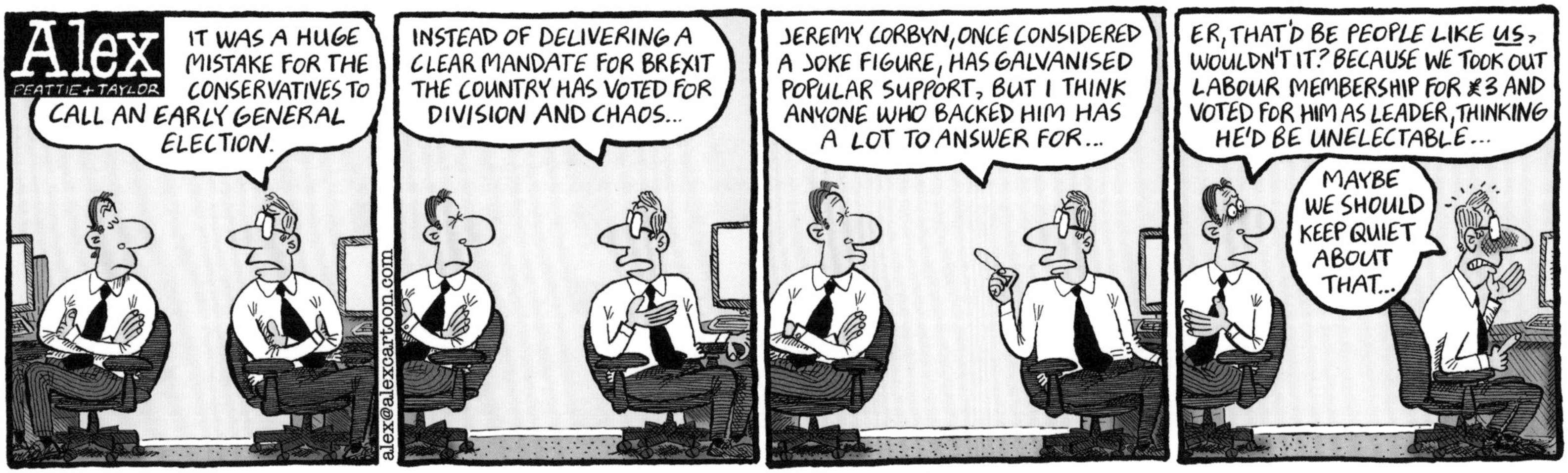
Alex
PEATTIE + TAYLOR
IT WAS A HUGE MISTAKE FOR THE CONSERVATIVES TO CALL AN EARLY GENERAL ELECTION.
alex@alexcartoon.com
INSTEAD OF DELIVERING A CLEAR MANDATE FOR BREXIT THE COUNTRY HAS VOTED FOR DIVISION AND CHAOS...
JEREMY CORBYN, ONCE CONSIDERED A JOKE FIGURE, HAS GALVANISED POPULAR SUPPORT, BUT I THINK ANYONE WHO BACKED HIM HAS A LOT TO ANSWER FOR...
ER, THAT'D BE PEOPLE LIKE US, WOULDN'T IT? BECAUSE WE TOOK OUT LABOUR MEMBERSHIP FOR £3 AND VOTED FOR HIM AS LEADER, THINKING HE'D BE UNELECTABLE...
MAYBE WE SHOULD KEEP QUIET ABOUT THAT...

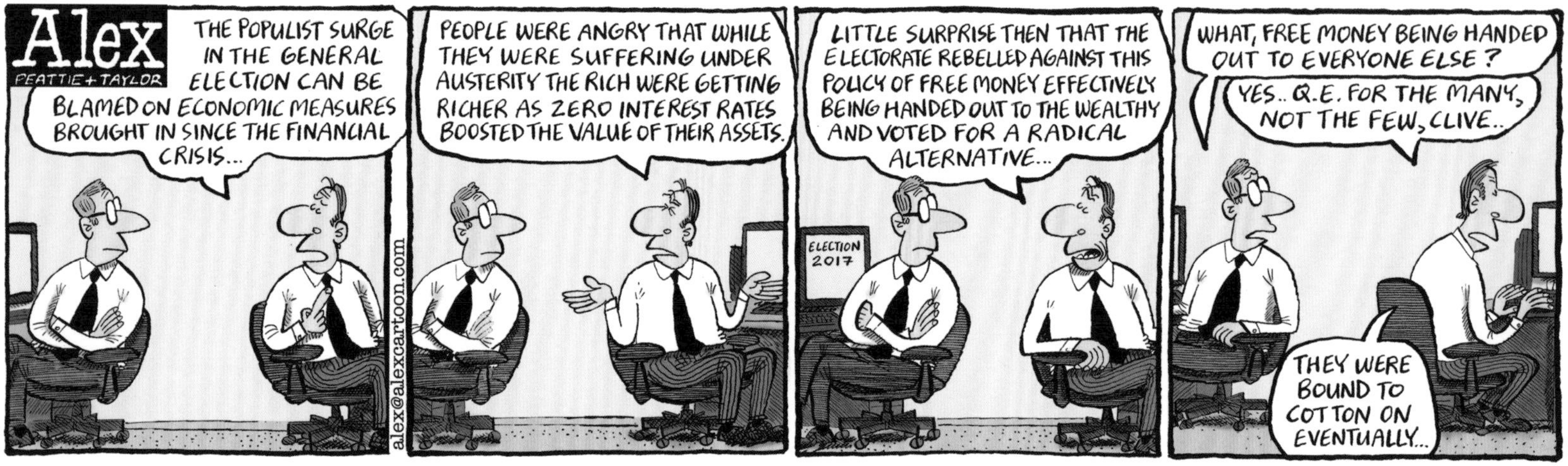
Alex
PEATTIE + TAYLOR
THE POPULIST SURGE IN THE GENERAL ELECTION CAN BE BLAMED ON ECONOMIC MEASURES BROUGHT IN SINCE THE FINANCIAL CRISIS...
alex@alexcartoon.com
PEOPLE WERE ANGRY THAT WHILE THEY WERE SUFFERING UNDER AUSTERITY THE RICH WERE GETTING RICHER AS ZERO INTEREST RATES BOOSTED THE VALUE OF THEIR ASSETS.
LITTLE SURPRISE THEN THAT THE ELECTORATE REBELLED AGAINST THIS POLICY OF FREE MONEY EFFECTIVELY BEING HANDED OUT TO THE WEALTHY AND VOTED FOR A RADICAL ALTERNATIVE...
ELECTION 2017
WHAT, FREE MONEY BEING HANDED OUT TO EVERYONE ELSE?
YES.. Q.E. FOR THE MANY, NOT THE FEW, CLIVE..
THEY WERE BOUND TO COTTON ON EVENTUALLY...

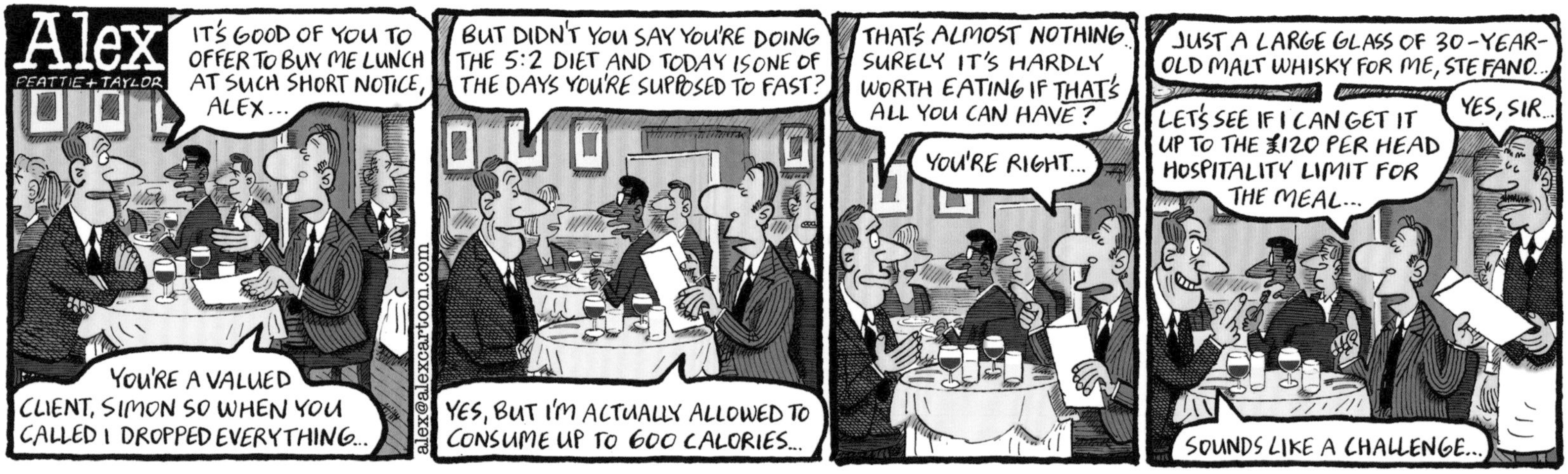
Alex
PEATTIE + TAYLOR
IT'S GOOD OF YOU TO OFFER TO BUY ME LUNCH AT SUCH SHORT NOTICE, ALEX...
YOU'RE A VALUED CLIENT, SIMON SO WHEN YOU CALLED I DROPPED EVERYTHING...
alex@alexcartoon.com
BUT DIDN'T YOU SAY YOU'RE DOING THE 5:2 DIET AND TODAY IS ONE OF THE DAYS YOU'RE SUPPOSED TO FAST?
YES, BUT I'M ACTUALLY ALLOWED TO CONSUME UP TO 600 CALORIES...
THAT'S ALMOST NOTHING. SURELY IT'S HARDLY WORTH EATING IF THAT'S ALL YOU CAN HAVE?
YOU'RE RIGHT...
JUST A LARGE GLASS OF 30-YEAR-OLD MALT WHISKY FOR ME, STEFANO...
YES, SIR...
LET'S SEE IF I CAN GET IT UP TO THE £120 PER HEAD HOSPITALITY LIMIT FOR THE MEAL...
SOUNDS LIKE A CHALLENGE...

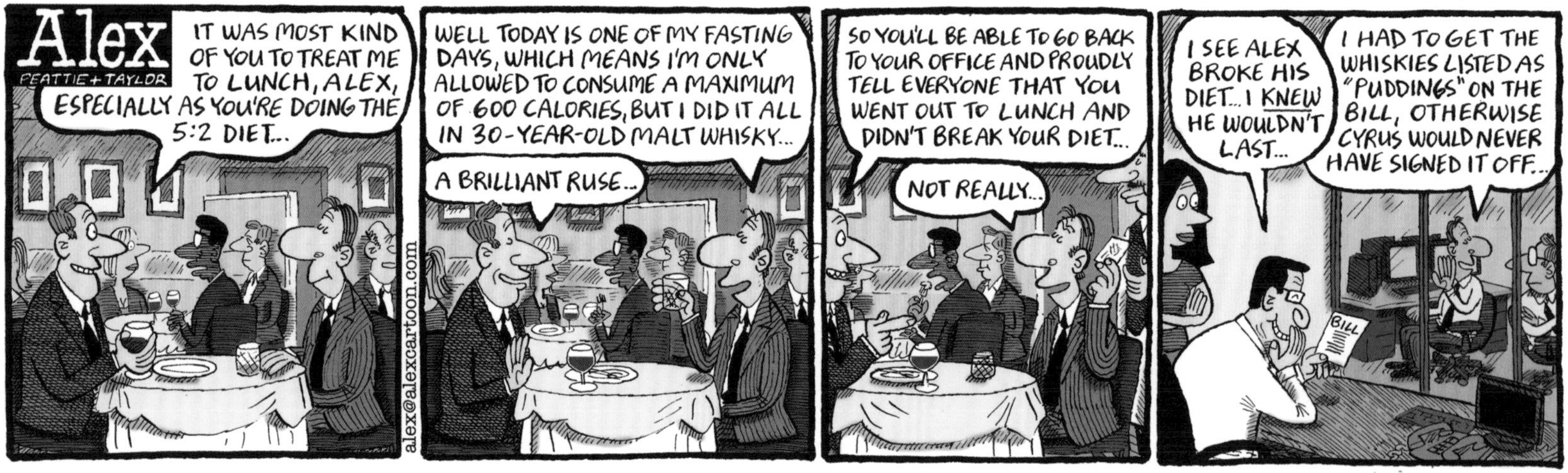
Alex
PEATTIE + TAYLOR
IT WAS MOST KIND OF YOU TO TREAT ME TO LUNCH, ALEX, ESPECIALLY AS YOU'RE DOING THE 5:2 DIET...
alex@alexcartoon.com
WELL TODAY IS ONE OF MY FASTING DAYS, WHICH MEANS I'M ONLY ALLOWED TO CONSUME A MAXIMUM OF 600 CALORIES, BUT I DID IT ALL IN 30-YEAR-OLD MALT WHISKY...
A BRILLIANT RUSE...
SO YOU'LL BE ABLE TO GO BACK TO YOUR OFFICE AND PROUDLY TELL EVERYONE THAT YOU WENT OUT TO LUNCH AND DIDN'T BREAK YOUR DIET...
NOT REALLY...
I SEE ALEX BROKE HIS DIET... I KNEW HE WOULDN'T LAST...
I HAD TO GET THE WHISKIES LISTED AS "PUDDINGS" ON THE BILL, OTHERWISE CYRUS WOULD NEVER HAVE SIGNED IT OFF...
BILL

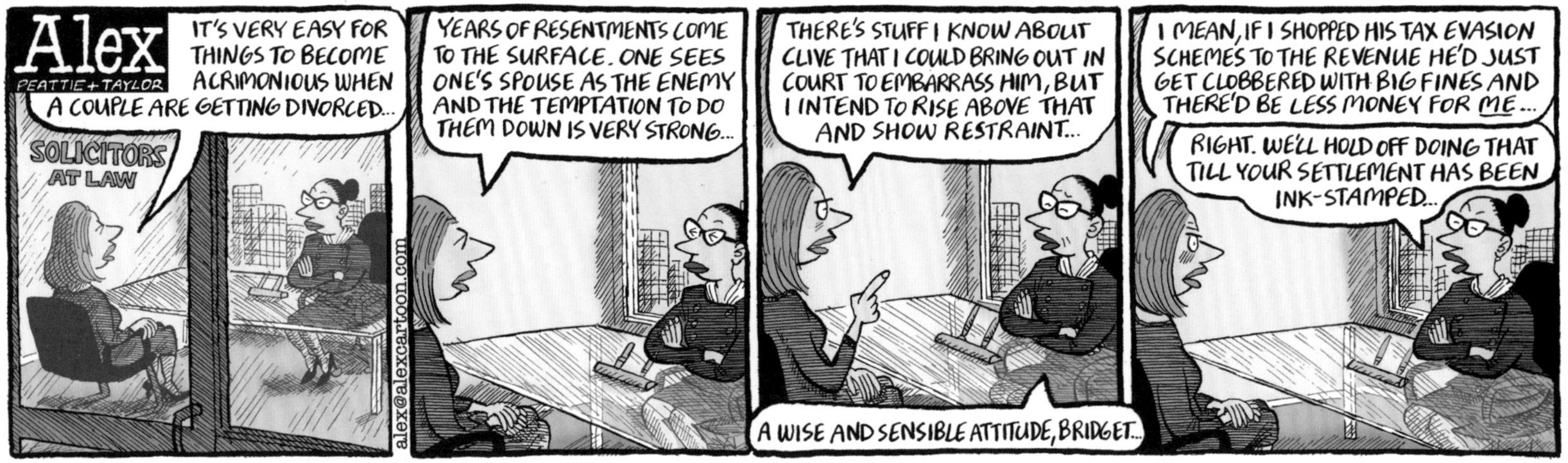
Alex
PEATTIE + TAYLOR
IT'S VERY EASY FOR THINGS TO BECOME ACRIMONIOUS WHEN A COUPLE ARE GETTING DIVORCED...
SOLICITORS AT LAW
alex@alexcartoon.com
YEARS OF RESENTMENTS COME TO THE SURFACE. ONE SEES ONE'S SPOUSE AS THE ENEMY AND THE TEMPTATION TO DO THEM DOWN IS VERY STRONG...
THERE'S STUFF I KNOW ABOUT CLIVE THAT I COULD BRING OUT IN COURT TO EMBARRASS HIM, BUT I INTEND TO RISE ABOVE THAT AND SHOW RESTRAINT...
A WISE AND SENSIBLE ATTITUDE, BRIDGET...
I MEAN, IF I SHOPPED HIS TAX EVASION SCHEMES TO THE REVENUE HE'D JUST GET CLOBBERED WITH BIG FINES AND THERE'D BE LESS MONEY FOR ME...
RIGHT. WE'LL HOLD OFF DOING THAT TILL YOUR SETTLEMENT HAS BEEN INK-STAMPED...

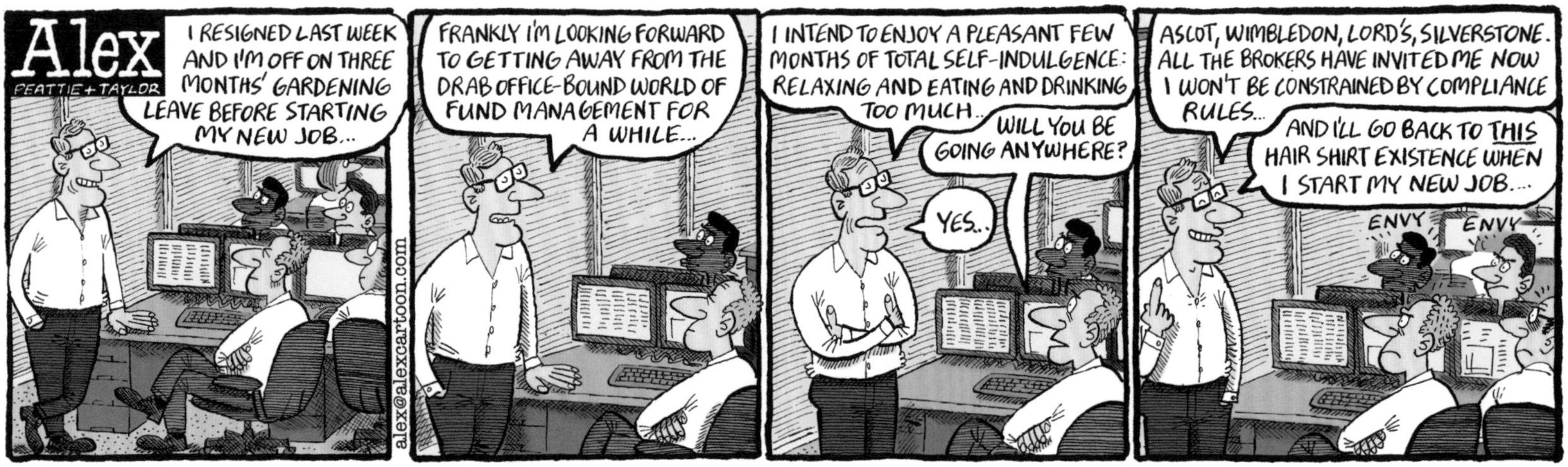
Alex
PEATTIE + TAYLOR
I RESIGNED LAST WEEK AND I'M OFF ON THREE MONTHS' GARDENING LEAVE BEFORE STARTING MY NEW JOB...
alex@alexcartoon.com
FRANKLY I'M LOOKING FORWARD TO GETTING AWAY FROM THE DRAB OFFICE-BOUND WORLD OF FUND MANAGEMENT FOR A WHILE...
I INTEND TO ENJOY A PLEASANT FEW MONTHS OF TOTAL SELF-INDULGENCE: RELAXING AND EATING AND DRINKING TOO MUCH...
WILL YOU BE GOING ANYWHERE?
YES...
ASCOT, WIMBLEDON, LORD'S, SILVERSTONE. ALL THE BROKERS HAVE INVITED ME NOW I WON'T BE CONSTRAINED BY COMPLIANCE RULES...
AND I'LL GO BACK TO THIS HAIR SHIRT EXISTENCE WHEN I START MY NEW JOB...
ENVY
ENVY

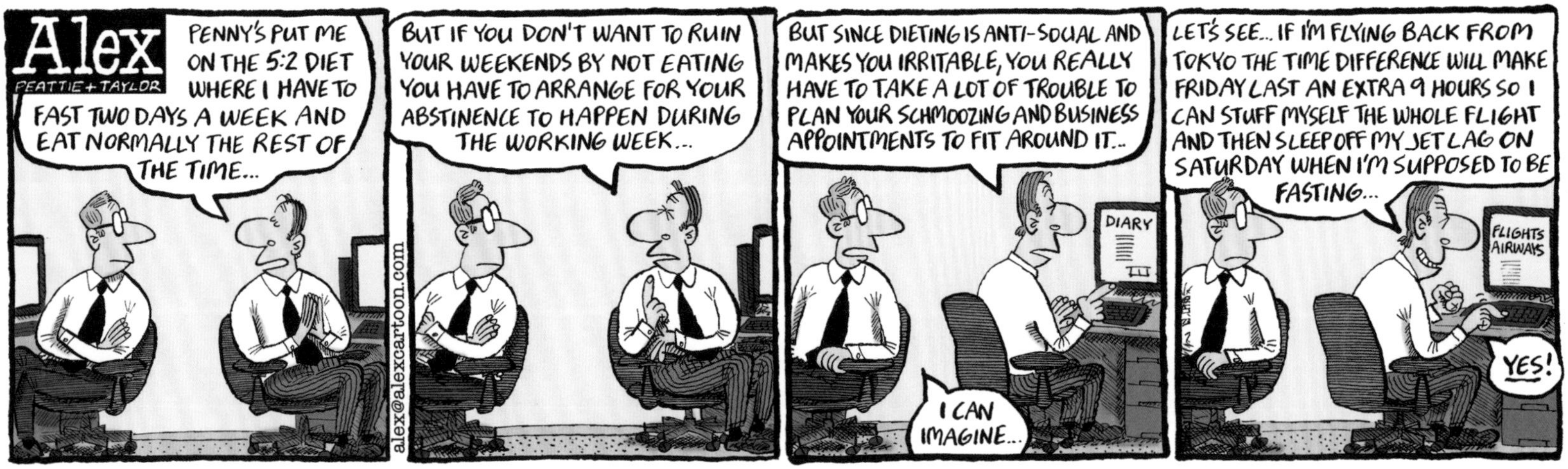
Alex
PEATTIE + TAYLOR
PENNY'S PUT ME ON THE 5:2 DIET WHERE I HAVE TO FAST TWO DAYS A WEEK AND EAT NORMALLY THE REST OF THE TIME...
alex@alexcartoon.com
BUT IF YOU DON'T WANT TO RUIN YOUR WEEKENDS BY NOT EATING YOU HAVE TO ARRANGE FOR YOUR ABSTINENCE TO HAPPEN DURING THE WORKING WEEK...
BUT SINCE DIETING IS ANTI-SOCIAL AND MAKES YOU IRRITABLE, YOU REALLY HAVE TO TAKE A LOT OF TROUBLE TO PLAN YOUR SCHMOOZING AND BUSINESS APPOINTMENTS TO FIT AROUND IT...
DIARY
I CAN IMAGINE...
LET'S SEE... IF I'M FLYING BACK FROM TOKYO THE TIME DIFFERENCE WILL MAKE FRIDAY LAST AN EXTRA 9 HOURS SO I CAN STUFF MYSELF THE WHOLE FLIGHT AND THEN SLEEP OFF MY JET LAG ON SATURDAY WHEN I'M SUPPOSED TO BE FASTING...
FLIGHTS AIRWAYS
YES!

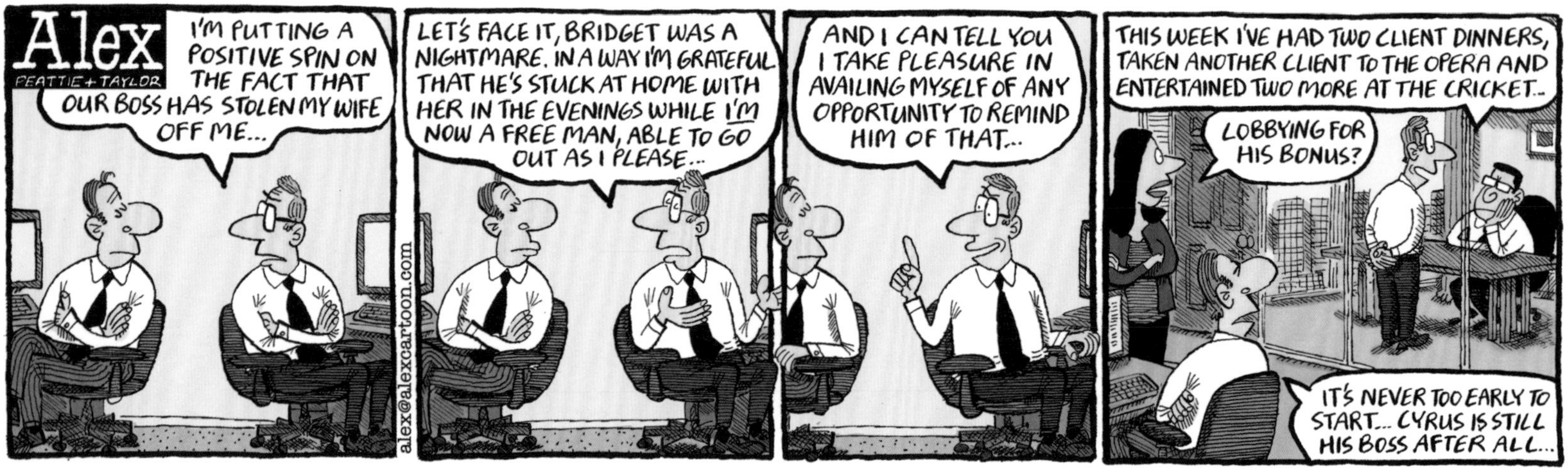
Alex
PEATTIE+TAYLOR
I'M PUTTING A POSITIVE SPIN ON THE FACT THAT OUR BOSS HAS STOLEN MY WIFE OFF ME...
LET'S FACE IT, BRIDGET WAS A NIGHTMARE. IN A WAY I'M GRATEFUL THAT HE'S STUCK AT HOME WITH HER IN THE EVENINGS WHILE I'M NOW A FREE MAN, ABLE TO GO OUT AS I PLEASE...
alex@alexcartoon.com
AND I CAN TELL YOU I TAKE PLEASURE IN AVAILING MYSELF OF ANY OPPORTUNITY TO REMIND HIM OF THAT...
THIS WEEK I'VE HAD TWO CLIENT DINNERS, TAKEN ANOTHER CLIENT TO THE OPERA AND ENTERTAINED TWO MORE AT THE CRICKET...
LOBBYING FOR HIS BONUS?
IT'S NEVER TOO EARLY TO START... CYRUS IS STILL HIS BOSS AFTER ALL...

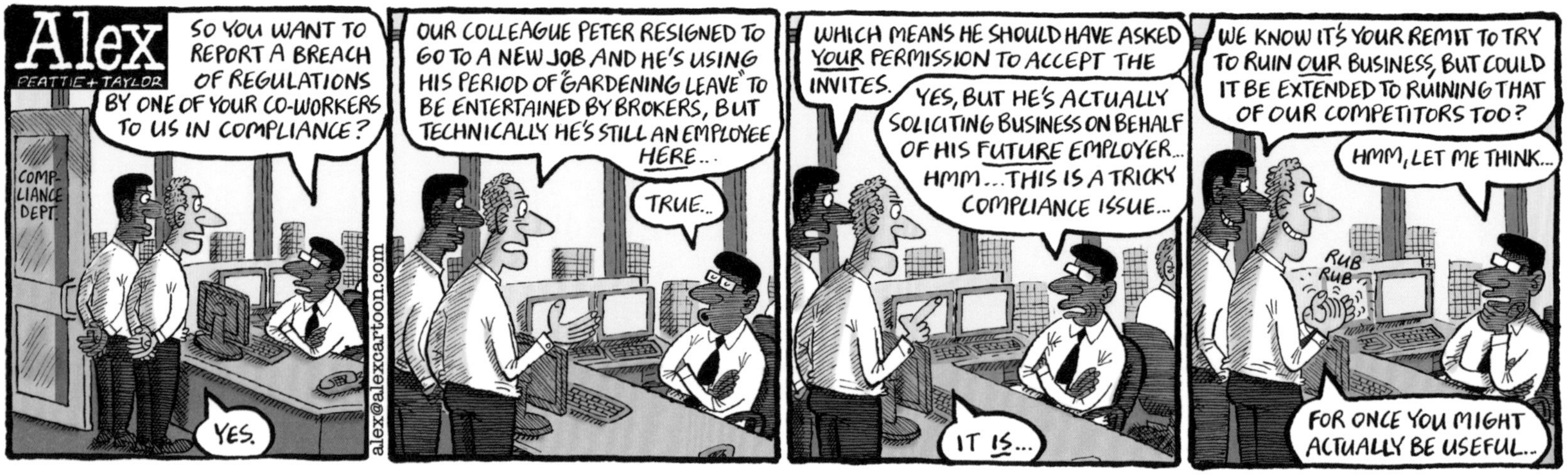
Alex
PEATTIE+TAYLOR
SO YOU WANT TO REPORT A BREACH OF REGULATIONS BY ONE OF YOUR CO-WORKERS TO US IN COMPLIANCE?
COMPLIANCE DEPT.
YES.
alex@alexcartoon.com
OUR COLLEAGUE PETER RESIGNED TO GO TO A NEW JOB AND HE'S USING HIS PERIOD OF "GARDENING LEAVE" TO BE ENTERTAINED BY BROKERS, BUT TECHNICALLY HE'S STILL AN EMPLOYEE HERE...
TRUE...
WHICH MEANS HE SHOULD HAVE ASKED YOUR PERMISSION TO ACCEPT THE INVITES.
YES, BUT HE'S ACTUALLY SOLICITING BUSINESS ON BEHALF OF HIS FUTURE EMPLOYER... HMM... THIS IS A TRICKY COMPLIANCE ISSUE...
IT IS...
WE KNOW IT'S YOUR REMIT TO TRY TO RUIN OUR BUSINESS, BUT COULD IT BE EXTENDED TO RUINING THAT OF OUR COMPETITORS TOO?
HMM, LET ME THINK...
RUB RUB
FOR ONCE YOU MIGHT ACTUALLY BE USEFUL...

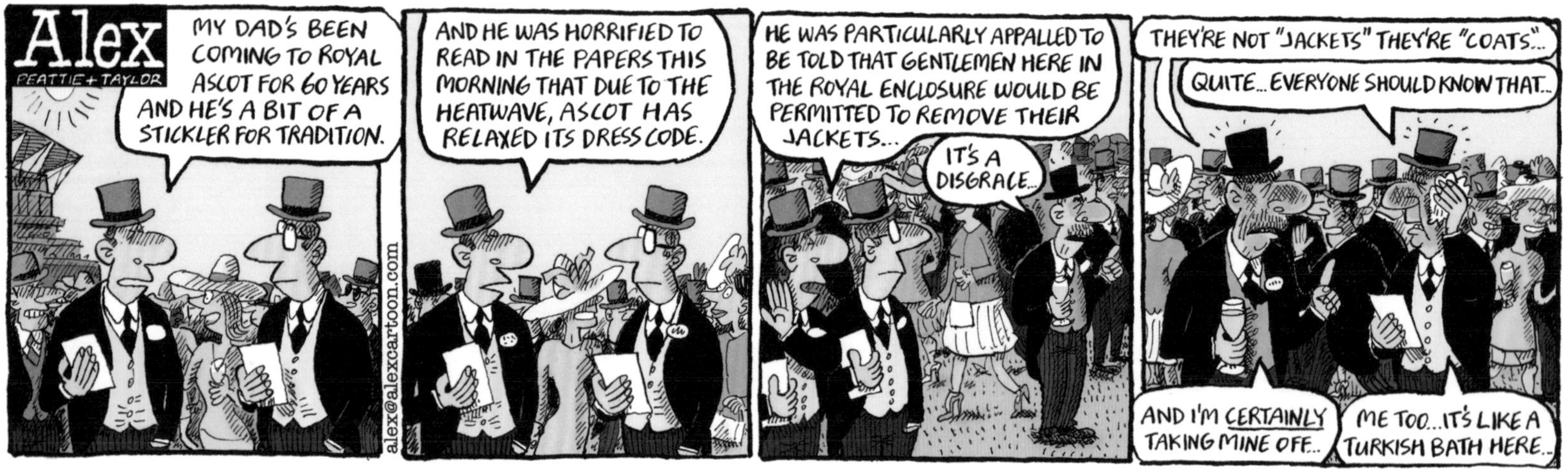
Alex
PEATTIE+TAYLOR
MY DAD'S BEEN COMING TO ROYAL ASCOT FOR 60 YEARS AND HE'S A BIT OF A STICKLER FOR TRADITION.
alex@alexcartoon.com
AND HE WAS HORRIFIED TO READ IN THE PAPERS THIS MORNING THAT DUE TO THE HEATWAVE, ASCOT HAS RELAXED ITS DRESS CODE.
HE WAS PARTICULARLY APPALLED TO BE TOLD THAT GENTLEMEN HERE IN THE ROYAL ENCLOSURE WOULD BE PERMITTED TO REMOVE THEIR JACKETS...
IT'S A DISGRACE...
THEY'RE NOT "JACKETS" THEY'RE "COATS"...
QUITE... EVERYONE SHOULD KNOW THAT...
AND I'M CERTAINLY TAKING MINE OFF...
ME TOO... IT'S LIKE A TURKISH BATH HERE...

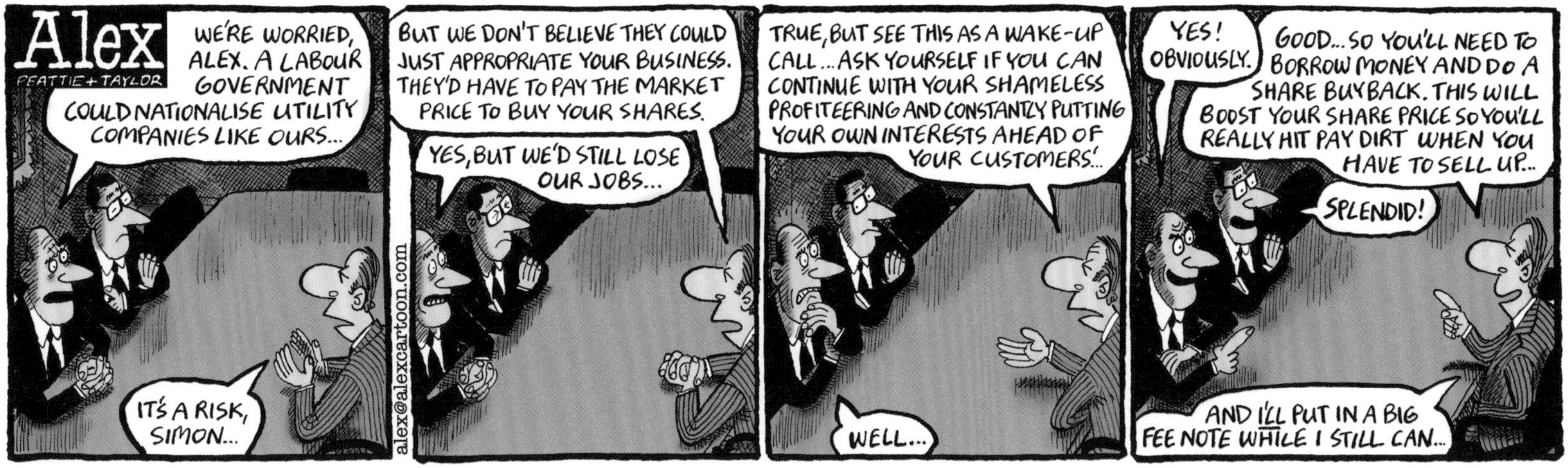
Alex
PEATTIE + TAYLOR
WE'RE WORRIED, ALEX. A LABOUR GOVERNMENT COULD NATIONALISE UTILITY COMPANIES LIKE OURS...
IT'S A RISK, SIMON...
BUT WE DON'T BELIEVE THEY COULD JUST APPROPRIATE YOUR BUSINESS. THEY'D HAVE TO PAY THE MARKET PRICE TO BUY YOUR SHARES.
YES, BUT WE'D STILL LOSE OUR JOBS...
alex@alexcartoon.com
TRUE, BUT SEE THIS AS A WAKE-UP CALL... ASK YOURSELF IF YOU CAN CONTINUE WITH YOUR SHAMELESS PROFITEERING AND CONSTANTLY PUTTING YOUR OWN INTERESTS AHEAD OF YOUR CUSTOMERS!..
WELL...
YES! OBVIOUSLY.
GOOD... SO YOU'LL NEED TO BORROW MONEY AND DO A SHARE BUYBACK. THIS WILL BOOST YOUR SHARE PRICE SO YOU'LL REALLY HIT PAY DIRT WHEN YOU HAVE TO SELL UP...
SPLENDID!
AND I'LL PUT IN A BIG FEE NOTE WHILE I STILL CAN...

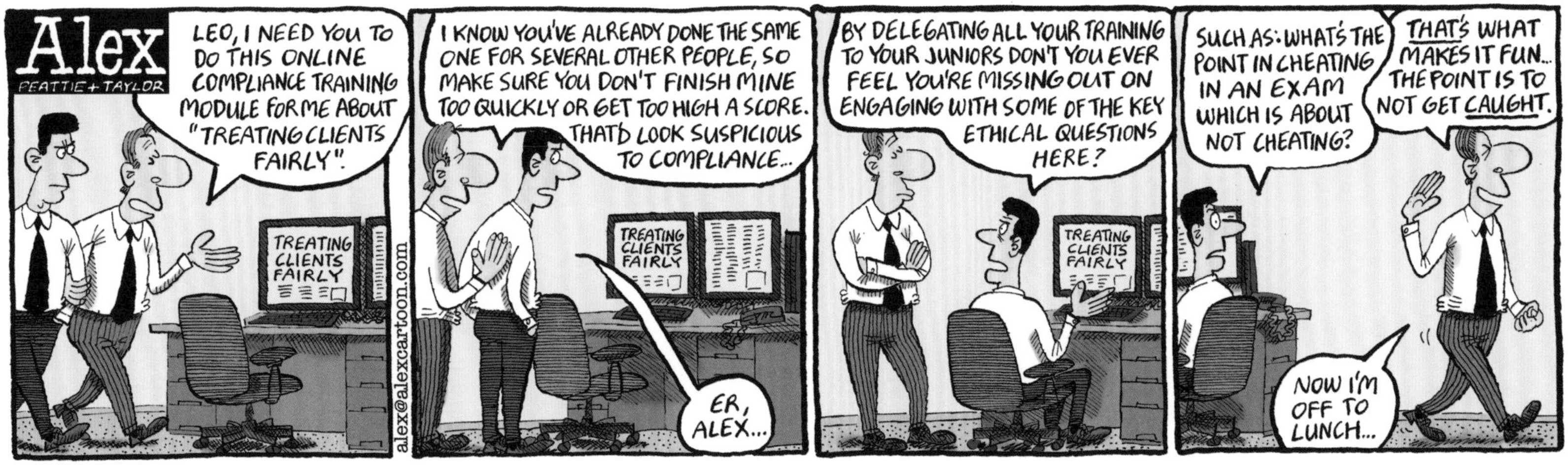
Alex
PEATTIE + TAYLOR
LEO, I NEED YOU TO DO THIS ONLINE COMPLIANCE TRAINING MODULE FOR ME ABOUT "TREATING CLIENTS FAIRLY".
TREATING CLIENTS FAIRLY
I KNOW YOU'VE ALREADY DONE THE SAME ONE FOR SEVERAL OTHER PEOPLE, SO MAKE SURE YOU DON'T FINISH MINE TOO QUICKLY OR GET TOO HIGH A SCORE. THAT'D LOOK SUSPICIOUS TO COMPLIANCE...
ER, ALEX...
alex@alexcartoon.com
BY DELEGATING ALL YOUR TRAINING TO YOUR JUNIORS DON'T YOU EVER FEEL YOU'RE MISSING OUT ON ENGAGING WITH SOME OF THE KEY ETHICAL QUESTIONS HERE?
SUCH AS: WHAT'S THE POINT IN CHEATING IN AN EXAM WHICH IS ABOUT NOT CHEATING?
THAT'S WHAT MAKES IT FUN... THE POINT IS TO NOT GET CAUGHT.
NOW I'M OFF TO LUNCH...

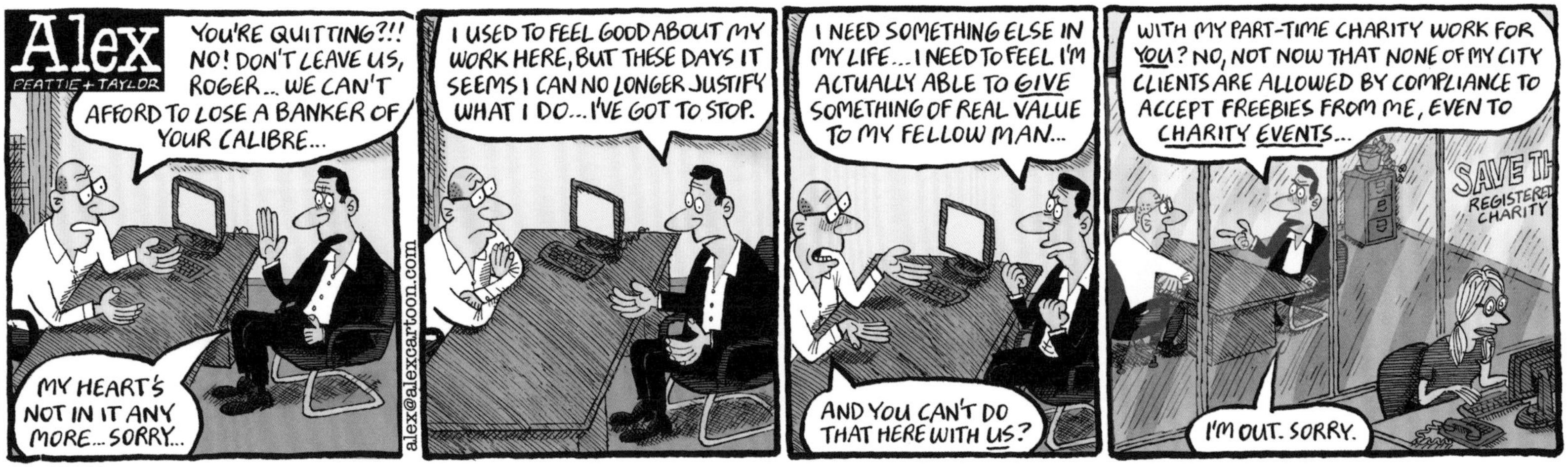
Alex
PEATTIE + TAYLOR
YOU'RE QUITTING?!! NO! DON'T LEAVE US, ROGER... WE CAN'T AFFORD TO LOSE A BANKER OF YOUR CALIBRE...
MY HEART'S NOT IN IT ANY MORE... SORRY...
I USED TO FEEL GOOD ABOUT MY WORK HERE, BUT THESE DAYS IT SEEMS I CAN NO LONGER JUSTIFY WHAT I DO... I'VE GOT TO STOP.
alex@alexcartoon.com
I NEED SOMETHING ELSE IN MY LIFE... I NEED TO FEEL I'M ACTUALLY ABLE TO GIVE SOMETHING OF REAL VALUE TO MY FELLOW MAN...
AND YOU CAN'T DO THAT HERE WITH US?
WITH MY PART-TIME CHARITY WORK FOR YOU? NO, NOT NOW THAT NONE OF MY CITY CLIENTS ARE ALLOWED BY COMPLIANCE TO ACCEPT FREEBIES FROM ME, EVEN TO CHARITY EVENTS...
SAVE TH
REGISTERED CHARITY
I'M OUT. SORRY.

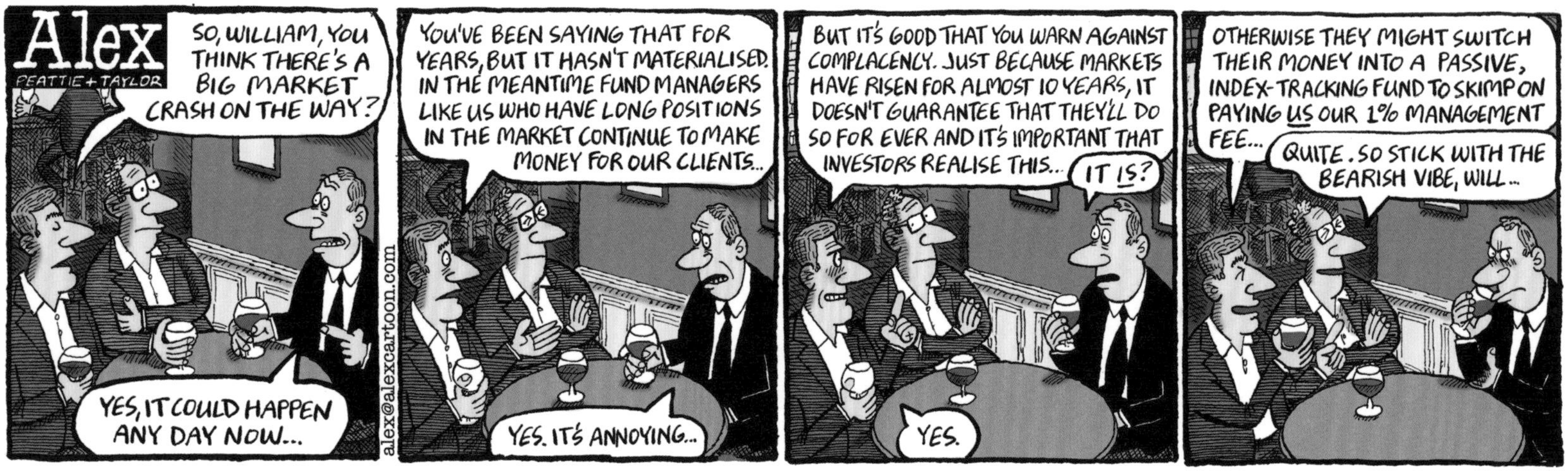
Alex
PEATTIE+TAYLOR
SO, WILLIAM, YOU THINK THERE'S A BIG MARKET CRASH ON THE WAY?
YES, IT COULD HAPPEN ANY DAY NOW...
alex@alexcartoon.com
YOU'VE BEEN SAYING THAT FOR YEARS, BUT IT HASN'T MATERIALISED. IN THE MEANTIME FUND MANAGERS LIKE US WHO HAVE LONG POSITIONS IN THE MARKET CONTINUE TO MAKE MONEY FOR OUR CLIENTS...
YES. IT'S ANNOYING...
BUT IT'S GOOD THAT YOU WARN AGAINST COMPLACENCY. JUST BECAUSE MARKETS HAVE RISEN FOR ALMOST 10 YEARS, IT DOESN'T GUARANTEE THAT THEY'LL DO SO FOR EVER AND IT'S IMPORTANT THAT INVESTORS REALISE THIS...
IT IS?
YES.
OTHERWISE THEY MIGHT SWITCH THEIR MONEY INTO A PASSIVE, INDEX-TRACKING FUND TO SKIMP ON PAYING US OUR 1% MANAGEMENT FEE...
QUITE. SO STICK WITH THE BEARISH VIBE, WILL...

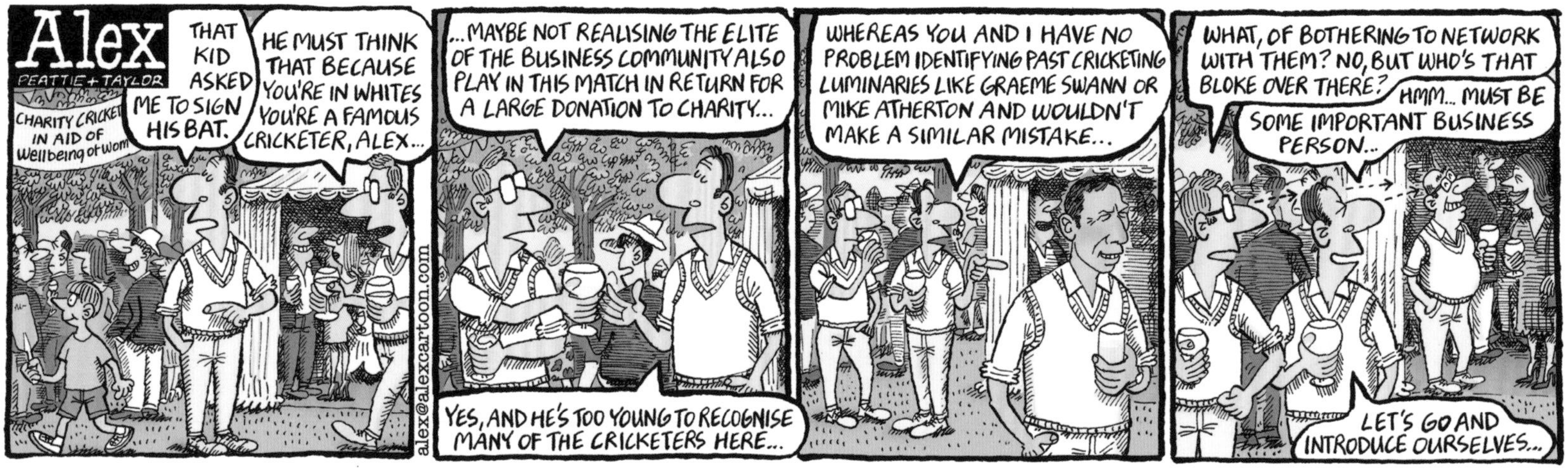
Alex
PEATTIE+TAYLOR
CHARITY CRICKET IN AID OF Wellbeing of Wom
THAT KID ASKED ME TO SIGN HIS BAT.
HE MUST THINK THAT BECAUSE YOU'RE IN WHITES YOU'RE A FAMOUS CRICKETER, ALEX...
alex@alexcartoon.com
YES, AND HE'S TOO YOUNG TO RECOGNISE MANY OF THE CRICKETERS HERE...
...MAYBE NOT REALISING THE ELITE OF THE BUSINESS COMMUNITY ALSO PLAY IN THIS MATCH IN RETURN FOR A LARGE DONATION TO CHARITY...
WHEREAS YOU AND I HAVE NO PROBLEM IDENTIFYING PAST CRICKETING LUMINARIES LIKE GRAEME SWANN OR MIKE ATHERTON AND WOULDN'T MAKE A SIMILAR MISTAKE...
WHAT, OF BOTHERING TO NETWORK WITH THEM? NO, BUT WHO'S THAT BLOKE OVER THERE?
HMM... MUST BE SOME IMPORTANT BUSINESS PERSON...
LET'S GO AND INTRODUCE OURSELVES...

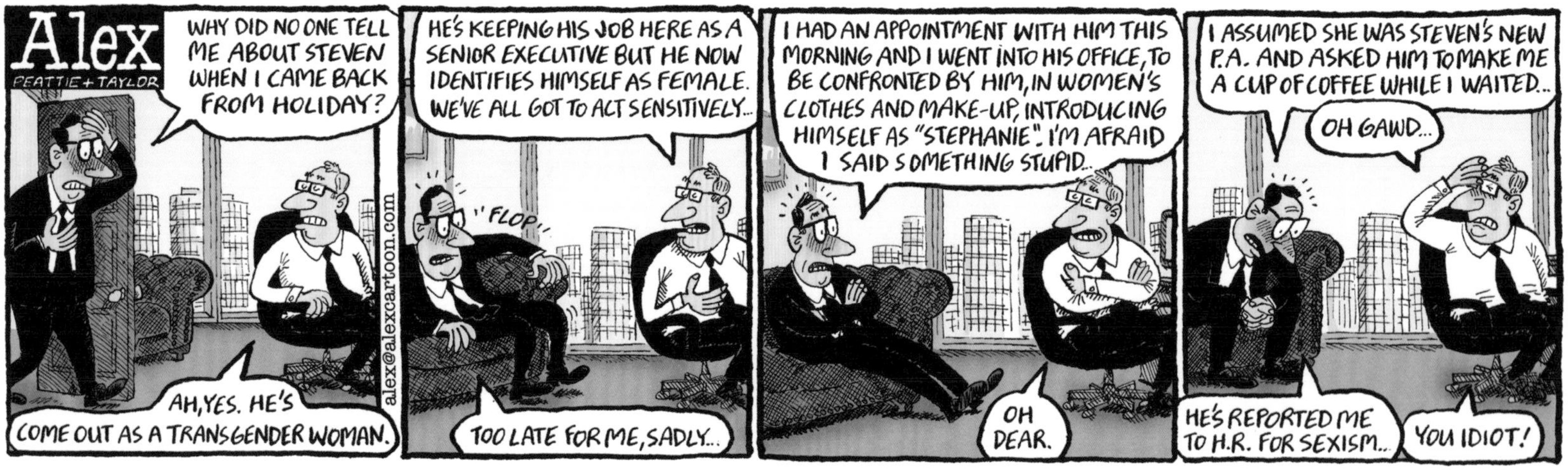
Alex
PEATTIE+TAYLOR
WHY DID NO ONE TELL ME ABOUT STEVEN WHEN I CAME BACK FROM HOLIDAY?
AH, YES. HE'S COME OUT AS A TRANSGENDER WOMAN.
alex@alexcartoon.com
HE'S KEEPING HIS JOB HERE AS A SENIOR EXECUTIVE BUT HE NOW IDENTIFIES HIMSELF AS FEMALE. WE'VE ALL GOT TO ACT SENSITIVELY...
FLOP
TOO LATE FOR ME, SADLY...
I HAD AN APPOINTMENT WITH HIM THIS MORNING AND I WENT INTO HIS OFFICE, TO BE CONFRONTED BY HIM, IN WOMEN'S CLOTHES AND MAKE-UP, INTRODUCING HIMSELF AS "STEPHANIE". I'M AFRAID I SAID SOMETHING STUPID...
OH DEAR.
I ASSUMED SHE WAS STEVEN'S NEW P.A. AND ASKED HIM TO MAKE ME A CUP OF COFFEE WHILE I WAITED...
OH GAWD...
HE'S REPORTED ME TO H.R. FOR SEXISM...
YOU IDIOT!

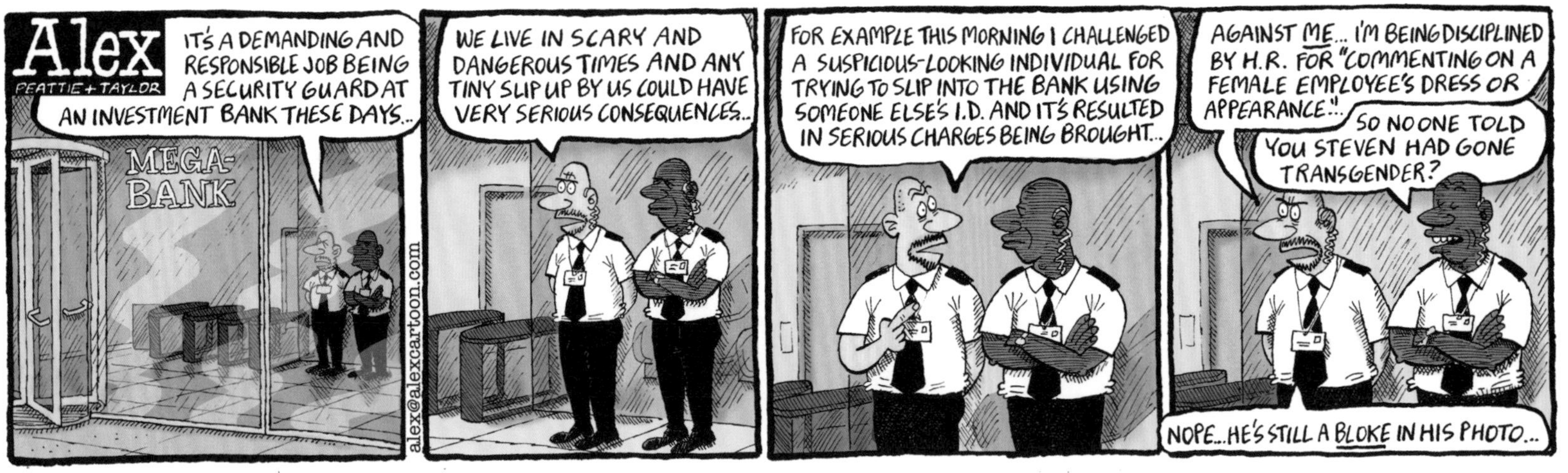
Alex
PEATTIE + TAYLOR
IT'S A DEMANDING AND RESPONSIBLE JOB BEING A SECURITY GUARD AT AN INVESTMENT BANK THESE DAYS...
MEGA-BANK
alex@alexcartoon.com
WE LIVE IN SCARY AND DANGEROUS TIMES AND ANY TINY SLIP UP BY US COULD HAVE VERY SERIOUS CONSEQUENCES...
FOR EXAMPLE THIS MORNING I CHALLENGED A SUSPICIOUS-LOOKING INDIVIDUAL FOR TRYING TO SLIP INTO THE BANK USING SOMEONE ELSE'S I.D. AND IT'S RESULTED IN SERIOUS CHARGES BEING BROUGHT...
AGAINST ME... I'M BEING DISCIPLINED BY H.R. FOR "COMMENTING ON A FEMALE EMPLOYEE'S DRESS OR APPEARANCE"!
SO NO ONE TOLD YOU STEVEN HAD GONE TRANSGENDER?
NOPE... HE'S STILL A BLOKE IN HIS PHOTO...

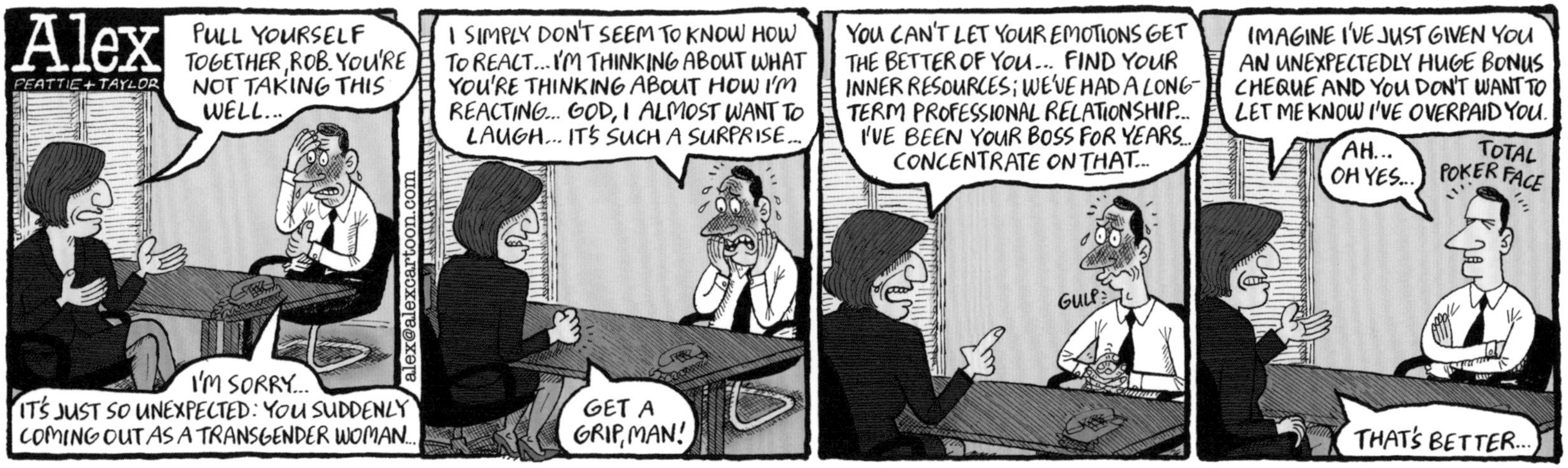
Alex
PEATTIE + TAYLOR
PULL YOURSELF TOGETHER, ROB. YOU'RE NOT TAKING THIS WELL...
I'M SORRY... IT'S JUST SO UNEXPECTED: YOU SUDDENLY COMING OUT AS A TRANSGENDER WOMAN...
alex@alexcartoon.com
I SIMPLY DON'T SEEM TO KNOW HOW TO REACT... I'M THINKING ABOUT WHAT YOU'RE THINKING ABOUT HOW I'M REACTING... GOD, I ALMOST WANT TO LAUGH... IT'S SUCH A SURPRISE...
GET A GRIP, MAN!
YOU CAN'T LET YOUR EMOTIONS GET THE BETTER OF YOU... FIND YOUR INNER RESOURCES; WE'VE HAD A LONG-TERM PROFESSIONAL RELATIONSHIP... I'VE BEEN YOUR BOSS FOR YEARS... CONCENTRATE ON THAT...
GULP
IMAGINE I'VE JUST GIVEN YOU AN UNEXPECTEDLY HUGE BONUS CHEQUE AND YOU DON'T WANT TO LET ME KNOW I'VE OVERPAID YOU.
AH... OH YES...
TOTAL POKER FACE
THAT'S BETTER...

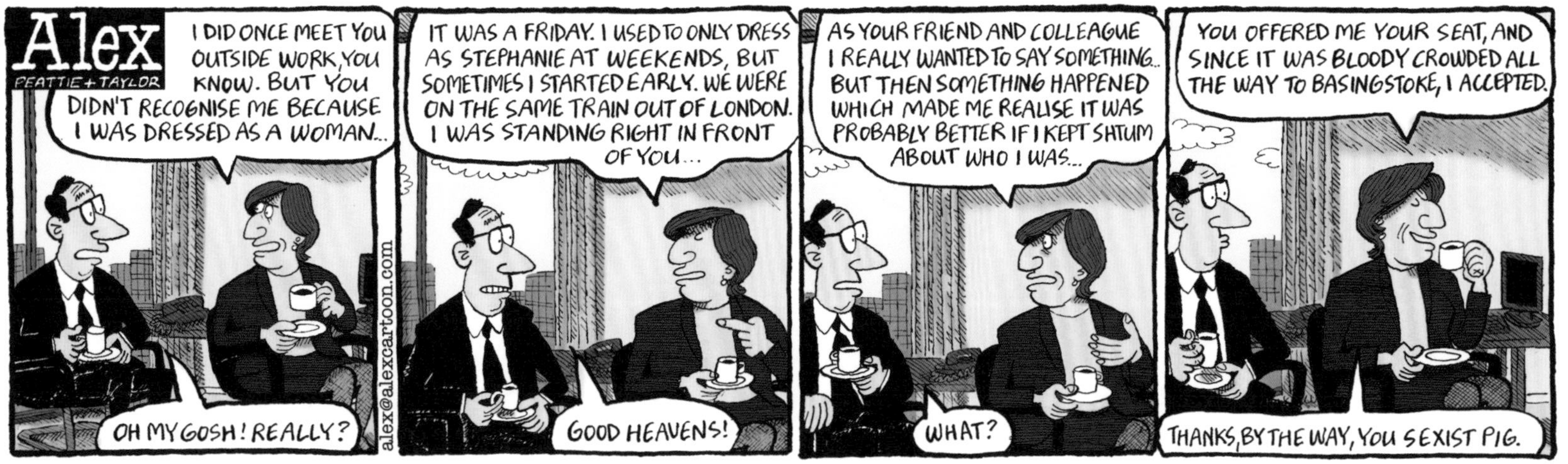
Alex
PEATTIE + TAYLOR
I DID ONCE MEET YOU OUTSIDE WORK, YOU KNOW. BUT YOU DIDN'T RECOGNISE ME BECAUSE I WAS DRESSED AS A WOMAN...
OH MY GOSH! REALLY?
alex@alexcartoon.com
IT WAS A FRIDAY. I USED TO ONLY DRESS AS STEPHANIE AT WEEKENDS, BUT SOMETIMES I STARTED EARLY. WE WERE ON THE SAME TRAIN OUT OF LONDON. I WAS STANDING RIGHT IN FRONT OF YOU...
GOOD HEAVENS!
AS YOUR FRIEND AND COLLEAGUE I REALLY WANTED TO SAY SOMETHING... BUT THEN SOMETHING HAPPENED WHICH MADE ME REALISE IT WAS PROBABLY BETTER IF I KEPT SHTUM ABOUT WHO I WAS...
WHAT?
YOU OFFERED ME YOUR SEAT, AND SINCE IT WAS BLOODY CROWDED ALL THE WAY TO BASINGSTOKE, I ACCEPTED.
THANKS, BY THE WAY, YOU SEXIST PIG.

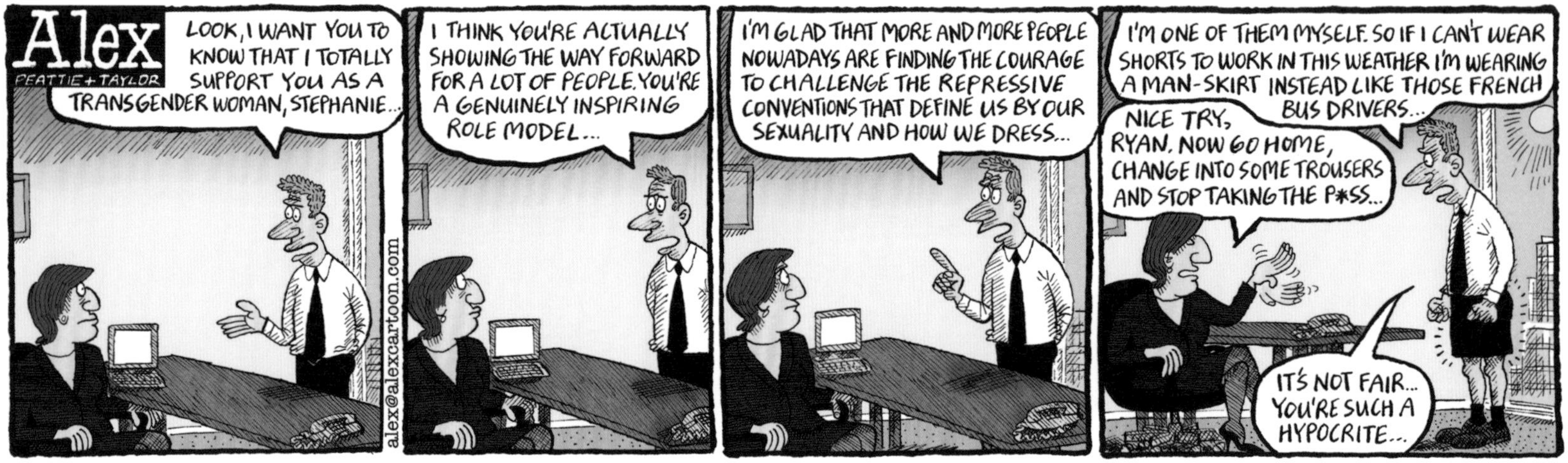
Alex
PEATTIE + TAYLOR
LOOK, I WANT YOU TO KNOW THAT I TOTALLY SUPPORT YOU AS A TRANSGENDER WOMAN, STEPHANIE...
I THINK YOU'RE ACTUALLY SHOWING THE WAY FORWARD FOR A LOT OF PEOPLE. YOU'RE A GENUINELY INSPIRING ROLE MODEL...
alex@alexcartoon.com
I'M GLAD THAT MORE AND MORE PEOPLE NOWADAYS ARE FINDING THE COURAGE TO CHALLENGE THE REPRESSIVE CONVENTIONS THAT DEFINE US BY OUR SEXUALITY AND HOW WE DRESS...
I'M ONE OF THEM MYSELF. SO IF I CAN'T WEAR SHORTS TO WORK IN THIS WEATHER I'M WEARING A MAN-SKIRT INSTEAD LIKE THOSE FRENCH BUS DRIVERS...
NICE TRY, RYAN. NOW GO HOME, CHANGE INTO SOME TROUSERS AND STOP TAKING THE P*SS...
IT'S NOT FAIR... YOU'RE SUCH A HYPOCRITE...

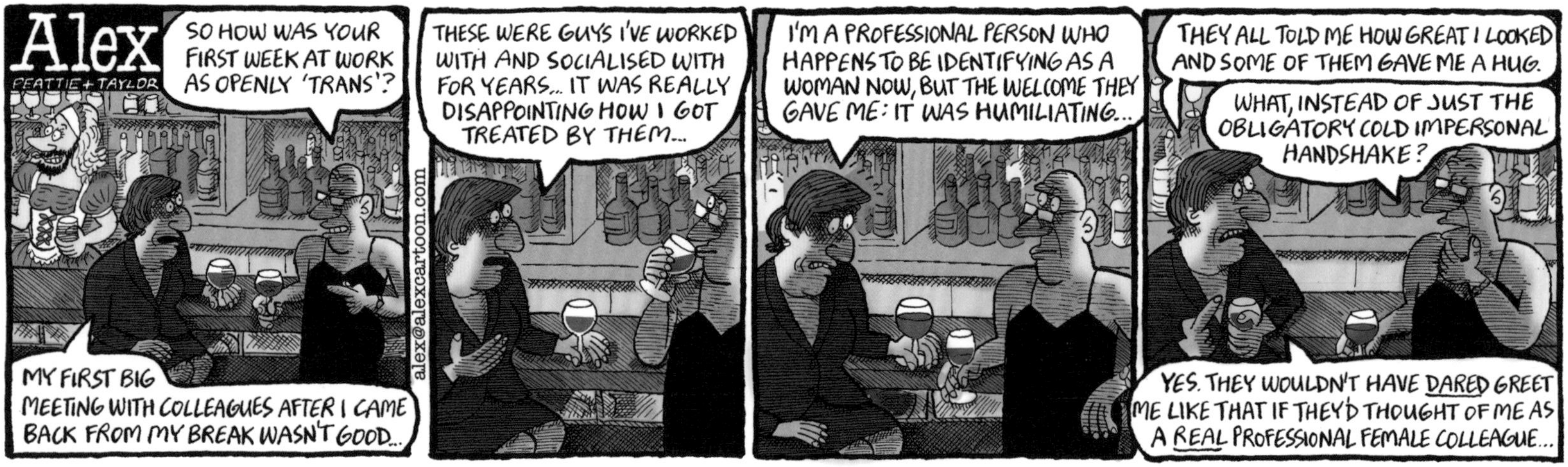
Alex
PEATTIE + TAYLOR
SO HOW WAS YOUR FIRST WEEK AT WORK AS OPENLY 'TRANS'?
MY FIRST BIG MEETING WITH COLLEAGUES AFTER I CAME BACK FROM MY BREAK WASN'T GOOD...
alex@alexcartoon.com
THESE WERE GUYS I'VE WORKED WITH AND SOCIALISED WITH FOR YEARS... IT WAS REALLY DISAPPOINTING HOW I GOT TREATED BY THEM...
I'M A PROFESSIONAL PERSON WHO HAPPENS TO BE IDENTIFYING AS A WOMAN NOW, BUT THE WELCOME THEY GAVE ME: IT WAS HUMILIATING...
THEY ALL TOLD ME HOW GREAT I LOOKED AND SOME OF THEM GAVE ME A HUG.
WHAT, INSTEAD OF JUST THE OBLIGATORY COLD IMPERSONAL HANDSHAKE?
YES. THEY WOULDN'T HAVE DARED GREET ME LIKE THAT IF THEY'D THOUGHT OF ME AS A REAL PROFESSIONAL FEMALE COLLEAGUE...

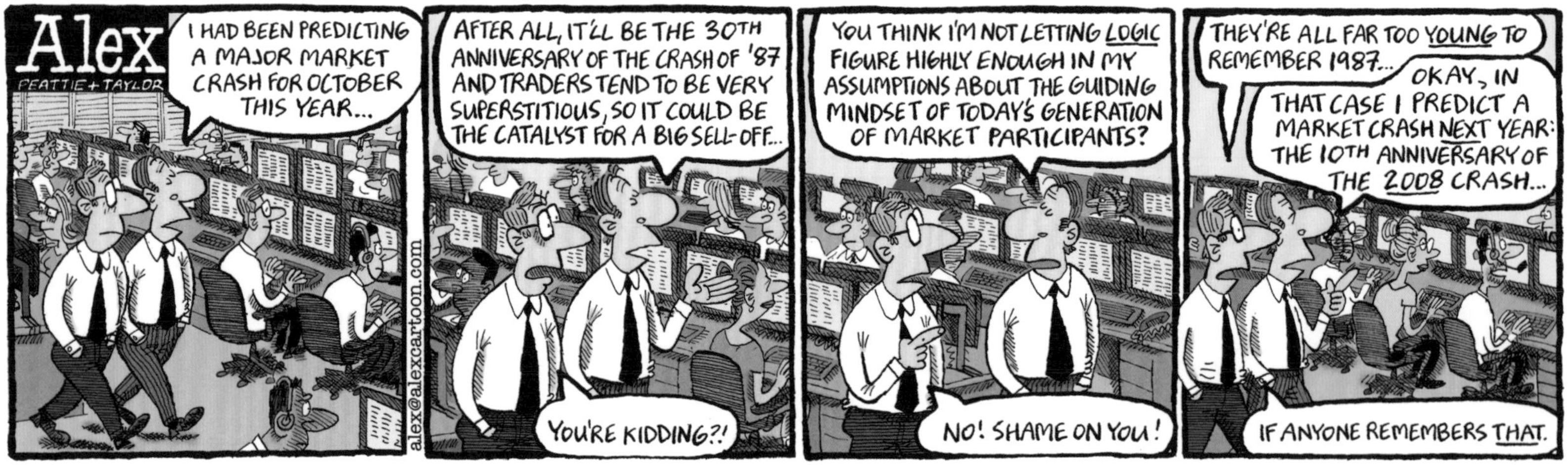
Alex
PEATTIE + TAYLOR
I HAD BEEN PREDICTING A MAJOR MARKET CRASH FOR OCTOBER THIS YEAR...
alex@alexcartoon.com
AFTER ALL, IT'LL BE THE 30TH ANNIVERSARY OF THE CRASH OF '87 AND TRADERS TEND TO BE VERY SUPERSTITIOUS, SO IT COULD BE THE CATALYST FOR A BIG SELL-OFF...
YOU'RE KIDDING?!
YOU THINK I'M NOT LETTING LOGIC FIGURE HIGHLY ENOUGH IN MY ASSUMPTIONS ABOUT THE GUIDING MINDSET OF TODAY'S GENERATION OF MARKET PARTICIPANTS?
NO! SHAME ON YOU!
THEY'RE ALL FAR TOO YOUNG TO REMEMBER 1987...
OKAY, IN THAT CASE I PREDICT A MARKET CRASH NEXT YEAR: THE 10TH ANNIVERSARY OF THE 2008 CRASH...
IF ANYONE REMEMBERS THAT.

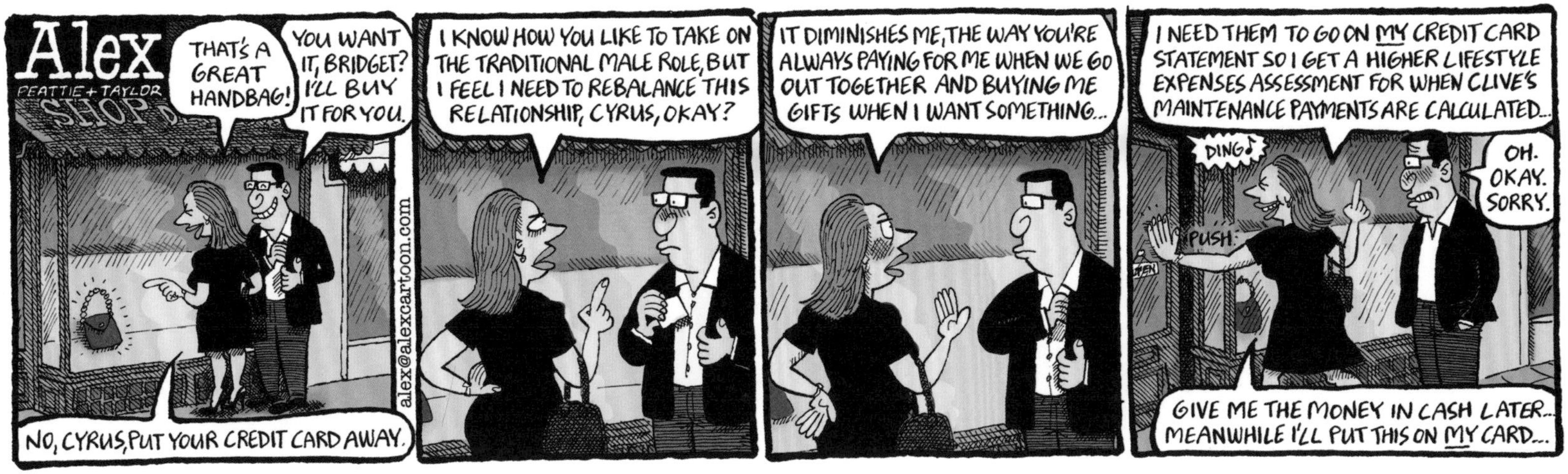

Alex
PEATTIE + TAYLOR
THAT'S A GREAT HANDBAG!
YOU WANT IT, BRIDGET? I'LL BUY IT FOR YOU.
NO, CYRUS, PUT YOUR CREDIT CARD AWAY.
alex@alexcartoon.com
I KNOW HOW YOU LIKE TO TAKE ON THE TRADITIONAL MALE ROLE, BUT I FEEL I NEED TO REBALANCE THIS RELATIONSHIP, CYRUS, OKAY?
IT DIMINISHES ME, THE WAY YOU'RE ALWAYS PAYING FOR ME WHEN WE GO OUT TOGETHER AND BUYING ME GIFTS WHEN I WANT SOMETHING...
I NEED THEM TO GO ON MY CREDIT CARD STATEMENT SO I GET A HIGHER LIFESTYLE EXPENSES ASSESSMENT FOR WHEN CLIVE'S MAINTENANCE PAYMENTS ARE CALCULATED...
DING
PUSH
OH. OKAY. SORRY.
GIVE ME THE MONEY IN CASH LATER... MEANWHILE I'LL PUT THIS ON MY CARD...

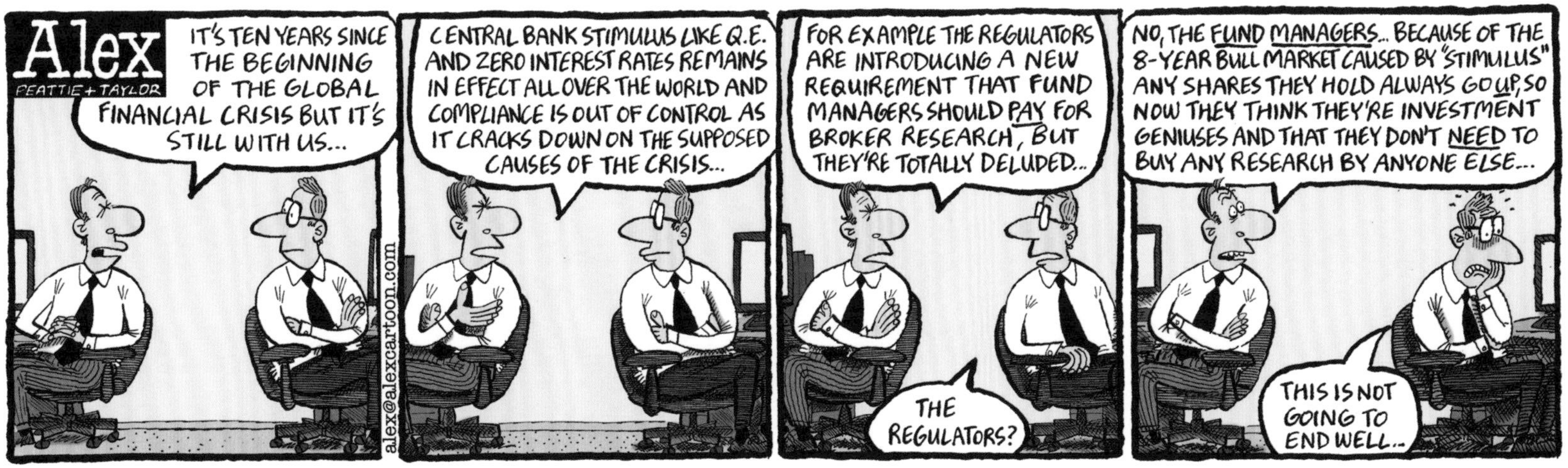

Alex
PEATTIE + TAYLOR
IT'S TEN YEARS SINCE THE BEGINNING OF THE GLOBAL FINANCIAL CRISIS BUT IT'S STILL WITH US...
alex@alexcartoon.com
CENTRAL BANK STIMULUS LIKE Q.E. AND ZERO INTEREST RATES REMAINS IN EFFECT ALL OVER THE WORLD AND COMPLIANCE IS OUT OF CONTROL AS IT CRACKS DOWN ON THE SUPPOSED CAUSES OF THE CRISIS...
FOR EXAMPLE THE REGULATORS ARE INTRODUCING A NEW REQUIREMENT THAT FUND MANAGERS SHOULD PAY FOR BROKER RESEARCH, BUT THEY'RE TOTALLY DELUDED...
THE REGULATORS?
NO, THE FUND MANAGERS... BECAUSE OF THE 8-YEAR BULL MARKET CAUSED BY "STIMULUS" ANY SHARES THEY HOLD ALWAYS GO UP, SO NOW THEY THINK THEY'RE INVESTMENT GENIUSES AND THAT THEY DON'T NEED TO BUY ANY RESEARCH BY ANYONE ELSE...
THIS IS NOT GOING TO END WELL...

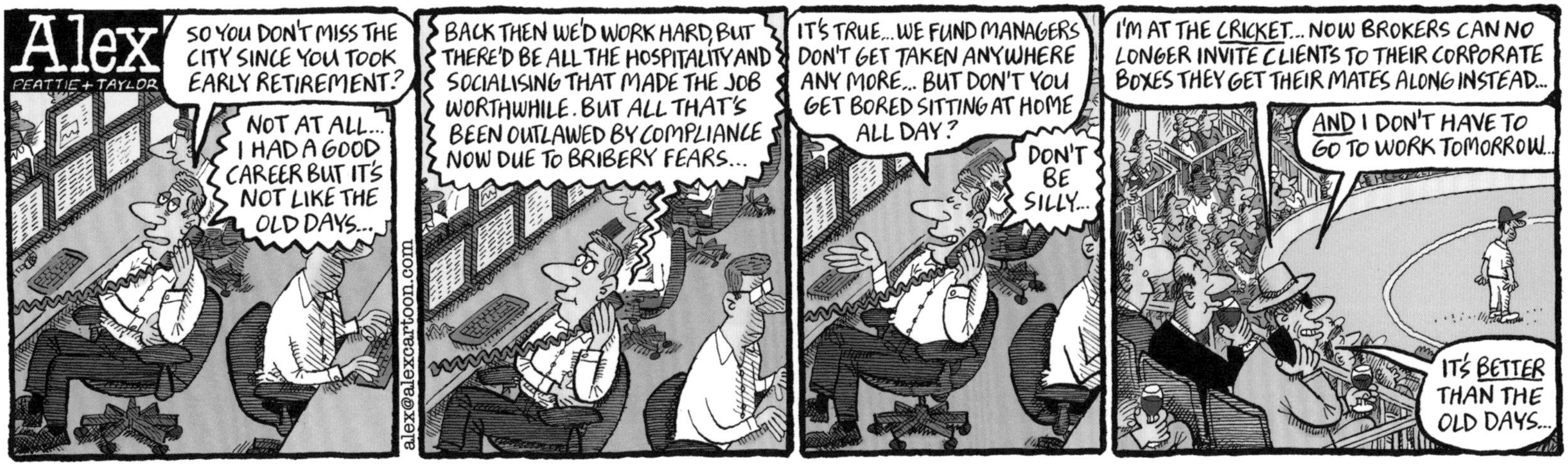

Alex
PEATTIE + TAYLOR
SO YOU DON'T MISS THE CITY SINCE YOU TOOK EARLY RETIREMENT?
NOT AT ALL... I HAD A GOOD CAREER BUT IT'S NOT LIKE THE OLD DAYS...
alex@alexcartoon.com
BACK THEN WE'D WORK HARD, BUT THERE'D BE ALL THE HOSPITALITY AND SOCIALISING THAT MADE THE JOB WORTHWHILE. BUT ALL THAT'S BEEN OUTLAWED BY COMPLIANCE NOW DUE TO BRIBERY FEARS...
IT'S TRUE... WE FUND MANAGERS DON'T GET TAKEN ANYWHERE ANY MORE... BUT DON'T YOU GET BORED SITTING AT HOME ALL DAY?
DON'T BE SILLY...
I'M AT THE CRICKET... NOW BROKERS CAN NO LONGER INVITE CLIENTS TO THEIR CORPORATE BOXES THEY GET THEIR MATES ALONG INSTEAD...
AND I DON'T HAVE TO GO TO WORK TOMORROW...
IT'S BETTER THAN THE OLD DAYS...

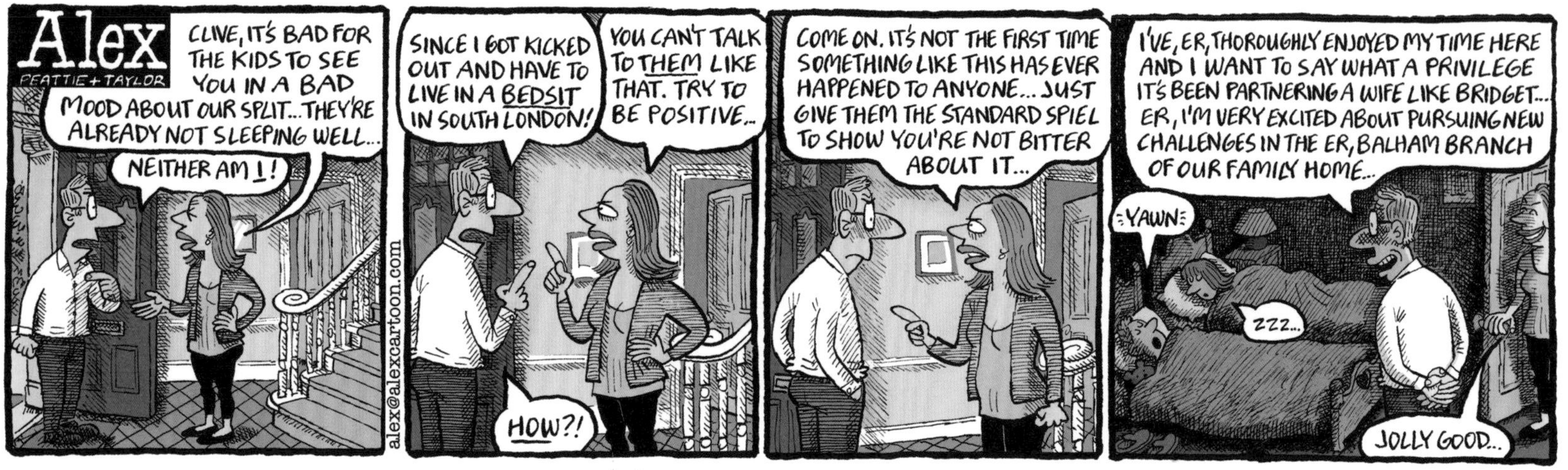
Alex
PEATTIE + TAYLOR
CLIVE, IT'S BAD FOR THE KIDS TO SEE YOU IN A BAD MOOD ABOUT OUR SPLIT... THEY'RE ALREADY NOT SLEEPING WELL...
NEITHER AM I!
alex@alexcartoon.com
SINCE I GOT KICKED OUT AND HAVE TO LIVE IN A BEDSIT IN SOUTH LONDON!
YOU CAN'T TALK TO THEM LIKE THAT. TRY TO BE POSITIVE...
HOW?!
COME ON. IT'S NOT THE FIRST TIME SOMETHING LIKE THIS HAS EVER HAPPENED TO ANYONE... JUST GIVE THEM THE STANDARD SPIEL TO SHOW YOU'RE NOT BITTER ABOUT IT...
I'VE, ER, THOROUGHLY ENJOYED MY TIME HERE AND I WANT TO SAY WHAT A PRIVILEGE IT'S BEEN PARTNERING A WIFE LIKE BRIDGET... ER, I'M VERY EXCITED ABOUT PURSUING NEW CHALLENGES IN THE ER, BALHAM BRANCH OF OUR FAMILY HOME...
YAWN
ZZZ...
JOLLY GOOD...

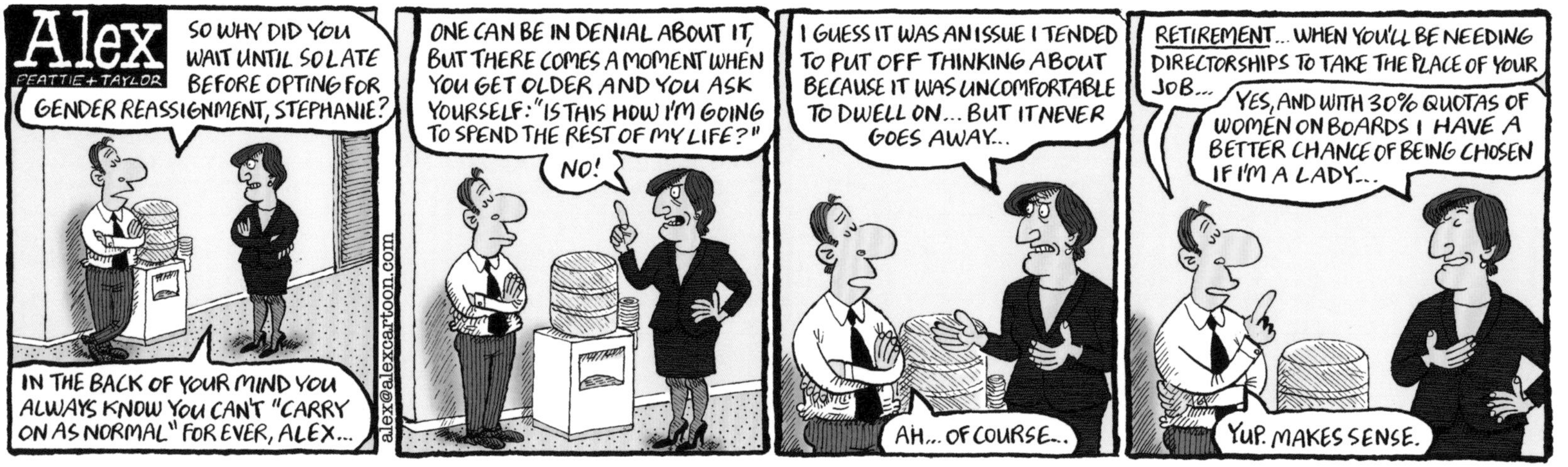
Alex
PEATTIE + TAYLOR
SO WHY DID YOU WAIT UNTIL SO LATE BEFORE OPTING FOR GENDER REASSIGNMENT, STEPHANIE?
IN THE BACK OF YOUR MIND YOU ALWAYS KNOW YOU CAN'T "CARRY ON AS NORMAL" FOR EVER, ALEX...
alex@alexcartoon.com
ONE CAN BE IN DENIAL ABOUT IT, BUT THERE COMES A MOMENT WHEN YOU GET OLDER AND YOU ASK YOURSELF: "IS THIS HOW I'M GOING TO SPEND THE REST OF MY LIFE?"
NO!
I GUESS IT WAS AN ISSUE I TENDED TO PUT OFF THINKING ABOUT BECAUSE IT WAS UNCOMFORTABLE TO DWELL ON... BUT IT NEVER GOES AWAY...
AH... OF COURSE...
RETIREMENT... WHEN YOU'LL BE NEEDING DIRECTORSHIPS TO TAKE THE PLACE OF YOUR JOB...
YES, AND WITH 30% QUOTAS OF WOMEN ON BOARDS I HAVE A BETTER CHANCE OF BEING CHOSEN IF I'M A LADY...
YUP. MAKES SENSE.

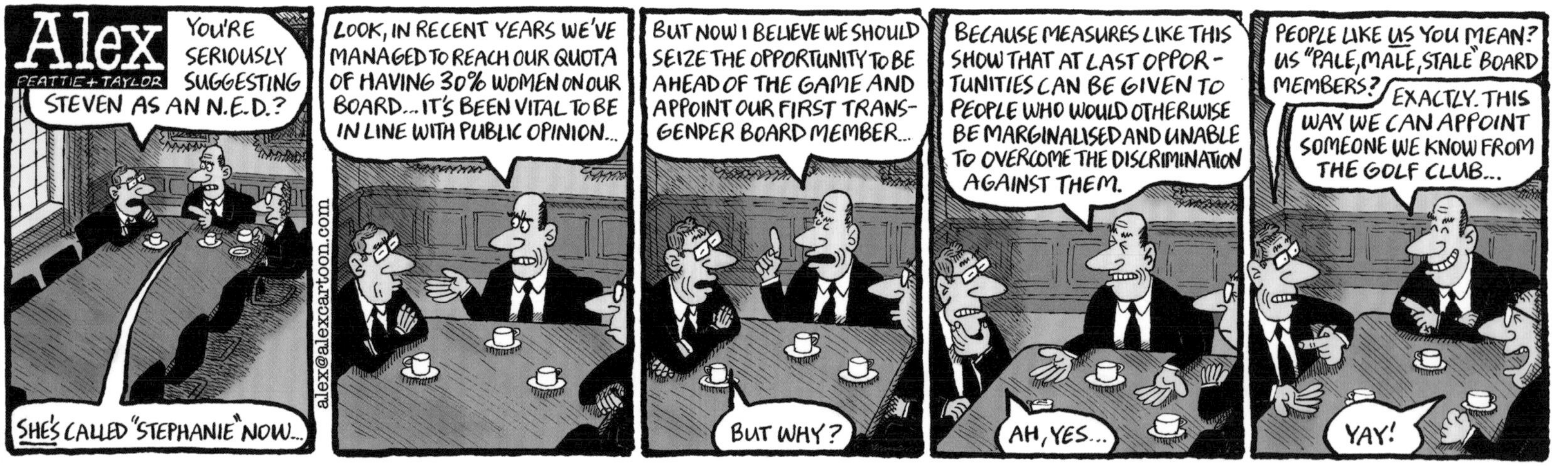
Alex
PEATTIE + TAYLOR
YOU'RE SERIOUSLY SUGGESTING STEVEN AS AN N.E.D.?
SHE'S CALLED "STEPHANIE" NOW...
alex@alexcartoon.com
LOOK, IN RECENT YEARS WE'VE MANAGED TO REACH OUR QUOTA OF HAVING 30% WOMEN ON OUR BOARD... IT'S BEEN VITAL TO BE IN LINE WITH PUBLIC OPINION...
BUT NOW I BELIEVE WE SHOULD SEIZE THE OPPORTUNITY TO BE AHEAD OF THE GAME AND APPOINT OUR FIRST TRANS-GENDER BOARD MEMBER...
BUT WHY?
BECAUSE MEASURES LIKE THIS SHOW THAT AT LAST OPPOR-TUNITIES CAN BE GIVEN TO PEOPLE WHO WOULD OTHERWISE BE MARGINALISED AND UNABLE TO OVERCOME THE DISCRIMINATION AGAINST THEM.
AH, YES...
PEOPLE LIKE US YOU MEAN? US "PALE, MALE, STALE" BOARD MEMBERS?
EXACTLY. THIS WAY WE CAN APPOINT SOMEONE WE KNOW FROM THE GOLF CLUB...
YAY!

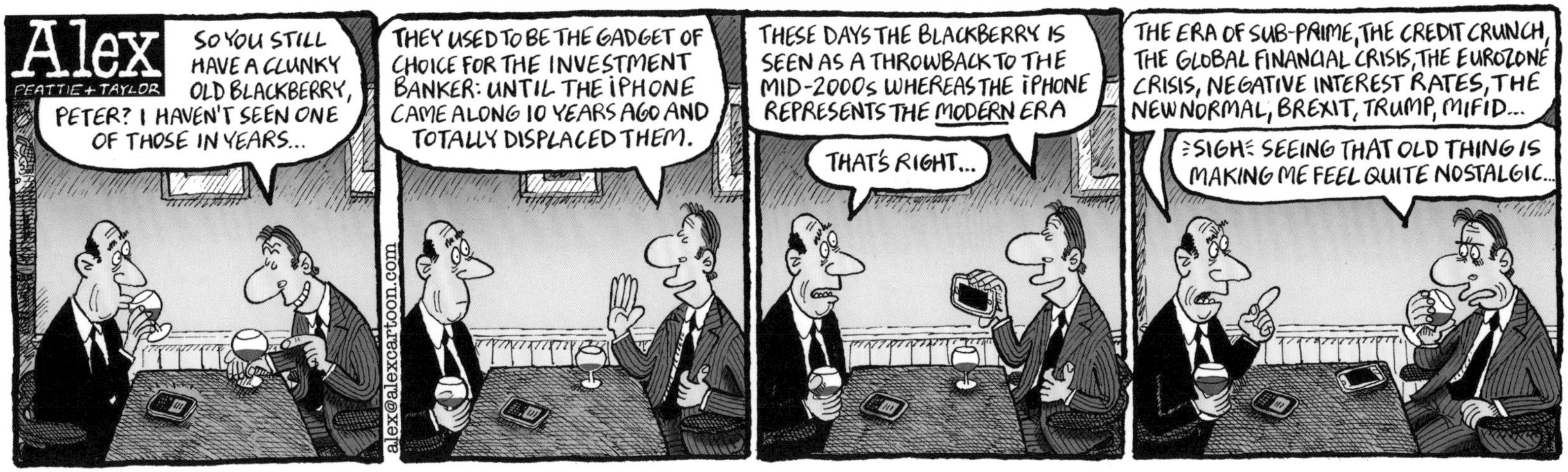
Alex
PEATTIE + TAYLOR
SO YOU STILL HAVE A CLUNKY OLD BLACKBERRY, PETER? I HAVEN'T SEEN ONE OF THOSE IN YEARS...
alex@alexcartoon.com
THEY USED TO BE THE GADGET OF CHOICE FOR THE INVESTMENT BANKER: UNTIL THE iPHONE CAME ALONG 10 YEARS AGO AND TOTALLY DISPLACED THEM.
THESE DAYS THE BLACKBERRY IS SEEN AS A THROWBACK TO THE MID-2000s WHEREAS THE iPHONE REPRESENTS THE MODERN ERA
THAT'S RIGHT...
THE ERA OF SUB-PRIME, THE CREDIT CRUNCH, THE GLOBAL FINANCIAL CRISIS, THE EUROZONE CRISIS, NEGATIVE INTEREST RATES, THE NEW NORMAL, BREXIT, TRUMP, MIFID...
SIGH SEEING THAT OLD THING IS MAKING ME FEEL QUITE NOSTALGIC...

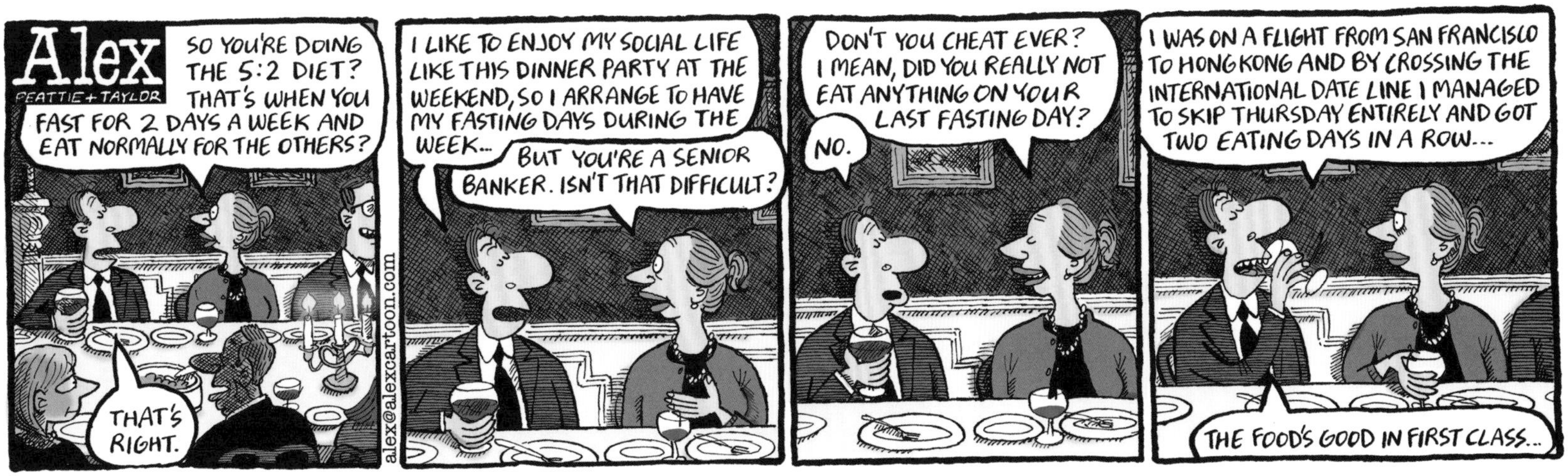
Alex
PEATTIE + TAYLOR
SO YOU'RE DOING THE 5:2 DIET? THAT'S WHEN YOU FAST FOR 2 DAYS A WEEK AND EAT NORMALLY FOR THE OTHERS?
THAT'S RIGHT.
alex@alexcartoon.com
I LIKE TO ENJOY MY SOCIAL LIFE LIKE THIS DINNER PARTY AT THE WEEKEND, SO I ARRANGE TO HAVE MY FASTING DAYS DURING THE WEEK...
BUT YOU'RE A SENIOR BANKER. ISN'T THAT DIFFICULT?
DON'T YOU CHEAT EVER? I MEAN, DID YOU REALLY NOT EAT ANYTHING ON YOUR LAST FASTING DAY?
NO.
I WAS ON A FLIGHT FROM SAN FRANCISCO TO HONG KONG AND BY CROSSING THE INTERNATIONAL DATE LINE I MANAGED TO SKIP THURSDAY ENTIRELY AND GOT TWO EATING DAYS IN A ROW...
THE FOOD'S GOOD IN FIRST CLASS...

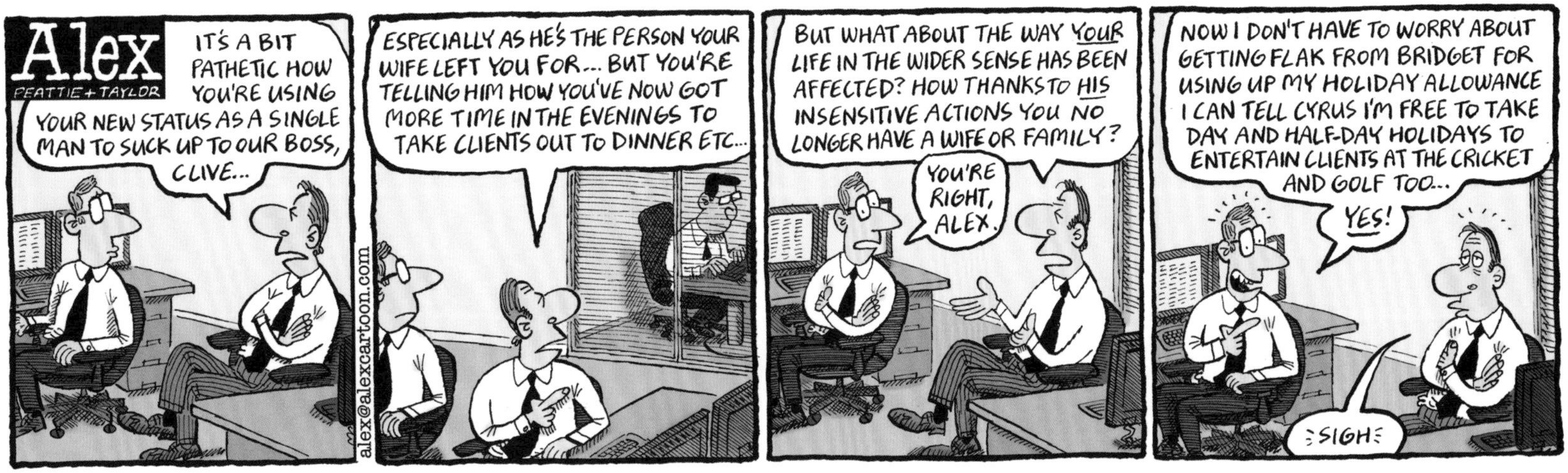
Alex
PEATTIE + TAYLOR
IT'S A BIT PATHETIC HOW YOU'RE USING YOUR NEW STATUS AS A SINGLE MAN TO SUCK UP TO OUR BOSS, CLIVE...
alex@alexcartoon.com
ESPECIALLY AS HE'S THE PERSON YOUR WIFE LEFT YOU FOR... BUT YOU'RE TELLING HIM HOW YOU'VE NOW GOT MORE TIME IN THE EVENINGS TO TAKE CLIENTS OUT TO DINNER ETC...
BUT WHAT ABOUT THE WAY YOUR LIFE IN THE WIDER SENSE HAS BEEN AFFECTED? HOW THANKS TO HIS INSENSITIVE ACTIONS YOU NO LONGER HAVE A WIFE OR FAMILY?
YOU'RE RIGHT, ALEX.
NOW I DON'T HAVE TO WORRY ABOUT GETTING FLAK FROM BRIDGET FOR USING UP MY HOLIDAY ALLOWANCE I CAN TELL CYRUS I'M FREE TO TAKE DAY AND HALF-DAY HOLIDAYS TO ENTERTAIN CLIENTS AT THE CRICKET AND GOLF TOO...
YES!
SIGH

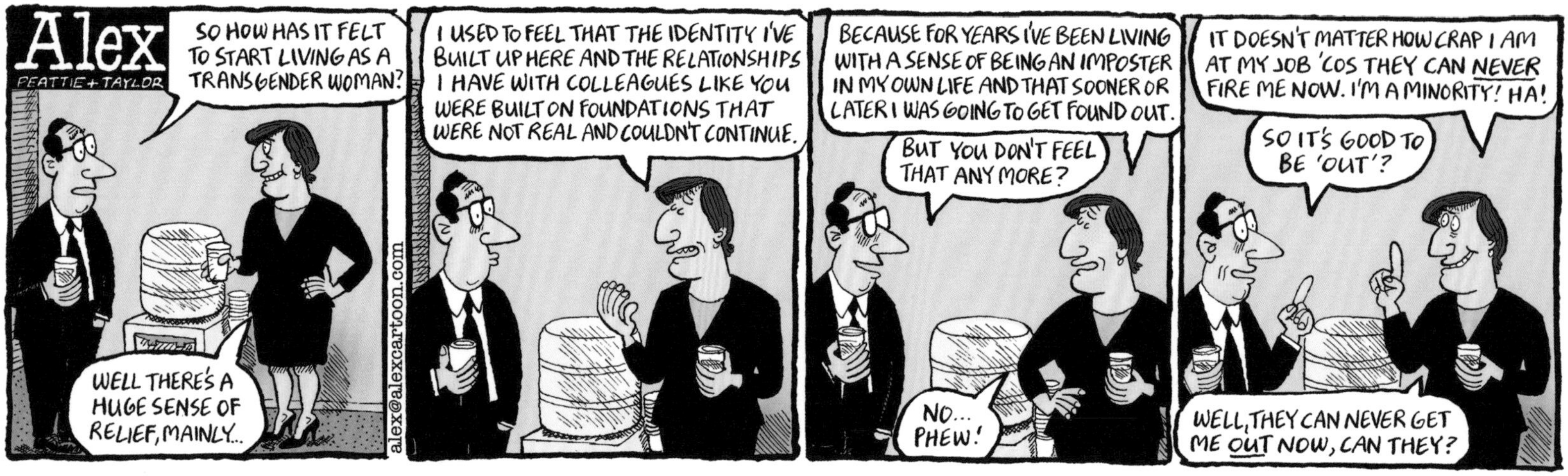
Alex
PEATTIE + TAYLOR
SO HOW HAS IT FELT TO START LIVING AS A TRANSGENDER WOMAN?
WELL THERE'S A HUGE SENSE OF RELIEF, MAINLY...
I USED TO FEEL THAT THE IDENTITY I'VE BUILT UP HERE AND THE RELATIONSHIPS I HAVE WITH COLLEAGUES LIKE YOU WERE BUILT ON FOUNDATIONS THAT WERE NOT REAL AND COULDN'T CONTINUE.
alex@alexcartoon.com
BECAUSE FOR YEARS I'VE BEEN LIVING WITH A SENSE OF BEING AN IMPOSTER IN MY OWN LIFE AND THAT SOONER OR LATER I WAS GOING TO GET FOUND OUT.
BUT YOU DON'T FEEL THAT ANY MORE?
NO... PHEW!
IT DOESN'T MATTER HOW CRAP I AM AT MY JOB 'COS THEY CAN NEVER FIRE ME NOW. I'M A MINORITY! HA!
SO IT'S GOOD TO BE 'OUT'?
WELL, THEY CAN NEVER GET ME OUT NOW, CAN THEY?

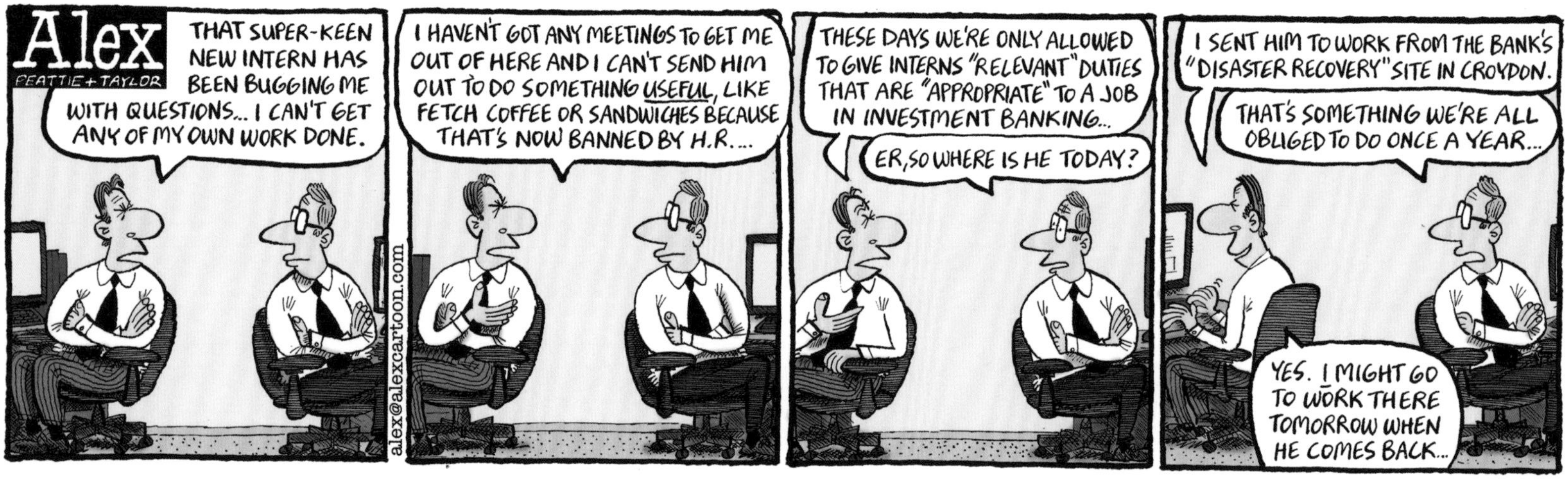
Alex
PEATTIE + TAYLOR
THAT SUPER-KEEN NEW INTERN HAS BEEN BUGGING ME WITH QUESTIONS... I CAN'T GET ANY OF MY OWN WORK DONE.
I HAVEN'T GOT ANY MEETINGS TO GET ME OUT OF HERE AND I CAN'T SEND HIM OUT TO DO SOMETHING USEFUL, LIKE FETCH COFFEE OR SANDWICHES BECAUSE THAT'S NOW BANNED BY H.R. ...
alex@alexcartoon.com
THESE DAYS WE'RE ONLY ALLOWED TO GIVE INTERNS "RELEVANT" DUTIES THAT ARE "APPROPRIATE" TO A JOB IN INVESTMENT BANKING...
ER, SO WHERE IS HE TODAY?
I SENT HIM TO WORK FROM THE BANK'S "DISASTER RECOVERY" SITE IN CROYDON.
THAT'S SOMETHING WE'RE ALL OBLIGED TO DO ONCE A YEAR...
YES. I MIGHT GO TO WORK THERE TOMORROW WHEN HE COMES BACK...

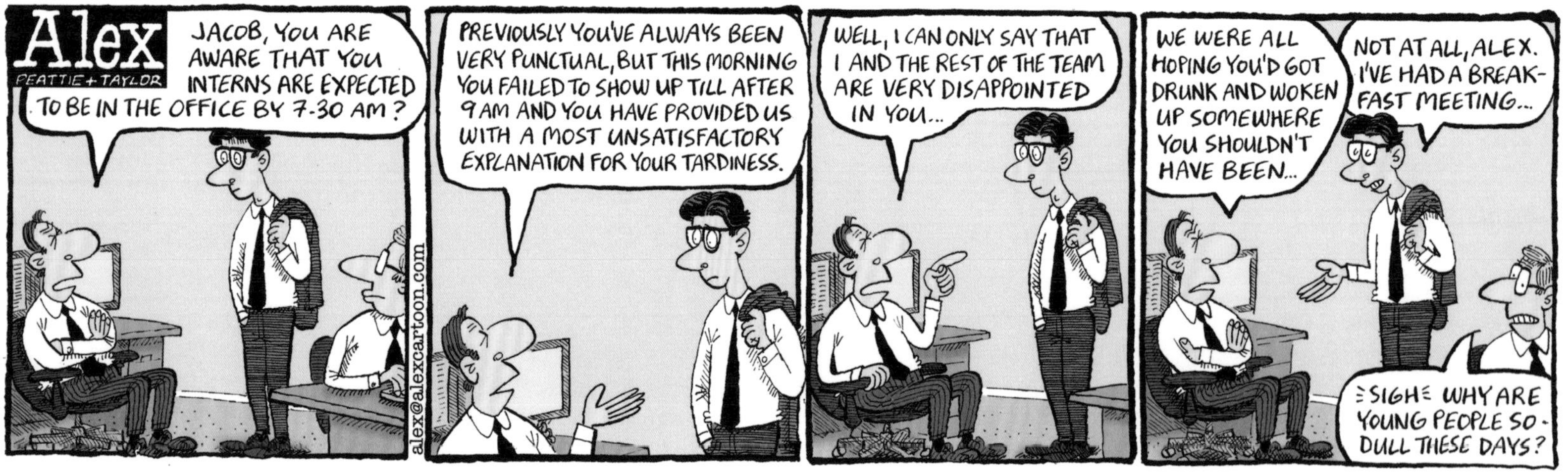
Alex
PEATTIE + TAYLOR
JACOB, YOU ARE AWARE THAT YOU INTERNS ARE EXPECTED TO BE IN THE OFFICE BY 7-30 AM?
alex@alexcartoon.com
PREVIOUSLY YOU'VE ALWAYS BEEN VERY PUNCTUAL, BUT THIS MORNING YOU FAILED TO SHOW UP TILL AFTER 9 AM AND YOU HAVE PROVIDED US WITH A MOST UNSATISFACTORY EXPLANATION FOR YOUR TARDINESS.
WELL, I CAN ONLY SAY THAT I AND THE REST OF THE TEAM ARE VERY DISAPPOINTED IN YOU...
WE WERE ALL HOPING YOU'D GOT DRUNK AND WOKEN UP SOMEWHERE YOU SHOULDN'T HAVE BEEN...
NOT AT ALL, ALEX. I'VE HAD A BREAKFAST MEETING...
≡SIGH≡ WHY ARE YOUNG PEOPLE SO DULL THESE DAYS?

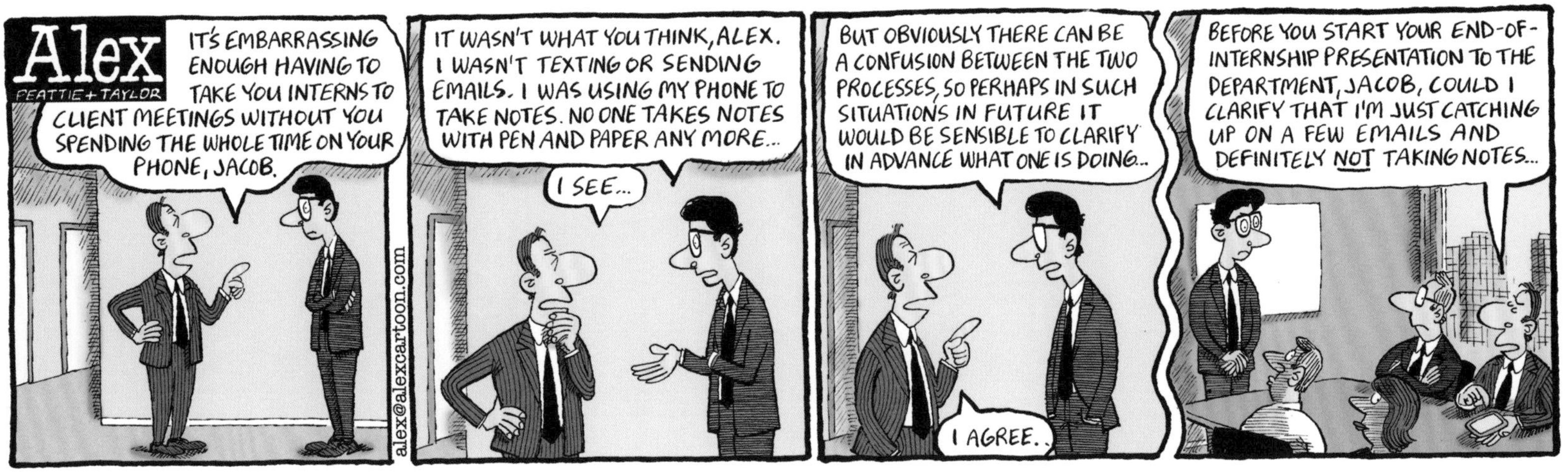
Alex
PEATTIE + TAYLOR
IT'S EMBARRASSING ENOUGH HAVING TO TAKE YOU INTERNS TO CLIENT MEETINGS WITHOUT YOU SPENDING THE WHOLE TIME ON YOUR PHONE, JACOB.
IT WASN'T WHAT YOU THINK, ALEX. I WASN'T TEXTING OR SENDING EMAILS. I WAS USING MY PHONE TO TAKE NOTES. NO ONE TAKES NOTES WITH PEN AND PAPER ANY MORE...
I SEE...
alex@alexcartoon.com
BUT OBVIOUSLY THERE CAN BE A CONFUSION BETWEEN THE TWO PROCESSES, SO PERHAPS IN SUCH SITUATIONS IN FUTURE IT WOULD BE SENSIBLE TO CLARIFY IN ADVANCE WHAT ONE IS DOING...
I AGREE...
BEFORE YOU START YOUR END-OF-INTERNSHIP PRESENTATION TO THE DEPARTMENT, JACOB, COULD I CLARIFY THAT I'M JUST CATCHING UP ON A FEW EMAILS AND DEFINITELY NOT TAKING NOTES...

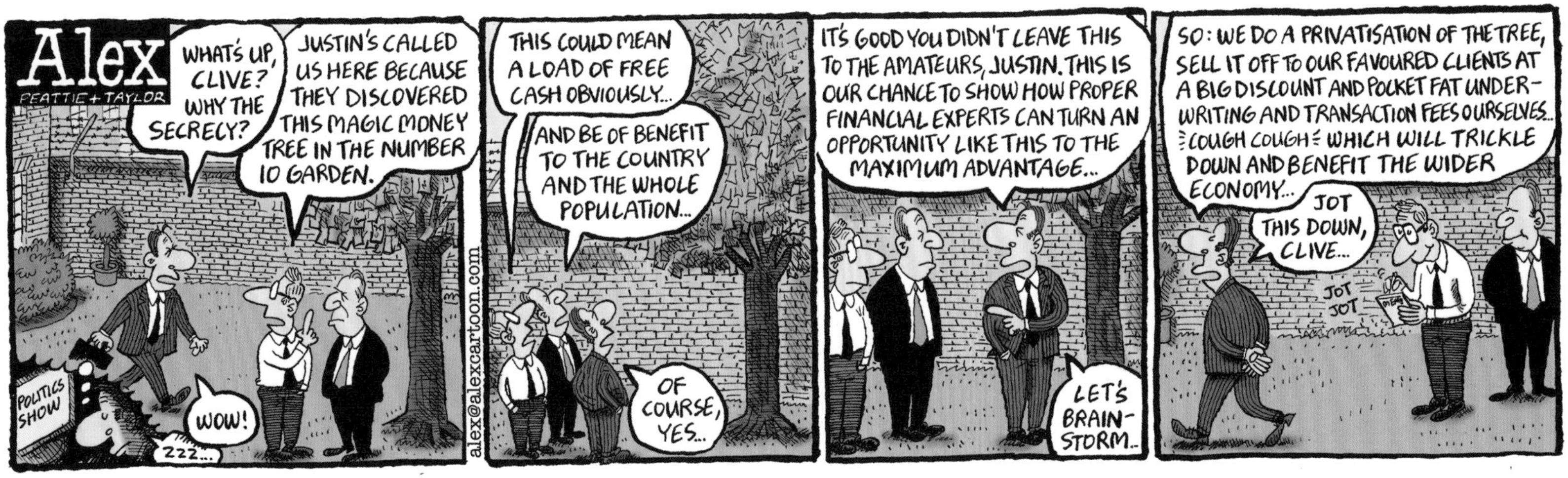
Alex
PEATTIE + TAYLOR
WHAT'S UP, CLIVE? WHY THE SECRECY?
JUSTIN'S CALLED US HERE BECAUSE THEY DISCOVERED THIS MAGIC MONEY TREE IN THE NUMBER 10 GARDEN.
WOW!
POLITICS SHOW
ZZZ...
alex@alexcartoon.com
THIS COULD MEAN A LOAD OF FREE CASH OBVIOUSLY...
AND BE OF BENEFIT TO THE COUNTRY AND THE WHOLE POPULATION...
OF COURSE, YES...
IT'S GOOD YOU DIDN'T LEAVE THIS TO THE AMATEURS, JUSTIN. THIS IS OUR CHANCE TO SHOW HOW PROPER FINANCIAL EXPERTS CAN TURN AN OPPORTUNITY LIKE THIS TO THE MAXIMUM ADVANTAGE...
LET'S BRAIN-STORM...
SO: WE DO A PRIVATISATION OF THE TREE, SELL IT OFF TO OUR FAVOURED CLIENTS AT A BIG DISCOUNT AND POCKET FAT UNDER-WRITING AND TRANSACTION FEES OURSELVES... COUGH COUGH WHICH WILL TRICKLE DOWN AND BENEFIT THE WIDER ECONOMY...
JOT THIS DOWN, CLIVE...
JOT JOT

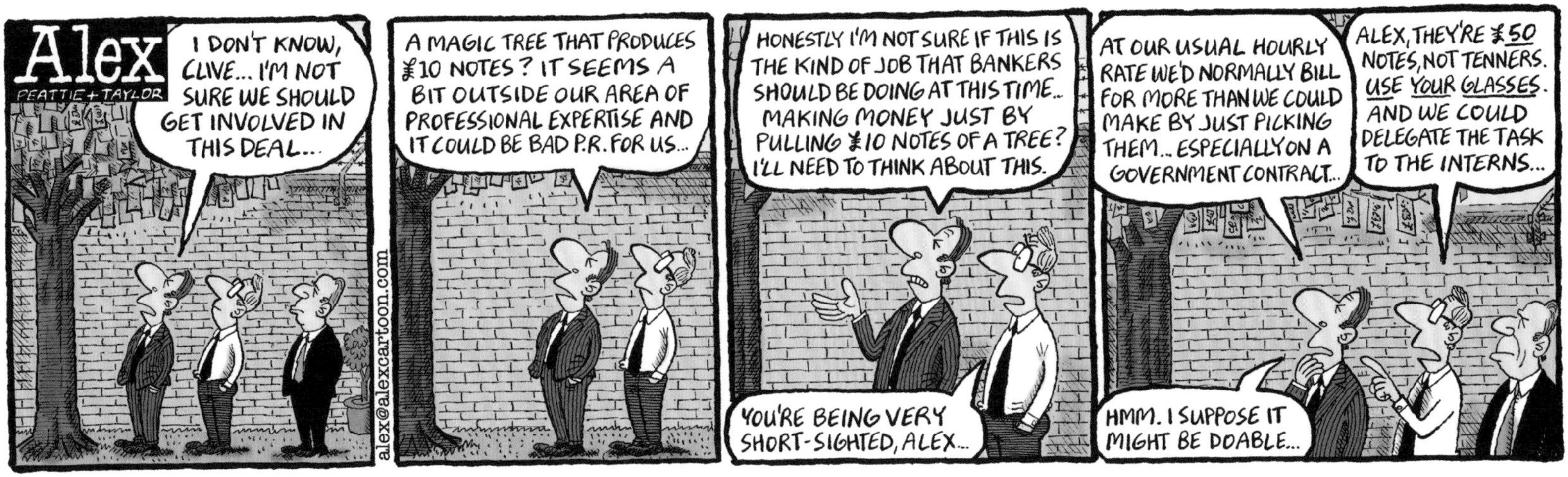
Alex
PEATTIE + TAYLOR
I DON'T KNOW, CLIVE... I'M NOT SURE WE SHOULD GET INVOLVED IN THIS DEAL...
alex@alexcartoon.com
A MAGIC TREE THAT PRODUCES ¥10 NOTES? IT SEEMS A BIT OUTSIDE OUR AREA OF PROFESSIONAL EXPERTISE AND IT COULD BE BAD P.R. FOR US...
HONESTLY I'M NOT SURE IF THIS IS THE KIND OF JOB THAT BANKERS SHOULD BE DOING AT THIS TIME... MAKING MONEY JUST BY PULLING ¥10 NOTES OF A TREE? I'LL NEED TO THINK ABOUT THIS.
YOU'RE BEING VERY SHORT-SIGHTED, ALEX...
AT OUR USUAL HOURLY RATE WE'D NORMALLY BILL FOR MORE THAN WE COULD MAKE BY JUST PICKING THEM... ESPECIALLY ON A GOVERNMENT CONTRACT...
ALEX, THEY'RE ¥50 NOTES, NOT TENNERS. USE YOUR GLASSES. AND WE COULD DELEGATE THE TASK TO THE INTERNS...
HMM. I SUPPOSE IT MIGHT BE DOABLE...

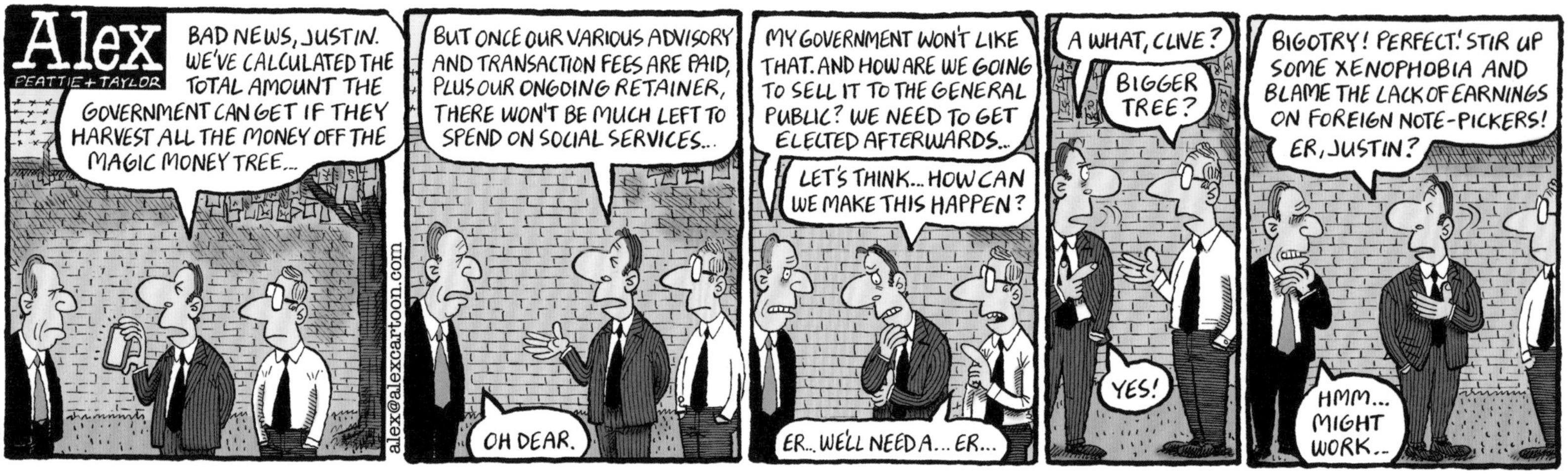
Alex
PEATTIE + TAYLOR
BAD NEWS, JUSTIN. WE'VE CALCULATED THE TOTAL AMOUNT THE GOVERNMENT CAN GET IF THEY HARVEST ALL THE MONEY OFF THE MAGIC MONEY TREE...
alex@alexcartoon.com
BUT ONCE OUR VARIOUS ADVISORY AND TRANSACTION FEES ARE PAID, PLUS OUR ONGOING RETAINER, THERE WON'T BE MUCH LEFT TO SPEND ON SOCIAL SERVICES...
OH DEAR.
MY GOVERNMENT WON'T LIKE THAT. AND HOW ARE WE GOING TO SELL IT TO THE GENERAL PUBLIC? WE NEED TO GET ELECTED AFTERWARDS...
LET'S THINK... HOW CAN WE MAKE THIS HAPPEN?
ER... WE'LL NEED A... ER...
A WHAT, CLIVE?
BIGGER TREE?
YES!
BIGOTRY! PERFECT! STIR UP SOME XENOPHOBIA AND BLAME THE LACK OF EARNINGS ON FOREIGN NOTE-PICKERS! ER, JUSTIN?
HMM... MIGHT WORK...

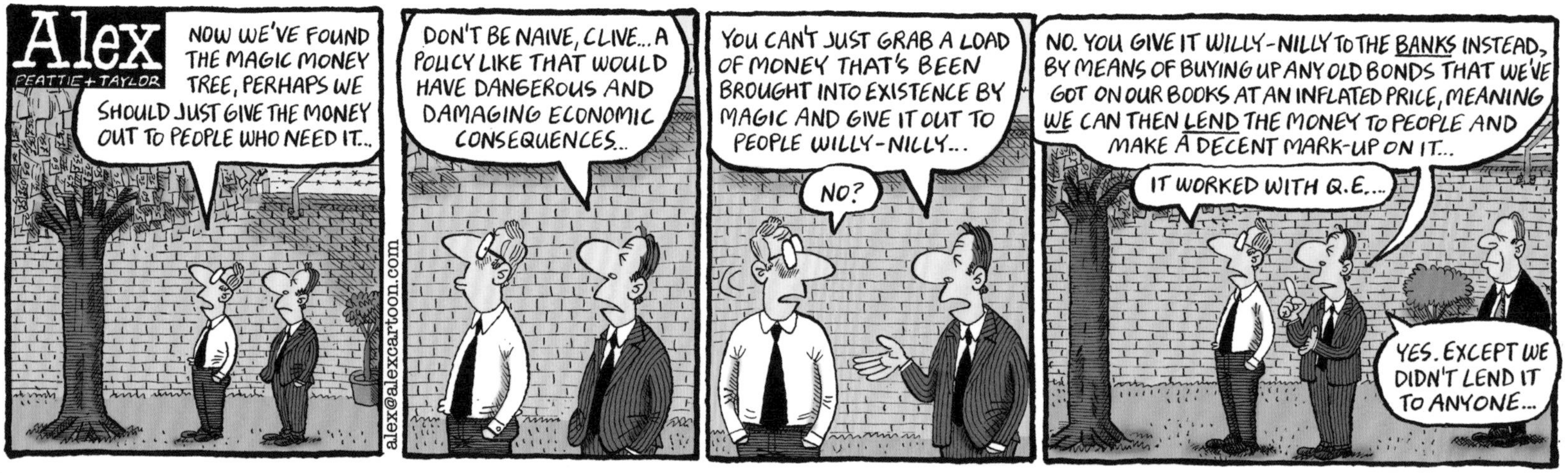
Alex
PEATTIE + TAYLOR
NOW WE'VE FOUND THE MAGIC MONEY TREE, PERHAPS WE SHOULD JUST GIVE THE MONEY OUT TO PEOPLE WHO NEED IT...
alex@alexcartoon.com
DON'T BE NAIVE, CLIVE... A POLICY LIKE THAT WOULD HAVE DANGEROUS AND DAMAGING ECONOMIC CONSEQUENCES...
YOU CAN'T JUST GRAB A LOAD OF MONEY THAT'S BEEN BROUGHT INTO EXISTENCE BY MAGIC AND GIVE IT OUT TO PEOPLE WILLY-NILLY...
NO?
NO. YOU GIVE IT WILLY-NILLY TO THE BANKS INSTEAD, BY MEANS OF BUYING UP ANY OLD BONDS THAT WE'VE GOT ON OUR BOOKS AT AN INFLATED PRICE, MEANING WE CAN THEN LEND THE MONEY TO PEOPLE AND MAKE A DECENT MARK-UP ON IT...
IT WORKED WITH Q.E....
YES. EXCEPT WE DIDN'T LEND IT TO ANYONE...

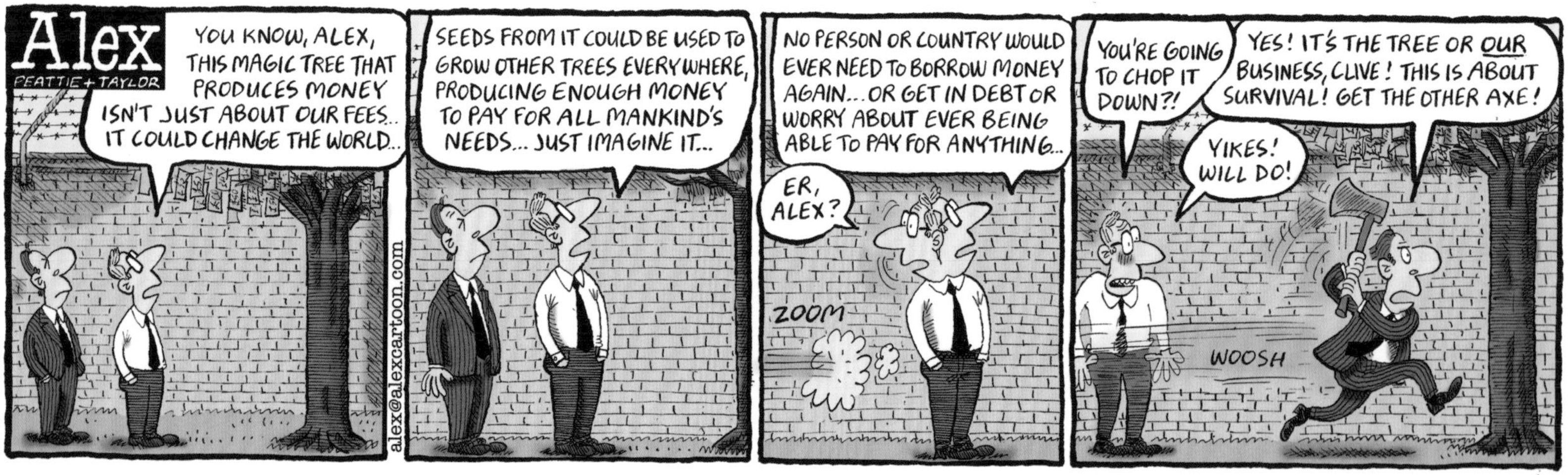
Alex
PEATTIE + TAYLOR
YOU KNOW, ALEX, THIS MAGIC TREE THAT PRODUCES MONEY ISN'T JUST ABOUT OUR FEES... IT COULD CHANGE THE WORLD...
alex@alexcartoon.com
SEEDS FROM IT COULD BE USED TO GROW OTHER TREES EVERYWHERE, PRODUCING ENOUGH MONEY TO PAY FOR ALL MANKIND'S NEEDS... JUST IMAGINE IT...
NO PERSON OR COUNTRY WOULD EVER NEED TO BORROW MONEY AGAIN... OR GET IN DEBT OR WORRY ABOUT EVER BEING ABLE TO PAY FOR ANYTHING...
ER, ALEX?
ZOOM
YOU'RE GOING TO CHOP IT DOWN?!
YES! IT'S THE TREE OR OUR BUSINESS, CLIVE! THIS IS ABOUT SURVIVAL! GET THE OTHER AXE!
YIKES! WILL DO!
WOOSH

ALEX WENT ON HOLIDAY TO CORNWALL

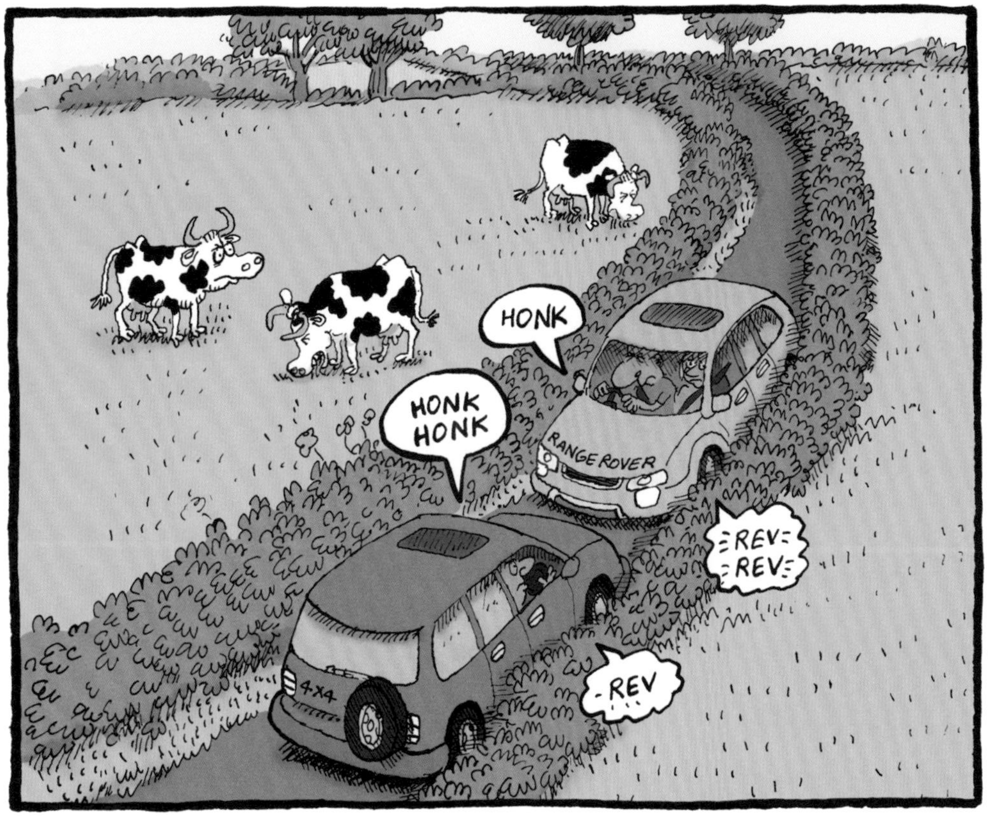
HONK
HONK HONK
RANGE ROVER
REV REV
4X4
REV

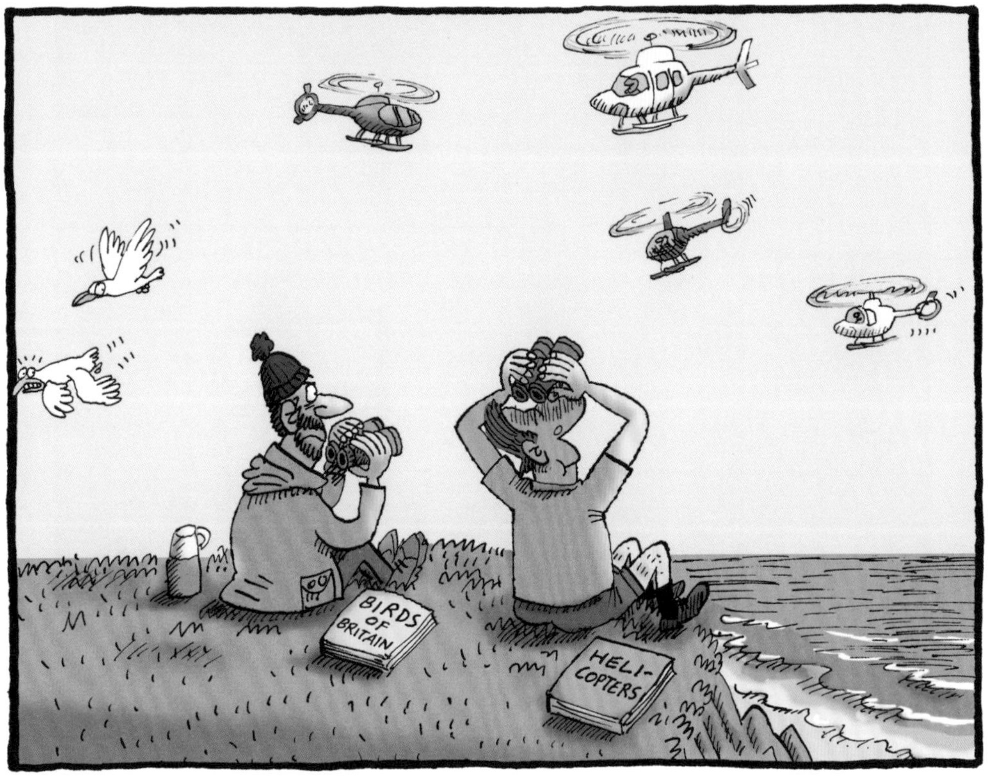
BIRDS OF BRITAIN
HELI-COPTERS

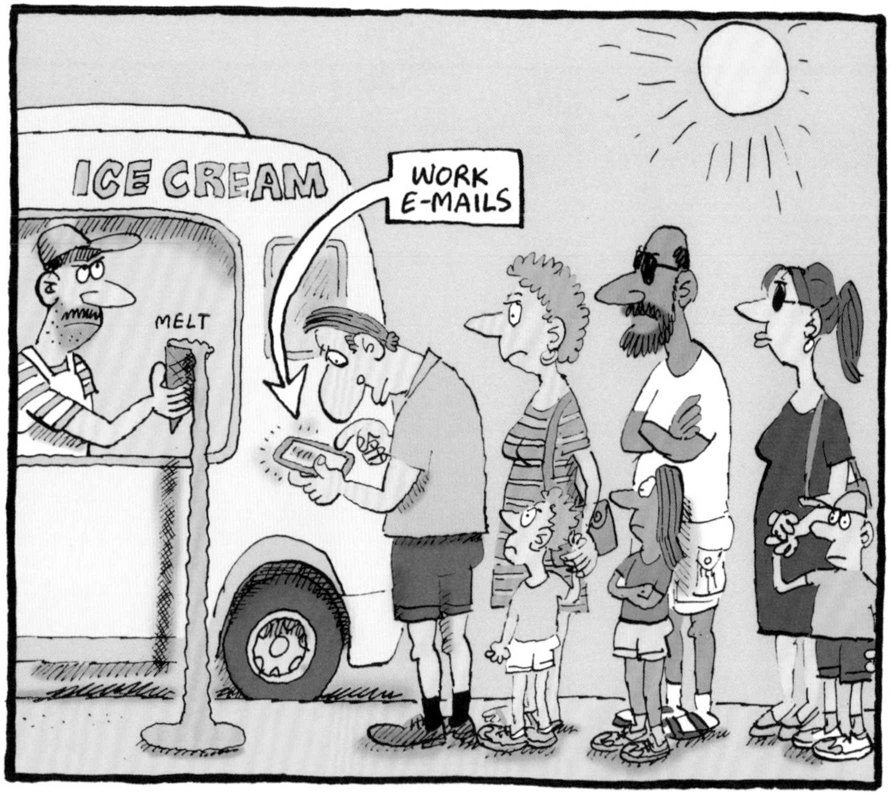
ICE CREAM
WORK E-MAILS
MELT

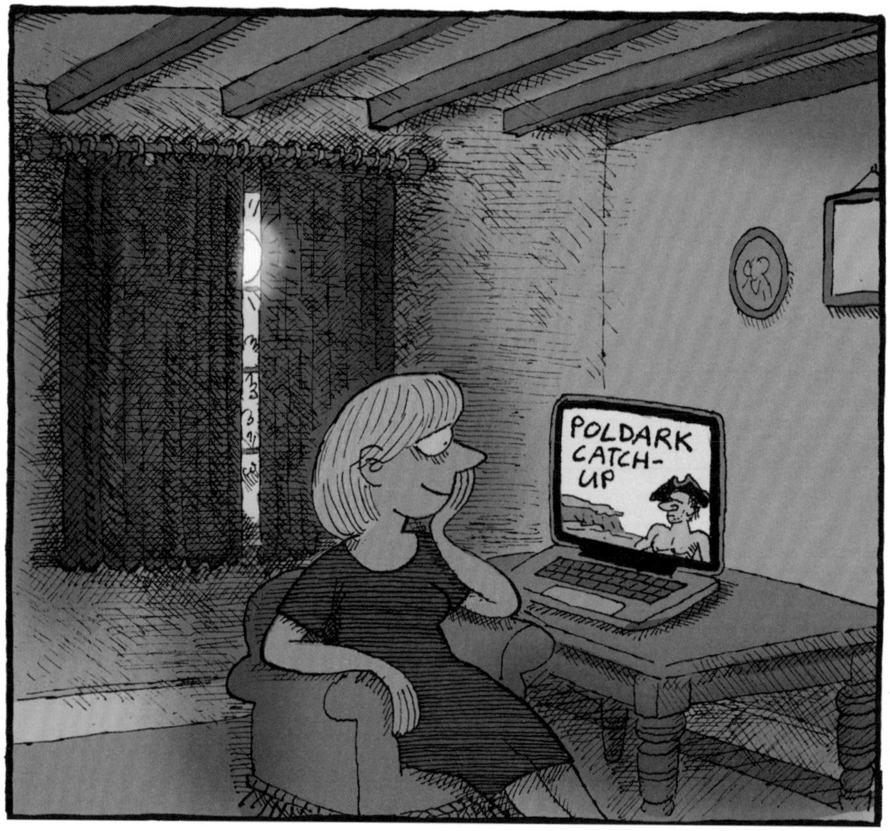
POLDARK CATCH-UP

Also available from Masterley Publishing

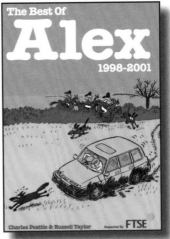

The Best Of
Alex
1998-2001
Charles Peattie & Russell Taylor
FTSE

The Best of Alex 1998 - 2001
Boom to bust via the dotcom bubble.

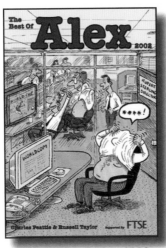

The Best Of
Alex
2002
WORLDCOM
****!
Charles Peattie & Russell Taylor
FTSE

The Best of Alex 2002
Scandals rock the corporate world.

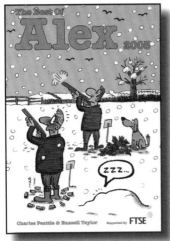

The Best Of
Alex
2003
ZZZ...
Charles Peattie & Russell Taylor
FTSE

The Best of Alex 2003
Alex gets made redundant.

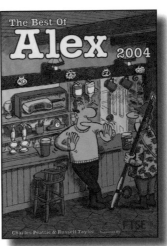

The Best Of
Alex
2004
Charles Peattie & Russell Taylor
FTSE

The Best of Alex 2004
And gets his job back.

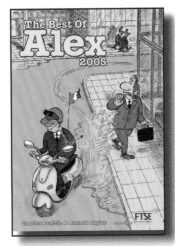

The Best Of
Alex
2005
Charles Peattie & Russell Taylor
FTSE

The Best of Alex 2005
Alex has problems with the French.

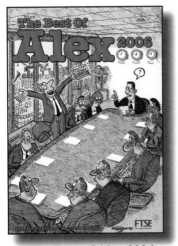

The Best Of
Alex
2006
?
FTSE

The Best of Alex 2006
Alex gets a new American boss.

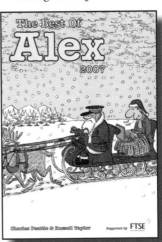

The Best Of
Alex
2007
Charles Peattie & Russell Taylor
FTSE

The Best of Alex 2007
Alex restructures Christmas.

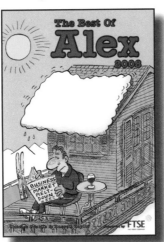

The Best Of
Alex
2008
BUSINESS
MARKET
MELT-
DOWN
FTSE

The Best of Alex 2008
The credit crunch bites

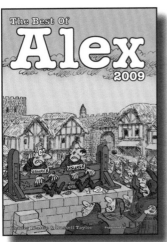

The Best Of
Alex
2009
USURER
USURER

The Best of Alex 2009
Global capitalism self-destructs.

The Best Of
Alex
2010
POST CARDS
TWITTER
FACE BOOK
Charles Peattie & Russell Taylor
FTSE

The Best of Alex 2010
Somehow the City lurches on.

The Best Of
Alex 2011
GOLD
GOLD
GOLD
Charles Peattie & Russell Taylor

The Best of Alex 2011
The financial crisis continues.

The Best Of
Alex 2012
OLYMPICS COVERAGE
Charles Peattie & Russell Taylor
FTSE

The Best of Alex 2012
The Olympics come to London.

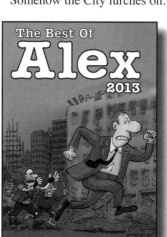

The Best Of
Alex
2013
Charles Peattie & Russell Taylor
FTSE

The Best of Alex 2013
It's a wonderful crisis.

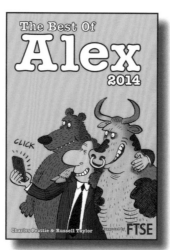

The Best Of
Alex
2014
CLICK
Charles Peattie & Russell Taylor
FTSE

The Best of Alex 2014
The 'New Normal' takes hold.

The Best Of
Alex 2015
COMPLIANCE DECLARATION
ON THE FIRST DAY OF CHRISTMAS MY CLIENT SENT TO ME... A PARTRIDGE IN
Charles Peattie & Russell Taylor
FTSE

The Best of Alex 2015
Compliance rules the roost.

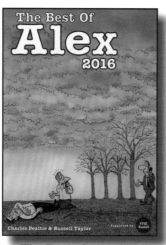

The Best Of
Alex
2016
Charles Peattie & Russell Taylor

The Best of Alex 2016
Alex battles Brexit and Bitcoin.

Celeb
The Original Gary Bloke From
PRIVATE EYE
Charles Peattie and Mark Warren

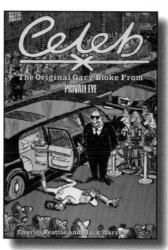

Celeb
Wrinkly rock star Gary Bloke.

Cartoon originals and prints
All our cartoon originals are for sale. They measure 4 x 14 inches. Prints are also available.
All originals and prints are signed by the creators.

For further details on prices and delivery charges for books, cartoons or merchandise:
Tel: +44 (0)1491 871 894
Email: alex@alexcartoon.com
Web: www.alexcartoon.com
Twitter: @alexmasterley

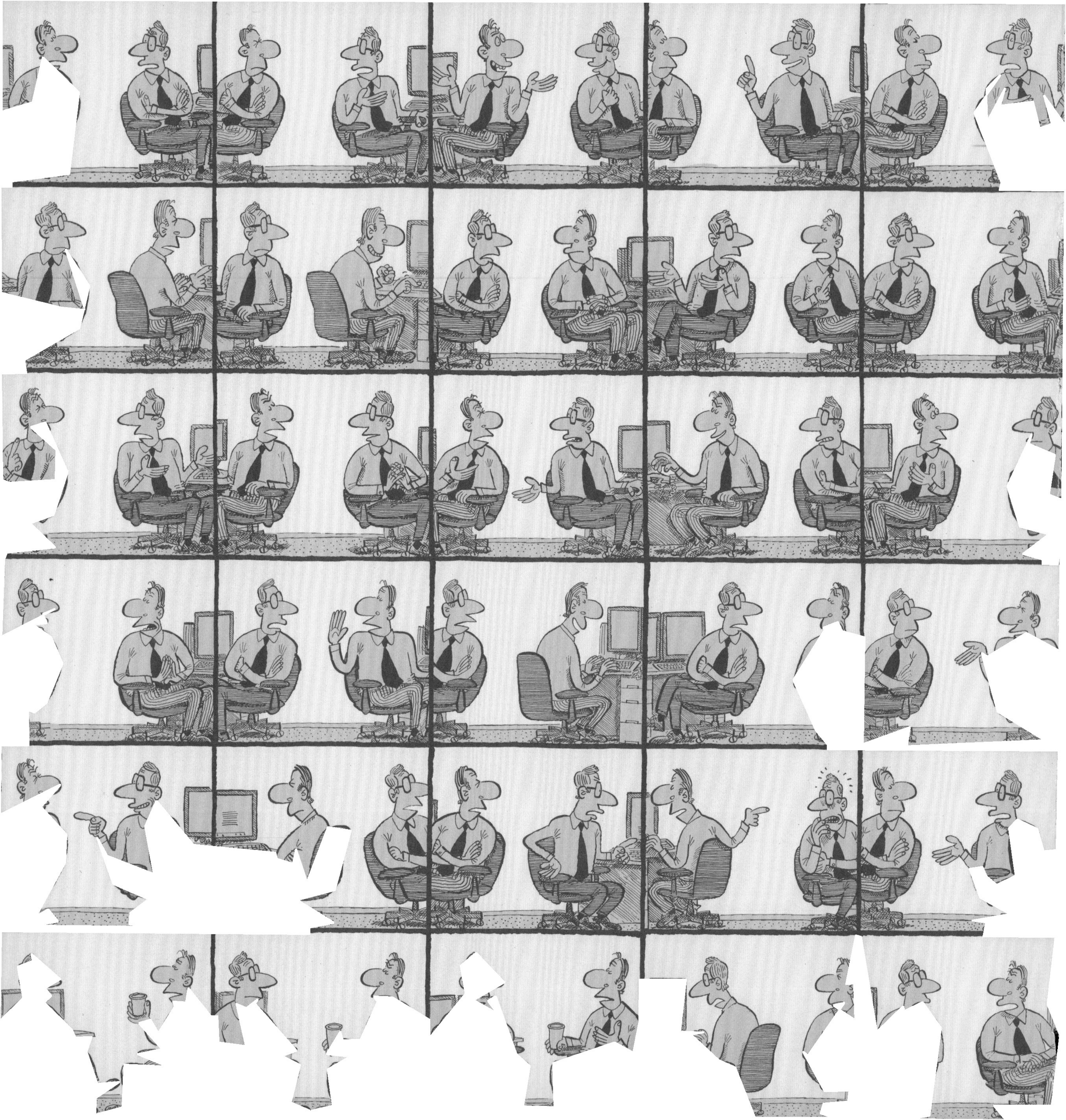